# THE

# COLORADO

# MOUNTAIN

# COMPANION

a potpourri of
useful miscellany from
the highest parts
of the highest state

m john fayhee

WestWinds Press®

**THE PRUETT SERIES**

WestWinds Press®
An imprint of Graphic Arts Books
P.O. Box 56118
Portland, OR 97238-6118
(503) 254-5591
www.graphicartsbooks.com

First Edition 2012

Library of Congress Cataloging-in-Publication Data

Fayhee, M. John, 1955–
    Colorado mountain companion : a potpourri of useful miscellany from the highest parts of the highest state / M. John Fayhee. — 1st ed.
        p. cm.
    Includes bibliographical references and index.
    ISBN-13: 978-0-87108-960-1
    ISBN-10: 0-87108-960-2
    1. Mountains—Colorado—Miscellanea. 2. Mountain life—Colorado—Miscellanea. 3. Outdoor life—Colorado—Miscellanea. 4. Natural history—Colorado—Miscellanea. 5. Colorado—History, Local—Miscellanea. 6. Colorado—Social life and customs—Miscellanea. 7. Colorado—Environmental conditions—Miscellanea. I. Title.
    F782.A16F39 2012
    978.8—dc23
                                              2012001616

Cover image by Larry Hubbell
Book design by Kay Turnbaugh

*This book is dedicated to Frank C. Smith, Jr.,*
*a gentleman, a scholar, and one of the few people I have*
*ever met who loves old maps as much as I do.*

*pooh -*
*live long &*
*prosper -*

# TABLE OF CONTENTS

# INTRODUCTION

## *I know for a fact...*

The seeds of this book first germinated in a watering hole several hundred miles from the Colorado mountains, in, of all places, arid Bisbee, Arizona. I must have looked like the tourist I assuredly was, and a gent a couple of barstools down asked me, by way of a mannerly conversational icebreaker, where I was from. After I told him, he said he was born in Leadville, although he left many decades before when he was still a youngster. That got the basic-social-interaction ball rolling, and somewhere along the line, with the brewskis flowing as fast as the stories, this gent stated for the benefit of his proximate Colorado-ignorant amigos that Leadville was the highest-elevationed municipality in the country. I know I ought to have left well enough alone, but, since tongue biting is, to say the least, not my usual barroom modus operandi, I felt compelled to interject a fact into what up until that point had been a perfectly pleasant period of innocuous, fairly fact-free, recreational yarn spinning.

"Ummm, actually," says I, sans sense, "Leadville is the *third*-highest incorporated municipality in the country. Alma is the highest, and Montezuma is second highest."[1]

I had not only rained on this man's storytelling parade, I had done so on his home turf, in his regular bar, in front of his drinking buddies—a social faux pas on so many levels that it now mortifies me to recollect the scene.

"I *know for a fact* that Leadville's the highest," the man snorted, crossing his arms in front of his chest, attempting to regain his footing. "Neither Alma nor Montezuma are incorporated."

"Ummm, actually..."

Instantly, our amicable chitchat disintegrated into the kind of disjointed petty one-upmanship that defines so much suds-enhanced discourse.

My retrospective mortification aside, as I was driving out of Bisbee the next morning, I started thinking about the many, many similar conversations I have either observed or been directly involved in over the years. Like the time at the Gold Pan, when fisticuffs nearly erupted between a couple of locals who *knew for a fact* that Arapahoe Basin is the oldest of Colorado's currently open ski areas.[2]

And the time I got into it with a *Denver Post* reporter in the Moose Jaw about Colorado's highest road. He *knew for a fact* that Trail Ridge Road, which traverses Rocky Mountain National Park, was the most-altitudinous stretch of blacktop in the country. I had to run out to my truck to fetch my Rand McNally before he believed me that the state's highest road goes near-bouts to the summit of 14,264-foot Mount Evans.[3]

And the tête-à-tête in the Lariat in Grand Lake about Colorado's coldest town, an issue, I stressed to several local boys who (1) looked inclined to stomp me on the spot and (2) *knew for a fact* that Fraser was the icebox of the nation, that could not be accurately settled because there is no universally accepted method for determining a given municipality's frigidity factor.[4]

Then, also, at various times: The highest vertical gain in the Colorado[5], the deepest abyss[6], the largest natural lake[7], the state's rank when it comes to avalanches[8] and lightning fatalities[9], the first chairlift[10], etc. etc., and on and on.

Although it ended up being far more than the sum of its conceptual parts, the original idea for this book was merely to compile a mountain of material specifically with the intention of having a handy-dandy, Colorado-high-country-based reference guide for settling such generally good-natured and, when you get right down to it, not-exactly-earth-shatteringly important, barroom arguments. I envisioned a copy in every altitudinous imbibery from Alamosa to Steamboat Springs, from Evergreen to Silverton. I thought as I was heading north out of Bisbee that long-ago day that such a notion could actually serve as a means by which John-Wayne-movie-esque bar brawls could be averted. Like: "OK, before we start duking it out over whether or not the summer rains in Colorado actually constitute a denotative monsoonal weather pattern, let's consult The Book."[11]

"Man, you're a genius, Fayhee!" I thought, as I pointed my truck back toward the high country. When I got home, Grim Reality began to sink in, as it always does when I experience a (usually short-lived) flash of brilliance. This, I soon realized, would require one serious amount of research, a word that has long caused near-terminal heart palpitations in my short-attention-spanned psyche. Heretofore, my books have consisted almost primarily of narratives revolving around multi-month backpacking trips I have taken along various long-distance trails. That's easy: "Today, I hiked some more. The mountains were once again mighty pretty." This project, obviously, would turn out to be a horse of a whole nuther color. Compared to the effort this book ultimately required, hiking a 1,000-mile trail and writing about it is relative child's play.

The intimidating toil factor aside, there were some serious structural decisions that needed to be made right off the bat if this volume was ever going to make its way from a pile of random notes scribbled onto cocktail napkins to actual coherency.

I decided immediately—predictably, some who know me might say—to follow no set research pattern. Like encyclopedias and dictionaries in the early 1700s, I elected to explore subjects that interest me personally while casting only a furtive glance toward the notion of traditional encyclopedic structure and comprehensiveness that, try though I might to ignore it, never wandered far from my peripheral vision during the process of molding this book into final form. Throughout this undertaking, I would find myself reading about, for example, the controversy regarding how many Fourteeners there actually are in Colorado[12], and, then, next thing I knew, I'd be investigating the story behind "America the Beautiful",[13] then, *next* thing I knew, I'd find myself wondering about why "Pikes" Peak is not "Pike's" Peak.[14] Whatever accidental systemization this book contains comes only by way of the fact that almost all of the subject matter herein contained relates in some way or another to the mountains of Colorado and the people who interact with those mountains. I understand that this reality "deals" with the concept of traditional organization by redefining, if not ignoring, that concept entirely but, well, there you have it.

Once I cast my lot with the research philosophy that, as Ani DiFranco sings, "everything is governed by the law of one thing leads to another"[15], I was liberated to follow my unencumbered muse, as it were. As a lifelong devotee of almanacs, I decided to include in this book ample quantities of pure, abashed, sometimes (and sometimes not) list- or chart-based miscellany and trivia—the kind of verbiage that, as I mentioned earlier, might be used as a means of diffusing a bar argument. I also decided to include much in the way of material best presented via a more journalistic narrative style—material that would, at a minimum, lose some of its essence if reduced to a list or a chart, or if condensed into mere trivia or miscellany.

After those conceptual decisions were essentially writ in stone, I jumped headlong into what ended up being a stunningly time-consuming and exhaustive research process. It was not long before I came to understand why encyclopedias come in sets. The word count I eventually compiled was at least twice as long as could be shoehorned into any reasonable book. And yet, by the time I finally pulled the plug, I truly considered that research to be about halfway done, because Colorado is an astoundingly interesting state on every imaginable level, from history, to natural history, to cultural anthropology, to vernacular, social perspective, and popular culture. It took me almost as much time to cull this manuscript into palpable form as it did to assemble the original mountain of words that came to dominate my life for more than two years.

I attempted to include as wide an array of subject matter as reasonably possible. After all, there are entire libraries dedicated to, as but one example of many, the individual tribes of Native Americans that have called the Colorado mountains home.[16] Obviously, I had to skim many surfaces that are worth further, more detailed exploration. I hope this book encourages you to do just that.[17]

A couple of necessary caveats: The overwhelming majority of the information I gathered and sluice-boxed into hopeful lucidity would make professional researchers collapse on the ground and start twitching apoplectically. Most of the skinny I gathered and collated comes from decidedly secondary and tertiary sources of the variety found via the most magic word known to those of us who majored in English by default rather than via any serious academic inclinations: Google. Although I attempted to verify much of the material herein contained, most was taken at face value from sources whose veracity I confirmed mainly via aggressive crossing of my fingers. Repeat after me: A doctoral dissertation this is not. I know that attitude may come across as a justification for what academic types might consider a lackadaisical research effort on my part. Anyone inclined to make that accusation is more than welcome to eyeball the chock-full boxes I have stacked in my office marked "The Colorado Mountain Companion."

I also did many personal interviews with Smart People, like professors, scientists, bureaucrats, and such, in hopes of presenting not only a wide array of material, but material that is mostly correct. Here would be a good time to stress that whatever errors these pages contain, whether those errors are factual, interpretive, or sins of omission, are my fault and my fault alone. I hope that when the inevitable boo-boos are found, readers will forgive me at least partially because, as any true high-country person knows, it's hard to dig one's way out from under an avalanche, whether that avalanche takes the form of snow or mounds of files. I would also hope that most readers will understand that very little, if any, of the material in this book is of the life-threatening variety, if you catch my drift.

Third last: One of the biggest concerns in putting this tome together was determining exactly what we mean by "the Colorado mountains"—to establish a boundary for the area supposedly delineated by this book's title. On the surface, making that determination would seem simple enough: If a place is located in the mountains, then, well, it falls into the proper realm. Well, not so fast. There are plenty of counties in Colorado that are partially mountainous and partially not. Boulder County, for instance. Should Boulder County be dis-included from this book because its eastern provinces are part of the Great Plains? And what about places that have mountains on the horizon so close you can almost reach out and touch them, like Denver, Fort Collins, Colorado Springs, Pueblo, and Grand Junction? There's definitely some rational hairsplitting involved, and I chose to deal with that situation by basically being more open than closed. If a county contains any vertical terrain whatsoever, I call it good. The last thing you want to do in Colorado is tell a whole bunch of otherwise pleasant people that they're not mountain people, unless they live closer to Kansas, Nebraska, or Oklahoma than they do to Idaho Springs or Woodland Park.

Second last: Some sections in this book are not directly specific to the Colorado mountains. The high country does not exist in a vacuum, even though it often seems like it does. A few years ago, ESPN, according to a buddy of mine who worked there, issued an edict to its staffers mandating that, whenever a comparative statement is made, such as "John Elway is the second-winningest quarterback of all time," it be made relative by saying that Dan Marino is number three and Brett Favre is number one. I believe that readers are interested in such relativity. Therefore, there are many instances in these pages when I say, for instance, that while Gunnison has been listed more times than any other Colorado town as having the nation's lowest temperature, it does not lead the nation in that frigid category.[18] One of the primary responsibilities of any journalist is to preemptively answer any reasonable questions that might be asked by any reasonable reader as a result of the words he or she pens, and, by sometimes broadening the scope of this book—not often, but often enough—I hope to do just that.

Last: There are going to be some sections that will be dated before this book even comes off the press. (I think of the Olympics, Wildfire, Elections and Wilderness chapters, for instance.) Not much I could do about that except to try to make the work as current as possible before the mean publisher started sending threatening letters with the nasty words "deadline" and "breach of contract" prominently displayed.

Last (seriously, this time): Although I spent more time on this book than I have on any other single project in a professional writing career that spans 30 years and literally thousands of published articles and millions of published words, I can say without compunction that this amounted to the most fun I've ever had with my clothes on. Matter of fact, I have never enjoyed working on a book this much, and, at the end of each day, unlike my backpacking books, I did not have to worry about tending to heel blisters.

So, there you have the story behind a book that I believe is unlike any other that has been penned in or about the highest part of the country's highest state. It was my goal to provide you with what amounts to a Bible of material that just might come in handy the next time you find yourself in a barroom argument with someone who *knows for a fact* that Leadville is the highest incorporated municipality in the country.[19]

— *M. John Fayhee, written in the Scarlet Saloon,*
*Leadville, Colorado, October 21, 2009*

## NOTES

1. As I explain in the "Highest Towns" chapter, there's actually a fourth municipality that has come lately to this argument: Winter Park.

2. That would be Loveland if you're thinking in terms of continuous operation, and Howelsen Hill if you don't mind a few down years added to your argument.

3. The "Colorado's Highest Roads" chapter (page 252) clears all this up.

4. As I explain in the "Icebox of the Nation" chapter (page 7), there's a lot to consider when attempting to ascertain which town is the state's coldest.

5. Go to the "Uphill Battles" chapter (page 216).

6. Go to the "Canyons Versus Gorges" chapter (page 187).

7. Go to the "Colorado Lakes and Reservoirs" chapter (page 61).

8. Go to the "Colorado Avalanches" chapter (page 56).

9. Go to the "Lightning" chapter (page 70).

10. Go to the "Ski History" chapter (page 126).

11. Go to the "Monsoon Season" chapter (page 73).

12. Go to the "Fourteeners" chapter (page 189).

13. Go to the "America the Beautiful" chapter (page 84).

14. Go to the "Non-Possessive Place Names" chapter (page 18).

15. "Hour Follows Hour," from the *Not A Pretty Girl* album.

16. Go to the "Native Americans in Colorado" chapter (page 160).

17. Almost every chapter contains sources at the end that serve at least partially as a bibliography.

18. Once again, go to the "Icebox of the Nation" chapter (page 7).

19. As I explain in the "Highest Towns" chapter (page 42), Colorado makes a distinction between a legal "town" and a "city." Therefore, Leadville rightfully maintains its claim as the country's highest *city.*

# THE "ICEBOX OF THE NATION"
# DESIGNATION NOT SO SIMPLE

In the spring of 2008, one of the longest-running climatological battles in the country was settled, not by the National Weather Service (NWS) or the faculty of some esteemed university, but, rather, by the U.S. Patent and Trademark Office. For many years, Fraser, Colorado (elevation 8,574 feet), and International Falls, Minnesota (elevation 1,122 feet), had battled for the legal right to use the term "The Icebox of the Nation." In 1989, the matter was supposedly settled when International Falls, with a population of about 6,500, paid Fraser, population about 1,000, $2,000 to essentially drop its frigid contention.

Once that check was cashed, International Falls registered its gelid acronym with the U.S. Patent and Trademark Office, and that was that. Fraser was still legally allowed to market itself as the "Icebox of Colorado," or the "Icebox of the Rockies," or "So Cold, Your Face Gets Frostbit Just Going to the Post Office," as long as that very specific term—the "Icebox of the Nation"—was not invoked.

Until 2007, all was well in the land of icicles and frozen nose hairs.

Then, International Falls committed a frosty faux pas: The city failed to file the paperwork required to renew its "Icebox" trademark. And Fraser pounced. The little town, located near Winter Park Ski Area, tried to hijack the chilly sobriquet. After a yearlong fight, the U.S. Patent and Trademark Office sided with International Falls when it granted the city, located near the Canadian border way the heck up in the Land of 10,000 Lakes, Trademark Registration Number 3,375,139.

But here's the thing: That trademark was in no way, shape, or form based upon climatic reality; it was, rather, based solely upon the fact that International Falls proved "longest continuous use" of "Icebox of the Nation" in a marketing and promotional sense. The city offered anecdotal proof that it first used "Icebox of the Nation" in 1948 and photographic proof—in the form of a PeeWee hockey team that traveled to Boston wearing jackets adorned with the slogan—since 1955. Fraser could not trump that evidence.

Although the U.S. Patent and Trademark Office decision was based solely on commercial history, it could not have integrated weather considerations into its decision, even if it wanted to, as there are no set criteria for determining what town is, in fact, the "icebox of the nation."

Yet, because all matters weather related are of import in mountain towns, if for no other reason than to have something to argue about in bars in February when it's -25 outside, the subject of relative frigidity is worth exploring.

Before doing so, however, it should be noted that both Fraser and International Falls ought to be somewhat ashamed of the specific wording of their legal battle because, as we all know, the true iceboxes of the nation are all found in Alaska. No matter how you define the term, rare is the day when the superlative bone-chilling stats are not found in the Last Frontier. When it comes to cold, neither International Falls nor Fraser can hold a candle to Barrow, Nome, and Chicken.

That aside, the ambiguous nature of climatic reality itself makes this a tough argument.

There are two main statistics (that is to say, weather-based data that have been measured and catalogued by reliable people over a long period of time) that can be invoked when this icebox-of-the-nation argument manifests itself. One is average annual temperature, which is kept by the NWS. And, there, International Falls comes in with a very respectable 37.4 degrees. But Fraser comes in even colder, with an average annual temperature of 34.4 degrees.

The other measured statistic that is applicable to this argument is the nation's low temperature, which is measured and archived daily by the NWS by way of its Cooperative Observer Program, which consists of about 11,000 people, mostly volunteers, scattered from sea to shining sea who, every day of the year, bond with thermometers and precipitation gauges.

The national low temperature is admittedly a specious prism through which this icebox-of-the-nation argument can be viewed, for at least two reasons.

First, many towns that find themselves often listed as having had the coldest temperature in the nation on a given day achieve that recognition in the summer. (Truckee, California, is a perfect example.) And while many people might argue that having the nation's low temperature in July actually trumps, or at least ties, the concept of having the nation's low in January, many other people would scoff at that notion.

Second, anyone bored enough to scrutinize the nation's low temperature list would, even if they were focusing solely on winter, immediately recognize that some towns—Embarrass, Minnesota, comes to mind—fairly regularly make the list with the nation's low temperature of, say, -40, while others will repeatedly make the list with lows of "only," say, -20.

Moreover, there are people who would rationally argue that the icebox of the nation ought to be based upon the number of times a town boasts the country's lowest daytime *high* temperature. And recently there has been some dialogue about establishing a nationally recognized weather miserability index that would include daytime low, daytime high, cloudiness, wind, humidity, and amount of snow. Were such an index established and implemented, few would argue that it would not be dominated by towns in the upper Midwest and Northeast, where entire months pass without the sun peeking out. The only way the mountain towns of the West might make their way onto such an aggregate index of hideous weather would be for duration to be included in the formula. After all, even places like International Falls (or, for that matter, Fairbanks, Alaska) rarely get snowstorms in June and July, as the mountain towns of Colorado sometimes do.

The main category that the mountains of the West dominate on this icebox argument front is the nation's low temperature on a given day. Therefore, it might be illuminating to examine some rudimentary regional stats.

Two towns rule Colorado's nation's-low-temperature statistics: Gunnison (elevation 7,703 feet) and Alamosa (elevation 7,544 feet). Between April 1, 1995, and August 31, 2010, Gunnison was home to the nation's low temperature 250 times, while Alamosa claimed that honor 193 times. Fraser, by comparison, was "only" the nation's cold spot 99 times during that period. All three of those Colorado towns have been the nation's coldest spot in all seasons, although almost half of Fraser's coldest-town dates have come in the summer.

Gunnison, more than any other Colorado mountain town, has been home to protracted periods of deep cold. In December 2002, for instance, Gunnison achieved the nation's coldest temperature eight times. Gunnison was the nation's cold spot 26 times in a two-month period—December 2005–January 2006—and 11 of those nation's low temperatures were −20 or colder.

Still, as nippy as Alamosa and Gunnison can be, they both pale by comparison to Stanley, Idaho, and West Yellowstone, Montana, both of which regularly make the nation's cold-temperature list in all seasons. Stanley was home to the nation's coldest temperature a staggering 661 times between April 1, 1995, and August 31, 2010, while West Yellowstone made the list 489 times in that time span.

Other towns that frequently are home to the lowest temperature in the Contiguous States are (all figures from April 1, 1995, to August 31, 2010):

- Truckee, California, which was home to the nation's cold spot 227 times. All but two of those low temperatures occurred in the summer.

- Saranac Lake, New York, has been home to the nation's low temperature more times than any other Eastern mountain town, with 168 listings, almost all of which occurred in winter.
- Jackson, Wyoming: 109 times, but almost all of those occurred between 1995 and 2001.
- Our old friend International Falls comes in with a dignified 85 times as the nation's low.

Other towns that are often listed as the nation's low include Embarrass, Minnesota; Boulder and Big Piney, Wyoming; Presque Isle and Caribou, Maine; Flagstaff, South Rim, and Bellemont, Arizona; Spincich Lake, Michigan; Berlin, New Hampshire; Mammoth Lakes, California; and Wisdom, Montana.

For the record, the coldest ambient temperature ever recorded in Colorado occurred in Maybell, way up in the northwest corner of the state. In January 1985, Maybell got down to a frosty –61. That temperature ranks number five when it comes to recorded all-time state-low temperatures.

**THE TOP-10 STATE LOW-TEMPERATURES LIST:**

- Prospect Creek, Alaska (elevation 1,100 feet), –80, February 3, 1947
- Rogers Pass, Montana (elevation 5,470 feet), –70, January 20, 1954
- Peters Sink, Utah (elevation 8,092 feet), –69, February 1, 1985
- Riverside, Wyoming (elevation 6,650 feet), –66, February 9, 1933
- Maybell, Colorado (elevation 5,920 feet), –61, February 1, 1985
- (Tie) Parshall, North Dakota (elevation 1,929 feet), February 15, 1936; Island Park Dam, Idaho (elevation 6,285 feet), January 18, 1943; Tower, Minnesota (elevation 1,430 feet), February 2, 1996, –60
- McIntosh, South Dakota (elevation 2,277 feet), –58, February 17, 1936
- Courderay, Wisconsin (elevation 1,300 feet), –55, February 4, 1996

**RECORD COLD TEMPERATURES FOR OTHER MOUNTAIN STATES ARE:**

- Arizona: Hawley Lake (elevation 8,180 feet), –40, January 7, 1971
- California: Boca (elevation 5,532 feet), –45, January 20, 1937
- Nevada: San Jacinto (elevation 5,200 feet), –50, January 8, 1937
- New Hampshire: Mount Washington (elevation 6,288 feet), –47, January 29, 1934
- New Mexico: Gavilan (elevation 7,350 feet), –50, February 1, 1951
- North Carolina: Mount Mitchell (elevation 6,525 feet), –34, January 21, 1985
- Oregon: Seneca (elevation 4,700 feet), –54, February 10, 1933

- Vermont: Bloomfield (elevation 915 feet), -50, December 30, 1933
- Washington: Mazama (elevation 2,120 feet) and Winthrop (elevation 1,755 feet), -48, December 30, 1968
- West Virginia: Lewisburg (elevation 2,200 feet), -37, December 30, 1917

The state with the highest low temperature ever recorded is Hawaii, where it got down to a frosty (barely) 12 at Mauna Kea (elevation 13,770 feet) on May 17, 1979.

Some weather statistics for select nippy Colorado towns that are home to National Weather Service (NWS) weather monitors between 1971 and 2000[1]:

- Alamosa: Average temperature: 41.2; average daily high: 58.9; average daily low: 23.4; average yearly snowfall: 31.3 inches
- Aspen: Average temperature: 40.7; average daily high: 55.7; average daily low: 26.5; average yearly snowfall: 137.5 inches (these statistics come from the 30-year NWS weather cycle, 1947-1979)
- Buena Vista: Average temperature: 43.3; average daily high: 58.9; average daily low: 27.8; average yearly snowfall: 33.3 inches
- Crested Butte: Average temperature: 33.9; average daily high: 53.4; average daily low: 21.8; average yearly snowfall: 200 inches (this is for the 2008-2009 winter only; statistics from 1971 to 2000 were not available)
- Dillon: Average temperature: 35.6; average daily high: 51; average daily low: 20.2; average yearly snowfall: 112.9 inches
- Durango: Average temperature: 47; average daily high: 63.4; average daily low: 30.5; average yearly snowfall: 68.8 inches
- Eagle County airport: Average temperature: 43.5; average daily high: 60.2; average daily low: 26.8; average yearly snowfall: 46.7 inches
- Evergreen: Average temperature: 43.8; average daily high: 60.4; average daily low: 27.3; average yearly snowfall: 85.1 inches
- Fraser: Average temperature: 34.4; average daily high: 51.8; average daily low: 17.1; average yearly snowfall: 151.1 inches
- Georgetown: Average temperature: 42.6; average daily high: 55.9; average daily low: 28.9; average yearly snowfall: 112.3 inches
- Grand Lake: Average temperature: 36.9; average daily high: 53; average daily low: 20.8; average yearly snowfall: 142.3 inches
- Gunnison: Average temperature: 37.8; average daily high: 55.4; average daily low: 20.3; average yearly snowfall: 47.3 inches.
- Kremmling: Average temperature: 38.7; average daily high: 55.2; average daily low: 22.1; average yearly snowfall: 56 inches
- Lake City: Average temperature: 39.1; average daily high: 55.8; average daily low: 22.3; average yearly snowfall: 82.5 inches

- Leadville: Average temperature: 34.5; average daily high: 49.5; average daily low: 19.5; average yearly snowfall: 147.2 inches
- Saguache: Average temperature: 41.8; average daily high: 58.3; average daily low: 25.3; average yearly snowfall: 25.1 inches
- Salida: Average temperature: 45.5; average daily high: 61.8; average daily low: 29.3; average yearly snowfall: 48.6 inches
- Silverton: Average temperature: 34.6; average daily high: 52.8; average daily low: 17.5; average yearly snowfall: 154.8 inches
- Steamboat Springs: Average temperature: 39.4; average daily high: 55.5; average daily low: 23.2; average yearly snowfall: 170.3 inches
- Walden: Average temperature: 37.5; average daily high: 53; average daily low: 22; average yearly snowfall: 64.8 inches
- Winter Park: Average temperature: 34.5; average daily high: 54.4; average daily low: 14.7; average yearly snowfall: 224.8 inches

Fraser also has the distinction of having the shortest growing season in the nation, with "growing season" being defined as the period between frosts. Fraser's official average growing season is four to seven days, with some years seeing essentially no growing season.

Other Colorado towns that have been listed as the nation's cold spot, between April 1, 1995, and August 31, 2010, are the following:

- Craig: 40 times
- Leadville: 20 times
- Grand Lake: 16 times
- Doyleville: 15 times
- Kremmling: 13 times
- Limon: 10 times
- Durango: 7 times
- Meeker: 5 times
- Winter Park, Trinidad, Aspen, Lake George, and Meredith: 3 times each
- Gould, Bailey, Conifer, Bridgeport, Walden, and Climax: 2 times each
- Crested Butte, Lamar, Redvale, Lake City, Dillon, Del Norte, Buena Vista, Steamboat Springs, Matheson, Roosevelt, Cheesman Reservoir, Yampa, Greeley, Climax, Berthoud Pass, Gould, and Boulder: 1 time each

## NOTES

1. The National Weather Service averages its data in 30-year cycles, meaning that the 1971–2000 cycle is the latest completed measurement cycle.

## SOURCES

www.usatoday.com/weather/news/extremes; encarta.msn.com/media; www.keno.org; National Weather Service.

# WHY ARE GUNNISON
# AND ALAMOSA SO COLD?

It is a very common misconception that altitude is the main variable when it comes to cold weather. You know—by and large, the higher, the colder. Yet, Gunnison, elevation 7,703 feet, and Alamosa, elevation 7,544 feet, reign supreme when it comes to frigidity in Colorado. Many less-frosty towns are significantly higher than that. So, what gives?

Both Gunnison and Alamosa are located in the bottom of big geographic bowls. Cold air is denser than warm air, and, like water, it flows downhill. Cold air accumulates in lower areas and remains there until meteorological circumstances move it out. The lower angle of the sun during the winter months, combined with snow cover, make it so that a fairly substantial quantity of wind is needed to move the cold air from Gunnison and Alamosa, which explains why those two towns are not only cold, but cold for long periods of time.

A good example of how a lower altitude can actually result in colder temperatures is found in the San Luis Valley. The weather station at the Great Sand Dunes National Park & Preserve has registered an average high temperature in January of 34.8°F and an average low temperature in January of 9.7°F (1951–present). Twenty miles away in Alamosa—500 feet lower than the dunes—the National Weather Service over that same period has registered an annual average high temperature in January of 34.4°F and an average low in January of minus 1.9°F.

The reason for this discrepancy? The dunes are located on the edge of the valley, above the area where the coldest air settles.

## SOURCES

Personal interview with Paul Wolyn, science operations officer, National Weather Service, Pueblo.

# WINDCHILL AND THE WEATHER
# MISERABILITY INDEX

The winter of 2007–2008 in the Colorado high country was, according to many a shell-shocked mountain dweller, among the most intense (read: worst) in recent memory. Many Colorado ski areas, such as Steamboat (489 inches of snow), Monarch (482 inches of snow), and Crested Butte (422 inches of snow) had record seasons. And it was not exactly warm either. Between November 1, 2007, and April 30, 2008, Colorado had the nation's cold temperature 36 times.

Still, long-time locals remarked that the conditions were reminiscent of the way things were back in the good old days—the days when temperatures routinely got low enough that, as but one random example, the pine bark beetles were kept in check by the frigid wrath of Mother Nature.

What was different about the winter of 2007–2008 was an aggregate climatic situation that was unusual to the point of freakish. During most winters in the high country, it might snow like crazy, but, when it's not snowing, it's generally clear, sunny, and flat-out wonderful. And, although when the sky is clear it can get cold as all get-out, at least there are generally palpable periods of time in the winter when, if you're not careful, you will get a facial sunburn the likes of which you likely have not experienced since your last vacation to the tropics. Not so in the winter of 2007–2008, a winter when shivering, seasonal-affective-disorder-stricken locals were trying mightily to verbally amalgamate a set of weather conditions little known in Colorado. "It was cold, snowy, gray, and windy" is the G-rated paraphrasing of what locals said through clenched dentition. And it was that way clear until the first week of June, when the last storm hit above 9,000 feet. People seemed to be scratching their noggins in search of some sort of composite miserability index by which they could express themselves vis-à-vis the bleak, blustery, bone-chilling, blizzard-based winter of their discontent. Something like, "It was 9.99 on the Richter scale of Endless Wretched Frigid Gloom."

Professional meteorologists offer little in the way of help in this regard. They can point toward snowfall statistics, average temperatures, and the number of sun-free days, but blending all that data into one usable statistic with which you can impress/perplex your friends back in Georgia is not something educated weather geeks do.

The closest thing to a weather-measurement aggregation that we have is the venerable windchill factor, and that is a statistic that has been assailed on all levels since it was first contrived by Antarctic explorer Paul A. Siple, who coined the term in a 1939 must-read dissertation, "Adaptation of the Explorer to the Climate of Antarctica." During the 1940s, Siple and Charles F. Passel conducted experiments on the time needed to freeze a bottle of water in a plastic cylinder that was exposed to the elements. They found that the time depends upon how warm the water is at the beginning of the experiment, combined with (duh!) the outside temperature and the wind speed. The result of their experiments was codified during World

War II, and, by the 1950s and 1960s, it was considered bonafide Scientific Gospel.

Throughout the lives of most of us, the windchill factor has been reported by well-meaning, straight-faced weather people, right alongside other gospel-like, though specious, statistics such as stock market numbers and gross national product.

Thing is, the windchill factor was flawed on many levels from the very beginning. It was so flawed that even the flaws were often contradictory, which is maybe a good way to keep scientists harmlessly occupied, but it's a bad way to figure out how many layers of clothes to put on before you step outside in January.

First of all, you must understand that the method by which Siple and Passel measured windchill factor was by way of a long and complex formula that makes those of us who studied the various Liberal Arts recoil in ignorant horror. Here it is: "$T_{wc}=0.817 (3.17V^{1/2}+5.81-0.25V)(T_f-91.4) + 91.4$, where $T_{wc}$ is the windchill factor, V is the wind speed in statute miles per hour, and $T_f$ is the temperature in degrees Fahrenheit." So, from the get-go, the foundation of the concept of windchill factor is inherently inaccessible to all but a few by its very nature. For most of us, it's some sort of nebulous combination of ambient temperature and wind.

More than that, though, the very nature of the formula is bunked up by its reliance on constants that are anything but. And that is where the entire concept of windchill factor comes unraveled. Sure, things like temperature and wind speed can indeed be viewed as objective, but windchill factor is by its very definition a measure of the effect of those supposed constants upon human skin. And human skin is definitely frustratingly dynamic. Go back to the initial experiments performed by Siple and Passel. They themselves said that the entire outcome was based on the temperature of the water inside the plastic cylinder. When people step outside, they do so in a dizzying array of circumstances. Some are warmer, while some are colder. Some are well hydrated—meaning there is ample blood flow through the capillary system—while others are dehydrated. Some are well insulated, while others have more exposed skin. Some are of Nordic extraction, while others are of Polynesian extraction. Some are skinny, some are fat. And on and on.

This reality is further exacerbated by a difference of opinion regarding how cold temperatures, combined with wind, actually chill exposed skin. One school of thought operates under the assumption that, as long as the air temperature is lower than the skin temperature, the body loses heat more quickly in the wind because each air molecule that touches the skin, via a process known as Inconceivable Quantum Mechanical Magic, carries away some body heat, and, if the wind blows faster, then more molecules touch your skin, and, consequently, more heat is removed.

Another perspective focuses on the thermal boundary layer surrounding the skin, which is several millimeters thick (don't even get me started on the effect that the metric system has had on all of these concepts and calculations!). This boundary acts as an insulator. When the wind kicks up, this thermal boundary layer gets compromised, but not in a linear fashion. The initial effects of wind upon the thermal layer are geometrically more intense than latter effects. Thus, once again, the constant figures upon which the initial windchill factor formula relies are kicked out the window.

But, if there's one aspect of the tried-and-(un)-true windchill factor, it's the application of the second degree of thermodynamics in this context. If windchill was an accurate measurement of the effects of wind on ambient temperature to produce an apparent temperature, then a windchill factor of 25° F would freeze water, which it won't if the ambient temperature remains above 32° F.

Hell, even the initial wind-speed measurement used to calculate windchill factor "temperatures" was compromised because anemometers of that era did not kick into action until the wind speed hit four miles per hour.

Understanding all of this, the National Weather Service in 2001 revised the windchill factor formula. That revision resulted in the establishment of a new windchill *index*, which is determined by "iterating" (their word, not mine) a model of skin temperature under various wind speeds and temperatures. Heat transfer was calculated for a bare face in wind, facing the wind, while walking into it at three miles per hour. The new model corrects the officially measured wind speed at face height, assuming the person is in an open field.

And, yes, there's another of those convoluted-looking formulas that proves we ought to get scientists out of the laboratory as often as possible so they can ski out into the woods on a frigid high country winter day. Only then will they learn what mountain dwellers have long known: that winter weather is best measured in the aggregate by using language rather than formulas.

"Blankety-blank-blank miserable" is about as accurate as weather observation gets.

SOURCES

National Science Digital Library; meteorologist Steve Horstmeyer (www.shortsmeyer.com); Wikipedia.

# HOW ARE SUNNY DAYS MEASURED?

Despite the fact that there is generally a shortage of attribution when the statements are made, Coloradans are justifiably proud of the fact that the state receives "300 days of sunshine per year." (The Durango Area Tourism Office website, for example, states exactly that.) And even though the actual number varies, to hear people tell it, Colorado gets about as much sun as the Sahara.

Well…not so fast.

The problem is that there's no official definition of "days of sunshine," so there is no data set where that information is collected.

For many years, the National Weather Service (NWS) has operated instruments called "sunshine switches" in three non-mountain Colorado locations—Denver, Pueblo, and Colorado Springs. These instruments measure and record, minute by minute, each day, when the sun is shining. Based upon a study conducted in the late 1990s at the Denver "sunshine switch," it was determined that, if you count every day that the sun came out for at least one hour, then you could come up with an average of around 300 "days of sunshine" each year in Denver.

The problem is that your average person probably equates a "day of sunshine" with "a sunny day." Few would contend that having the sun come out for an hour during an otherwise cloudy day is the same as having a day completely void of cloud cover. Yet, the "300 days of sunshine per year" claim still maintains traction in Colorado, especially among marketing and real estate people.

The NWS has recently established a criterion for determining "clear," "cloudy," and "partly cloudy" days based upon sky cover. Any day with an average sky cover of 30 percent or less is considered a "clear" day. If the sky cover is 80 percent or more, it's consider a "cloudy" day. Anything in between is a "partly cloudy" day. (These measurements are averaged from hourly sky-condition reports taken between sunrise and sunset.)

Based upon these definitions, Denver receives 115 "clear" days, 130 "partly cloudy" days, and 120 "cloudy" days on average per year. In Grand Junction, the number of "clear" days is high—137 on average per year—but the number of cloudy days (121) is almost the same.

According to the NWS, the most total sunshine per year in Colorado occurs around Alamosa, while the least occurs around Boulder and in the northern mountains.

SOURCE

Colorado Climate Center.

# NON-POSSESSIVE PLACE NAMES

Grammatically, you would think that the seemingly pluralized place names like "Pikes" Peak would appear on maps and in marketing brochures in the possessive form: "Pike's Peak." But, in 1891, the newly formed U.S. Board on Geographic Names, an organization obviously staffed with scientists rather than English majors, recommended against the use of apostrophes in place names.

Thus, we have in Colorado, in addition to Pikes Peak, Grays and Torreys peaks, Longs Peak, and the Eagles Nest Wilderness.

Very often, magazine and newspaper editors, unaware of that 1891 place-name recommendation, will—purposefully or otherwise—trump officialdom with proper grammar and use the possessive forms of those names in print.

In addition, in 1978, the Colorado State Legislature actually passed a resolution specifically mandating the use of the non-possessive Pikes Peak, resulting in more than one person wondering just how many Pikes there actually were. There is no record of what punishment the state legislature proposed for those grammatical purists, or even those wallowing in ignorance, who continued to use "Pike's" Peak.

Understanding the apparent aversion of both the state and federal governments toward possessive-ized place names, it would be tempting to assume that aversion made its way down to the eastern plains, where is found the unincorporated hamlet of Joes. This town name is not a victim of the grammar-challenged employees of the U.S. Board on Geographic Names, or even of the Colorado State Legislature. It is, rather, the result of the fact that three of the town's first settlers were named Joe (what are the chances?). At one time, people called the town, located in Yuma County, "Three Joes," but that would have caused confusion had a fourth Joe defied all odds and moved to town. Now, no matter how many Joes move to Joes, everyone feels as though an entire town, albeit a modest one, was named after them. It's the Johns who feel left out.

And, speaking of Johns…

One other place that boasts confusing pluralization-based appellation is the mostly ghost town of Saints John (founded in 1863 or 1864 and originally called Coleyville), located at an elevation of 10,763 in Summit County, near Montezuma. The temptation for most people is to call the town "Saint John's," which, based upon the aforementioned U.S. Board on Geographic Names, would have to appear on maps as "Saint Johns."

But Saints John, site of one of Colorado's first silver discoveries, is indeed Saints John. Although there is some disputation on how the town came to be thusly named, the most commonly accepted version these days is that two of the people who founded this town, which used to house the largest private library in Colorado, were Masons. And the patron saints of the Masons are Saint John the Baptist and Saint John the Evangelist. Nothing like covering your bets with one easy place naming.

SOURCES

*Colorado Ghost Towns and Mining Camps* by Sandra Dallas; Wikipedia.

# A SENSE OF SCALE

Colorado, at 104,069 square miles, is the country's eighth-largest state. With a population of about 5,024,748, it's the twenty-second most populated state. That amounts to 48.28 inhabitants per square mile, not including tourists and second-homeowners.

Many people lament the fact that, since 1980, when the state had 2,907,526 residents, Colorado's population has increased more than 50 percent. Even though that is surely a significant statistic that manifests itself in venues as disparate as Interstate 70 congestion on Sunday afternoons during ski season and the fact that more and more wilderness areas now require camping permits, some context is still enlightening.

Colorado is slightly smaller than Ecuador and the African nation of Burkina Faso. It is almost exactly the same size as another African nation, Gabon.

Colorado and New Zealand, at 103,737 square miles, are within eight square miles of being exactly the same size. And, with 3.8 million residents, New Zealand's population density of 37 people per square mile is similar to Colorado's population density, which falls between the population density of Equatorial Guinea (43 people per square mile) and Sweden (51 people per square mile). Peru, with 53 people per square mile, is also in the population density ballpark, as is Finland, at 40 people per square mile.

The population density for the entire United States is 76 people per square mile, so Colorado is well under the national average.

In the West, Colorado tends toward the top of the population density pack.

- **Alaska:** 570,374 square miles; 710,231 people; 1.25 people per square mile
- **Wyoming:** 97,105 square miles; 563,626 people; 5.8 people per square mile

- **Montana:** 145,556 square miles; 989,415 people; 6.8 people per square mile
- **New Mexico:** 121,364 square miles; 2,059,179 people; 16.9 people per square mile
- **Idaho:** 82,751 square miles; 1,567,582 people; 18.9 people per square mile
- **Nevada:** 109,806 square miles; 2,700,551 people; 24.6 people per square mile
- **Utah:** 82,168 square miles; 2,763,885 people; 33.6 people per square mile
- **Oregon:** 96,033 square miles; 3,831,074 people; 39.9 people per square mile
- **Arizona:** 113,642 square miles; 6,392,017 people; 56.2 people per square mile
- **Washington:** 66,582 square miles; 6,724,540 people; 101 people per square mile
- **California:** 155,973 square miles; 37,253,956 people; 238.9 people per square mile

As for a continental population–density comparison, the whole of the United Kingdom—including England, Scotland, Wales, Northern Ireland, and the Channel Islands — comprises 94,525 square miles, or roughly 91 percent of Colorado's land area. Yet, with 60 million inhabitants, the population density of the United Kingdom is 634.75 people per square mile. With that in mind, Colorado seems sparsely populated indeed.

SOURCES

2010 U.S. Census Bureau population estimates; *Rand McNally Road Atlas; Covent Garden Books' World Reference Atlas.*

# JUST EXACTLY HOW BIG IS COLORADO?

Were there one seemingly unarguable Colorado statistic, you would think it would be the state's actual physical area. Alas...

While there is no dispute regarding relativity—Colorado is the country's eighth-largest state, well behind seventh-largest Nevada (109,826 square miles) and well ahead of ninth-largest Wyoming (97,100 square miles)—there is very little absolute consensus regarding exactly how big Colorado actually is.

According to Rand McNally, Colorado's total area is 103,718 square miles. Both www.city-data.com/states/Colorado.html and National Geographic contend that the state covers 104,091 miles.

But www.netstate.com/states/geography/co_geography.htm contends that it's 104,100 square miles, while both Wikipedia and www.answerbag.com say that it's 104,185 square miles. The *Historical Atlas of Colorado* states that the correct number is 104,247 square miles[1].

What's up here?

Because Colorado is one of only three states—Wyoming and Utah being the others—whose boundaries are defined totally by lines of latitude and longitude rather than by natural boundaries such as rivers or the crests of mountain ranges, it would seem fairly easy for numbers geeks to ascertain exactly how many square miles are found within the state's borders. Such is not the case, for a number of reasons.

First things first. Although many people are inclined to say that Wyoming and Colorado are the country's only rectangular states (verily, www.netstate.com/states/geography/co_geography.htm echoes a lot of sources by stating that Colorado is "…shaped in an almost perfect rectangle"), such a statement is not only inaccurate but also physically impossible. Because lines of longitude are not parallel (they all eventually meet at the North Pole), the northern boundary of Colorado (Wyoming and Nebraska) is by definition shorter than the southern (New Mexico and Oklahoma) boundary (about 364.6 miles to about 385.9 miles, respectively). It is likely that some of the inexactitude regarding measurements of the state's area stems from calculations mistakenly treating Colorado as a pure rectangle.

Colorado is, in fact, a trapezoid that was physically established by Congress during the period leading up to the Organic Act that established the Colorado Territory in 1861. Congress decreed that the Colorado Territory stretched south to north from 37 degrees north latitude to 41 degrees north latitude. Its east–west dimensions went from 102 degrees west latitude to 109 degrees west latitude. There is disputation on the accuracy of virtually every one of those lines.

Wikipedia, citing the U.S. Geological Survey, contends that the state's east and west borders are actually located at 103-03 west longitude to 109-03 west longitude, respectively.

The *Colorado Atlas & Gazetteer* shows on its maps that:
- The southwest corner of the state is actually located at 36-59-56 degrees north latitude, 109-02-39 degrees west latitude.
- The northwest corner is located at 40-59-58 degrees north latitude, 109-02-56 degrees west longitude.
- The northeast corner is located at 41-00-08 degrees north latitude, 102-02-56 degrees west longitude.

- The southeast corner is located at 36-59-40 degrees north latitude, 102-02-41 degrees west longitude.

These inconsistencies alone would result in discrepancies when the state's area is being calculated.

But a more likely scenario is that those doing the state-area calculations mistakenly treated Colorado's borders as straight lines, when, in fact, the northern, western, and southern boundaries all contain fairly significant surveying errors, which, when aggregated, amount to several hundred square miles of measurement irregularity.

It should come as no surprise that Colorado's mountainous terrain made accuracy difficult for surveyors. Since the state's boundaries were based upon specific lines of latitude and longitude[2], surveyors had to work in territory that was ill suited to regular demarcation. As well, given the fact that all surveys made when Colorado's boundaries were being physically established originated from a single point more than 1,500 miles away—the Old Naval Observatory in Washington. D.C.—it's easy to see how mistakes were made. Verily, it's a testament to the skills of the early surveyors that there weren't more noteworthy errors.

The first significant boundary survey error occurred in 1868, when the Ehud N. Darling Survey completed its work along Colorado's southern boundary. Sadly, in Archuleta County, near the tiny town of Edith, an error led to a dispute between Colorado and New Mexico that was not settled until the U.S. Supreme Court ruled in 1960 that an official boundary survey—even if it was erroneous— was still valid. (Darling's miscalculation resulted in parts of Colorado extending below 37 degrees north latitude, a reality that was discovered during a re-survey in 1903. In 1919, as it was applying for statehood, New Mexico claimed the inaccurately surveyed turf, which would have moved several Colorado villages and post offices into the Land of Enchantment.)

Darling's miscalculation was followed in 1873, when A.D. Richards made a surveying error along the border between Wyoming and Weld County.

The most glaring blunder occurred in 1879, when Rollin J. Reeves's survey of the Colorado–Utah border resulted in an error of such magnitude that it is visible today on even poorly produced highway maps. (Hint: Look at the southwestern corner of Montrose County.)[3]

For the record, Vincent Matthews, state geologist and director of the Colorado Geological Survey, and his staff performed calculations specifically for this book in early 2009, taking into account every surveying irregularity, and determined that the state's actual area is 104,069 square miles (66,604,124 acres).[4]

# NOTES

1. There is even disputation regarding how much of Colorado's total area is covered by water, with sources varying from between 371 square miles to 496 square miles.

2. In most boundary surveys, such as those following the courses of rivers or the crests of mountain ranges, points would be marked, and then surveyors would ascertain the latitude and longitude of those points using benchmarks whose latitude and longitude had already been established. Colorado's boundaries were set by doing exactly the opposite—a much more difficult and tedious process.

3. Although the Darling, Richards, and Reeves boo-boos eventually impacted Colorado's physical boundaries, they are far from the only major surveying mistakes known in Colorado. In 1875, Chandler Robbins mistakenly located the famed Four Corners Monument—one of the most iconic surveying markers in the entire country—about a half-mile east of where it ought to have been placed. At least that's what people in the know thought for many years. In May 2009, the U.S. Geodetic Survey announced that the Four Corners Monument is either 1,807.14 feet, or 2.5 miles, off—depending on where one starts one's measurements. The original mandate called for the only location in the United States where the boundaries of four states—Colorado, Utah, New Mexico, and Arizona—met would be at 109 degrees west longitude, 37 degrees north latitude. While the latitude part is simple enough (no one argues that all latitude measurements begin at the Equator), longitude is another matter. According to Dave Doyle, chief geodetic surveyor for the U.S. Geodetic Survey, the Four Corners measurement should have been taken at 32 degrees longitude west of the Washington Meridian, which passes through the Old Naval Observatory in the Foggy Bottom neighborhood of Washington, D.C. That calculation yields the 1,807.14-foot disparity. Measuring instead to the 109th meridian west of Greenwich, United Kingdom, would result in the much larger disparity of 2.5 miles. Either way, when tourists walk around the Four Corners Monument assuming that they just visited four states in one fell swoop, what they actually did was walk around a point in southwestern Colorado. There are no plans to relocate the monument itself, and its inaccurate location does not affect the actual, physical borders between Colorado, Utah, New Mexico, and Arizona.

4. Matthews stressed that the whole notion of measuring a state's surface area is inherently flawed, especially if that state contains as much in the way of vertical terrain as does Colorado. State area measurements are based upon two-dimensional observations. Yet, were a flexible skin to be spread over the top of Colorado, so that it molded itself to the state's actual three-dimensional physical topography, then stretched out, it would cover far more than the official, two-dimensional area measurement. For this reason, were you to add up the total acreage that has been actually surveyed in Colorado, it would greatly exceed the amount of acreage the State Geological Survey came up with because land surveyors measure actual surface area, which takes into account vertical topography.

## SOURCES

*Historical Atlas of Colorado* by Thomas J. Noel, Paul F. Mahoney, and Richard E. Stevens (a must-have book for Colorado-philes); personal interviews with Vincent Matthews, state geologist and director of the Colorado Geological Survey; Wikipedia; *How the States Got Their Shapes* by Mark Stein; www.econ.umn.edu/~holmes/data/BorderData.html; the Associated Press.

# COLORADO MOUNTAIN LEXICON

So, there you are, enjoying a frothy beverage in a mountain-town watering hole, not really meaning to eavesdrop on the conversation three barstools down, but the people are talking so ebulliently that you can't help it. Thing is, this is what you overhear:

"Dude, that was one righteous ride, except for that gnarly endo and all that quag."

"Yeah, dude, that was one mondo drop, but you stuck it."

"Epic."

For many people, such sentences might as well be uttered in Navajo. Like plenty of other places where certain palpable lifestyle demographics reign supreme—ranch country, coastal areas where boating, surfing, and fishing are big, military bases, college campuses, prisons—the Colorado high country is a hub of activity-(and, often, age-) specific lingo that seemingly exists as much to nonplus non-members of the tribe as it is to actually communicate with one's bro-brahs. To make life easier for those interfacing with the mountains, whether on a short-term or long-term basis, a series of mountain lexicons might be helpful, at least so you can ascertain whether the two youngsters in the lift line just insulted you.

Even though there are a number of activity-specific translation matrices strategically placed throughout this book in appropriate sections, covering literally hundreds of words, please remember that each of the activities upon which the lexicons are centered boasts respective vocabularies big enough to each fill volumes in and of themselves. The words included in this book are only the tip of a lexicographic iceberg that keeps expanding and changing season by season. Also remember that there are unavoidable overlaps between the various lexicons. Here is some general mountain-based terminology.

- **Action Figure:** Those folks who do it all, do it all well, and are buff about it. The lean mountain biker who rides every day, kayaks, climbs, and telemark skis, skinning up the ski hill rather than being lame and riding the lift like mere mortals—and they still manage to get five runs in before happy hour. They have all the toys, roof racks, etc., and their mountain-fashion ensembles consist of all the right brands—Patagonia, The North Face, Carhartt, Kavu—which, while being well-scuffed, do not approach the level of rags that would be worn by dirtbags and bottom feeders (*see* "Dirtbag" and "Bottom Feeder"). Action figures are also proficient users of mountain lingo, moving seamlessly between paddling and skiing lexicons in a sort of pidgin mountain patois.

- **Affordable/Attainable Housing:** Government-controlled housing, typically built by private developers in return for being allowed to construct more non-controlled, non-affordable/attainable housing or larger homes. Typically, mountain towns use such schemes to create employee housing without the employers having to pay for same.
- **Agro:** Short for "aggressive," often unnecessarily so. "Dude, every time you chug three cans of Red Bull before you go skiing, you get all agro toward the mountain and everyone on it!"
- **Aprés Ski:** Literally, "after skiing." Most often applied to sitting quietly and contentedly with one's chums—all of whom are wearing matching Icelandic wool sweaters—in front of a crackling fire and sipping a recreational beverage while listening to quiet folk music and reflecting upon the beauty of the mountains and mountain life. Has evolved to mean raucous frat boys doing repeated shots of tequila in a slope-side imbibery while requesting Jimmy Buffet song after Jimmy Buffet song from the exasperated 50-year-old guitar player who viscerally hates Jimmy Buffet songs and who, if you would have told him 30 years ago that he would *still* be playing Buffet covers at après-ski bars for poor-tipping, inebriated frat boys, would have gone Back Home (*see* "Back Home") to get an MBA.
- **Aspenized:** Loosely, a term to mean anything screwed up because of being glitzy beyond belief and priced beyond the reach of all but the kinds of folks who are often the first to get snuffed during a revolution. Named, of course, after Aspen, the most glitzy and expensive resort town of them all. "Dude, Breck is still a great place to visit, but it's been Aspenized all to hell."
- **Back Home:** The place where almost every mountain dweller is "from," and where a high percentage of mountain dwellers will return—a decision they will likely regret for the rest of their lives.
- **Bartering:** The process by which, say, a local ski tech will tune a bartender's boards for free with the understanding that the bartender will slide him a couple of uncharged-for pitchers of beer down the road. This is, of course, a purely theoretical concept that does not deserve any macro-scrutiny whatsoever from the IRS.
- **Beater:** An all-star among area POS mountain cars (*see* "POS").
- **Black Ice:** Nearly invisible ice coating on roadways. Caused by snow melting across the road when the sun is up and freezing once the sun goes down. One of the leading objective causes of road accidents in Colorado.
- **Bottom Feeder:** A person who is perfectly willing to sleep on a beer-stained floor and who harbors absolutely no shame when it comes to mooching, stealing, cajoling, bribing, or "borrowing," as long as they don't have to work. Also: A secondary character in former *Aspen Daily News* reporter Dan Dunn's rum-soaked semi-novel *Nobody Likes A Quitter, and Other Reasons to Avoid*

*Rehab.* Also, and not by chance, it is the name of a song by Aspen-area musician Steve Skinner, who therefore has first dibs on the term.

- **Bro-Brahs:** Muchachos.
- **Brown Ice:** Snow that has been warmed by a doggie deposit enough to partially melt it and that, when the sun goes down, re-freezes.
- **Buddy Pass:** A cut-rate, ski-area season pass designed specifically to raise as much pre-season operating cash as possible for the owners of the ski area. While seeming like a great deal for skiers and snowboarders, buddy passes are universally regarded as having caused a degree of crowding on the slopes and highways that was at one time unthinkable.
- **Butt Tucker:** Lift operator at a downhill ski area.
- **Company:** (1) A corporate entity, usually a limited-liability corporation, which creates customers to annoy workers; (2) people who just won't freakin' leave your hovel: "Dude, you still have company?" (*See also* "Bottom Feeders" and "Couch Surfing.")
- **Couch Surfing:** The process of "visiting" enough different people in a given mountain town that one can stay an entire season without ever having to pay rent.
- **Dirtbag:** Generally a young person who is willing to live a style well out of the American mainstream in order to be able to ski, paddle, and bike as often as possible. Often confused with hippies (*see* "Hippie"), except that dirtbags are far more into recreational hedonism than they are into peace, love, and granola—unless said granola is both free and washed down with free beer.
- **Dog:** Four-legged cousin of the domesticated wolf. Considered necessary lifestyle accoutrement for mountain dwellers, especially those who just moved to the mountains. Often named for mountain features, like "Talus" and "Tundra," which serves to show others that the dog owner is a true mountain aficionado. Rarely trained, a reality explained away by words to the effect of, "Training would negate [Tundra's] true spirit."
- **Down Valley:** An otherwise literal geographic term filled with all manner of social connotation. Generally, where the worker bees live. Applied to towns like Gunnison, Edwards, Carbondale, Fraser, and Dillon, which are "down valley," respectively, from Crested Butte, Vail, Aspen, Winter Park, and Keystone.
- **Dude:** Slang for human being. Doesn't have to be a cool or hip human being, only a human being. Likewise, a dude can be male or female, though he is usually male. Females are often called "dudettes." Once reserved to describe certain individuals who boasted at least minimal distinguishing characteristics (e.g., ability to score free food at closing time from the kitchen staff at the local Arby's), "dude" is now so common that it can serve many roles in conversation: "(Sigh) Dude, I know a lotta dudes who

skied that line, but, dude, you bailed, you wuss." Other dude: "Duuuude!"

- **DUI (a.k.a. Dewey):** Driving under the influence (of an intoxicating substance). Considered by many to be an unavoidable component of mountain living, like high rents and black ice. (*See* "Rent" and "Black Ice.*")

- **Firewood:** Mostly archaic term that once described dead tree parts that were used to heat mountain homes back before most high-country municipalities started outlawing wood-burning devices as a means of fighting inversion-caused air pollution, which, in turn, often caused righteous sniffles on the part of newcomers whose mountain fantasies were based more upon crystal-clear air than they were on long-time locals being able to scavenge for free means of heating their hovels.

- **First/Last/Security Deposit:** First month's rent, last month's rent, and a security deposit generally equal to one month's rent. The often-astounding amount of money that renters in mountain country usually have to come up with before they are allowed to rent a housing unit. (*See* "Security Deposit.")

- **Gaper:** Tourist.

- **Gaper Tan:** Bright-white, non-sunburned goggle marks left on an otherwise extremely fried red face.

- **Going Down:** Leaving the mountains, for either the short term (going down to a concert in Denver, for instance) or the long term (returning to Ohio to attend graduate school).

- **Gonzo:** A form of personalized journalism created and personified by Dr. Hunter S. Thompson (1937–2005), a long-time resident of Woody Creek, a rural enclave NearAspen, Colorado (see "NearAspen"). The gonzo alchemy combines first-person point of view with actual participation in the story, sometimes applying the tools of the novel to situations that are, well, novel. "Gonzo" freed many journalists from staid strictures of the "inverted pyramid" style of writing that still defines a high percentage of newspapers that are, as we speak, not un-coincidentally, fighting for their business lives. The term "gonzo" is inexorably intertwined with Thompson's oeuvre, but it was actually coined by *Boston Globe* magazine editor Bill Cardoso in a 1970 story about Thompson's article, "The Kentucky Derby Is Decadent and Depraved," which appeared first in *Scanlan's Monthly* magazine, then in Thompson's personal anthology *The Great Shark Hunt*. Cardoso claimed that "gonzo," which he used to describe Thompson's writing style, was South Boston Irish slang for the "last man standing after an all-night drinking marathon." Other etymologists contend that the word evolved from a 1950s hipster term made up of "gone" (as in ecstatic, uncontrolled) and an "o" suffix that appeared on several other hipster words, like "daddy-o." Still others believe that the term was directly borrowed from the Italian word for "buffoon" or "simpleton." The last definition that Hunter gave of gonzo journalism was, "Journalism that doesn't automatically accept as truth what the authorities say." The term is now so misused that it has lost much of its original meaning. "Gonzo" these days is used to describe anything from the most tepid, first-person writing style that lacks even a semblance of the insight or participatory part of the alchemy that defined Thompson's work or, worse, by extreme athletes to mean "crazily intense," a reality evidenced by a motel in Moab—which primarily caters to mountain bikers—named the "Gonzo Inn." Also used these days in the porn industry to mean a movie that goes straight from the opening credits to the sex part without even pretending to establish plot and character beforehand.

- **Happy Hour:** Times when watering holes offer reduced-price beverages as well as, sometimes, free food. Magnets for dirtbags, bottom feeders, hippies, ski bums, woodsies (*see* "Woodsies"), and, increasingly, real estate professionals hard hit by the economic downturn.
- **Health Insurance:** An increasingly mythical concept that pays for the inevitable miscues that accompany life at altitude. Usually comes with a high price (*see* "Job").
- **Hippie:** Usually a derivative person young enough that he or she was not yet born during the Summer of Love. Dresses in vibrantly colored clothing, often procured from hippie.com. Would not be caught dead at a Rainbow Family Gathering. Also: Real-estate professional-in-training.
- **Job:** That which interferes with skiing and biking and usually does not provide enough in the way of actual remuneration to make the trade-off worth it, unless part of that remuneration includes a season ski pass and maybe even health insurance (*see* "Health Insurance").
- **Jonesing:** In very bad need; enthusiastically desiring. "Dude, I'm jonesing for another powder day."
- **Lease:** A housing-related legal document that, at the beginning of ski season, seems like such a wonderful idea, but, toward the end of the season, seems like a form of unreasonable indenture promulgated by The Man. Generally meant to be broken.
- **"Like":** Ordinarily an innocent preposition that now is used so often as a combination preposition/conjunction that most sentences, especially those uttered by people under age 30, do not have structure or cohesiveness without it. "It was like he was like jonesing like to like go like skiing, but he like couldn't like find his like skis."
- **Local:** Significant disputation surrounds this ambiguous term. Most folks will call themselves a "local" as soon as they sign a lease (*see* "Lease") and get a post office box in a mountain town, even if they only plan to stay for one ski season. Generally, moun-

tain dwellers feel that, in order to be a true local, you have to have lived in the high country at least as long as they have.

- **Local's/Locals' Discount(s):** The mostly unspoken agreement wherein business owners will charge locals (*see* "Local") less for products and services than they charge tourists and second homeowners. On occasion, individual members of a business owner's staff—especially wait staff—will unilaterally implement de facto locals' discount policies involving friends, lovers, potential lovers, out-of-town family, in-town family, and/or co-workers. It is customary to tip (*see* "Tips") based upon the what-would-have-been amount up to $100. That would be at least $20 for those who are tip-mathematics-challenged.
- **Mondo:** Huuuuuuuuuge. "Now that you've successfully hucked this cliff, you're ready for that mondo drop over on Vail Pass."
- **Mountain Betty/River Betty:** Tomboy-type females who very, very, very often ski, climb, bike, and paddle better than the boys who chase them. Added points if she owns a reliable car.
- **Mountain Town:** Any town located at an elevation no less than 1,000 vertical feet lower than the town in which you live. In Colorado, barroom consensus indicates that it's mighty hard for any town less than 6,000 feet in elevation feet to be called a "mountain town." Most mountain-town dwellers start rolling their eyes at the thought of a true mountain town being less than 7,000 feet, a reality that admittedly excludes otherwise important sociological factors that are very evident in such sub-7,000-foot towns as Steamboat Springs and Boulder.
- **NearAspen:** Versions are found in most resort communities, like NearBreck or NearSteamboat, but the term is thought to have originated in Aspen because that was the first resort town to be Aspenized (*see* "Aspenized"). Typical of the famous resort town, it's the place people are from who would like to live in Aspen and who culturally and socially gravitate toward the town but don't actually live there, often for economic reasons. "Yeah, baby, let's ski and we can stay in my condo NearAspen." (*See* "Down Valley.")
- **Newbie:** New arrival to mountain country, whether of the 19-year-old, living-in-car variety or the newly retired, second-homeowning variety. Both usually tend to act like they've lived there forever and that people, even lifelong locals, ought to immediately care what they think. (*See* "Local.")
- **POS:** Piece of [dung]. (Use your imagination.) Generally refers to mountain cars of a certain vintage whose rust "spots" actually cover more area than the non-rust "spots." Registration and proof of insurance are often not easily located.
- **Quarter Beer Night:** Very dignified affairs at certain classy types of mountain bars that have figured out a way to draw people who would likely be there anyhow by offering half-filled plastic cups of flat, tepid, low-rent beer that you couldn't give away in a pris-

on yard. Quarter beer nights often present great opportunities for people to hone their bar-fighting skills.

- **Raccoon Face:** See "Gaper Tan."
- **Real Estate:** Mountain-based investment opportunity that used to increase in value.
- **Rent:** Stunningly high monthly expenditure made by mountain-dwelling people who actually hold jobs (*see* "Job") and who wonder why they have become suddenly so popular among their bottom-feeder and dirtbag bro-brahs. (*See* "Bottom Feeder," "Dirtbag," and "Bro-Brah.")
- **Righteous:** Very cool. Synonym: bitchin'.
- **Roommate(s):** Co-dwellers who, in return for helping with rent, prove the old saying that familiarity breeds contempt.
- **Safety Meeting:** A group session in, say, a van or a backcountry cabin. Rumor has it that safety meetings sometimes imply the use of illegal substances, but this has never been substantiated.
- **Security Deposit:** That part of a rental agreement (*see* "First/ Last/Security Deposit") theoretically designed to cover the costs incurred by the landlord for the inevitable damage that comes from renting out property in a resort town and that is supposed to be returned to the renter(s) in the extremely unlikely case that damage does not occur. Either way, the security deposit often goes directly into the retirement account of the landlord at the end of the term of the lease (*see* "Lease") without explanation. Most renters consider this to be just another part of the cost of doing business in the high country.
- **Ski Bum:** Archaic term referring to people who used to sacrifice what most people would consider a normal American lifestyle in order to ski as many days per year as possible. Dishwashing and janitorial services have long been considered appropriate ski-bum vocations. The term has lost much of its cachet in recent years because it is now often co-opted by middle-aged stockbrokers referring to the amount of time they spend in their ski-in/ ski-out condo.
- **Sucker Hole:** A slight parting of the clouds and concomitant exposure of a small section of blue sky indicating to optimistic outdoorspeople that the stormy weather is about to break. Often followed by a thunderous downpour and much in the way of colorful expletives.
- **Swag (sometimes "Schwag"):** Believed to come from the Hollywood term for "stuff we all get." Something, usually worthless, you receive, usually for free, from a contest or a promoter, like a T-shirt or a sunglass holder. The vast majority of this stuff one could definitely live without, but, out of principle, every person in mountain country seeks swag out and then acts as though it's actually worth schlepping home. "Bobby stuffed all the swag he

scored at the X-Games into the back of his closet, never to be seen again."

- **Technical:** Anything that requires expertise, focus, experience, etc., usually using all of those things to avoid hitting something undesirable, like a rock in the middle of the river or the trail.
- **"The Odds Are Good, But the Goods Are Odd":** Term highly overused by mountain women to refer to the available stock of eligible males in the various mountain towns.
- **Tips:** A generally small amount of money that has an astounding effect on the ability of a bartender to remember your name and what you drink the next time you enter the bar.
- **Townie:** A kind of bicycle generally made from scavenged parts and of a value low enough that, if it's stolen, it's no biggie. In recent years, numerous bike manufacturers have jumped on the townie trend and now make townies that are worth more than many POS cars. (*See* "POS.")
- **Trustfunder:** Technically, a person who has inherited enough money, placed in a trust fund by forward-thinking parents who, after all, know their offspring better than anyone. A trustfunder does not, like, have to, like, work. Generally a derisive term used by people who, more than anything else in the world, wish they were trustfunders.
- **Trustifarian:** A trustfunder (*see* "Trustfunder") who tries to cover up whatever bourgeois-based guilt he or she has regarding his or her trustfunder status at least partially by wearing secondhand clothing, sporting stylishly unkempt locks, and driving a POS mountain car (*see* "POS") adorned with "Free Tibet" and "Think Globally, Act Locally" bumperstickers.
- **Turkey:** Tourist.
- **Up Valley:** Opposite of "Down Valley" (*see* "Down Valley"). Generally where the more affluent folks and second homeowners live. Aspen, Crested Butte, Breckenridge, Winter Park, and Vail are generally considered "Up Valley" locales.
- **Vacation Rage:** Stressful anger brought into the mountains by vacationers who often seem to forget that they are on vacation. Often caused by a combination of high prices, tight scheduling, missed connections, long hours on the highway with screaming kids, and a stunning lack of understanding regarding the entire concept of what a "vacation" is meant to be.
- **White Ribbon of Death:** Term used to define the first couple of ski runs that open at the beginning of a ski season. Often consisting of little more than one strip of icy, man-made snow filled top to bottom, side to side with skiers and riders. (*See* "Buddy Pass.")
- **Woodsie:** A person who lives outside affluent mountain towns in the woods, sometimes year-round. Woodsies generally interface with their mountain towns the same as non-woodsies (as in having jobs and visiting local bars and restaurants), but they choose

to forego rent, leases, and all of the other detritus of conventional living in favor of tents, lean-tos, hovels, and slapped-together plywood shacks and shanties. (*See* "Rent" and "Lease.")

- **Yard Sale:** A scattering of accessories after taking a particularly captivating fall on a ski run.
- **"You Don't Break Up, You Lose Your Turn":** Overused mountain term often employed by men who were just left by their girlfriend, who has taken up with someone else in the same small town and therefore often runs into the person who was just broken up with.

## SOURCES

Curtis Robinson, ex-publisher of the *Roaring Fork Sunday* newspaper in Basalt, Colorado; Devon O'Neil, freelance writer, Breckenridge, Colorado; Malcolm McMichael, writer, Carbondale, Colorado.

# HOW COLORADO'S MOUNTAIN TOWNS GOT THEIR NAMES

There are two necessary caveats before we delve into how, as but one example, Almont came to be named Almont.

First: This section does not deal with the actual processes by which towns are named, which is an area of study that covers history, psychology, and oftentimes overt backroom politicking. The best book on the market that deals with toponymy—the study of place names—is *Names on the Land: A Historical Account of Place-Naming in the United States*, by George R. Stewart, which contains numerous references to Colorado's mountain country.

Second caveat: There is often significant disputation regarding how Colorado's mountain towns came to be named. Sources often vary in their contentions, and, too often, sources rely upon inaccurate hearsay or speculation that was itself based upon inaccurate hearsay or speculation.

The historic/speculative roots of the herein-listed mountain towns have all been checked with at least two sources. Still, one would be advised to not bet the farm on the information herein contained, as none of it can be considered even close to original, primary-source research.

- **Alamosa** (established 1878[1]): Spanish for "place of cottonwood trees" or "full of cottonwood trees." Derived from "alamo," which means "cottonwood tree." First briefly known as Rio Bravo.

- **Alma** (established 1872): Disputed. While some may think that Alma was named after the Spanish word for "soul," it is more likely named after either Alma James, a merchant's wife; Alma Graves, whose husband ran the Alma Mine; Alma Trevor, reportedly the first child born in what is now Alma; or Alma Jaynes, daughter of an early settler. With that many early-day Almas, though, the naming of the country's highest incorporated municipality was a no-brainer.
- **Almont** (established 1881): Sam Fisher, an early and prominent Gunnison County rancher, purchased a stallion that was the offspring of a well-known Kentucky stallion named Almont. When the Denver and Rio Grande Railroad came through, this hamlet was named after Almont the horse.
- **Aspen** (established 1880): Originally named Ute City, prospector/surveyor B. Clark Wheeler named the town site after the splendid aspen forests that to this day cover the mountainsides of the Upper Roaring Fork Valley.
- **Avon** (established 1884): Thought to be named by an Englishman for England's Avon River, but an early spelling, "Avin," casts a small amount of doubt on that story.
- **Bailey** (established 1864): Named after settler William Bailey, who constructed a hotel and stage station during the penultimate year of the Civil War.
- **Basalt** (established 1882): First known as Fryingpan and Fryingpan Junction (for the river that flows through town and here joins the Roaring Fork River), this community later became Aspen Junction. It was finally named Basalt after the prevalent dark igneous rock found in the area.
- **Black Hawk** (established 1859): A mining company brought in a stamp mill that was made by the Black Hawk Company of Illinois. Black Hawk was a chief of the Sauk and Fox tribe in Illinois and Wisconsin.
- **Boulder** (established 1859): First known as Boulder City and named after the large rocks in the area.
- **Breckenridge** (established 1859): Disputed. The most accepted story is that the town fathers, in an attempt to grease the political wheels in hopes of getting a post office approved, named the town after vice-president John C. Breckinridge. When the Civil War started, Breckinridge, then a Kentucky senator, joined the Confederacy, which prompted the pro-Union residents of the Colorado mountain town that bore his name to retaliate by changing the spelling to its current form. A second theory states that the town was named for Thomas E. Breckenridge, a renowned prospector, who later was a part of the historic John C. Fremont Expedition. Both theories are contradicted on maps and in letters, diaries, and newspaper articles from the 1860s, which show spellings with both an "i" and "e."

- **Buena Vista** (established 1879): Spanish for "good view," which this Chaffee County town most certainly has. Despite its Spanish roots, Buena Vista is properly pronounced in a decidedly Anglo fashion: BYOO-nuh VIS-ta.
- **Carbondale** (established 1883): Named by John Mankin, one of the town's founders, for his hometown in Pennsylvania.
- **Central City** (established 1859): Soon after John H. Gregory discovered Colorado's first lode gold in May 1859, thousands of prospectors flocked to the headwaters of the North Fork of Clear Creek. *Rocky Mountain News* publisher William N. Byers suggested the name because of the town's central location among the gold camps of Black Hawk, Mountain City, and Nevadaville.
- **Climax** (established 1884): Not what you think. When the Denver, South Park and Pacific Railroad completed its line to Leadville over Fremont Pass in 1884, it named the station, now home to the massive Climax Molybdenum Mine, "Climax," because the name evinced a brave effort to overcome the obstacles associated with laying tracks to 11,300 feet.
- **Como** (established 1879): Despite the temptation to think that this small town in Park County was named after the Spanish word for "how," it was actually named by Italian coal miners after the lake and city of the same name back in their native land.
- **Copper Mountain** (established 1977): Named after nearby Copper Mountain, a peak rich with, not surprisingly, copper. Construction on this Summit County ski area began in 1971. Copper Mountain is located near Wheeler Junction (1880), which was named after homesteader John S. Wheeler. There is little evidence left of Wheeler Junction, but the name of the popular bike path trailhead at the junction of Ten Mile Creek and West Ten Mile Creek bears the name.
- **Crawford** (established 1882): Named for George A. Crawford, who was elected governor of the Kansas Territory in 1861, but that election was nullified. When the lands of western Colorado were opened up to settlement following an 1881 "agreement" between the Ute Indians and the U.S. government, Crawford turned to speculation and helped found Grand Junction, Delta, and his namesake community.
- **Creede** (established 1890): Named after prospector Nicholas C. Creede, who discovered the nearby Amethyst Lode. Creede absorbed the adjacent mining camps of Weaver, Willow, Upper Creede, Bachelor, Amethyst, Sunnyside, and Gintown.
- **Crested Butte** (established 1879): Took its name from the 12,162-foot mountain that was christened Crested Butte by the 1874 Hayden Survey. The peak is often described as having the appearance of a rooster's comb or a helmet.
- **Crestone** (established 1879): Takes its name from the nearby peak of the same name. From the Spanish "creston," meaning

"cock's comb," "crest of a helmet in which feathers are placed," and "an outcropping or vein of ore."

- **Cripple Creek** (established 1891): Disputed. Named after a creek into which a cowboy on horseback chased a cow that stumbled, causing the horse to fall over the cow and throwing the rider to the ground. Both cow and horse supposedly suffered broken legs, while the cowboy suffered a broken arm. Another version states that the creek was so named merely because a cow fell and broke its leg. Still another version attributes this bad-luck nomenclature to the fact that a man fell off of a roof nearby, and, shortly thereafter, a cowboy was thrown from his horse, suffering a broken leg.
- **Dillon** (established 1879): Gold prospector Tom Dillon got lost in the mountains west of the Continental Divide in what is now Summit County. When he finally emerged in Golden, he described a wide valley where three rivers met—the Blue and Snake rivers and Ten Mile Creek. Later prospectors located the area and named the new town that they founded after Dillon. That town, now known as "Old Dillon," was submerged when the Dillon Dam was built in 1961. "New" Dillon, known just as "Dillon," was moved one mile north to its current location.
- **Durango** (established 1880): The most accepted version is that it was named by former territorial governor Alexander C. Hunt after a visit to Durango, Mexico.
- **Eagle** (established 1885): Disputed. Once known as Castle, Rio Aguila (Spanish for "Eagle River"), and MacDonald, the town was definitely named after the Eagle River. It's how the Eagle River got its name that's disputed. Some say it's because the river has as many tributaries coming into it as there are feathers in an eagle's tail. Others contend that the river got its name because, about a quarter-mile upriver from the town of Red Cliff, there was for many years a prominent eagle's nest.
- **Edwards** (established 1882): Named for Melvin Edwards after he became Colorado secretary of state in 1883. First known as Berry's Ranch, after Harrison Berry, owner of the town site land.
- **Eldora** (established 1896): First called Happy Valley, then Eldorado, after the Spanish, "El Dorado," "The Gilded One." Shortened to Eldora when an application was made to get a post office, to avoid confusion with Eldorado Springs, also in Boulder County.
- **Empire** (established 1860): Originally Valley City. Henry De-Witt, Clinton Cowles, and three other New Yorkers renamed the town Empire City, after the nickname of their home state. Later shortened to Empire.
- **Estes Park** (established 1905): Named after Joel Estes, who in 1859 built a cabin on Fish Creek. Name was first used by *Rocky Mountain News* publisher William N. Byers in 1864 to describe

the lush valley at the base of Lumpy Ridge. It should be noted that the word "park" in the 1800s did not have the same connotation it does today. From the French "parc," the word back then meant an open place with abundant wildlife. Thus, South, Middle, and North parks.

- **Evergreen** (established 1866): Named by D.P. Wilmot after the abundant evergreen trees surrounding the town. Was at first known as The Post, after Amos F. Post, son-in-law of Thomas Bergen, first settler of nearby Bergen Park, in 1859.
- **Fairplay** (established 1859): Prospectors seeking gold along the headwaters of the South Platte in South Park considered the miners of nearby Tarryall so greedy that they nicknamed the camp "Grab-all." In righteous reaction, they decided to name their new town Fair Play, which evolved into Fairplay. Earlier, the town, one of at least 11 towns in the country so named, was known as Platte City, then South Park City.
- **Fraser** (established 1871): First known as Easton, for George Easton, who laid out the town site. The town was then named after the nearby Fraser River, which was, in turn, named after Ruben Frazier, an early settler. Postal authorities adopted the easier spelling when the first post office was opened in 1876.
- **Frisco** (established 1879): Taken from the nickname for San Francisco, probably as a joke being applied to the small cluster of primitive cabins that defined the town. Supposedly, the name "Frisco City" was nailed by Henry Learned, who later became mayor, to the front of the cabin of miner H.C. Recen, Frisco's first resident, who arrived in 1873 from Sweden.
- **Georgetown** (established 1864): Named after George Griffith, who, along with his brother David, discovered gold here in 1859. Two mining camps sprang up. One was Georgetown; the other was Elizabethtown. Elizabeth is usually identified as a Griffith sister, but she may in fact have been the wife of another brother, John Griffith. In 1867, by public vote, the two camps merged into Georgetown.
- **Glenwood Springs** (established 1882): Once known as Defiance, and, for a brief time, Barlow, the town was named after Glenwood, Iowa, where two early residents once lived. The "Springs" part of Glenwood Springs springs from all of the hot springs located thereabouts.
- **Granby** (established 1904): Named after Granby Hillyer, whose distinguished legal career included a stint as U.S. district attorney for Colorado.
- **Grand Lake** (established 1879): Named after Grand Lake, next to which this town sits. Grand Lake, in turn, was named after the Grand River, which was the name of the Colorado River, the source of which is near Grand Lake. In 1921, an act of Congress changed the name to the Colorado River.

- **Gunnison** (established 1876): Originally known as Richardson's Colony, Gunnison was named after the Gunnison River, which, in turn, was named after Captain John W. Gunnison, who led a surveying party though the area in 1853 in search of a railroad route to the west. About six weeks later, Gunnison and seven of his men were killed by Indians near Sevier Lake, Utah. Gunnison, Utah, was also named after Captain Gunnison.
- **Hot Sulphur Springs** (established 1874): Named for the, well, hot sulphur springs that surround the area. The town site was once owned by *Rocky Mountain News* publisher William N. Byers, who used his paper to promote the healing benefits associated with the town's warm, odiferous waters.
- **Idaho Springs** (established 1860): Disputed. In all of America, few are the place names that hold by their very essence as much disagreement as "Idaho," one of the numerous nomenclatural options considered by Congress for what ended up being designated the Colorado Territory. For many years, "Idaho" was long considered to be an Indian word, "Ea-da-HOW," supposedly meaning "light on the mountain." But no one studying Native American etymology has ever been able to prove that. Others argue that "Idahoe" is the Arapahoe Indian word for "gem of the mountains." Still others argue that it is a Plains Apache word, "idaahe," for "enemy," which was used to describe the Comanche. Lalia Boone, in her 1988 book *Idaho Place Names*, is of the opinion that the word "Idaho" is a totally coined word. No matter the linguistic history of "Idaho," the "Springs" part of the town's name clearly comes from the many springs found in the area.
- **Keystone** (established 1917): A Denver, South Park and Pacific Railroad station named after nearby Keystone Gulch, which was likely named by miners from Pennsylvania, the Keystone State. In 1970, Keystone Ski Resort opened, and most signs of "Old Keystone" are now found in a cluster of cabins used by the Keystone Science School as part of that organization's campus.
- **Kremmling** (established 1885): Named after Rudolph Kremmling, who, in 1884, had established a store on the north bank of the Muddy River on the Harris Ranch. Once the town site was platted, local ranchers John and Aaron Kinsley proposed that the town be named Kinsley, which it was. (It was also called Kinsley City.) Kremmling moved his store across the river, which soon became known as Kremmling. It was the new site that endured, and the name stuck.
- **Lake City** (established 1875): Named after nearby Lake San Cristobal, one of the largest natural bodies of water in Colorado.
- **Lake George** (established 1886): Local rancher George Frost dammed the South Platte River as it emerged from Elevenmile Canyon to form a reservoir from which he cut and sold ice. First

called Lidderdale Reservoir, it was commonly known as George's Lake. When a post office was established in 1891, the town's name officially became Lake George.

- **Leadville** (established 1876): Gold discoveries in 1860 brought the first prospectors to the area, and Oro City, located at the base of California Gulch, sprang up almost overnight just down the Arkansas River from where Leadville now stands. Leadville came into existence at least partially because of the discovery of silver, which is found in lead carbonate. Other names considered for Leadville when the post office was established in 1877 included Carbonateville, Agassiz (after famed Swiss naturalist Louis Agassiz), and Harrison, for Edwin Harrison, president of the Harrison Reduction Works. Storekeeper Horace Tabor, one of Colorado's most famous historic characters, lobbied in favor of Leadville, and Leadville it was.

- **Manitou Springs** (established 1871): Disputed. The "spring" part of the name is pretty self-explanatory in this spring-dense part of the world. Some argue that the "Manitou" part of the name apparently comes from a reference made by English adventurer George Ruxton in his 1846 book *Adventures in Mexico and the Rocky Mountains*. The Arapahoe Indians, Ruxton wrote, "Never fail to bestow their votive offerings upon the water spirit, in order to propitiate the 'Manitou' of the fountain." Others assert that English investor William Blackmore suggested "Manitou," which he contended was the Algonquin word for "spirit." It was taken from one of his favorite poems, Henry Wadsworth Longfellow's "Song of Hiawatha," which inspired many place names after its 1855 publication.

- **Marble** (established 1889): Named after the large deposits of marble found along Yule Creek. Marble from Marble was used for the construction of the Colorado State Capitol, the Lincoln Memorial, and the Tomb of the Unknown Soldier.

- **Meeker** (established 1880): Named for Nathan Meeker, a founder of Greeley and former agricultural editor of the *New York Post*. Meeker was named agent to the White River Ute in 1878. After outlawing the Indians' favorite sport, pony racing, the Utes killed Meeker and several agency employees and abducted his wife and daughter, as well as another woman. After what became known as the Meeker Massacre, a military post on the White River was established four miles above the ruined agency. When the camp was abandoned in 1883, all of the buildings were sold to residents of the surrounding area, giving them a ready-made town that was officially platted soon thereafter.

- **Minturn** (established 1885): Briefly called Rocco, for a local family, the Denver and Rio Grande train station was renamed in honor of Robert B. Minturn, an officer of the railroad.

- **Montezuma** (established 1865): Named after the Aztec emperor of the same name. Prospectors supposedly would have been familiar with Montezuma because of William H. Prescott's 1843 book *History of the Conquest of Mexico*.
- **Nederland** (established 1871): Known first as Brownsville, then as Middle Border or Tungsten Town. After Dutch investors bought into the nearby Caribou Mine, the town took the Dutch name for the Netherlands.
- **Ophir** (established 1878): Hopeful miners named this town after the location of the biblical reference to the site of King Solomon's Mines (1 Kings 9:28).
- **Ouray** (established 1875): Named after Ouray, one of the most famous chiefs of the Ute Indians. Modern-day Utes say the word means either "main pole of a tipi" or "king." Chief Ouray himself said his name was nothing more than the first word he said as a baby. The city was first a silver camp known as Uncompahgre or Uncompahgre City.
- **Pagosa Springs** (established 1878): From the Ute word "PAH-go-sa," meaning "hot-spring water," "boiling water," or "healing."
- **Paonia** (established 1881): Founded by Samuel Wade, a rancher who built the first general store. After he helped secure a post office, he suggested the name "Paeonia," the formal botanical name for the peony flower, roots of which he had carried with him from his native Ohio. The post office changed the spelling to "Paonia," presumably for its simplified spelling.
- **Parachute** (established 1885): Disputed. Named after Parachute Creek, the branches of which, when viewed from on high, resemble the shrouds of a parachute. Another take is that hunters on the cliffs above town once exclaimed that they would need a parachute to get back down to town. The name was at one time changed to Grand Valley. In the 1970s, it was changed back to Parachute.
- **Paradox** (established 1882): Named after the paradox associated with the Dolores River as it makes its way through the Paradox Valley at a right angle, rather than flowing down the valley.
- **Pitkin** (established 1879): First known as Quartzville, then renamed after Colorado Governor Frederick W. Pitkin, who was supposedly a friend of Pitkin's first postmaster. The name is also applied to Pitkin County, of which Aspen is the county seat.
- **Poncha Springs** (established 1868): Significant head scratching is associated with this name, which is also applied to nearby Poncha Pass. Some say the word originates from either a New Mexican Spanish word or a Ute word, "punche," which refers to a kind of local weed used as a tobacco substitute. Others believe it comes from the Spanish word, "pancho," meaning "paunch" or "belly," supposedly used to describe the low altitude of Poncha Pass. Still others say that "pancho" can also mean "mild," in reference to Poncha Spring's benign climate.

- **Rico** (established 1879): First known as Carbon City, Carbon-ville, Lead City, and Dolores City, town fathers came together and decided on the Spanish word for "rich."
- **Ridgway** (established 1890): Named for Robert M. Ridgway, superintendent of the mountain division of the Denver and Rio Grande Railroad.
- **Rifle** (established 1882): Named after nearby Rifle Creek, where several soldiers were working on placing mileposts between the Colorado (then the Grand) and White rivers. One of the soldiers lost his rifle and found it next to the creek. Another version speaks of a soldier finding a rifle left by a previous traveler. Either way, there was a rifle that left its name for, first, a creek, then a town.
- **Saguache** (established 1866): From the Ute "sagwachi," referring to a color range that includes both green and blue, or "Sa-gua-gua-chi-pa," which means either "blue earth" or "the water at the blue earth." Some modern-day Ute speakers believe the place name refers to green vegetation, while others believe it refers to bluish stones or earth. A different spelling is applied to the Sawatch Mountain Range, Colorado's highest.
- **Salida** (established 1880): Spanish for "outlet" or "exit," referring either to the place where the Arkansas River opens out or to a point that is the outlet for the numerous mining camps in the area. Former territorial governor Alexander Hunt, who at the time worked for the Denver and Rio Grande Railroad, and his wife have been credited with suggesting the name.
- **San Luis** (established 1851): Known for many years as Culebra (Spanish for "snake"), San Luis de Culebra, and Plaza del Medio. "San Luis" is Spanish for "Saint Louis." San Luis claims to be Colorado's oldest town, although it was not officially incorporated until 1968. Other towns in the San Luis Valley, such as Garcia, dispute the claim.
- **Silt** (established 1898): Originally called Ferguson, it was renamed by the Denver and Rio Grande Railroad after the nature of the local soil. There have been several contemporary attempts to change the name to something less earthy. In 1992, local residents voted to stay with Silt over two alternatives: Grandview and, of all things, Pistol (Silt being just downriver from Rifle).
- **Silver Plume** (established 1870): Disputed. Some claim that "Commodore" Stephen Decatur, then editor of nearby George-town's *Colorado Miner* newspaper, suggested naming the town after the Silver Plume Mine, which was, in turn, named because feathery streaks of silver could be seen in the first ore discovered. Others argue that the mine and, therefore, the town was named for a miner named Plume, or for James G. Blaine, a prominent congressman whose nickname was the "Plumed Knight."

- **Silverthorne** (established 1962): Named for Marshall Silverthorn, a Pennsylvanian who came West during the gold rush and established the Silverthorn Hotel in Breckenridge. When the town was established to house employees working on the Dillon Dam, Silverthorn was remembered nearly a century later. When the town was incorporated, the last "e" was added.
- **Silverton** (established 1874): First known as Baker's Park, then Quito (after Ecuador's lofty capital), then Reeseville and Greenville. One story states that the town got its name because a miner once exclaimed, "We may not have much gold, but we've got silver by the ton!"
- **Snowmass** (established 1889): Named after nearby Snowmass Mountain, which, according to Ferdinand V. Hayden Survey topographer Henry Gannett, was so named because of "the immense field of snow on its eastern face." Snowmass Village, a completely different town, serves as the base area for Snowmass Ski Area.
- **Steamboat Springs** (established 1875): This spring-happy town took its name from the Steamboat Spring, which, according to early trappers, emitted noise that sounded like a steamboat chugging down a river. The spring after which this town was named was destroyed by railroad construction in 1908.
- **Stoner** (established 1890): Tempting though it might be to assume that this name came from Colorado's hippie past, it came from nearby Stoner Creek, which was likely thus named because of all of the rocks and stones on the creek's bed. It has also been suggested that an early settler named Stoner might have given his name to the creek.
- **Tabernash** (established 1905): Named for a Ute Indian of the same name who was killed in a battle with white settlers in a battle that served as a precursor for the Meeker Massacre.
- **Telluride** (established 1878): Known as Columbia until the Denver, Rio Grande and Southern Railroad came to town in 1890. Named after the tellurium ore found in the area. Tellurium is a rare element related to sulphur and is usually combined with metals such as gold and silver, which were found in abundance in the San Juan Mountains.
- **Vail** (established 1959): Named for Vail Pass, which, in turn, was named after state highway engineer Charles D. Vail. When Vail passed away in 1945, Colorado had 5,000 miles of paved roads, 10 times more than existed in 1930 when Vail was appointed to his post.
- **Walden** (established 1881): Fans of Henry David Thoreau will be disappointed to learn that this North Park town was named after early settler Marcus A. Walden.

- **Westcliffe** (established 1881): Disputed. Known first as Clifton. One side argues that the town was given its current name when the Denver and Rio Grande narrow gauge came to town. Dr. William A. Bell, a prominent local landowner who was friends with Denver and Rio Grande founder William Jackson Palmer, is alleged to have named the town after his birthplace, Westcliffe-on-the-Sea, England. The other side argues that the town was named simply because of its location a mile west of Silver Cliff.
- **Winter Park** (established 1923): Originally settled as a work camp for the nearby Moffat Tunnel, with the poetic name "West Portal." The name was changed in 1940 shortly after Winter Park Ski Area opened.
- **Wolcott** (established 1889): First known as Bussells. The name was changed to honor Edward O. Wolcott, U.S. senator from Colorado from 1879 to 1883.
- **Woodland Park** (established 1888): Originally known as Manitou Park, the new name reflected the heavily forested hills surrounding the town.
- **Woody Creek** (established 1890): Named after the nearby creek of the same name, which was in turn named for the forested nature of the area.

## NOTES

1. Date of establishment can mean several things: The date the first people settled in an area that was to become the town, the date the town was first named (understanding that first name might be different than the current name), the date a post office was opened, and/or the date the town was incorporated. Generally, we're using the oldest of those potential dates.

## SOURCES

Much of this section was gleaned from two books that should have a home on every Colorado resident's bookshelf: *1001 Colorado Place Names,* by Maxine Benson, and *Colorado Place Names,* by William Bright. Both of these books are treasure troves of important Colorado-based information. A lot of information was also provided by the town clerks of the various towns listed in this section.

# HIGHEST TOWNS A MATTER OF PERSPECTIVE

You would think that the determination of which Colorado municipality is the highest above sea level would be a straightforward, well-established process in this altitude-crazy state. It is anything but, for a number of reasons.

It's not unusual for people to think (and argue vociferously) that Leadville, at 10,152 feet above sea level (according to the Colorado Department of Transportation highway signs on both ends of town), is the highest city in the United States. After all, for many decades, Leadville itself made that claim, which has long been picked up and transmitted by media used to quoting itself without further verification. And Leadville is big enough and known well enough (it once boasted a population of more than 50,000 people and, when Colorado was admitted to the Union in 1876, was a serious contender for the site of the new state's capital) that people have heard its name.

Thing is, Alma (population 270) is located at 10,578 feet above sea level, and Montezuma (population about 50) is located at 10,400 feet. And, despite protestations to the contrary, both of these hamlets are officially incorporated, although both are far less serious about making their altitudinous presence known to the rest of the world than is tourist-dollars-seeking Leadville. It was because of a lack of desire for notoriety that the good folks in Alma for many years kept their lips pursed while Leadville continued to make its lofty, superlative claim.

Then, in the early 1990s, the Almaniacs, as they call themselves, put on the fighting gloves.

The town government heard or read that Leadville was again making claims about being the highest town in the country. It was mud season, and things were slow, so the Alma town government decided to investigate.

The result of that investigation was twofold. First, the good people of Alma, located in Park County just south of Hoosier Pass, learned that there was no established criteria by which towns are legally obligated to measure their altitude, save the fact that whatever altitude they claimed had to exist somewhere within the town's boundaries.

The Alma town government was under the impression that towns measured their elevation at their post office or town hall. But attempts to verify that requirement proved inconclusive.

Therefore, Alma's Powers That Be adopted as the town's high point a place that had the convenience of already boasting an official U.S. Geological Survey benchmark: the cemetery, 10,578 feet above sea level.

A letter was sent to Leadville's municipal government. Leadville responded by threatening to annex some adjacent higher ground, and Alma responded by threatening to annex nearby Mount Democrat, the summit of which lies at 14,148 feet. Thing is, if such an annexation battle had actually transpired, Leadville would have ultimately emerged victorious, as its entire western skyline is dominated by the two highest peaks in the Rockies: Mount Elbert (14,443 feet) and Mount Massive (14,420 feet).

Although the battle of the highest towns waged long enough to get some media coverage, in the end, it was settled amicably enough. By gentlemen's agreement, Leadville got to retain the title of highest "city" in the nation, while Alma laid claim to being the highest "town." (Colorado maintains an arcane distinction between towns—incorporated municipalities with fewer than 2,000 residents—and cities—more than 2,000 residents. The U.S. Census Bureau estimated Leadville's population to be 2,700 in 1996.)

But the plot thickens. In 2007, in an effort to bypass the complicated planning process required by the Grand County government, the Winter Park Town Council annexed part of Winter Park Ski Area—up to 12,060 feet. Shortly after the annexation, the Winter Park city government said that there were no plans to market the town as the country's highest incorporated municipality, because the town's new high point consisted of a mountainside where not one single person lived. But, the town's official Web site, www.winterparkgov.com, now does just that.

**Colorado's highest incorporated municipalities are:**

- **Winter Park** (12,060 feet). Measured on the slopes of newly annexed Winter Park Ski Area, where no one lives, save a few ptarmigan.
- **Alma** (10,578 feet). Measured from a USGS benchmark at the town's cemetery, where also no one lives.
- **Montezuma** (10,400 feet). Measured at the Montezuma town hall.
- **Leadville** (10,152 feet). Measured at the first step of the old city hall, now the Heritage Museum. It should be noted, however, that the www.Leadville.com Web site lists Leadville's elevation at 10,430 feet. Efforts to hunt down where this number came from were unsuccessful.
- **Blue River,** population 849 (10,020 feet). Measured at the Blue River town hall.
- The unincorporated town of **St. Mary's,** in Clear Creek County (10,079 feet).
- The unincorporated town of **St. Elmo,** in Chaffee County, (10,052 feet).

There is great disputation as to what the highest-ever town was in Colorado, at least partially because there is disputation about what defined a town back in the mining-era heyday. Here are several contenders.

- **Carson,** located near Lake City, is officially referred to as a "camp." It was located at 12,000 feet.
- **Boreas,** located at 11,481 feet on the summit of Boreas Pass, between Breckenridge and Como, consisted of a railroad section house and several cabins, some of which have been renovated by the Summit Huts Association for winter recreational use.
- **Climax,** between Leadville and Copper Mountain, lies above Fremont Pass at an elevation of 11,300 feet. The Climax Molybdenum Mine, around which the old town of Climax was built, was scheduled to reopen by the time this book hits the streets, but that did not happen. Climax was once home to the highest post office and highest train station in the country.
- The **Independence** ghost town between Aspen and Independence Pass is located at 11,000 feet.

## THE HIGHEST STATE CAPITALS

Many people mistakenly believe that Denver—the world-famous Mile High City—is the highest state capital in the United States. Well, it's not even second. It is third.

Santa Fe, New Mexico, located at an elevation of 6,989 feet, is the country's highest state capital. Cheyenne, Wyoming, at 6,067 feet, is second.

After Denver come Carson City, Nevada (4,730 feet), Salt Lake City, Utah (4,266 feet), and Helena, Montana (4,090 feet)

---

### ADDITIONAL MOUNTAIN TOWN ELEVATIONS

- Fairplay: 9,950 feet (second-highest county seat in the country, after Leadville)
- Copper Mountain: 9,720 feet
- Victor: 9,695 feet
- Breckenridge: 9,603 feet
- Cripple Creek: 9,508 feet
- Silverton: 9,305 feet
- Twin Lakes: 9,220 feet
- Keystone: 9,166 feet
- Divide: 9,165 feet
- Silver Plume: 9,100 feet
- Snowmass Village: 9,100 feet
- Dillon: 9,087 feet
- Frisco: 9,097 feet
- Crested Butte: 8,908 feet
- Rico: 8,827 feet
- Telluride: 8,792 feet
- Silverthorne: 8,751 feet
- Lake City: 8,658 feet
- Empire: 8,614 feet
- Grant: 8,591 feet
- Fraser: 8,574 feet
- Georgetown: 8,512 feet

- Central City: 8,496 feet
- Allenspark: 8,450 feet
- Grand Lake: 8,437 feet
- Woodland Park: 8,437 feet
- Vail: 8,380 feet
- Red Feather Lakes: 8,342 feet
- Glendevey: 8,292 feet
- Nederland: 8,233 feet
- South Fork: 8,208 feet
- Hesperus: 8,110 feet
- Shawnee: 8,103 feet
- Walden: 8,099 feet
- Powderhorn: 8,080 feet
- Black Hawk: 8,056 feet
- Almont: 8,018 feet
- Lake George: 7,968 feet
- Buena Vista: 7,955 feet
- Granby: 7,939 feet
- Fort Garland: 7,932 feet
- Aspen: 7,907 feet
- Westcliffe: 7,888 feet
- Antonito: 7,882 feet
- Del Norte: 7,879 feet
- Minturn: 7,847 feet
- Ouray: 7,811 feet
- Bailey: 7,750 feet
- Gunnison: 7,703 feet
- Saguache: 7,694 feet
- Nathrop: 7,690 feet
- Hot Sulphur Springs: 7,680 feet
- Monte Vista: 7,663 feet

- Alamosa: 7,544 feet
- Idaho Springs: 7,524 feet
- Estes Park: 7,522 feet
- Poncha Springs: 7,465 feet
- Avon: 7,430 feet
- Kremmling: 7,362 feet
- Edwards: 7,226 feet
- Palmer Lake: 7,225 feet
- Redstone: 7,190 feet
- Pagosa Springs: 7,105 feet
- Salida: 7,080 feet
- Evergreen: 7,040 feet
- Mancos: 7,030 feet
- La Veta: 7,013 feet
- Ridgway: 6,988 feet
- Dolores: 6,936 feet
- Bayfield: 6,892 feet
- Pine: 6,754 feet
- Steamboat Springs: 6,728 feet
- Basalt: 6,620 feet
- Eagle: 6,600 feet
- Durango: 6,523 feet
- Crawford: 6,520 feet
- Manitou Springs: 6,320 feet
- Cortez: 6,201 feet
- Carbondale: 6,170 feet
- Glenwood Springs: 5,763 feet
- Eldorado Springs: 5,762 feet
- Golden: 5,674 feet
- Paonia: 5,645 feet
- Boulder: 5,344 feet

## SOURCES

Colorado Municipal League; *Colorado Ghost Towns and Mining Camps* by Sandra Dallas; numerous personal interviews with town officials in Leadville and Alma.

# ESTABLISHING COLORADO'S LOWEST POINT

In an altitude-proud state like Colorado, it should come as no surprise that less effort has been spent establishing the state's low point as has been spent establishing the state's high points.

As a matter of fact, the dialogue regarding Colorado's low point was still getting sorted out as recently as 2005.

In April 2000, the *Rocky Mountain News,* in reaction to a reader's question regarding the specifics of Colorado's low point, asserted that it could be found along the banks of the Arkansas River in Prowers County, just west of the Kansas border, at an elevation of 3,350 feet.

Thing is, the Colorado Department of Transportation (CDOT) map indicated that the state low point was along the North Fork of the Republican River, just west of the Nebraska border, at an elevation of 3,337 feet. An astute reader opted to investigate. He learned that the low point was actually along the Arikaree River as it flows out of the state near the Colorado/Nebraska/Kansas corner, near the town of Wray, at an elevation of 3,315 feet.

The *Rocky Mountain News* ran a correction two weeks later, naming the Arikaree elevation as the state's low point.

In May 2000, the America's Basement Web site became the first source to acknowledge that the state's low point was indeed to be found on the banks of the Arikaree.

In June 2001, the United States Geological Survey listed the Arikaree River as the state's lowest point, giving the elevation official government status. However, on the USGS Web site, the river was misspelled as "Alikaree." The correct spelling was posted in August 2001.

In May 2002, an updated CDOT highway map listed the Arikaree as the state's low point. Sadly, although it was spelled correctly on the map itself, on the information section of the map, CDOT incorrectly spelled the name of the state's low point as "Arickaree."

In September 2003, the *Rocky Mountain News* once again ran a short item on the state's low point. The paper incorrectly reported the same information that it ran in April 2000, stating that the 3,350-foot elevation along the Arkansas River was the state's low point. The paper was once again forced to run a correction shortly thereafter, listing once again the Arikaree's 3,315-foot elevation.

Until September 2005, the Wikipedia page, "List of U.S. States by Elevation," continued to run the incorrect Arkansas River elevation as the state's low point. It was finally listed correctly on Wikipedia on September 10, 2005.

SOURCE

www.geocities.com.

# STATES WHOSE HIGHEST POINTS ARE LOWER THAN COLORADO'S LOWEST POINT

Eighteen states, plus the District of Columbia, in the United States have highest points that are lower than Colorado's lowest point:

- **Florida:** Point in Walton County– 345 feet (lowest high point in the country)
- **District of Columbia:** Tenleytown– 410 feet
- **Delaware:** In New Castle city limits– 448 feet
- **Louisiana:** Driskill Mountain– 535 feet
- **Mississippi:** Woodall Mountain– 806 feet
- **Rhode Island:** Jerimoth Hill– 812 feet
- **Illinois:** Charles Mound– 1,235 feet
- **Indiana:** In Franklin Township– 1,257 feet
- **Ohio:** Campbell Hill– 1,549 feet
- **Iowa:** In Osceola County– 1,670 feet
- **Missouri:** Taum Sauk Mountain– 1,772 feet
- **New Jersey:** High Point– 1,803 feet
- **Wisconsin:** Timms Hill– 1,951 feet
- **Michigan:** Mount Arvon– 1,979 feet
- **Minnesota:** Eagle Mountain– 2,301 feet
- **Connecticut:** Side of Mount Frissell– 2,380 feet (Connecticut doesn't even have the honor of boasting as its highest point the summit of a mountain– the actual summit of Mount Frissell, at 2,453 feet, lies in Massachusetts)
- **Alabama:** Cheaha Mountain– 2,405 feet
- **Arkansas:** Magazine Mountain– 2,753 feet
- **Pennsylvania:** Mount Davis– 3,213

Four other states have high points that are barely higher than Colorado's lowest point:

- **Maryland:** Backbone Mountain– 3,360 feet
- **Massachusetts:** Mount Greylock– 3,487 feet

- **North Dakota:** White Butte– 3,506 feet
- **South Carolina:** Sassafras Mountain– 3,560 feet

SOURCE

Rand-McNally.

# HOW DOES COLORADO COMPARE?

## HIGHEST TOWN ELEVATIONS IN OTHER MOUNTAIN STATES

- **New Mexico:** Taos Ski Valley: 9,800 feet
- **Arizona:** McNary: 7,316 feet; Note: The unincorporated town of Alpine, Arizona, is located at 8,050 feet, and the unincorporated town of Summerhaven is at 8,000 feet.
- **Utah:** Brian Head: 9,800 feet
- **Idaho:** Island Park: 6,290 feet
- **Montana:** West Yellowstone: 6,667 feet
- **Wyoming:** Centennial: 8,076 feet
- **Washington:** Lyman: 3,752 feet
- **Oregon:** Greenhorn: 6,410 feet
- **California:** Mammoth Lakes: 7,920 feet
- **Nevada:** Mount Charleston: 7,760 feet
- **Alaska:** Chisina: 3,318 feet

## Highest Towns in Select Mountainous Eastern States

- Fancy Gap, Virginia: 2,920 feet
- Beech Mountain, North Carolina: 4,200 feet
- Davis, West Virginia: 3,099 feet
- Jenkins, Kentucky: 1,526 feet
- Roan Mountain, Tennessee: 2,575 feet
- Jacksonville, Vermont: 1,334 feet
- Greenville, Maine: 1,308 feet

SOURCE

www.maps-n-stats.com.

▲

## POPULATION OF COLORADO'S MOUNTAIN TOWNS IN 2010

Followed by the Populations of Those towns in 2000, and the Percentage Increase or Decrease Over Ten Years

- Alamosa: 8,780 (7,960, plus 10.3%)
- Alma: 270 (179, plus 50.8%)
- Aspen: 6,658 (5,914, plus 12.6%)
- Basalt: 3,857 (2,681, plus 43.9%)
- Black Hawk: 118 (118, stayed the same)
- Blue River: 849 (685, plus 23.9%)
- Breckenridge: 4,540 (2,408, plus 88.5%)
- Buena Vista: 2,617 (2,195, plus 19.2%)
- Carbondale: 6,427 (5,196, plus 23.7%)
- Central City: 663 (515, plus 29%)
- Creede: 290 (2000 Census numbers unavailable)
- Crested Butte: 1,487 (1,529, minus 2.8%)
- Crestone: 127 (73, plus 74%)
- Cripple Creek: 1,189 (1,115, plus 6.6%)
- Dillon: 904 (802, plus 12.7%)
- Durango: 16,887 (13,922, plus 21.3%)
- Eagle: 6,505 (3,032, plus 115%—the highest percentage population increase over the previous decade of any Colorado mountain town, as well as the highest actual population increase)
- Empire: 282 (355, minus 20.6%)
- Fairplay: 679 (610, plus 11.3%)
- Fraser: 1,224 (910, plus 35%)
- Frisco: 2,683 (2,443, plus 9.8%)
- Georgetown: 1,034 (1,088, minus 5%)
- Glenwood Springs: 9,614 (7,736, plus 24.3%)
- Granby: 1,864 (1,525, plus 22.2%)
- Grand Lake: 471 (447, plus 5.3%)
- Gunnison: 5,854 (5,409, plus 8.2%)
- Hot Sulphur Springs: 663 (521, plus 27.3%)
- Idaho Springs: 1,717 (1,889, minus 9.1%)
- Kremmling: 1,444 (1,578, minus 8.5%)
- Lake City: 408 (375, plus 8.8)
- Leadville: 2,602 (2,821, minus 7.8%—the biggest actual population decrease over the previous decade of any Colorado mountain town)
- Montezuma: 65 (42, plus 55%)
- Nederland: 1,445 (1,394, plus 3.7%)
- Ouray: 1,000 (813, plus 23%)
- Pagosa Springs: 1,727 (1,591, plus 8.6%)
- Paonia: 1,451 (1,497, minus 3%)

- Pitkin: 66 (124, minus 47%—the biggest percentage decline over the previous decade of any Colorado mountain town)
- Poncha Springs: 737 (466, plus 58%)
- Red Cliff: 267 (289, minus 7.6%)
- Rico: 265 (205, plus 29%)
- Ridgway: 924 (713, plus 30%)
- Salida: 5,236 (5,504, minus 4.9%)
- Silver Plume: 170 (203, minus 16%)
- Silverthorne: 3,887 (3,196, plus 22%)
- Silverton: 637 (531, plus 20%)
- Snowmass Village: 2,826 (1,822, plus 55%)
- South Fork: 386 (604, minus 36%)
- Steamboat Springs: 12,088 (9,815, plus 23%)
- Telluride: 2,325 (2,221, plus 5%)
- Vail: 5,305 (4,531, plus 17%)
- Victor: 397 (445, minus 11%)
- Walden: 608 (734, minus 17.2%)
- Ward: 150 (169, minus 11%)
- Westcliffe: 568 (417, plus 36%)
- Winter Park: 999 (662, plus 51%)
- Woodland Park: 7,200 (6,515, plus 10.5%)

SOURCE

2010 U.S. Census.

# MOUNTAIN LICENSE PLATES

Forever and ever, you could eyeball a Colorado automobile license plate and discern from whence that vehicle hailed. From 1959 to 1982, the Colorado Department of Revenue, which includes the Division of Motor Vehicles (which, in turn, supervises all matters related to license plates), issued what were known as the "2/4 plates." These plates basically started with two county-specific letters, followed by a series of numbers that could be anywhere from one digit to four. There was some crossover in the latter years of the 2/4-plate program when plate numbering started running out. However, for the most part, that overlap was found in the more populated counties of the Front Range.

In the early 1980s, the Department of Corrections, which oversees the actual manufacture of license plates in Colorado (yes, the prisoners-making-license-plates stereotype is accurate), came to the conclusion that, because of increases in the state's population and the resultant increased number of registered vehicles, it would have to scrap the 2/4 system, a decision that caused a surprising amount of ire, especially in the more chauvinistic rural counties in Colorado.

The change resulted in a non-county-specific system with license plates generally containing three letters, followed by three numbers. The new system sometimes seems like it is county specific. County clerks, who issue license plates on the local level, may order, say, 500 plates at a time. These plates will likely appear in sequence (e.g., WRF-000, WRF-001, etc.). But a county on the complete other side of the state might get the next 500 in the WRF sequence.

The Division of Motor Vehicles did resurrect county-specific plates from 1989 to 1992, when it offered its "denim plates." These plates were blue and actually had the name of the county in which the vehicle was registered written on the bottom. The plates proved far less popular than the green-on-white or white-on-green mountain background plates, and so the denim-plate program was scrapped.

The state does allow for 2/4 plates issued before July 1, 2003, to remain legal. Thus, it is still possible to see license plates in the Colorado high country that read: ZB-14 or ZA-2. Whenever you see someone whose ride sports such plates, best not to get into an argument with that person about who has lived in the county the longest.

The old mountain-county 2/4 license plate prefixes are:

- Alamosa: XE-XG
- Archuleta: YU
- Boulder: ML-NF, FH-FP, CT, CZ, FL-FZ
- Chaffee: XH-XK
- Clear Creek: YY-YZ
- Conejos: WS-WT
- Costilla: YA
- Custer: ZA
- Delta: VL-VR
- Dolores: ZH
- Eagle: YM-YN
- El Paso: JX-LL, GA-GN
- Fremont: UP-UV
- Garfield: WM-WR
- Gilpin: ZK
- Grand: ZB-ZC
- Gunnison: YD-YE
- Hinsdale: ZN
- Huerfano: VE-VF
- Jackson: ZJ
- Jefferson: RS-TD, HG-HX, FA-FK
- La Plata: VV-WA
- Lake: YF-YH
- Larimer: LU-MK
- Mesa: NG-NZ
- Mineral: ZM
- Montezuma: XL-XN
- Ouray: ZF
- Park: ZD
- Pitkin: ZG-ZS, UM-UN
- Rio Blanco: YV-YW
- Rio Grande: WJ-WL
- Routt: WZ-XV
- Saguache: XU-XV
- San Juan: ZE
- San Miguel: YX
- Summit: ZL, ZR
- Teller: YL, XY

SOURCES

Colorado Department of Revenue.

# MOUNTAIN AREA CODES

Until 1988, Colorado was home to only one area code: 303. However, with the population burgeoning, more area codes were needed.

On March 5, 1988, a second code—719—was added, to much consternation among long-time locals who fretted that this change was yet another example of things going down the toilet. The 719 code comprised much of Colorado's mountain country, including Leadville and the upper Arkansas River Valley, Alamosa, the San Luis Valley, Trinidad, and Cañon City, although it lost much mountain cachet because 719 also included the entire southeastern part of the state, clear down to the Kansas and Oklahoma borders.

In 1995, a third area code—970—was added. Many people consider 970 to now be the official area code of Colorado's mountain country, even though it includes the entire northeastern part of the state, out where the sugar beets grow. The 970 code includes Aspen, Vail, Steamboat Springs, Summit County, South Park, Telluride, Silverton, Ouray, Creede, Lake City, Gunnison, Crested Butte, Durango, Grand Junction, and Fort Collins.

In 1998, a fourth area code was added to Colorado—720—which is overlaid with the last remaining vestiges of the original 303 code. Both 303 and 720 are now limited to the Denver Metropolitan area.

SOURCES

Wikipedia.com.

▲

## AREA AND POPULATION OF COLORADO'S MOUNTAIN COUNTIES

- Alamosa: 1,182 square miles. 15,445 people, up from 14,996 in 2000, an increase of 3.2%.
- Boulder: 740 square miles. 294,567 people, up from 269,768 in 2000, an increase of 1.1%.
- Chaffee: 1,014 square miles. 17,809 people, up from 16,262 in 2000, an increase of 9.6%.
- Clear Creek: 396 square miles. 9,088 people, down from 9,322 in 2000, a decrease of 2.5%.
- Conejos: 1,290 square miles. 8,256 people, down from 8,400 in 2000, a decrease of 1.7%.
- Costilla: 1,229 square miles. 3,425 people, down from 3,663 in 2000, a decrease of 3.8%.

- Custer: 740 square miles. 4,255 people, up from 3,503 in 2000, a 21.5% increase.
- Delta: 1,149 square miles. 30,952 people, up from 27,834 in 2000, an 11.2% increase.
- Eagle: 1,700 square miles. 52,197 people, up from 41,675 in 2000, a 25.3% increase.
- Fremont: 1,533 square miles. 46,824 people, up from 46,145 in 2000, a 1.5% increase.
- Garfield: 2,958 square miles. 56,389 people, up from 43,791 in 2000, an increase of 28.8%, the biggest percentage and actual population increase of any Colorado mountain county between 2000–2010.
- Gilpin: 150 square miles. 5,441 people, up from 4,771 in 2000, a 14.4% increase.
- Grand: 1,868 square miles.14,843 people, up from 12,442 in 2000, a 19.3% increase.
- Gunnison: 3,259 square miles.15,324 people, up from 13,956 in 2000, a 19.3% increase.
- Hinsdale: 1,123 square miles. 843 people, up from 790 in 2000, a 6.7% increase.[1]
- Jackson: 1,619 square miles.1,394 people, down from 1,577 in 2000, an 11.6% decrease.
- Lake: 383 square miles. 7,310 people, down from 7,812 in 2000, a 6.4% decrease.
- La Plata: 1,700 square miles. 51,334 people, up from 43,949 in 2000, a 16.8% increase.
- Mineral: 878 square miles. 712 people, down from 831 in 2000, a decrease of 14.3%, which is the largest population percentage decrease of any Colorado mountain county between 2000–2010.
- Montrose: 2,035 square miles. 41,276 people, up from 33,432 in 2000, a 23.5% increase.
- Ouray: 542 square miles. 4,436 people, up from 3,742 in 2000, an 18.5% increase.
- Park: 2,209 square miles. 16,206 people, up from 14,523 in 2000, an 11.6% increase.
- Pitkin: ; 970 square miles. 17,148 people, up from 14,872 in 2000, a 15.3% increase.
- Rio Grande: 913 square miles.11,148 people, down from 12,413 in 2000, a 3.5% decrease, which is the largest actual population drop of any Colorado mountain county between 2000–2010.
- Routt: 2,362 square miles. 23,509 people, up from 19,688 in 2000, a 19.4% increase.
- Saguache: 3,168 square miles. 6,108 people, up from 5,917 in 2000, a 3.2% increase.
- San Juan: 389 square miles. 699 people, up from 558 in 2000, a 25.3% increase.
- San Miguel: 1,290 square miles. 7,359 people, up from 6,594 in 2000, an 11.6% increase.

- Summit: 619 square miles. 27,994 people, up from 23,548 in 2000, an 18.9% increase.
- Teller: 558 square miles. 23,350 people, up from 20,555 in 2000, a 13.6% increase.

## NOTES

1. For many years, Hinsdale County, with Lake City as its seat, was described in many Colorado newspaper articles as the country's least-populated county. In fact, Loving County, Texas, with a 2008 population of 82 (an increase of 15 residents since 2000), has been the country's least-populated county for more than 30 years.

## SOURCE

2010 U.S Census; Wikipedia.

# COLORADO MOUNTAIN COUNTY HIGH POINTS

- **Lake:** Mount Elbert (14,433 feet)
- **Chaffee:** Mount Harvard (14,420 feet)
- **Alamosa:** Blanca Peak (14,345 feet)
- **Costilla:** Blanca Peak (14,345 feet)
- **Huerfano:** Blanca Peak, northeast slope (14,320 feet)
- **Hinsdale:** Uncompahgre Peak (14,309 feet)
- **Saguache:** Crestone Peak (14,294 feet)
- **Park:** Mount Lincoln (14,286 feet)
- **Clear Creek:** Grays Peak (14,270 feet)
- **Summit:** Grays Peak (14,270 feet)
- **Gunnison:** Castle Peak (14,265 feet)
- **Pitkin:** Castle Peak (14,265 feet)
- **Boulder:** Longs Peak (14,265 feet)
- **Dolores:** Mount Wilson (14,246 feet)
- **Custer:** Crestone Peak, East Peak (14,240+ feet)
- **Ouray:** Mount Sneffels (14,150 feet)
- **El Paso:** Pikes Peak (14,110 feet)
- **La Plata:** Mount Eolus (14,083 feet)
- **San Miguel:** Wilson Peak (14,017 feet)
- **Eagle:** Mount of the Holy Cross (14,005 feet)
- **Mineral:** Creede Crest (13,895 feet)
- **San Juan:** Vermillion Peak (13,894 feet)
- **Las Animas:** West Spanish Peak (13,626 feet)

- **Larimer:** Hagues Peak (13,560 feet)
- **Grand:** Pettingell Peak (13,553 feet)
- **Archuleta:** Summit Peak (13,300 feet)
- **Gilpin:** James Peak (13,294 feet)
- **Montezuma:** Lavender Peak (13,240 feet)
- **Rio Grande:** Bennett Peak (13,203 feet)
- **Conejos:** Conejos Peak (13,172 feet)
- **Fremont:** Bushnell Peak (13,105 feet)
- **Teller:** Devils Playground (13,060+ feet)
- **Jackson:** Clark Peak (12,951 feet)
- **Garfield:** Flat Top Mtn. (12,354 feet)
- **Pueblo:** Greenhorn Mtn. (12,347 feet)
- **Routt:** Mount Zirkel (12,180 feet)
- **Rio Blanco:** Rio Blanco County High Point (12,027 feet)
- **Jefferson:** Buffalo Peak (11,589 feet)
- **Montrose:** Castle Rock (11,453 feet)
- **Delta:** Mount Lamborn (11,396 feet)
- **Mesa:** Leon Peak (11,236 feet)
- **Moffat:** Black Mtn. (10,840+ feet)

SOURCE

peakbagger.com.

# AVALANCHES IN COLORADO

Colorado is ground zero when it comes to avalanches and avalanche deaths in the United States. On average, about 2,300 avalanches are reported each year to the Colorado Avalanche Information Center (CAIC). This includes natural, deliberately set, and accidentally triggered avalanches. As sobering as that number might be, CAIC estimates that 10 times that number of avalanches occur in Colorado every year but go unreported.

The preponderance of avalanches in Colorado is a result of a combination of geographic and climatological factors. Colorado has what avalanche experts call a "continental snow climate," which is characterized by shallow snow events, cold temperatures, and lots of wind. The shallow snow and cold temperatures create weak layers within the snowpack. The wind creates very hard slabs on top of these weak layers. This combination creates very dangerous avalanche conditions and lingering weaknesses within the snowpack that might not release on their own but can be triggered by a human.

Additionally, Colorado boasts in spades another necessary component of avalanche superlatives: vertical terrain, much of which is home to slopes in the 30–45-degree range, which is perfect for slides. Less steep, and there's not enough slope for snow to slide. Any more steep, and the snowpack would not adhere to the slope long enough to build up those aforementioned windblown, weak slabs.

Those physical conditions, combined with the fact that Colorado's backcountry gets significant human visitation, result in the sad fact that the Centennial State has suffered more avalanche-based fatalities than any other state—by far.

Between 1950 and the winter of 2009–2010, 1,005 avalanche deaths were reported in the United States. More than a quarter of those took place in Colorado. Colorado's avalanche death total during that time exceeded that of the next two states—Alaska and Washington—combined. Of the 37 avalanche deaths reported nationally during the winter of 2009–2010, seven took place in Colorado. Of the 27 avalanche fatalities that took place in the United States during the winter of 2008–2009, four occurred in Colorado. In the winter of 2007–2008, there were 36 avalanche fatalities in the United States, eight of which took place in Colorado.

### STATE-BY-STATE LIST OF AVALANCHE DEATHS IN THE UNITED STATES FROM 1950 THROUGH THE WINTER OF 2009–2010

- Colorado: 240
- Alaska: 130
- Washington: 106
- Utah: 103
- Montana: 98
- Wyoming: 68
- Idaho: 67
- California: 60
- New Hampshire: 15
- Oregon: 12
- Nevada: 11
- New Mexico and New York: Tied with 4
- Maine and North Dakota: Tied with 2; one of the two avalanche deaths reported in North Dakota, in the winter of 2007–2008, was from a slide coming off of a roof
- Arizona and Vermont: Tied with 1 each

## COLORADO AVALANCHE FATALITIES
## BY COUNTY, 1950–2010

- Pitkin: 40
- Summit: 37
- Clear Creek: 24
- Gunnison: 18
- Eagle and Ouray: 14 each
- Chaffee: 13
- Lake: 11
- San Miguel and Larimer: 10 each
- Grand: 7
- San Juan and Mineral: 5 each
- Boulder: 4
- Routt: 3
- Jackson, Garfield, Mesa, and La Plata: 2 each
- Dolores, Hinsdale, Costilla, Conejos, Huerfano, Saguache, and El Paso: 1 each

## CUMULATIVE AVALANCHE FATALITIES IN
## THE UNITED STATES BY ACTIVITY, 1950–2007

- Backcountry/out-of-bounds skiing: 242
- Climbers/hikers: 181
- Snowmobilers: 170
- Snowboarders: 50
- In-bounds skiers: 30
- Snowshoers: 28
- Snow sliding off of roofs: At least 10
- Child standing at a bus stop in the middle of town: 1

## CUMULATIVE AVALANCHE FATALITIES
## IN THE UNITED STATES BY ACTIVITY,
## WINTERS OF 2007–2008, 2008–2009, AND 2009–2010*

- Snowmobilers: 62
- Backcountry/out-of-bounds skiers: 27
- Snowshoers/climbers/hikers: 14
- Backcountry/out-of-bounds snowboarders: 9
- In-bounds skiers/snowboarders: 8
- Other (including roof slides): 8

*Categories for avalanche deaths were modified in the winter of 2007–2008 to more closely reflect modern activity realities.

## Avalanches and Colorado Highways

The Colorado Department of Transportation (CDOT) administers highways in winter that have a total of 457 avalanche paths crossing them. CDOT controls 176 of the most active paths by using explosives.

CDOT has a convoluted formula for determining which are Colorado's most dangerous mountain passes when it comes to avalanches. This formula takes into account the number of avalanche paths crossing the pass, the frequency with which those paths slide, and the number of vehicles using the highway. Therefore, according to CDOT's hazardous pass formula, Berthoud Pass is ranked more dangerous than Wolf Creek Pass, even though Wolf Creek has more avalanche paths crossing the highway (55 versus 26), because Berthoud gets significantly more traffic than Wolf Creek.

And Loveland Pass is ranked more dangerous than Wolf Creek Pass, even though, again, it has fewer avalanche paths (24 versus 55) because the paths that cross Loveland run more frequently. And Vail Pass, which has only two avalanche paths crossing it, is rated more dangerous than Monarch Pass (eight paths) because of the amount of traffic crossing Vail Pass via Interstate 70.

### CDOT'S MOST DANGEROUS PASSES

- U.S. Highway 550 over Red Mountain, Molas, and Coal Bank passes: 162 avalanche paths cross this section of highway, of which 83 are controlled using explosives
- U.S. Highway 40 over Berthoud Pass: 26 paths, 8 controlled
- U.S. Highway 6 over Loveland Pass: 24 paths, 22 controlled
- U.S. Highway 160 over Wolf Creek Pass: 55 paths, 20 controlled
- Interstate 70, Silver Plume to Frisco: 34 paths, 12 controlled
- Colorado Highway 145 over Lizard Head Pass: 47 paths, 15 controlled
- Interstate 70 over Vail Pass: 2 paths, 1 controlled
- U.S. Highway 50 over Monarch Pass: 8 paths, 1 controlled
- Colorado Highway 110 over McClure Pass: 24 paths, 1 controlled
- Colorado Highway 14 over Cameron Pass: 14 paths, 6 controlled
- Colorado Highway 65 over Grand Mesa: 3 paths, 2 controlled
- Colorado Highway 17 over La Manga Pass: 3 paths, 2 controlled
- Colorado Highway 24 over Battle Mountain Pass: 16 paths, 0 controlled
- Colorado Highway 139 over Douglas Pass: 8 paths, 0 controlled
- Colorado Highway 91 over Fremont Pass: 13 paths, 0 controlled

- Colorado Highway 83 over Independence Pass: 82 paths, 14 of which are controlled prior to the road's seasonal opening before Memorial Day; the avalanche paths on Independence Pass are not counted in the state total because the pass is closed in winter

SOURCES

The Colorado Avalanche Information Center (CAIC): avalanche.state.co.us; Colorado Department of Transportation.

# IMPOTENCE DRUGS REACH NEW PEAKS

Any high-altitude-dwelling person looking for an excuse to talk to the doctor about procuring a prescription for one of the many available erectile dysfunction medications now has a perfect pretense for bringing that subject up without having to get into any potentially embarrassing discussions about flaccidity. A 2007 study by the American Psychological Society concluded that Viagra improved the cardiovascular and exercise performance of trained cyclists at high altitude by up to 45 percent.

The conclusion came on the heels of a 2004 German study that found that Viagra increased the ability of people to exercise at altitude.

Viagra causes blood vessels to relax—in various parts of the body (not just the parts one normally thinks about when pondering ED medications). Originally developed to relieve high blood pressure, Viagra improves blood flow and increases oxygen transport to working muscles throughout the body, including the lungs, creating the potential for enhanced performance in oxygen-thin mountain country.

Viagra and its competitors, such as Cialis and Levitra, have already received a lot of publicity regarding their ability to combat high-altitude pulmonary edema (HAPE), a potentially life-threatening illness causing shortness of breath, fatigue, cough, and sometimes a pink, frothy sputum as fluid collects in the lungs. While it is certainly a major concern for serious mountain climbers, HAPE also affects beaucoup regular-Joe mountain recreationists at altitudinous Colorado resorts.

Cialis is more frequently prescribed for HAPE than Viagra, since it lasts longer. Two pills are required per day, rather than Viagra's every-eight-hours, 50-milligram dosage.

High-altitude medical specialists are now recommending that serious mountain climbers carry Viagra in their medical kits to address problems as they arise.

It is suspected at this point that erectile dysfunction medications will be more beneficial to those who already have trouble with pulmonary function at high altitude than they will be for the 80 to 90 percent of the population that already adjusts well to thin air.

It must be stressed that Viagra, Cialis, and Levitra do nothing to combat acute mountain sickness (AMS) or the worst of the altitude-based maladies—high-altitude cerebral edema (HACE). No word yet on whether women's athletic performance might benefit from ED drugs, as they were not included in the cycling study.

And, like all the TV commercials state, there are potential side effects to using ED medications, such as headaches, a bluish coloration in vision, or blind spots.

As to the question about potential sexual side effects, which center on whether your ugly climbing buddy's going to start looking attractive after you ingest a dosage of ED medication 30 miles back in the wilderness, the answer is "no." That aspect of ED medication requires very specific physiological stimulation.

## SOURCES

"Cause for Excitement: Impotence Drugs Reach New Peaks," by Kim Marquis, in the October 2007 issue of *Mountain Gazette.* Marquis's story was based to a large extent on interviews with the man whom many people consider the foremost expert on the physiological effects of altitude, Dr. Peter Hackett, of Telluride's Institute for Altitude Medicine.

# COLORADO LAKES AND RESERVOIRS

Unlike most other western states, Colorado suffers a dearth of large natural bodies of water. As a matter of fact, Colorado has the second-smallest "largest lake" of all the western states. You don't have to worry about any Loch Ness–type monsters in Colorado, unless they were more like Loch Ness minnows, because they simply wouldn't fit into any of the state's diminutive lakes and reservoirs.

There is disputation regarding what is actually Colorado's largest natural body of water. Common belief is that Grand Lake, at 506 surface acres, is the state's largest lake and that Lake San Cristobal, near Lake City, is Colorado's second-largest natural body of water, with 346 surface acres. Not so fast. Near Alamosa lies San

Luis Lake, which boasts a surface area of 890 acres, making it the largest natural body of water in the state. Thing is, there are major fluctuations of water levels in San Luis Lake; when it is full, however—which is actually fairly often (depending upon snowpack levels and spring runoff)—there is no doubt it is Colorado's largest natural body of water. This means that Grand Lake is actually the state's second-largest natural body of water, and Lake San Cristobal comes in third. Surface area, though, is only one way to measure a lake's "size." San Luis Lake achieves a maximum depth of only 25 feet while maintaining an average depth of about five feet. Grand Lake, on the other hand, achieves a maximum depth of 265 feet, easily making it the state's most voluminous natural body of water.

There is further confusion about all of this, as a very obvious sign near Twin Lakes proclaims that otherwise splendid body of water to be "Colorado's largest glacial lakes." To the sympathetic eye, Twin Lakes do indeed seem to be larger than either Lake San Luis, Grand Lake, or Lake San Cristobal. Sadly, for argumentative purists, there's that small matter of the Twin Lakes Dam, which was built in 1978 to increase the capacity of the lakes so that additional water could be made available to the Fryingpan/Arkansas Project of the U.S. Department of the Interior's Water and Power Resources Project.

Thus, despite its natural beginnings, Twin "Lakes," which provide the name for Lake County, now must be classified as a reservoir, as do almost all of the dammed-up bodies of water in Colorado that, despite their dammed-ness, are often still called "lakes" (official maps and documents often mix plural with singular by naming the feature "Twin Lakes Reservoir"). Verily, since the construction of the dam, what used to be Twin "Lakes" now, during a strong runoff year, becomes one seamless body of water.

THE LARGEST BODIES OF WATER IN COLORADO[1], IN *SURFACE ACRES*[2], ARE:

1. John Martin Reservoir (in the Arkansas River Valley, out on the Great Plains): 11,000[3]
2. Blue Mesa Reservoir (near Gunnison): 9,000
3. Lake Granby (actually a reservoir between Granby and Grand Lake): 7,256
4. Adobe Creek Reservoir (north of Las Animas, out of the Great Plains): 5,029
5. Pueblo Reservoir (west of Pueblo): 4,646
6. Meredith Reservoir (on the Great Plains, near Ordway): 4,525
7. McPhee Reservoir (near Dolores): 4,470
8. Eleven Mile Reservoir (near Hartsel): 3,400
9. Dillon Reservoir (in Summit County): 3,233

10. Vallecito Reservoir (near Durango): 2,718
11. Jackson Lake (a reservoir near Goodrich, on the Great Plains): 2,700
12. Spinney Reservoir (near Hartsel): 2,520
13. Antero Reservoir (near Fairplay): 2,500
14. Twin Lakes Reservoir (between Leadville and Buena Vista): 2,440
15. Taylor Park Reservoir (near Almont): 2,400
16. Green Mountain Reservoir (between Silverthorne and Kremmling): 2,125
17. Horsetooth Reservoir (near Fort Collins): 1,899
18. Williams Fork Reservoir (near Kremmling): 1,810
19. Turquoise Lake (a reservoir near Leadville): 1,788
20. Wolford Reservoir (near Kremmling): 1,550

## THE *DEEPEST*[4] BODIES OF WATER IN COLORADO ARE[5]:

1. Blue Mesa Reservoir (near Gunnison): 338 feet
2. McPhee Reservoir (near Dolores): 270 feet
3. Grand Lake (near Grand Lake): 265 feet
4. Lake Granby (near Granby): 221 feet
5. Strontia Springs Reservoir (southwest of Denver): 212 feet
6. Ridgway Reservoir (near Ridgway), Rampart Reservoir (near Woodland Park), and Trinidad Lake (near Trinidad): 200 feet

## THE LARGEST BODIES OF WATER IN OTHER WESTERN STATES

- **Utah:** The Great Salt Lake, at 1,700 square miles (1,088,000 acres), is the largest body of water between the Great Lakes and the Pacific Ocean.
- **New Mexico:** Stinking Lake, which was obviously not named by the local chamber of commerce, boasts 1,300 very seasonal surface acres. Elephant Butte Reservoir is the Land of Enchantment's largest impounded body of water at 36,500 surface acres.
- **Arizona:** The Grand Canyon State is partial home to the two largest reservoirs in the United States—Lake Mead and Lake Powell—both of which boast almost exactly the same surface area, about 250 square miles (160,000 acres). Arizona's largest natural body of water is 600-surface-acre Mormon Lake, which has the distinction of being the smallest largest natural body of water in any western state. Worse, Mormon Lake only achieves a maximum depth of 10 feet and many years finds itself completely lacking one of the most fundamental denotative components of

the word "lake," because in many years, Mormon Lake, south of Flagstaff, is completely dry.

- **Wyoming:** Yellowstone Lake has a surface area of 136 square miles (87,040 acres). It is located at an elevation of 7,732 feet and achieves a maximum depth of 390 feet. Its shores are frequently home to some of the nation's coldest winter temperatures.
- **Montana:** Flathead Lake, at 191.5 square miles (122,560 surface acres), is the largest freshwater natural lake between the Great Lakes and the Pacific Ocean.
- **Idaho:** Lake Pend Oreille has a surface area of 148 square miles (94,720 acres).
- **Nevada:** Pyramid Lake is a closed-basin salt lake with a surface area of 188 square miles (120,320 acres).
- **Washington:** Lake Chelan, at 50 miles in length, is one of the longest western lakes. With a surface area of 52.1 square miles (33,344 acres), though, it's quite skinny. And at a depth of 1,486 feet, it's the third deepest lake in the country and the twenty-fourth deepest in the world. But there is an asterisk, because a dam, built in the 1920s, raised Lake Chelan's water level by about 20 feet. The largest un-asterisked lake in Washington is Lake Washington, with a surface area of 21,500 acres.
- **Oregon:** Klamath Lake has a surface area of 91,000 acres, literally 179 times as large as Colorado's largest natural lake. But it only has a maximum depth of 50 feet, making it five times shallower than Grand Lake. Oregon is home to the country's deepest lake, Crater Lake, which achieves a depth of 1,949 feet.
- **California:** This is another asterisk state. Technically, the Salton Sea, at 376 square miles (240,640 surface acres), is the Golden State's largest lake. It is hardly natural, however, yet neither is it a reservoir per se. It was created quite by accident in 1905, when heavy snowmelt combined with heavy rainfall to swell the Colorado River, which then breached the Imperial Valley Dike. The water flowed into what had been a dry lake bed 227 feet below sea level, meaning that the Salton Sea has no outflow and, thus, as its name would indicate, is very salty. Lake Tahoe (which boasts a maximum depth of 1,645 feet, making it the country's second deepest lake), at 191 square miles (122,240 surface acres), is the largest natural, freshwater lake in California, although much of Tahoe lies in Nevada. California also shares Goose Lake (186 square miles, or 119,000 surface acres) with another state. Its northern half lies in Oregon. Some years, Goose Lake is bone dry. Clear Lake, at 43,785 surface acres, is the largest natural freshwater lake entirely in California. It has a maximum depth of only 27 feet and is also one of the oldest lakes in the United States.

## LAKES VERSUS RESERVOIRS

If you drive on U.S. Highway 50 west of Gunnison toward the Curecanti National Recreation Area, you may notice two signs that, even though they look conceptually similar, are in reality as different as night and day. One sign says, "Blue Mesa Lake." Farther up the road, another sign says, "Blue Mesa Reservoir." For most people, these two signs amount to little more than "you say to-MAY-to, I say to-MAH-to." To water experts, however, there is much more to it than that.

Dave Wegner, for instance, is a Durango-based ecosystem management facilitation specialist who, following a 21-year career with the federal Bureau of Reclamation (the folks who built most of the dams in the West), now works for the prestigious Glen Canyon Institute. Wegner is perhaps best known as the man who organized the much-ballyhooed 1996 Colorado River release from "Lake" Powell (through Glen Canyon Dam) that was supposed to emulate natural river-flow patterns through the Grand Canyon. Wegner has been working for years in hopes of getting reservoirs nomenclaturally listed as such on all USGS maps. He feels that, for instance, by referring to Summit County's Dillon Reservoir—Denver's primary source for drinking water—as "Lake Dillon," citizens lose sight of the natural dynamics that are found in lake ecosystems and that assuredly are not found in artificial reservoirs.

"People need to understand the effects that reservoirs have on the natural environment," Wegner stresses. "If something is called a 'lake,' when it's actually a reservoir, then people, especially newcomers, might not think about the fact that millions of dollars were spent and a natural ecosystem destroyed in order to impound that water."

While he harbors no illusions that reservoirs now referred to as "lakes" on USGS maps will be renamed, Wegner has taken his argument to the federal Board on Geographical Names in the hope that all new reservoirs are accurately described on all future federal maps.

His efforts so far have failed, at least partially because of organized opposition from developers and marketing entities who feel that the word "lake" sounds a lot more attractive to potential tourists and those wanting to acquire mountain real estate than does the word "reservoir."

NOTES

1. Navajo Reservoir, at 15,610 surface acres, is the largest single body of water that is partially located in Colorado. Most of the reservoir, however, is in New Mexico.

2. It needs to be stressed that the water levels of all reservoirs fluctuate dramatically. Figures cited reflect the surface area of a given reservoir when it is full, which, some years, does not happen.

3. As a perfect example of footnote number 2, John Martin Reservoir has an official surface area of "between 1,000 and 11,000 acres."

4. Once again, it needs to be stressed that the water levels and, thus, the depths of reservoirs can vary significantly from season to season and from year to year.

5. Navajo Reservoir, of which a small part lies in Colorado, reaches a depth of 400 feet near the dam, which lies in New Mexico.

## SOURCES

Colorado Lakes & Reservoirs: Fishing and Boating Guide, Outdoor Books and Maps (an imprint of Adler Publishing Company), Castle Rock, Colorado, 2008; information about San Luis Lake comes from Colorado State Parks; Oregon State Parks & Recreation Department; Town of Grand Lake; Wikipedia.

# LAKES AND ICE

Because of one of the true miracles of physics, those who enjoy fishing in Colorado's mountain country are greeted each spring by lakes full of hungry trout rather than fishsicles. That's because, except for the shallowest alpine tarns, Colorado's mountain lakes rarely freeze all the way to the bottom. If they did, whatever fish that call those lakes home would obviously not survive.

The reason why Colorado's mountain lakes rarely freeze all the way to the bottom is because water, unlike almost every other substance on earth, boasts a solid form—ice (duh!)—that is less dense than its liquid form. (At one atmosphere, water reaches its greatest density at 34°F; water freezes at 32°F.)

We all see ample evidence of that fact every time we down a beverage with ice cubes, which, as we all know, float. When lakes freeze, the ice stays at the top. This further insulates the remaining water from the colder air above.

Additionally, as you go deeper, the water pressure in a lake becomes greater than one atmosphere. When pressure is increased, the temperature necessary to freeze water decreases. It is a perfect, self-fulfilling loop that is so significant some scientists even state that, without this loop, life as we know it would not exist on earth. That, and, well, the mountain lake fishing would not be as fruitful.

This physical trait of water also has a lot to do with the survival of beavers, which are unable to ingress and egress their domiciles if the water backed up by their dams freezes all the way to the bottom. (This is why beavers are continually building their dams higher and higher.)

## SOURCE

answers.yahoo.com.

# SAFE ICE THICKNESS AND
# COLD-WATER HYPOTHERMIA

In a state dominated for half the year by frozen ponds, tarns, lakes, rivers, and reservoirs, it is beneficial to have a grip on how thick ice needs to be before venturing out to cross-country ski, skate, snowmobile, ice sail, snow kite, or fish.

Note that these figures apply to solid, clear blue/black lake ice. Slush ice has half the strength of lake ice, and the strength value of river ice is 15 percent less than lake ice.

- 2 inches or less: Stay off!
- 3 inches: Holds a single person on foot.
- 4 inches: Holds a group in single file, ice fishing.
- 5 inches: Holds a snowmobile or ATV, or Texans ice fishing.
- 7½ inches: Holds a passenger car.
- 8–12 inches: Holds a small pickup.
- 12–15 inches: Holds a medium truck.
- 15 inches: Holds 10 tons (this is getting into *Ice Road Truckers* territory).
- 20 inches: Holds 25 tons.
- 30 inches: Holds 70 tons.
- 38 inches: Holds 110 tons.

Ice thickness can easily be measured using an ice chisel, an ice auger, a ¼-inch cordless drill with a long bit, and a tape measure. This might sound like a lot of trouble, but consider the alternative.

Other things to keep in mind when checking ice:

- Ice is seldom the same thickness over an entire body of water. It can be two feet thick in one place and one inch thick a few yards away due to currents, springs, or rotting vegetation. You need to check the ice at least every 150 feet, especially early in the season or for any situation where the thickness varies widely.
- White ice, sometimes called "snow ice," is only about half as strong as new, clear ice; therefore, the above thicknesses should be doubled.
- Refrain from driving on ice whenever possible. If you must drive a vehicle, be prepared to leave it in a hurry—i.e., keep windows down, unbuckle your seat belt, and have a simple emergency plan of action that you also have discussed with your passengers.
- Vehicles weighing about one ton, such as cars, pickups, or SUVs, should be parked at least 50 feet apart and moved every two hours to prevent sinking. It's not a bad idea to make a hole next

to the car. If water starts to overflow the top of the hole, the ice is sinking, and it's time to move the vehicle!

- Check for known areas of thin ice with a local resort or bait shop.
- Don't "overdrive" your snowmobile's headlight. At even 30 miles per hour, it can take a much longer distance to stop on ice than your headlight shines. Many fatal snowmobile through-the-ice accidents occur because the machine was traveling too fast for the operator to stop when the headlamp illuminated the hole in the ice.
- Wear a life vest under your winter gear. Or wear one of the new flotation snowmobile suits. And it's a good idea to carry a pair of ice picks or ice pins that may be home made or purchased from most well-stocked sporting goods stores that cater to winter anglers. It's amazing how difficult it can be to pull yourself back onto the surface of unbroken but wet and slippery ice while wearing a snowmobile suit weighted down with 60 pounds of water. The ice picks really help pulling yourself back onto solid ice.
- Do *not* wear a flotation device when traveling across the ice in an enclosed car or truck, as it may inhibit your ability to egress the vehicle.
- Snow is a good insulator. It slows down the ice-forming process and keeps the ice from freezing hard. And, snow is heavy—it adds to the load on the ice.
- Ice near the shore is weakest. The shifting, expansion, and buckling action of the lake or stream over the winter continually breaks and refreezes ice along the shoreline.
- Protruding logs, brush, or docks can absorb heat from the sun and weaken the surrounding ice.
- Stay away from alcoholic beverages. (Yeah, right.) Even "just a couple of beers" are enough to cause a careless error in judgment that could cost you your life. And contrary to common belief, alcohol actually makes you colder rather than warming you up.

What if you, a companion, or a pet fall through the ice?

- As with any emergency, don't panic! (Yeah, right.) If you fall through the ice, briefly call for help. It doesn't take long for the cold water to start slowing your physical and mental functions, so you must act quickly. Air will remain trapped in your clothes for a short time, aiding your buoyancy. Kick your legs while you grasp for firm ice. Try to pull your body up using the ice picks or ice pins that should be hanging around your neck. (You didn't forget your ice pins, did you?) Once your torso is on firm ice, roll toward thicker ice. This will better distribute your weight. Remember that ice on which you have previously walked should be the safest. After you reach safe ice, don't waste precious time, because you need to warm up quickly to prevent hypothermia. Go to the nearest fishing shanty, warm car, or home.

• If a companion falls through the ice, remember the phrase "Reach-Throw-Go." If you are unable to reach your friend from shore, throw him or her a rope, jumper cables, a tree branch, or other object. If this doesn't work, go for help before you also become a victim. Get medical assistance for the victim immediately.

• When you are walking on or near ice, keep your pets on a leash. If a pet falls through the ice, do not attempt to rescue the pet. (Yeah, right.) Go for help. Well-meaning pet owners can too easily become rescue victims when trying to assist their pets.

Next is a list of water temperatures and their corresponding potentials for causing hypothermia. This is also known as a motivational tool in case, even after reading all the above-related skinny, you still manage to break through the ice.

• Water temperature: 32.5°F (which it often is in the Colorado high country): Exhaustion or unconsciousness comes in less than 15 minutes. Expected time of survival is 15–45 minutes.

• Water temperature: 32.5–40°F (which it often is in the high country): Exhaustion or unconsciousness occurs in 15–30 minutes. Expected time of survival is 30–90 minutes.

• Water temperature: 40–50 degrees (which it often is in the high country): Exhaustion or unconsciousness occurs in 30–60 minutes. Expected time of survival is 1–3 hours.

• Water temperature: 50–60°F (getting a little warm for the high country, but still possible): Exhaustion or unconsciousness occurs in 1–2 hours. Expected time of survival is 1–6 hours.

• Water temperature: 70–80°F (otherwise known as a tropical vacation): Exhaustion or unconsciousness occurs in 3–12 hours. Expected time of survival is 3 hours–indefinitely, but keep your eyes peeled for sharks!

SOURCES

Minnesota Department of Natural Resources; *Old Farmer's Almanac;* Massachusetts Division of Fisheries & Wildlife; www.athropolis.com/arctic-facts/fact-ice-safety.htm.

# LIGHTNING: THE FEARSOME FLASH FROM ABOVE

This seems to surprise many people (and many of us are surprised by that surprise), but Colorado is one of the most dangerous states in the country when it comes to lightning fatalities. Sixtynine people perished as a result of lightning in Colorado between 1980 and 2004. Between 1997 and 2006, there were 30 lightning deaths in Colorado, second only to Florida's 71. No matter what time frame you examine, Colorado is perennially in the top three states for lightning injuries and fatalities, even though it ranks only 28th in terms of actual lightning strikes hitting the ground (499,888 times between 1997 and 2001).

Other interesting facts about lightning are:

- Lightning is the number-two weather killer in the United States, after floods.
- The air within a lightning strike can reach 50,000° F.
- Lightning can heat its path five times hotter than the surface of the sun.
- Of all lightning fatalities in Colorado, 89 percent were males.
- Between 1980 and 2003, the worst day of the week for lightning deaths in Colorado was Saturday, when 43 people died. The best day was Thursday, when "only" 23 people died.

In the early summer of 2004, 19 linksmen playing on a makeshift golf course on a bluff outside Kremmling were all knocked on their posteriors by one single blast of lightning. No single lightning

## COLORADO MOUNTAIN COUNTY LIGHTNING FATALITIES, 1980–2009

- El Paso: 10*
- Park: 5
- Boulder* and Teller: 4 each
- Montezuma, Pitkin, Rio Grande, and Routt: 3 each
- Chaffee, Eagle, Garfield, and Summit: 2 each
- Custer, Fremont, Jackson, La Plata, Mesa, Mineral, Moffat, Montezuma, Ouray, Rio Blanco, Saguache, and San Juan: 1 each

* Obviously, large portions of El Paso and Boulder counties do not lie in the mountains. These numbers apply to the entire counties, including non-mountainous terrain.

strike in U.S. history has ever impacted more people at once, and it is a miracle that no one died. Those who were hit reported that the lightning arced its way from person to person. One man told NBC's Today Show that, when he came to, he felt "totally paralyzed" before feeling a surge of heat and pain that left him feeling "like he was on fire." Another survivor reported a "dead feeling" from his chest down. Yet another said that the blast felt like someone hit him over the head with a baseball bat. The strike occurred as the golfers made their way back onto the course from their cars, where they had been waiting out a storm. Thinking the storm had passed, the victims returned to the bluff. Four of the 19 people struck were airlifted to Denver with life-threatening injuries, but all recovered. This incident underscores common lightning-avoidance advice: Stay indoors or in your vehicle until a minimum of 30 minutes after the last bolt of lightning is observed.

**LIGHTNING FATALITIES IN WESTERN STATES, 1990–2003**

- Colorado: 39
- Arizona: 17
- New Mexico and Wyoming: 14 each
- California: 8

To illustrate the capricious nature of lightning, here is a smattering of recent lightning-fatality narratives from the Colorado mountains:

- Just prior to 1 P.M. on July 25, 2000, an 18-year-old male was killed by a cloud-to-ground lighting flash on top of Pikes Peak. He was standing in a boulder field approximately 100 feet from the summit and was the tallest object in a very exposed area. He was with two other friends on the mountain, and they were each spaced about 30 feet apart. The friend closest to the victim who was struck by the flash was thrown to the ground but was not injured. The other companion was still standing after the flash. No thunder was heard prior to this deadly flash.
- At 4:37 P.M., July 27, 2003, a 25-year-old female was struck and killed by a lightning flash while hiking along the Willow Creek Trail just east of Crestone. The woman, along with her 33-year-old husband, was coming down the trail after hiking Kit Carson and Challenger peaks. The couple was approximately 2.5 miles from the trailhead near Crestone when the flash occurred. According to rescue officials, the couple was located at midslope in heavy timber when the flash occurred. Although the male was thrown to the ground by the flash, he received no injuries related to the flash.
- On August 24, 2003, a 59-year-old male motorcyclist was traveling eastbound on Colorado Highway 24. At approximately 4:45

P.M., 1.5 miles southeast of Lake George, he was struck and fatally wounded by a lightning flash. After being struck, the bike and rider crossed into the westbound lane and crashed into an embankment on the north side of the highway. A witness in an automobile who was immediately behind the cyclist did not observe any deviant motion of the cycle after the rider was hit. The witness stated: "The bike gradually turned to the left (crossing into the westbound lane) and crashed into the embankment." The witness also stated that rain was falling at the time of the flash, and lightning was visible prior to the flash that struck the cyclist. Although the cyclist was still alive when emergency authorities arrived, he succumbed to his injuries while being transported to the hospital. According to the coroner, the cause of death was due to the lightning flash, not the ensuing crash.

- At approximately 5:30 P.M. on July 19, 2006, a 17-year-old male who was playing soccer with friends was struck and killed by lightning at Cavanaugh Field, located in Woodland Park. According to media reports, the flash entered near his collarbone and exited his left foot. None of the other players were injured by this flash.

- On September 2, 2007, a 21-year-old male was killed by lightning while inside a tent that was located in the foothills eight miles southwest of Colorado Springs. Three other people were also in the tent when the flash occurred, but they received only minor injuries. An autopsy report indicated that the victim was lying down on the ground inside the tent at the time of the flash. The electrical current entered through his elbow, on which he was leaning at the time, traveled through his torso, and exited his buttocks. The other three occupants in the tent were standing at the time of the flash.

- On the afternoon of July 3, 2008, a 16-year-old male was killed by a lightning flash while riding a mountain bike on a dirt road in the Wet Mountains in Custer County. The fatal flash occurred about half a mile to the north-northwest of Colorado Highway 96 and Custer County Road 271. The victim was riding toward the southeast on County Road 271 with five others and was second in line of the five cyclists. At the actual time of the flash, the riders were spaced about two miles apart, with three of the riders in the lead pack (including the victim), while the other two were much farther behind. The first cyclist in the lead pack was approximately seven yards in front of the victim when the flash occurred. This first cyclist felt the electrical shock from the flash and was knocked off of his bike but received no injuries. The cy-

clist who was behind the victim was approximately 25 yards behind and was not affected by the flash.

## SOURCES

The National Oceanic and Atmospheric Administration; www.msnbc.com;
www.lightningsafety.com; www.infoplease.com/science/weather/lightning-
deaths.html.

# MONSOON SEASON

In the summer in the Colorado mountains, you often hear
someone say words to the effect: "It's like clockwork. Every afternoon, the thunderstorms move in. You can set your watch."

You will sometimes hear the word "monsoon" attached to
those observations.

Although the weather patterns of the high country are not as
clockwork-ish as some would argue, pretty much, during summer
months, sometime toward late morning or midday, clouds start to
form on the western horizon and, following the prevailing winds,
they move eastward. Then, sometime in early to mid-afternoon,
the rains will come, as will lightning, thunder, and wind. Then, the
weather front will pass by and the world left behind will be moist,
fresh, and wonderful.

Of course, sometimes the rains come later in the day, and every
once in a good while, mountain dwellers will wake up to grayness
and drizzle. And often high-pressure systems will descend upon the
high country, forcing moisture-bearing, low-pressure systems to the
north and south, resulting in days of perfect, dry, bluebird skies.
However, by and large, Colorado's mountain rains are as much like
clockwork as dynamic weather systems can be. But are those systems accurately considered "monsoons," as many folks assert?

The answer is a guarded "yes."

The word "monsoon" entered the English vernacular in the
sixteenth century, during the Age of Exploration, and referred not
only specifically to a certain seasonal weather pattern but also to
a specific part of the world. When your average person thinks in
terms of "monsoon season," a vision of inundated rice paddies and
overflowing sewage systems in India and Bangladesh will surely
emerge. That's the part of the world where the word "monsoon" was
first used—entering English by way of the Dutch bastardization of
the Arabic *mawsim* ("season")—and it's the part of the world where
that which weather nerds call "monsoons" are the most intense.

But that's pretty much where universal agreement on the concept of monsoons ends.

The most basic definition of "monsoon" does not even include rain as a fundamental component. The term means nothing more than a seasonal shifting of the wind. Thus, in India and Bangladesh, there is the "wet monsoon," when the wind blows from the southwest between May and September, bringing with it quantities of tropical moisture that are inconceivable in the Rockies, and, to add a bit more confusion to the discussion, there is also the "dry monsoon," when the wind shifts and blows in from the arid central Asian steppes.

In its purest, historic context, the word "monsoon" likely ought never have left the Indian subcontinent and the other malaria-infested mud holes that make their way onto CNN every summer when entire villages are washed into snake-infested rivers as wide as lakes. However, in the last couple of centuries, it has indeed emigrated to points as far away as North America's Mountain Time Zone, where it has found a nice summer home.

There are a lot of terms used to describe the fairly predictable precipitation situation in the summer in the United States, particularly in the Southwest and the southern Rockies. People used to just call it the "rainy season." In the past decade, though, we have started applying the monsoon concept, as well as the term itself, to weather conditions in North America that mimic weather conditions in southern and southwestern Asia.

Those conditions consist of the seasonal shift of wind, combined with a transference of moisture from tropical seas—in our case, the Gulf of Mexico and the Sea of Cortez—to otherwise relatively dry points inland.

In the summer, global climatic circumstances result in low-pressure systems building up over Mexico's Sierra Madre. We therefore see winds rotating in from the south and southwest and picking up moisture in the Gulf of Mexico and the eastern Pacific. Because it's summer, that air is warmer and, therefore, it can hold more moisture. It then carries that moisture as far north as the central Rockies.

While there is still some barroom disputation among weather wonks regarding the correct application of monsoon terminology to the Rockies, that terminology has now reached official status in the Sonoran Desert of Arizona. Until the late 1970s, even weather experts were still debating what to call the summer precipitation systems that hit Arizona and New Mexico. As in Colorado, terms like "summer thunderstorm season" and "rainy season" were still being used in a very unscientific manner. It wasn't until 2004 that scientists decided that the summer weather patterns that hit the Southwest and, by extension, the Colorado mountains, were indeed "monsoons."

And it wasn't until literally 2008 that "monsoon season" was institutionalized by the National Weather Service the same way that "hurricane season" was institutionalized years ago. Now, "North American Monsoon Season" officially begins June 15 and runs through the end of September. The idea is that, by lending official nomenclature to the weather pattern, efforts to educate the public about monsoon-related dangers—flash floods, thunderstorms, lightning—will be easier.

## MONSOON SEASON TIDBITS

The most notorious manifestation of monsoon season in Colorado was the infamous Big Thompson Flood. On July 31, 1976, an estimated 12 to 14 inches of rain fell on the headwaters of Big Thompson Canyon, on the east side of the Continental Divide upriver from Loveland. A wall of water 20 feet deep raced down the canyon at 14 miles per hour. One hundred forty-three people were killed.

The official record rainfall in Colorado over a 24-hour period actually took place down on the plains. On June 7, 1965, Holly, Colorado, received a whopping 11.08 inches of rain.

The Antelope Canyon Flash Flood that took 11 lives in northern Arizona on August 12, 1997, came from a mere 0.75 inches of monsoonal rain that fell 10 miles away from where the victims perished.

## SOURCE

Timothy Schott, a meteorologist with the National Weather Service headquarters office in Washington, D.C.

# CLOUD SEEDING

For most people, the notion of cloud seeding lies somewhere between water dowsing, rain dances, and the sacrificing of virgins to appease the gods of precipitation in hopes that the skies will yield liquid bounty. Yet, cloud seeding got something of an image boost during the 2008 Summer Olympics with the Chinese government's much-ballyhooed efforts to use cloud seeding over Beijing to, first, induce rain to help eliminate that city's world-class air pollution before the Olympics began, then, days later, when they used upwind cloud seeding in hopes of assuring that no precipitation would fall upon the games' opening ceremonies. Given the fact that the Chinese wowed the world with every other aspect of their Olympic extravaganza, it became a bit easier for people to think that just maybe there is something to this cloud-seeding idea.

Scientists half a world away in Colorado said, "See…we told you so!"—a sentiment with direct applicability to the Centennial State, as Colorado is among the cloud-seeding leaders of the country. Within Colorado lie more than 90 operational cloud-seeding sites working to increase the state's rain and snow factor. (Utah, by comparison, has 138 cloud-seeding generators.) Ten other western states put money into Colorado's cloud-seeding coffers in hopes that those dollars will result in more water being transported by gravity from the precipitous Rockies downriver to their thirsty, often golf-course-filled, lands.

Cloud seeding was invented by accident by people smart enough to recognize the potential ramifications of their serendipitous discovery. In July 1946, Vincent Shaefer, following ideas generated between himself and Nobel Laureate Irving Langmuir while climbing New Hampshire's Mount Washington—at 6,288 feet, the highest mountain in New England—created a way of experimenting with super-cooled clouds using a deep-freeze unit lined with velveteen (a type of cotton cloth made to imitate velvet). Schaefer tried hundreds of potential agents to stimulate ice growth, including salt, talcum powder, soils, dust, and various chemical agents, all with very limited success. Then, one hot, humid day in July, Schaefer wanted to try a few related follow-up experiments at General Electric's Schenectady (New York) Research Lab. While so doing, he was astonished to learn that the deep freezer he was using was not cold enough to produce a cloud using exhaled air. So, he added a chunk of dry ice just to lower the temperature. To his utter amazement, as soon as he exhaled into the then-colder chamber, he noted a bluish haze, followed by the display of millions of ice crystals. He immediately realized that he had stumbled upon a way to change super-cooled water into ice crystals.

Within a month, noted atmospheric scientist Dr. Bernard Vonnegut (brother of the late, great writer Kurt Vonnegut) piggybacked off of Schaefer's work and discovered, while sitting at a desk using information in a basic chemistry text, a more efficient method for "seeding" (a term he is credited with coining) super-cooled cloud water. Other scientists, including crystallographer Henry Chessin, then piggybacked off of Vonnegut's calculations, which pointed toward silver iodide as being the best substance for instigating "seeding." (The crystallography of ice later played a role in Kurt Vonnegut's 1963 science-fiction novel *Cat's Cradle*.) Both methods—Schaefer's use of dry ice and Vonnegut's use of silver iodide—were adopted for use in the earliest days of cloud seeding in 1946. Schaefer's method altered a cloud's "heat budget," while Vonnegut's altered its formative crystal structure.

The first attempt to seed natural clouds occurred during an airplane flight in Upstate New York on November 13, 1946, when Schaefer was able to cause snow to fall atop proximate Mount Greylock—at 3,487 feet, Massachusetts's highest mountain—after he dumped six pounds of dry ice into a target cloud.

The theory behind cloud seeding is that, as warm air rises from the Earth, it begins to cool and forms tiny droplets of water that condense into cloud droplets. Cloud droplets are formed around particles of dust, salt, or soil (called "cloud condensation nuclei") that are always present in the atmosphere. These droplets group together into clouds, which can form precipitation in one of two ways. In warm temperatures, the droplets in the clouds merge with many other droplets and become heavy enough to fall to the Earth as rain. (It takes millions of cloud droplets to form a single raindrop.) In colder temperatures, the droplets of water form ice crystals. Other droplets freeze onto these ice crystals, which grow larger and heavier until they fall to the ground as rain, snow, or hail.

In 1969, at the famed Woodstock Music Festival in Watkins Glen, New York, various people claimed to have witnessed clouds being seeded by the U.S. military. This was said to have resulted in the rainstorms that besieged the festival for most of its three days.

Cloud seeding, in the simplest terms, introduces other particles into a cloud to serve as cloud condensation nuclei and aid in the formation of precipitation. There are three types of cloud seeding: static mode, dynamic mode, and hygroscopic seeding. Static-mode cloud seeding seeks to increase rainfall by adding ice crystals (usually in the form of silver iodide or dry ice) to cold clouds. Dynamic-mode cloud seeding increases rainfall by enhancing vertical air currents in clouds and thereby vertically process more water through the clouds. Basically, in this method of seeding, a much larger number of ice crystals are added to the cloud than in the static mode. In hygroscopic seeding, salt crystals are released into a cloud. These particles grow until they are large enough to cause precipitation to form. Clouds can be seeded from above with the help of airplanes that drop pyrotechnics or from the ground by using artillery, ground-to-air rockets, or other mechanical devices.

In Colorado, all of the 90-plus cloud-seeding generators are ground based. They are known as ice-nuclei generators, which put out the right-sized silver iodide particles in solution. When the particles are released into the atmosphere, this method resembles a smoke plume heading skyward.

Cloud seeding in Colorado, which began with a pilot program on the Grand Mesa in the 1950s that was funded and supervised by the federal Bureau of Reclamation, now falls under the purview of the state's Water Conservation Board, which oversees permitting and implementation of seeding operations in four distinct target areas.

- The Vail and Upper Arkansas Target Area has 25 generators and covers 372 square miles.
- The Grand Mesa Target Area has 13 generators and covers 869 square miles.
- The San Juan/Dolores River Basins Target Area has 30 generators and covers 2,237 square miles.
- The Gunnison Basin Target Area has 23 generators and covers 3,116 square miles.

All told, roughly 6 percent of Colorado's total land area is found within the state's four cloud-seeding target areas, although the effect of those 91 generators covers a much larger area via runoff.

There are three main questions people ask about cloud seeding:

1. **Does it work?** This is the $64,000 question. There have literally been dozens of scientific papers addressing this issue. The main issue here is not knowing for certain how much precipitation would have occurred naturally had the seeding not taken place. Part of the problem comes from the logical impossibility of proving a negative. The World Meteorological Organization has very ambiguously concluded that cloud seeding does not produce positive results in all cases and is dependent on specificity of clouds, wind speed and direction, terrain, and other factors. The Weather Modification Association, which has as members numerous for-profit companies that have vested fiscal interests in positive data, has concluded that, for "well-designed and properly conducted projects," precipitation increases of 5 to 20 percent can be expected in winter in continental regions, whereas, in warm seasons, single-cloud experiments have produced precipitation increases of at least 100 percent." The Colorado Water Conservation Board's (CWCB) Weather Modification Program, which has an annual budget of about $775,000 ($177,000 of which comes from other states in hopes that Colorado's cloud-seeding efforts will help raise river levels downstream), cautiously states that a 10-percent positive effect is realized on snowpack. The CWCB officially states that its cloud-seeding efforts have a great effect in some areas sometimes, and not such great effects in other areas at other times. The CWCB spends considerable effort focusing on the "well-designed and properly executed projects" component of the above-stated Weather Modification Association's efficacy

statement. Generators are constantly moved, often to higher elevations, to improve targeting accuracy. The official line in Colorado is that, very often, when cloud seeding is not efficacious, it's less because cloud seeding itself does not work and more because the targeting is off, meaning that the silver oxide is not getting to the clouds.

2. **Is it a case of robbing Peter to pay Paul?** As demonstrated at the Beijing Olympics, cloud seeding in one place can have a direct precipitation effect on downwind areas. When Vail Ski Area started investing in cloud seeding in 1972, there were howls of righteous indignation in neighboring Summit County that Vail, a definite ski-area competitor, was "stealing" snow that, were it not coaxed out of the clouds via cloud seeding, would likely have made its way downwind to Summit's slopes. At least 40 scientific papers conclude that cloud seeding has little, if any, effect on downwind locations. But some experts admit that, if cloud seeding has an effect on precipitation downwind, the range is more likely to be 20 to 250 miles. And, if the upwind seeding results in more precipitation filling river drainages that flow toward that downwind area, then it's a moisture wash.

3. **What is its effect on the environment?** Cloud seeding is not without its environmental controversies. Many people have wondered about the effects of the silver iodide that is used to actually seed the clouds, the concern being based around the common understanding the silver itself is highly toxic. The official position from the CWCB is that, in soluble form, silver oxide is inert and poses no threat to the environment or to public health. Long-term studies performed by the Australian government back up that assertion, according to the CWCB.

The two main things to remember about cloud seeding are: (1) even people who argue that it is an effective endeavor stress that cloud seeding needs to be considered as a long-term solution to drought (i.e., using it as a means of filling reservoirs now to make sure water is available down the road), because, (2) it really only works when there is cloud cover into which dry ice and/or silver oxide can be released. Cloud seeding gets its most enthusiastic support from the public during dry years, when there are few clouds to work with and, therefore, it is less likely to produce the desired drought-busting results.

SOURCES

www.ask.yahoo.com; North American Weather Consultants, Inc.; the North American Weather Modification Council; Wikipedia; personal interviews with Joe Busko, Colorado Weather Modification Program coordinator.

# JUST HOW MUCH WATER IS THAT?

When word hit the national news in 2007 that there was a serious quantity of toxic water backing up in the Leadville Mining and Drainage Tunnel (LMDT), there was twofold justifiable unease in the Cloud City: First, there were concerns about the overall funkiness quotient of the water, which was laden with all manner of heavy metals that could, in the words of one elected official, pretty much biologically sterilize the Arkansas River headwaters for 100 years. (Important note: This situation has been dealt with. The danger has passed!)

Then, there was unease about the sheer *quantity* of water that had backed up in the LMDT. As much as 1.5 billion gallons of tainted water were in the tunnel, ready to unleash themselves upon Leadville and the Arkansas River Valley.

When anything starts getting measured in the billions, people sit up and pay attention, be it oxygen molecules, grains of rice, federal bailout dollars, or gallons of funky water backing up in a crumbling mine tunnel directly above your town, wherein dwell you and yours. Thing is, few people really had a grip on just how much water there was in the LMDT. Is 1.5 billion gallons enough to wash away an entire town? Or does it just *sound* like a lot of water?

Part of the tangibility-based comprehension conundrum stems from the fact that water in mountain country is measured in many ways, almost none of which are designed to translate easily into the day-to-day life of Joe Blow the Ragman. With regard to the LMDT threat, a significant percentage of the people of Leadville could do some basic palpable mental calculations: They knew that, if the tunnel broke, it would be the water equivalent of 2.67 billion six packs of Budweiser suddenly bursting forth and rushing down toward the Arkansas like something out of a bad sci-fi movie.

Sadly, people who are paid significant quantities of tax dollars to ponder things like flood impacts and stream flows are not inclined to measure things in six packs, at least in public. Rather, they use a dizzying array of measurements that rarely translate into anything as patently understandable as beer.

The main terms one hears in Colorado when the discussion turns to water are: "acre feet," "cubic feet per second" (cfs), and, when things are really getting dicey, "crest" or "stream stage." It would be one thing if, whenever water experts used these measurements, they made them relative to measurements most of us use every day, like gallons or, well, six packs. But, often, there will be inter-arcane-term translation that, by the time the number crunching is done, most of us have no earthly idea whether we're talking about a tempest in a teapot or some wrath-of-God-type action straight out of the Old Testament.

Here, for instance, is a paragraph taken verbatim from the U.S. Geological Survey (USGS) Web site: "Stream flow, or discharge, is the volume of water flowing past a fixed point in a fixed unit of time. For water flow in streams, the [USGS] expresses the value in cubic feet per second (cfs). For example, when rain has not fallen in a while, Peachtree Creek often is at a base-flow stage of about 3 feet. The rating curve shows that at a stage of 3 feet, stream flow is 76 cfs. Since one cubic foot of water contains 7.48 gallons, it might be easier to understand this stream-flow value if you consider that 76 cfs is about 568 gallons of water flowing each second."

In other words: By the time the USGS people got to the end of that paragraph, they themselves were so confused they just threw in the towel and reverted to using gallons the same way a non-egghead would have. It is somewhat surprising that they did not just go ahead and make some sort of scientific six-pack translation.

Anyhow, like the USGS Web site says, one cubic foot per second of water amounts to 7.48 gallons (since many of us were liberal arts majors, let's round it up to 7.5). This form of measurement is used mainly by river rafters because it serves, in their river-rafting mindset, as a simultaneous measurement of water volume and speed.

The Arkansas River through Brown's Canyon, near Buena Vista, can run anywhere between 200 cfs up through 6,000 cfs during an especially heavy spring runoff. If you want to start looking at the potential torrent presented in 2007 by the LMDT the way a rafter or kayaker would, then—hmmm—let's see: Take that 1.5 billion gallons of pent-up funky water and divide it by 7.5, and, boy howdy, that gives us a very respectable-sounding 200,000,000 cubic feet of heavy-metal-contaminated water backed up in the LMDT just itching to burst forth. At 200 cfs, that would translate to 1 million seconds, or 16,666 minutes, or 277 hours, or 11.54 days of funky flow. At 6,000 cfs, that would translate to 33,333 seconds, or 555 minutes, or 9.2 hours of flow. Of course, no one knows whether those 1.5 billion gallons of water would have spewed forth all at once or over a long period of time, so those numbers serve mainly as conversational fodder for those tired of watching *Jeopardy* reruns at the local tavern.

Another water-measurement term that you read in newspapers whenever someone is talking about wanting to build a new dam is the "acre foot." Technically, an acre foot is the amount of water necessary to cover one acre of land one foot deep, which means, of course, that the now-really-nonplussed Joe Blow the Ragman has to mentally map how much area an acre covers in order to gain any cranial traction whatsoever with this measurement. It's enough to drive a man to drink!

Let's go back to the LMDT. It takes about 325,851 gallons to make an acre foot of water. Windy Gap Reservoir, between Granby and Hot Sulphur Springs, holds 445 acre feet of water. So that means, let's see here: 1.5 billion divided by 325,851 equals, well, 4,603, which further equals 10.3 Windy Gap Reservoirs–worth of water that was held in the LMDT. Of course, that sounds like a lot, especially if you're worried about all that water maybe flowing through your living room while you're watching *The Simpsons*. But, when you consider that Dillon Reservoir in Summit County—the main source of drinking water for Denver—can hold 254,036 acre feet of water, and, therefore, 82,777,884,636 gallons (or, if you really get your jollies by comparing apples to kumquats, 11,065,808,160 cubic feet), you come to realize that the amount of water that was pent up in the LMDT was only 1/55th the capacity of Dillon Reservoir! Now, that doesn't sound so bad, does it? (Oh, by the way, the acre-foot measurement is not to be confused with a reservoir's surface-area measurement. Dillon Reservoir's *surface area* is 3,233 acres.)

The third main way you hear water being measured in the mountains is "stream stage," which can also be, and most often is, articulated for public consumption by saying something like, "The stream will crest at 14 feet," or, "The wall of water that swept all of those nice people away was 12 feet high."

According to our hyper-articulate friends at the USGS, stream stage is "…the height of the water surface, in feet, above an established datum plane where the stage is zero. The zero level is arbitrary but is often close to the streambed."

Sigh.

Anyhow, it's undeniable that water measurement in the mountains is a mixed bag often requiring much in the way of pondering and translation and a heartfelt desire to throttle an egghead. Whenever things get too complicated as you sit there trying to ascertain whether or not your house might get washed away, you might want to wander down to the closest bar and order yourself a beer. That would be 12 ounces per bottle or can, unless, of course, you order a pint. Then things get really complicated.

SOURCES

Personal interviews with various local sources in Leadville; the *Summit Daily News*; a calculator.

All of Colorado lies between 36 degrees, 59 minutes, 40 seconds and 41 degrees, 00 minutes, 08 seconds north latitude.

Vail, which we choose as the point of orientation because it is centrally located in Colorado, lies just south of 40 degrees north latitude. That makes Vail more or less at the same latitude north as

- Springfield, Illinois
- Indianapolis, Indiana
- Columbus, Ohio
- Philadelphia, Pennsylvania
- Madrid, Spain
- The Mallorca Islands, Spain
- The island of Sardinia, Italy
- Northern Greece
- Ankara, Turkey
- Yerevan, Armenia
- Baku, Azerbaijan
- Tashkent, Uzbekistan
- The middle of Inner Mongolia
- Beijing, China
- Pyongyang, North Korea
- Akita, Honshu, Japan
- Reno, Nevada

Very little in the way of land mass lies at 40 degrees south latitude. However, at the Southern Hemisphere's equivalent of Vail's Northern Hemisphere latitude can be found:

- Valdivia, Chile
- San Carlos de Bariloche, Argentina
- The Bass Strait, which separates the island of Tasmania from the Australian mainland
- The southern part of New Zealand's North Island

All of Colorado lies between 102 degrees, 02 minutes, 41 seconds and 109 degrees, 02 minutes, 39 seconds west longitude. Vail lies at about 106 degrees west longitude. That makes Vail more or less at the same west longitude as:

- The Guadalupe Mountains of Texas
- Durango, Mexico
- Puerto Vallarta, Mexico
- Easter Island
- Mount Seeling, Antarctica
- Regina, Saskatchewan
- Cambridge Bay, Nunavut

At the exact opposite side of the world, where the time zone is 12 hours different than the Mountain Time Zone, lie most of India, most of Pakistan, the Hindu Kush Mountains, and most of eastern Kazakhstan.

The point on the planet exactly opposite Vail lies in the middle of the Indian Ocean.

SOURCES

Numerous world atlases.


## "AMERICA THE BEAUTIFUL": COLORADO'S MOST FAMOUS MUSICAL SUMMIT

Few are the states that have inspired lyricists, songwriters, and various and sundry melody-makers more than Colorado. That's primarily because Colorado was one of those ground-zero hippie states, and homegrown music was a huge part of the hippie lifestyle/consciousness. Sure, it would be hard to top California, New York, and Texas for pure volume of produced musical material, but, when it comes to the tuneful passion and creative inspiration associated with a given state, Colorado more than holds its own.

You'll get little debate that the two best-known Colorado songs are "America the Beautiful" by Katherine Lee Bates (which does not mention Colorado by name) and "Rocky Mountain High" by Henry John Deutschendorf, Jr., otherwise known by his nom de guerre, John Denver (which does).

It has often been suggested that "America the Beautiful," which Bates penned in 1893 (with revisions in 1904 and 1913), replace the structural awkwardness of Francis Scott Key's "The Star-Spangled Banner" as our national anthem. Verily, in 1926, five years before Congress cast its official lot with the "The Star-Spangled Banner," there was a vociferous movement afoot to get "America the Beautiful" named the national anthem. ("The Star-Spangled Banner" reportedly won out because of its undeniable venerability.)

Still, "America the Beautiful" is considered by many people to be the country's unofficial second national anthem, and, before sporting events, it often replaces Key's song, which, despite that aforementioned structural awkwardness and the fact that it requires a rarely successfully achieved vocal range of an octave-and-a-fifth, maybe gains some additional style points because it was set to the tune of a popular British drinking song, the "Anacreontic Song," written by John Stafford Smith. (You've got to admire the chorus of the "Anacreontic Song": "And besides I'll instruct you like me to intwine/the Myrtle of Venus with Bacchus's wine"—which, translated, sounds very much like Jimmy Buffet's "Why Don't We Get Drunk and Screw.")

Bates (1859–1929) was a professor of English at Wellesley College in Massachusetts. In 1893, she came West to teach some summer courses at Colorado College in Colorado Springs. On July 22, she bagged her first and only Fourteener, 14,110-foot Pikes Peak. Bates did not exactly don her La Sportiva boots and hike to the summit. She took a horse-drawn carriage most of the way before actually summiting on mule back, which may seem like cheating by today's Fourteener-bagging standards, but, then again, few Fourteener baggers today manage to pen a song for the ages while standing atop a mountain.

Bates and her group, which was made up mostly of other Wellesley faculty members, were on top of Pikes Peak for only half an hour or so, because one member of the party got stricken with altitude sickness, a situation that maybe we all ought to be thankful for, because, had Bates spent any more time on top of Pikes Peak, we may have been treated to a full-fledged opera libretto instead of a mere seven verses that, undeniably, were fast fizzling in quality by the time the fat lady sang.

After that summit visit, Bates wrote, "An erect and decorous group, we stood at last on the Gate-of-Heaven summit…and gazed in wordless rapture over the far expanse of mountain ranges and sealike sweep of plain. Then and there the opening lines of 'America the Beautiful' spring into being…I wrote the entire song on my return that evening to Colorado Springs."

When Bates said that she "wrote the entire song," that's not exactly correct. What she wrote was a poem that first appeared in the weekly journal, *The Congregationalist* (surely the *Rolling Stone* of the era), on July 4, 1895. It was first sung to the melody of "Materna," which was written by Samuel A. Ward more than a decade before Bates stood atop Pikes Peak. For 15 years, the lyrics of "America the Beautiful" were applied to many different folk melodies, most notably "Auld Lang Syne," which, you've got to admit, changes the overall tone significantly. Bates' lyrics were not published with "Materna," the melody we now think of as being as much a part of "America the Beautiful" as "amber waves of grain," until 1910.

Even after that, the tune part of "America the Beautiful" continued to be challenged. In 1926, the National Federation of Music Clubs held a contest in hopes of attaching Bates' words to a more upbeat melody. But no other tune was deemed acceptable. Bates apparently never chose her favorite tune for her words before she passed on to the great fruited plain in the sky in 1929.

Despite the fact that it has never succeeded in displacing "The Star-Spangled Banner" as the official national anthem, it's highly likely that more Americans can recite the entire first verse of "America the Beautiful" than its more officious patriotic counterpart. (Only 61 percent of Americans can sing "The Star-Spangled Banner" all the way through the first verse.) What is equally likely is that most Americans could not make their way past verse one of "America the Beautiful" if their lives depended on it.

Here, for instance, is verse 2:

*O beautiful for pilgrim feet*
*Whose stern impassioned stress*
*A thoroughfare of freedom beat*
*Across the wilderness!*
*America! America!*
*God mend thine every flaw,*
*Confirm thy soul in self-control,*
*Thy liberty in law!*

You can see why we generally do not generally venture much past the first eight lines of Bates' immortal patriotic ode.

In all likelihood, few people are going to be inclined to hunt down a recorded version of "America the Beautiful," because it's just sort of out of vogue these days. But, if either your patriotism or your attachment to Colorado via her undeniably most famous song overcomes your natural aversion to pilgrim feet with stern impassioned stress, you can download a version of the state's almost-national anthem by Neil Young on his *Living with War* CD. Other artists who have covered "America the Beautiful" are: the immortal Ray Charles, who sang the song at Super Bowl 35 (January 28, 2001—Baltimore Ravens, 34; New York Giants, 7); Elvis; Little Richard; Gladys Knight; Reba McIntyre; and Boys II Men.

SOURCE

Wikipedia.

# BATES NOT THE ONLY FAMOUS PERSON TO SUMMIT PIKES PEAK

Although Katherine Lee Bates' beast-of-burden-aided ascent of Pikes Peak in 1893 is likely the most famous climb of a Fourteener in state history, she was not the only luminary to stand atop Colorado's 31st-highest mountain.

In the late 1880s, Zalmon Simmons, inventor of the Simmons Beauty Rest Mattress Company, rode to the summit of Pikes Peak on horseback, partly to enjoy the view and partly to check on the status of one of his inventions: an insulator for telegraph lines that ran to the army signal station on the summit.

After an arduous two-day round-trip journey, Simmons, whose posterior was likely feeling worse for wear, found himself relaxing in one of Manitou Springs's mineral baths. The owner of the hotel at which Simmons was staying broached the subject of building a railway to the top of Pikes Peak. Simmons agreed to capitalize the venture, and on June 30, 1891, the first passenger train, carrying a church choir from Denver, made it to the summit of Pikes Peak.

The 8.9-mile route is the world's highest "cog" railway. Conventional railroads use the friction of their wheels upon the tracks to gain and maintain momentum. Because only a small portion of the wheels are making contact with the tracks at any given moment, the amount of potential friction is relatively small, despite the great weight of locomotives. Therefore, conventional railroads are only able to climb grades of 4 to 6 percent, with very short sections as steep as 9 percent, and that's only with a good head of steam.

Not surprisingly, the sides of Pikes Peak are far steeper than that. Therefore, Simmons opted to utilize cog railway technology, which had only been invented in New Hampshire in 1869.

Cog railways—otherwise known as rack railways—use a gear (a "cog wheel") that meshes into a special rack rail mounted in the middle of the track, between the outer rails. This cog maintains constant contact with the rail by way of the gear. It therefore cannot slip backwards when the friction of the wheels becomes insufficient to maintain the weight of the train on a steep grade. This technology enables the Manitou & Pikes Peak Railway, as it is properly known, to ascend grades as steep as 25 percent.

The Pikes Peak cog railway has never experienced a mishap. It now runs year-round.

## SOURCES

www.cograilway.com.

# ROCKY MOUNTAIN HIGH

When one makes the claim that "America the Beautiful" is the most famous "Colorado song," you'd best be prepared for some retort by John Denver fans, who will argue that "Rocky Mountain High" is both better known and *better*. While certainly more people would recognize "America the Beautiful," not everyone realizes that it was inspired by Katherine Lee Bates' 1893 trip to the summit of Pikes Peak. The fact that the song—actually a poem later set to music—mentions neither Pikes Peak nor Colorado compels even sympathetic listeners to think it is only marginally a bona fide "Colorado song."

There is no disputation about "Rocky Mountain High," the lyrics of which mention Colorado a total of 11 times (depending on how many times you are inclined to sing the chorus).

Denver, who was born Henry John Deutschendorf, penned the lyrics of "Rocky Mountain High" (Mike Taylor composed the music) after watching the Perseid meteor shower with friends near Williams Lake. It was recorded in August 1972 and released the following year.

Almost since the exact minute it was written, there have been many efforts to replace the official state song, "Where the Columbines Grow," with the more upbeat and contemporary "Rocky Mountain High."

Finally, in March 2007, after years of lobbying (most often by schoolchildren), the Colorado State Legislature passed a resolution proclaiming "Rocky Mountain High" as Colorado's second official song. (It was an encore honor for Denver, who passed away in a plane crash in 1997. West Virginia had previously adopted Denver's "Take Me Home, Country Roads" as its number-two state song. "West Virginia Hills," by Ellen King and H.E. Engle, is the official song of the Mountaineer State.)

"Rocky Mountain High," which went as high as number 9 on the Billboard Charts, was embroiled in a bit of controversy shortly after it was released. The Federal Communications Commission had been granted powers to crack down on music deemed to promote drug use, which covered about half the country's discography in those days, and "Rocky Mountain High" was actually banned from some radio stations as a result.

Stunningly, inferences were drawn that a "Rocky Mountain High" was in fact a drug-induced state of being!

In 1985, Denver testified before Congress in the Parents Music Resource Center hearings about his experience:

*This was obviously done by people who had never seen or been to the Rocky Mountains, and also who had never experienced the elation, celebration of life, or the joy in living that one feels when he observes something as wondrous as the Perseid meteor shower on a moonless, cloudless night, when there are so many stars that you have a shadow from the starlight, and you are out camping with your friends, your best friends, and introducing them to one of nature's most spectacular light shows for the first time.*

Despite that non sequitorius quote, Denver made no reference during that testimony to whether or not drugs were indeed involved in the experience that eventually gave the world "Rocky Mountain High."

The song gained even more mainstream credence when it was performed by a soloist before a Denver Nuggets basketball game in 2005. "Rocky Mountain High" has also been used in an advertisement for Colorado-based Coors Beer, hardly a bastion of counterculture consciousness.

In late 2007, "Rocky Mountain High" once again drew some controversy when the last two lines of the song ("Friends around the campfire/and everybody's high") were left off a stone that was placed in the John Denver Sanctuary in Aspen.

Here are notes on some of the references in the lyrics of "Rocky Mountain High":

- "He was born in the summer of his 27th year." Denver was 27 when he saw that Perseid meteor shower.
- "Coming home to a place he'd never been before." He and his wife Annie, the title subject of another of Denver's best-known songs, "Annie's Song," had just made Aspen their home.
- "And he lost a friend but kept his memory." A good friend from Minnesota had come to visit and was killed riding Denver's motorcycle.
- "Why they try to tear the mountains down to bring in a couple more." This referred to the debate at that time about bringing the Olympics to Colorado (*see* the separate section on the Olympics in Colorado).

# "WHERE THE COLUMBINES GROW"—THE STATE SONG THAT NO ONE KNOWS

Three years after Katherine Lee Bates penned "America the Beautiful," the poem that would morph into America's unofficial second national anthem, Arthur John Flynn (born 1857), penned "Where the Columbines Grow," which would morph into the state song that no one knows. Flynn had come to Colorado in 1889 after being educated in New York. In 1896, Flynn, who was a teacher in both Central City and Alamosa before joining the faculty at Colorado State University in 1898, was traveling by horse and wagon to visit Indian tribes in the San Luis Valley. He came upon Schinzel Flats when it was resplendent in blossoming columbines. This vision provided the inspiration for "Where the Columbines Grow," but it did not provide inspiration for prompt creative action, as Flynn did not start writing "Where the Columbines Grow" until 1909. It was first performed in 1911 and was adopted on May 8, 1915, by the Colorado legislature as the official state song.

But, of course, there was controversy that lasted clear up until the hippies started descending upon Colorado in droves with their guitars in hand. This controversy was based upon the fact that "Where the Columbines Grow" does not even once contain the word "Colorado"—something you would think would be important in a state song. In 1916, the Colorado Federation of Women's Clubs unanimously voted to repeal "Where the Columbines Grow." Faced with a cadre of irate women's clubs, the state legislature did the only reasonable thing: It backpedaled and held a state song competition in 1917. Four songs were performed for the legislators, who, one can presume, were happy for the distraction, given that the First World War was then raging in Europe. "Where the Columbines Grow" won hands-down, with 34 votes. Finishing a distant second was "Skies Are Blue in Colorado," by John Ramsey, which only garnered 17 votes.

The anti–"Where the Columbines Grow" faction, however, was not placated by something as bothersome as the democratic process. In 1947, Senator John J. Harpel proposed replacing "Where the Columbines Grow" with a military march, "Hail Colorado." It did not pass. As late as 1969, a mere four years before John Denver released "Rocky Mountain High," Representative Betty Anne Dittemore initiated a bill to have "Colorado," otherwise known as "If I Had a Wagon," named as the official state song. The proposal died in committee.

The weirdest thing about having "Where the Columbines Grow" as the official state song is not its lack of the word "Colorado" within its lyrics. The weirdest thing is its dark heart. After the obligatory effusive opening stanza, the song turns rather "Where Have All the Flowers Gone?"-ish.

Here's verse two of "Where the Columbines Grow":

*The bison is gone from the upland,*
*The deer from the canyon has fled,*
*The home of the wolf is deserted,*
*And the antelope moans for its dead,*
*The war whoop re-echoes no longer,*
*The Indian's only a name,*
*And the nymphs of the grove in their loneliness rove,*
*But the columbines bloom just the same.*

So, after reading those words, you can see where, when John Denver came along singing happily about being born in the summer of his 27th year, people were ready for a change.

It's not like you're going to get tired of hearing people sing "Where the Columbines Grow." After 24 years of living in Colorado, I've never heard it sung a single time. Still, it's entirely possible to download at least two versions of this tune. One version is, of all things, by head-banger band Pinhead Circus and is found on their *Coolidge 50* album. The next version is very, very different. On *Melanie's Melodies of the Rockies: Soothing Songs of the Old West for Home and Fireside*, there's a nice folksy version. It should be noted, as you're scrambling to download "Where the Columbines Grow," that no other album that has ever been produced contains the word "Colorado" in as many song titles as does *Melanie's Melodies of the Rockies*. It should also be noted that this is not THE Melanie (Safka), of "Lay Down (Candles in the Rain)" fame.

SOURCE

www.netstate.com/states/symb/song/co_song.htm.

# COLORADO SONGS

There is no doubt that there will be many exclamations sounding very much like, "That guy's an idiot! How could he not include [such and such a song] or at least something by [fill in the blank]." I realize that many Hot Rize and Dotsero and Leftover Salmon and String Cheese Incident fans might propose downloads that they would like to add to this list. I am all ears. Please send gently worded suggestions (as well as any corrections to this list) to mjfayhee@ yahoo.com. Anyway, here goes!

- Because he lived most of his adult life in Colorado, a large percentage of John Denver's discography hailed from the Centennial State. Many of his tunes make reference to his adopted home state, but, if you're going to seek out a Denver song not named "Rocky Mountain High" that is about Colorado, your best bet is "I Guess He'd Rather Be in Colorado."
- Bob Dylan, another singer who, like John Denver changed his name (from Robert Allen Zimmerman), still maintains a second home in Telluride. In "Man of Constant Sorrow" (a traditional song first recorded in 1913 by partially blind Kentucky fiddler Dick Burnett and covered by many musicians, including Waylon Jennings, Peter, Paul and Mary, Jackson Browne, Jerry Garcia, and made famous by The Foggy Bottom Boys in the 2000 movie, *O Brother, Where Art Thou!*), he sings (first verse): "I am a man of constant sorrow/I've seen trouble all my days/I'll say good-bye to Colorado/Where I was born and partly raised." And (fourth verse): "I'm going back to Colorado/The place that I started from/If I'd known how bad you'd treat me honey/I would never have come." And, in "Wanted Man," (the only song Dylan ever co-wrote with Johnny Cash, who released it on his 1969 album, *At San Quentin*), he sings: "I might be in Colorado or Georgia by the sea/Working for some man who may not know at all who I might be." (Note: Contrary to some published reports, Dylan's "Romance in Durango" is not about the southwestern Colorado town that is home to Fort Lewis College, but, rather, the nice big city that is in Mexico.)
- While still with The Flying Burrito Brothers, Rick Roberts wrote, "Colorado," which was included on that group's self-titled 1971 album. "Colorado" was covered by Linda Ronstadt on her 1973 album, "Don't Cry Now." Roberts went on to help found Firefall. Several versions of "Colorado," as performed by both The Flying Burrito Brothers and Ronstadt, can be found on YouTube.
- Stephen Stills's "Colorado" is an example (of many) of a great mountain-based song with lyrics so disjointed that you wonder how much pot these folkies were actually smoking back in the earliest days of the Rocky Mountain High era.
- James McMurtry, the son of Pulitzer-Prize-winning author Larry McMurtry (of *Lonesome Dove* fame) wrote in "No More Buffalo" ("Live in Aught-Three"): "We headed south across those Colorado plains/just as empty as the day/we looked around at all we saw/remembered all we hoped to see/looking out through the

bugs on the windshield/somebody said to me/no more buffalo, blue skies, or open road/no more rodeo/no more noise/take this Cadillac/park it out in back/mama's calling/put away the toys."

- Merle Haggard recorded two Colorado-based songs, "Colorado" and "Lucky Old Colorado."
- Townes Van Zandt's "Colorado Girl," from his *Rear View Mirror* album, is one of the most fetching songs about the state. Steve Earl does a wonderful cover of "Colorado Girl" on his *Townes* album, which is a tribute to the late Van Zandt.
- If you are inclined to travel to the deep, dark, musical past—a past that was hilariously skewered by the 2003 movie *A Mighty Wind*—you can download the Kingston Trio's folk classic, "The Colorado Trail," which was written by Carl Sandburg and Lee Hayes. Though it may be tempting to wonder how this song was birthed a solid decade before the Colorado Trail was even conceived, much less constructed, edification comes when you realize this tune is not about the 500-mile hiking trail that connects Denver to Durango, but, rather, an old cattle-drive trail from days of yore. Either way, any song that contains the near-Wordsworthian words, "Weep, all ye little rains. Wail, winds, wail. All along, along, along the Colorado Trail," is worth a listen, if for no other reason that to thank the gods that the early 1960s folk music scene was short lived. Melanie, referenced in the "Where the Columbines Grow" chapter, covers this tune on her *Melodies of the Rockies* album. One listen and you won't be able to resist lacing on your boots and hiking 500 miles from Denver to Durango on the Colorado Trail, even if it's the wrong Colorado Trail.
- Even though it may be considered a mildly good-natured anti-Colorado song, National Lampoon's "Colorado," sung by, of all people, Chevy Chase, is actually a surprisingly melodic satire of "Rocky Mountain High." "Colorado" is found on the 1973 *Lemmings* album.
- Folk singer Chuck Pyle is often referred to as the official singer/ songwriter of the high country. His 2007 album, *Higher Ground: Songs of Colorado,* contains one song named "Colorado" and another named "Moonlight on the Colorado." But it's his "Little Town Tour," which begins, "Bayfield, Cascade, Manitou, Palisade…" that is most interesting in that it includes the names of almost every single mountain town in the state.
- While, admittedly, its Colorado connection is somewhat oblique, Tom Waits's "Nighthawk Postcards (From Easy Street)," which appeared on his seminal 1975 live album *Nighthawks at the Diner,* contains the line, "Maybe you're standing on the corner of 17th and Wazee streets, yeah, out in front of the Terminal Bar,

there's a Thunderbird moving in a muscatel sky." Those words were penned long before LoDo—which Waits would hate—spontaneously combusted. The Terminal Bar is long gone, but the building, which now houses Jax Fish House, remains.

- One of the great musical shames of the past decade is that Denver-based DeVotchKa is not a household name from Maine to Australia. That changed a bit with the release of the Academy-Award-nominated film, *Little Miss Sunshine,* which was completely scored with DeVotchKa songs. It did not appear in the film, but "Commerce City Sister," with its line, "You know I ain't never going back to Commerce City," expresses the sentiment of many people who have actually visited Commerce City, an industrial Denver suburb. Hopefully, *Little Miss Sunshine* will serve as a gateway drug for many future DeVotchKa fans. This is truly a wonderful musical ensemble.

- No Colorado-based song list would be complete without mention of the Nitty Gritty Dirt Band, which spent a lot of time in the state. One of its long-time members, Jimmy Ibbotson, still lives in Woody Creek, where he performs often. One of the Dirt Band's best-known songs that contains the state's name is "Colorado Christmas," which was actually written by the late, great Steve Goodman, who served as a mentor for folk/rock legend John Prine. (Goodman and Prine co-owned a bar in Chicago named Somebody Else's Troubles, after one of Goodman's best-known tunes.)

- You'll be forgiven if the words "Ozark Mountain Daredevils" have not entered your thought processes for many years. In the mid-1970s, this band from Springfield, Missouri, was one of the hottest acts in the country, and their "Colorado Song" (by Steve Cash and John Dillon) was released on their first album, *The Ozark Mountain Daredevils.* This song is highly recommended, despite its second-to-the-last verse, which consists entirely of "aaaahhhhh" being repeated over and over, and the last verse, which consists of "lalalalala" being repeated over and over.

- So, OK, it's technically a song about leaving Colorado, but that can easily be overlooked due to the fact that Emmylou Harris's "Boulder to Birmingham" is flat-out one of the best songs ever penned. It has been covered by many artists, including Joan Baez, Dolly Parton, and the Starland Vocal Band (yes, they of "Afternoon Delight" fame). The lines "I was in the wilderness and the canyon was on fire/And I stood on the mountain in the night and I watched it burn/ I watched it burn/I watched it burn" are lovely.

- Folk diva Judy Collins was actually born in Seattle, but she grew up in Denver, where she attended East High School. Many of her songs contain references to Colorado. Few songs about the state are more accurately evocative than Collins's "The Blizzard (The Colorado Song)," which contains lines that show the singer was intimate with the realities of Colorado life: "One night on the mountain, I was headed for Estes/When the roads turned to ice and it started to snow/Put on the chains in a whirl of white powder/Halfway up to Berthoud near a diner I know." You never heard Stephen Stills or the Ozark Mountain Daredevils singing about chaining up in the middle of a blizzard.

- So far, these Colorado songs have been a bit on the heavy, philosophical side. Fun needs to be part of the download equation, and that's where Bowling For Soup's "Surf Colorado" comes in. With lines like, "She's traded rattlesnakes for bunny runs in Colorado Springs," it's easy to overlook the fact that this song is essentially a rant by a Texan who's angry that his paramour left the Lone Star State to move to Colorado without him. Also, the fact that the album upon which "Surf Colorado" appears is titled *Drunk Enough to Dance* ought to gain it some style points in the hedonistic high-country resort towns.

- There's no denying that, when John Denver released "Rocky Mountain High" in 1973, it marked the first time that many Americans gave the Mountain Time Zone the mental time of day. Many people even believe that "Rocky Mountain High" was in and of itself responsible for drawing nationwide attention to Colorado, the same way Edward Abbey's *Desert Solitaire* drew attention to Utah's slickrock country. But Denver was not the only person singing about the Rockies in 1973. While it does not mention Colorado specifically (and, hey, if the official state song doesn't even mention Colorado, then all bets are off), Joe Walsh's "Rocky Mountain Way" was in the top 20 at the very same time as "Rocky Mountain High." Walsh was living outside Nederland in Boulder County when he recorded "Rocky Mountain Way." The fact that it makes no sense at all does not diminish its place in musical history.

- Continuing the folk-rock trend that defined Colorado music for so many years, Pure Prairie League, which hailed from decidedly un-altitudinous Ohio, released "Boulder Skies" in 1972 on its second album, *Bustin' Out*. The second verse commences, "Colorado canyon girl could set me free/Brown eyes in the mornin' lookin' back at me." "Boulder Skies" was written by PPL co-founder Craig Fuller and was recorded on a horse farm outside Toronto, Canada, while Fuller was on the lam for draft evasion. He eventually returned to the U.S. to face the music and was sentenced to six months in the slammer before his conscientious objector status could be established.

- Richie Furay (who used to play in Buffalo Springfield with Stephen Stills and Neil Young) was an architect of country rock while living on Sugarloaf Mountain outside Boulder in the '70s. Furay was also founding member of Poco. The song "A Good Feelin' to Know," which Furay wrote and which appears on an album of the same name (Poco's fifth, released in 1972), contains the lyrics, "Colorado mountains/I can see your distant skies/ You're bringin' a tear of joy to my eyes." In 1983, Furay became a senior pastor at Calvary Chapel in Broomfield, a Denver suburb. In 1997, Furay was inducted into the Rock & Roll Hall of Fame as a member of Buffalo Springfield. He also performed at the 2010 Rock & Roll Hall of Fame induction ceremony.

- On Jimmy Buffett's 11th studio album *Coconut Telegraph*, released in 1981, appears the song, "Incommunicado, " which Buffett co-write with Deborah McCall and M.L Benoit. On that song, Buffett sings: "Now on the day that John Wayne died/I found myself on the Continental Divide/Tell me where do we go from here?/Think I'll ride into Leadville and have a few beers."

- In the mid-'70s, Dan Fogelberg wintered outside Nederland, Colorado, otherwise known as Ned (its residents are known as "Nedheads"). A decade later, with his popularity definitely on the downslide, Fogelberg released *High Country Snows*. The title song will never become a mosh pit favorite, unless there's irony at play (although, now that I think about it, if "Where the Columbines Grow" can be covered by a headbanger group, then anything's possible), but it still does justice to life at altitude, as does "Nether Lands"—which is close enough to "Nederland" that we'll call it good. Fogelberg later had a home in Durango. Thus the lyric, "I'm in Colorado, when I'm not in some hotel" from his hit, "Leader of the Band." On *High Country Snows*, he also wrote an instrumental titled "Wolf Creek." Finally, on his *Wild Places* CD, the song of the same name notes, "I was walking alone, through the lofty San Juans."

- The Grateful Dead performed at least two songs that contained references to Colorado. "Me and My Uncle" ("Me and my uncle went ridin' down/South Colorado, West Texas bound...") was actually written by John Phillips, of Mamas and Papas fame (Judy Collins and Neil Young were anecdotally connected to the song by way of extreme drunkenness in a hotel room in 1963). And "I Know You Rider" ("I'd shine my light through a Colorado rain...") is considered "traditional."

- Even though none of his songs contain the word "Colorado," Elton John did record his 1974 album *Caribou* at the famed Caribou Ranch outside Nederland. The best-known song from that album was "Don't Let the Sun Go Down on Me," but one of the lesser-known tunes was "Cold Highway," which contains the lyrics, "Where the corners turn blind like the graveyard ground/ Oh your black icy snare once cut down my friend/In the deepest dark winter when the world seemed to end." Before it burned down in 1985, Caribou Studios housed recording efforts by dozens of world-class acts such as America, Badfinger, the Beach Boys, Chicago, Phil Collins, Rick Derringer, Earth, Wind & Fire, Emerson, Lake & Palmer, Waylon Jennings, Billy Joel, Carole King, John Lennon, Jerry Lee Lewis, Tom Petty, Rod Stewart, U2, War, and Frank Zappa. Rumor has it that, in addition to its isolation, the main attraction to the Caribou Ranch was its altitude, which anecdotally allowed singers to hit, appropriately enough, high notes that they could only dream of at sea level.

- It was never released, but Jackson Brown wrote a song, "Bound for Colorado." Efforts to locate a recorded version have not been successful.

- Any song containing the lyrics, "I didn't kill that man, I called it self-defense/Now I watch the world go by through a twelve-foot barbed-wire fence" deserves to be listed, especially if it's titled "Colorado." That would be performed by 19 Wheels (from the album *Six Ways from Sunday*).

## SOURCES

Google, Wikipedia, personal music collection, and input from *Mountain Gazette* readers Kevin Masters, Randy Wyrick, Mark Besoke, and Tim Payne.

# COLORADO AS A MOVIE SET

Given its scenic splendor, Victorian architecture, mining-era ghost towns, and world-class ski resorts, it's no wonder that the Colorado Rockies have long attracted filmmakers like flies to honey.

Since 1898 (that would be only 10 years after the generally agreed-upon date of the invention of the first motion-picture camera, which was designed by Frenchman Louis le Prince, who conducted his groundbreaking work in Leeds, England), more than 400 films have been set in part or totally in Colorado—and that number does not include the myriad offerings from the relatively new adrenaline-based ski/snowboard/climbing/kayaking/mountain-biking genre that are churned out each year by people like Warren Miller.

A high percentage of the movies that have been filmed in Colorado are eminently and justifiably forgettable. But some stand out, either because they boasted some intrinsic artistic value or because they were as bad as anything placed on celluloid can possibly be.

Meaning no insult by omission to the lofty cinemagraphic likes of *Mr. Dungbeetle* (2005), *American Beer* (2004), *Cheerleader Massacre* (2003), *Stolen Women, Captured Hearts* (1997), and *The Inside of the White Slave Traffic* (1913)—all of which were shot at least partially in Colorado—here are some of the more noteworthy (read: both good and bad) films with Colorado mountain connections, however tenuous.

- *Procession of Mounted Indians and Cowboys* (1898). *Colorado mountain connection:* Shows the grandstand, corner of Broadway and Colfax Avenue [in downtown Denver], with Indian braves and squaws passing; also rough cowboys on half-tamed bronchos [*sic*].
- *The Great K&A Train Robbery (*1926). Starring Tom Mix as Tom Gordon, Dorothy Dwan as Madge Cullen, and Tony the Horse as Tony the Wonder Horse. *Plot summary:* Cullen has hired Tom to try and stop the robberies on her railroad, all the while knowing that Cullen's secretary is tipping off the bad guys. *Colorado mountain connection:* Train scenes shot in Glenwood Springs and the Royal Gorge.
- *The Searchers* (1956). Starring John Wayne as Ethan Edwards, Jeffrey Hunter as Martin Pawley, Vera Miles as Laurie Jorgensen, and Natalie Wood as the older Debbie Edwards. *Plot summary:* As a Civil War veteran spends years searching for a young niece captured by Indians, his motivation becomes increasingly questionable. *Colorado mountain connection:* Much footage filmed in Aspen and Gunnison.
- *The Maverick Queen* (1956). Starring Barbara Stanwyck as Kit Banion, Barry Sullivan as Jeff Younger, and Scott Brady as Sundance. *Plot summary:* Based on a Zane Grey novel published more than a decade after the author's death. As head of the outlaw gang called the Wild Bunch, Kit Banion (Stanwyck) wreaks havoc on the banks and railroads of the West. Pinkerton detective Jeff Younger (Barry Sullivan) infiltrates the gang, falling in love with Kit along the way. *Colorado mountain connection:* Filmed in Durango, Silverton, and the Royal Gorge.
- *Around the World in Eighty Days* (1956). Starring David Niven as Phileas Fogg, Cantinflas as Passepartout, and Finlay Currie as Whist Partner. *Plot summary:* Adaptation of a Jules Verne novel about a Victorian Englishman who bets that, with the new steamships and railways, he can travel, well, around the world in, well, 80 days. *Colorado mountain connection:* Train scenes shot on the Durango–Silverton Narrow Gauge Railroad.

- *How the West Was Won* (1962). Starring Carroll Baker as Eve Prescott Rawlings, Lee J. Cobb as Marshal Lou Ramsey, Henry Fonda as Jethro Stuart, and Karl Malden as Zebulon Prescott. *Plot summary:* A family saga covering several decades of westward expansion in the nineteenth century—including the Gold Rush, the Civil War, and the building of the railroads. *Colorado mountain connection:* Large number of scenes filmed in Durango and Delta.
- *Cat Ballou* (1965). Starring Jane Fonda as Catherine "Cat" Ballou, Lee Marvin as Kid Shelleen, and Michael Callan as Clay Boone. *Plot summary:* A woman seeking revenge for her murdered father hires a famous gunman, but he's very different from what she expects. *Colorado mountain connection:* Most of the movie was filmed in and around Cañon City.
- *Butch Cassidy and the Sundance Kid* (1969). Starring Paul Newman as Butch Cassidy, Robert Redford as the Sundance Kid, and Katharine Ross as Etta Place. *Plot summary:* Two western bank/ train robbers flee to Bolivia when the law gets too close. *Colorado mountain connection:* Butch and Sundance leaped to safety, robbed trains, and visited bars in Durango, Telluride, and Silverton.
- *Downhill Racer* (1969). Starring Robert Redford as David Chappellet, Gene Hackman as Eugene Claire, and Camilla Sparv as Carole Stahl. *Plot summary:* Quietly cocky David Chappellet joins the U.S. Ski Team as a downhill racer and clashes with the team's coach, played by Hackman. Lots of good skiing. *Colorado mountain connection:* The training scenes were filmed in Boulder, while other scenes were filmed in Durango.
- *True Grit* (1969). Starring John Wayne as Marshal Reuben J. "Rooster" Cogburn, Glen Campbell as La Boeuf, and Kim Darby as Mattie Ross. *Plot summary:* A drunken, hard-nosed U.S. marshal and a Texas ranger help a stubborn young woman track down her father's murderer in Indian territory. *Colorado mountain connection:* Parts were shot in Cañon City, Castle Rock, Gunnison, Montrose, and Ridgway.
- *Vanishing Point* (1971). Starring Barry Newman as Kowalski, Cleavon Little as Super Soul, and Dean Jagger as Prospector. *Plot summary:* Kowalski works for a car delivery service. He takes delivery of a 1970 Dodge Challenger to drive from Colorado to San Francisco. Shortly after pickup, he takes a bet that he can get the car there in less than 15 hours. Negative interactions with law enforcement ensue. Includes lots of chase scenes, gay hitchhikers, and a naked woman riding a motorcycle. *Colorado mountain connection:* Barry Newman races away from police in Glenwood Springs and Rifle. During a chase in Denver, long-time local TV newsman/Colorado icon Bob Palmer plays the role of a reporter.

- *The Cowboys* (1972). Starring John Wayne as Wil Andersen, Roscoe Lee Browne as Jebediah Nightlinger, and Bruce Dern as Long Hair. *Plot summary:* When his cattle drivers abandon him for the goldfields, rancher Wil Andersen is forced to take on a collection of young boys as his drivers in order to get his herd to market in time to avoid financial disaster. The boys learn to do a man's job under Andersen's tutelage, however, neither Andersen nor the boys know that a gang of cattle thieves is stalking them. *Colorado mountain connection:* Filmed in Castle Rock, Cañon City, and Pagosa Springs.
- *Sleeper* (1973). Starring Woody Allen as Miles Monroe, Diane Keaton as Luna Schlosser, and John Beck as Erno Windt. *Plot summary:* A nerdish store owner is revived out of cryostasis 200 years in the future, where he falls in love with a woman he hates and fights an oppressive government. *Colorado mountain connection:* Allen, who also directed this film, made a home overlooking Interstate 70 near the Genesee exit a national landmark by using it in *Sleeper*. The home is to this day known as the "Sleeper House," although, when it was constructed in 1963 by architect Charles Deaton, it was known as the "Sculptured House." Until recently, it had never been lived in full time. Additional shooting took place in Boulder, Denver, Greenwood Village, and Lakewood.
- *The White Buffalo* (1977). Starring Charles Bronson as Wild Bill Hickok, Slim Pickens as Abel Pinkney, and John Carradine as Amos Briggs. *Plot summary:* In this strange, western-genre mating of *Jaws* and *Moby Dick*, two enemies unite to fight a white buffalo that Bronson has seen in a dream. *Colorado mountain connection:* Filmed in and around Cañon City.
- *Every Which Way But Loose* (1978). Starring Clint Eastwood as Philo Beddoe, Sondra Locke as Lynn Halsey–Taylor, and Geoffrey Lewis as Orville Boggs. *Plot summary:* Philo Beddoe is an easygoing trucker and a great fistfighter. With two friends—Orville, who promotes prizefights for him, and Clyde, the orangutan he won on a bet—he roams the San Fernando Valley in search of cold beer, country music, and the occasional punch-up. But he is floored himself by a dainty little country and western singer who gives him the slip when she realizes he's getting too serious. *Colorado mountain connection:* Filmed partially in Georgetown.
- *The Shining* (1980). Starring Jack Nicholson as Jack Torrance, Shelley Duvall as Wendy Torrance, and Danny Lloyd as Danny Torrance. *Plot summary:* A family heads to an isolated hotel, where an evil and spiritual presence influences the father to violence, while his psychic son sees horrific images from the past and forebodings of the future. *Colorado mountain connection:*

Many scenes were shot in and around Estes Park, although the majority of the movie was filmed in Oregon. The 1997 TV miniseries of the same name, starring Steven Weber, was filmed mostly at Estes Park's Stanley Hotel.

- *Copper Mountain* (1983). Starring Jim Carrey as Bobby Todd, Alan Thicke as Jackson Reach, and Richard Gautier as Sonny Silverton. Includes a cameo by Jean-Claude Killy, playing himself. *Plot summary:* Two friends travel to a ski resort, one looking to hit the slopes, the other looking to pick up women. *Colorado mountain connection:* Much footage filmed at Copper Mountain Ski Resort, the Copper Mountain Club Med, and the White River National Forest.

- *Red Dawn* (1984). Starring Patrick Swayze as Jed, Lea Thompson as Erica, and Charlie Sheen, in his feature-film debut, as Matt. *Plot summary: Red Dawn* follows the exploits of a group of Colorado teenagers who manage to defeat, by a combination of guerrilla-warfare tactics, bad acting, and highly improbable plot twists, a joint Soviet/Cuban invasion force that has taken over most of the United States. *Colorado mountain connection:* Much to the chagrin of the entire state, *Red Dawn* was shot almost entirely in the Arapahoe National Forest.

- *American Flyers* (1985). Starring Kevin Costner as Marcus Sommers, David Marshall Grant as David, and Rae Dawn Chong as Sarah. *Plot summary:* Sports physician Marcus persuades his unstable brother David to come with him to train for a bicycle race across the Rockies. *Colorado mountain connection:* Filmed almost entirely in Colorado. Locations included Boulder, Grand Junction, Colorado National Monument, Echo Lake/Mount Evans Road, Golden, and Superior. The race portrayed in the movie is based upon the famed Red Zinger Bicycle Classic, which ran from 1975 to 1979 and which was organized by Boulder-based Celestial Seasonings Tea to promote their signature blend. In 1979, the race morphed into the Coors Classic, which ran for eight years.

- *Christmas Vacation* (1989). Starring Chevy Chase as Clark Griswold, Beverly D'Angelo as Ellen Griswold, Juliette Lewis as Audrey Griswold, and Johnny Galecki as Russell "Rusty" Griswold. *Plot summary:* The Griswold family's plans for a big family Christmas predictably turn into a big disaster. *Colorado mountain connection:* Almost all of the opening sequence, where the Griswolds are driving down a mountain highway, engaging in one of the worst car scenes ever placed on film (and the movie goes downhill from there), was shot along Colorado Highway 9 between Silverthorne and Green Mountain Reservoir.

- *Indiana Jones and the Last Crusade* (1989). Starring Harrison Ford as Indiana Jones, Sean Connery as Professor Henry Jones,

Alison Doody as Dr. Elisa Schneider, and the late River Phoenix as the young Indiana Jones. *Plot summary:* When Dr. Henry Jones suddenly goes missing while pursuing the Holy Grail, eminent archeologist Indiana Jones must follow in his father's footsteps and stop the Nazis from gaining possession of the Grail. *Colorado mountain connection:* The train scenes wherein the young Indiana Jones first gained his fear of snakes was the Cumbres & Toltec Scenic Railroad, which connects Antonito, Colorado, with Chama, New Mexico. Also: The house wherein Dr. Henry Jones tells his son to calm down by asking him to count to 10 backwards in Greek is located in Antonito.

- *Conagher* (1991) (Made for TV). Starring Sam Elliot as Conn Conagher, Katharine Ross as Evie Teale, and Barry Corbin as Charlie McCloud. *Plot summary:* Mrs. Evie Teale is struggling to stay alive while raising her two children on a remote homestead. Conn Conagher is an honest, hardworking cowboy. Their lives are intertwined as they fight the elements, Indians, outlaws, and loneliness. *Colorado mountain connection:* Filmed at Buckskin Joe, near the Royal Gorge outside Cañon City.

- *Thelma & Louise* (1991). Starring Susan Sarandon as Louise, Geena Davis as Thelma, Harvey Keitel as Hal, and Brad Pitt, in his feature-film debut, as J.D. *Plot summary:* An Arkansas waitress and her housewife friend shoot a rapist and take off for Mexico, via Utah, in a '66 Thunderbird. *Colorado mountain connection:* Thelma phones the FBI agent from the Bedrock General Store. Some filming took place in Unaweep Canyon, Grand Junction, and Interstate 70 in the far western part of the state.

- *Under Siege 2: Dark Territory* (1995). Starring Steven Seagal as Casey Ryback, Eric Bogosian as Travis Dane, Everett McGill as Marcus Penn and Katherine Heigl as Sara Ryback. *Plot summary:* After pretty much saving the world in *Under Siege,* Casey Ryback has retired from the Navy and is now a chef at the Mile High Cafe in Denver. Ryback takes his niece Sarah Ryback on a vacation. They board a train traveling through the Rocky Mountains from Denver to Los Angeles. Travis Dane takes the train hostage and starts using the train as a control center… in his effort to take control of a top-secret government outer space super-weapon. *Colorado mountain connection:* Filmed in Glenwood Springs, Leadville, and Pinecliff, as well as outside Kremmling in the Gore Canyon area.

- *Aspen Extreme* (1993). Starring Paul Gross as T.J. Burke, Peter Berg as Dexter Rutecki, and Finola Hughes as Bryce Kellogg. *Plot summary:* T.J. and his friend Dexter quit their jobs in Detroit, where—stunningly!—the skiing in Michigan has become boring, to become ski instructors in Aspen. While T.J. advances to become the most popular instructor of the school during the season, he has to take care of Dexter, whose future is less bright and who's eventually thinking about jobbing as a drug courier— bringing their friendship to a test. Meanwhile, rich business-woman Bryce supports T.J. in his writing ambitions and invites him to live at her home. But in her absence, he falls in love with the stunningly beautiful blond radio moderator Robin. *Colorado mountain connection:* Mortifyingly enough, there is a big one. Although most of the skiing scenes were filmed in British Columbia, many vistas and local venues were indeed filmed in Aspen, much to the chagrin of the local citizenry.

- *Cliffhanger* (1993). Starring Sylvester Stallone as Gabe Walker, John Lithgow as Eric Qualen, and Michael Rooker as Hal Tucker. *Plot summary:* A botched midair heist results in suitcases full of cash being searched for by various groups throughout the Rocky Mountains. *Colorado mountain connection:* Some of the film's most exciting scenes were filmed in Jefferson County. Additional footage was shot in the Durango area.

- *Dumb and Dumber* (1994). Starring Jim Carrey as Lloyd Christmas, Jeff Daniels as Harry Dunne, and Lauren Holly as Mary Swanson. *Plot summary:* The cross-country adventures of two good-hearted but incredibly stupid friends. *Colorado mountain connection:* Substantial. Many scenes filmed in and around Aspen, Breckenridge, and Estes Park. Ski scenes shot at Copper Mountain.

- *Cannibal! (Alferd Packer): The Musical* (1996). Starring Trey Parker as Alferd Packer, Dian Bachar as George Noon, Stephen Blackpool as Black Cat, and Stan Brakhage as Noon's Father. *Plot summary:* The sole survivor of an ill-fated mining expedition tells how his taste for gold was replaced by that of human flesh. *Colorado mountain connection:* Major. Before he teamed with Colorado native Matt Stone to produce *South Park* (itself set in the Colorado mountains), Trey Parker, also a Colorado native, wrote and directed *Alferd Packer*. Filmed in the Black Canyon of the Gunnison, Boulder, Cañon City, and Ouray.

- *Scrapple* (1998). Starring Ryan Massey as Beth Muller, L. Kent Brown as Kurt Hinney, and Grady Lee as Phil Brandel. *Plot summary:* Small-time drug dealer Al Dean (Geoffrey Hanson) sells pot to his friends in the Colorado ski town of Ajax, in hopes of raising enough money to buy a house for himself and his brother, who is in the VA hospital. He will finally be able to afford the house once his shipment of "Nepalese Temple Balls" comes in. When they finally arrive, a pig named Scrapple, which was procured at a pig chase, eats the hash balls, and Al finds himself drawn into a big-time drug deal in order to purchase the house.

(Note: The name "Scrapple" comes from a seasoned pork hash by that name.) *Colorado mountain connection:* Filmed almost entirely in the San Miguel County towns of Telluride, Ophir, and Placerville, with a detour to Gateway. Interiors shot inside the New Sheridan Bar in Telluride, with exteriors shot of Wilson Peak, one of Colorado's famed Fourteeners.

- *Phantoms* (1998). Starring Ben Affleck as Sheriff Bryce Hammond, Peter O'Toole as Dr. Timothy Flyte, and Rose McGowan as Lisa Pailey. *Plot summary:* In the peaceful town of Snowfield, Colorado, something evil has wiped out the community. And now, it's up to a group of people to stop it, or at least get out of Snowfield alive. *Colorado mountain connection:* Filmed on location in Georgetown.

- *For the Love of the Game* (1999). Starring Kevin Costner (a part-time Aspen resident) as Billy Chapel, Kelly Preston as Jane Aubrey, and John C. Reilly as Gus Sinski. *Plot summary:* Thank goodness—yet another syrupy Kevin Costner baseball movie. This time, a baseball legend (played by guess who?), almost finished with his distinguished career at the age of forty, has one last chance to prove who he is and what he is capable of and win the heart of the woman he has loved for the past four years. *Colorado mountain connection:* Filmed in and around Aspen and Glenwood Springs.

- *Silver City* (2004) (Made for TV). Starring Chris Cooper as Dickie Pilager, Richard Dreyfuss as Chuck Raven, and Cajardo Lindsey as Lloyd. *Plot summary:* Set against the backdrop of a mythic "New West," a satire that follows grammatically challenged, "user-friendly" candidate Dickie Pilager, scapegrace scion of Colorado's venerable Senator Jud Pilager, during his gubernatorial campaign. When Pilager finds that he's reeled in a corpse while fishing during the taping of an environmental political ad, his ferocious campaign manager, Chuck Raven, hires former idealistic journalist turned rumpled private detective Danny O'Brien (played by Danny Huston) to investigate potential links between the corpse and the Pilager family's enemies. Danny's investigation pulls him deeper and deeper into a complex web of influence and corruption, involving high-stakes lobbyists, media conglomerates, environmental plunderers, and undocumented migrant workers. *Colorado mountain connection:* Entire film set and filmed in Colorado, with locations including Cherokee Ranch & Castle in Sedalia and the Argo Gold Mine in Idaho Springs, as well as exterior filming locations in Leadville.

- *Mr. & Mrs. Smith* (2005). Starring Brad Pitt as John Smith, Angelina Jolie as Jane Smith, and Vince Vaughn as Eddie. *Plot summary:* John and Jane Smith are a normal married couple, living a normal life in a normal suburb, working normal jobs... if you can call secretly being assassins "normal." But neither Jane nor John knows about their spouse's secret until they are surprised to find each other as targets! On their quest to kill each other, they learn a lot more about each other than they ever did in five (or six) years of marriage. *Colorado mountain connection:* Angelina Jolie's climbing sequences were filmed in Glenwood Canyon.

▲

## OTHER MOVIES FILMED IN THE COLORADO MOUNTAINS

- *Glenn Miller Story* (1954): Boulder and other Colorado locations
- *Badlands* (1973): La Junta, Las Animas, and Otero counties
- *The Duchess and the Dirtwater Fox* (1976): Central City and Buckskin Joe Frontier Town near the Royal Gorge
- *National Lampoon's Vacation* (1983): Alamosa, Durango
- *Starman* (1984): Scenes in Fruita
- *Lightning Jack* (1994): Buckskin Joe Frontier Town near the Royal Gorge
- *Tall Tale* (1995): Glenwood Springs, Carbondale
- *Nurse Betty* (2000): Durango

SOURCES

Considerable material for this section came from imbd.com, the Internet Movie Database, surely one of the best and most comprehensive and entertaining Web sites in existence. If you are even slightly inclined to learn about a particular movie, this is the site to visit. Additional research came from Colorado.com; cbs4denver.com; movies.yahoo.com; infernofilm.com; Wikipedia.com.

# THE GREAT DEMONYMIC DEBATE: COLORADANS OR COLORADOANS?

The seemingly trite descriptive conundrum—Coloradan or Coloradoan—can actually cause a great deal of heartburn within the boundaries of Colorado.[1] Verily, in the 2008 Colorado senatorial election between Dan Schaffer and Mark Udall (which Udall won handily), the Coloradan/Coloradoan battle reached contentious proportions. Congresswoman Diana DeGette's (D–Denver) journalist sister, Cara DeGette, was quoted as saying during the election, in a barb pointed directly toward Schaffer, "Colorado Confidential noted back in August how you can always tell when something is likely coming from inside the [D.C.] Beltway when material refers to 'Coloradoans' rather than the commonly accepted use of 'Coloradan.'"

To which Schaffer responded: "I have been a Colorado resident since 1990 and lived in the state for five more years than that as a non-resident military officer. I personally use 'Coloradoan' in my writing. Since I saw [DeGette's] comment, I have rolled the term off of my tongue several times and might actually pronounce it 'Coloradan.'"

So, that didn't exactly clear things up.

First, a little background. The way one describes oneself based upon where one is from is called a "demonym" (also referred to as a "gentilic"). *National Geographic* attributes demonym—which comes from the Greek word for "populace" ("demos"), with the suffix for "name" ("-onym")—to *Merriam-Webster* editor Paul Dickson, who later brought "demonym" into the furthest fringes of the linguistic mainstream in his 1997 book *Labels for Locals*. Dickson attributed the term to George H. Scheez, who used it in his book *Name's Names: A Descriptive and Prescriptive Onymicon*. The term was foreshadowed by "demonymic," which the *Oxford English Dictionary* (OED) defines as "the name of an Athenian citizen according to the deme (subdivisions of land surrounding Athens) to which he belonged." The *OED* traced first usage of "demonymic" to 1893.

In a 2007 column for the Denver Post, noted Colorado writer the late-Ed Quillen entertained this exact question. He cited the wonderful 1945 book, *Names on the Land* by George R. Stewart, which states that, when a place name ends in an "o," you add an "-an" to achieve its demonymic form. The exception, Quillen correctly notes when he interprets Stewart's words, is if the place name is of Spanish origin. Then, you drop the "o" and add an "-an."[2] Since "Colorado" is a Spanish word meaning "colored," it would seem logical that the state's demonym would be achieved by dropping the last "o" and replacing it with "-an." Thus, "Coloradan."

Quillen goes on to quote various newspaper copy editors throughout the state who all agree that the proper style is "Coloradan." Even the *Fort Collins Coloradoan* daily newspaper, despite its name, uses as its preferred style "Coloradan" within its pages.

Michael Rudeen, in his "Denver Wacky Questions Examiner" column, observes, "If the name is derived from an American Indian word (such as Chicago or Idaho), the ending is "-oan" (Chicagoan, Idahoan). If it comes from a Spanish word (Mexico, San Francisco), the ending is "-an" (Mexican, San Franciscan). This means that residents of Colorado, a Spanish derivation, should be called 'Coloradans.'"[3]

Several sources refer to "Coloradoan" as an archaic term, albeit one that is still acceptable. As well, at least 13 other states have alternate demonyms.

## DEMONYMS FOR COLORADO MOUNTAIN TOWNS

- Alamosa: Alamosans
- Alma: Almanites or Almanians (informal) or Al-Maniacs (very informal)
- Aspen: Aspenites
- Basalt: Basaltines
- Black Hawk: No commonly accepted demonym
- Blanca: Blancans
- Boulder: Boulderites
- Breckenridge: Breckenridgians or Breckies (informal)
- Buena Vista: Buena Vistans
- Carbondale: Carbondalians
- Central City: Central Citians or Zeeks (very informal, after the old ZK license plates that used to be issued in Gilpin County)
- Cortez: Cortezians
- Crawford: Crawfordites
- Creede: Creedites
- Crested Butte: Buttians or Crusty Butts (very informal)
- Cripple Creek: Cripple Creekers
- Durango: Durangoans or Durangatans (very informal)
- Estes Park: Estes Parkers or Estes Parkians
- Evergreen: No commonly accepted demonym
- Fraser: Fraserites
- Frisco: Friscoites (pronounced Frisco-ites)
- Georgetown: Georgetowners
- Glenwood Springs: Glenwoodites or Glenwoodians
- Granby: Granbyites
- Grand Lake: Grand Lakers
- Gunnison: Gunnisonites
- Hotchkiss: Hotchkissers
- Idaho Springs: No commonly accepted demonym
- Lake City: Lake Citians
- Leadville: Leadvillites or Leadvillians or Pb-ers (very informal, and any reference to Pabst Blue Ribbon beer is purely coincidental)
- Montezuma: Zumans or Zuman Beings
- Montrose: Montrosians
- Morrison: Morrisonites
- Nederland: No commonly accepted demonym; Nedheads (very informal)
- Olathe: Olatheans

- Ouray: Ourayites or Ourangatans (very informal)
- Pagosa Springs: Pagosans
- Paonia: Paonians or P-towners (informal)
- Parachute: Stunningly, no commonly accepted demonym
- Rifle: Rifleites (pronounced Rifle-ites)
- Saguache: Saguachians
- Salida: Salidans
- Silt: True shame that it is, no commonly accepted demonym
- Silver Cliff: Silver Cliphonians (spelled thus because it was taken from the name of a 1980s local rock band of the same name that chose to go with the "ph" rather than the double "f")
- Silverton: Silvertonians
- Silver Plume: Plumies
- Steamboat Springs: Steamboaters
- Telluride: Telluridians or, less commonly, Telluriders or To-Hell-You-Riders (very informal)
- Vail: Vailites or Vailians (very informal)
- Victor: Victorites
- Walden: Waldenites
- Westcliffe: West Cliffians
- Wetmore: Wetmorons (very informal)
- Winter Park: No commonly accepted demonym
- Honorary Mention: Although the Denver suburb of Bow Mar is not a mountain town, it deserves honorary altitude status based upon the fact that its demonym is Bowmartians.

## NOTES

1. The state government has not issued an official edict about this one way or another, although ex-Governor Bill Ritter uses "Coloradan."

2. It needs to be stressed that this is an English-ization of Spanish de-monymic tendencies. In Spanish, demonyms—*gentilicios*—are achieved in a variety of ways, most notably by dropping the final vowel and adding "-iano" (californiano/a, for someone from California; -eño (guanajuateño, for some-one hailing from Guanajuato); or, most commonly, a variation on "-ense" (chi-huahuense for someone from Chihuahua or guerrerense for someone from Guerrero). (Note: In Spanish, demonyms are never capitalized.) Given these linguistic realities, Coloradans or Coloradoans, if they stick with the undeni-able Spanish roots of the state's name, ought to call themselves coloradenses or coloradeños. (Note: This obvious awkwardness is at least partially caused by the fact that, even though "Colorado," when applied to the name of the country's thirty-eighth state, becomes a proper noun, in Spanish, it is a participle used as an adjective. Spanish adjectives do not have natural demonymic forms.)

3. Numerous Rudeen readers vehemently disagreed with his assertion. One woman wrote, "As a Denver, Colorado, native, I take great exception at the use of 'Coloradans.' I have polled many of my friends who are either natives or long-time Coloradoans, and, without exception, they insist it should be Coloradoans. We were taught, well over 70 years ago, that we lived in Colorado, not Colorada."

Another reader wrote to Rudeen: "I'm a third-generation Colorado native, and we ALWAYS called ourselves COLORADOANS until the TV and newspaper people from back East decided they knew better. It still grates on me to be called a Coloradan, and I think it sounds uneducated. I think that if someone from Chicago can be a Chicagoan, then I should be allowed to stay a Coloradoan."

## SOURCES

Wikipedia; http://everything2.com; http://schaffervudall.blogspot.com; http://blogs.rockymountainnews.com; http://gazettewonderblogspot.com; www.denverpost.com; http://nevadaculture.org. The Colorado mountain town demonyms were obtained from a wide variety of sources, including local town governments, local newspaper professionals, chambers of commerce, tourist offices, historical societies, and long-time Saguachians, Basaltines, Zeeks, etc. In almost all cases, at least two sources were checked.

# COLORADO OLYMPIC ATHLETES

Given the geophysical nature of the state, the active nature of the state's population, and the abundance of sport-specific facilities[1]—to say nothing of the fact that the U.S. Olympic Complex is located in Colorado Springs[2]—it should come as no surprise that Colorado has been home to many Olympic athletes: A total of 138 were born in Colorado. Forty-one of those were born in mountain towns. Seven Olympic athletes who were born in Colorado mountain towns have medaled in the Olympics:

- **Shalane Grace Flanagan** was born in Boulder. She won a bronze medal in the 10,000m run in the 2008 Summer Games in Beijing. She also competed in the 2008 Summer Games in the 5,000m run, as well as at the 2004 Summer Games (Athens) in the 5,000m run.
- **Paul J. Forester** was born in Rangley. He competed in sailing at four Olympic Games—1988 (Seoul), 1992 (Barcelona), 2000 (Sydney), and 2004 (Athens). He won a gold medal in the 470 (double-handed dinghy) in 2004 and silver medals in the 470 (double-handed dinghy) in 2000 and the Flying Dutchman in 1992.
- **Kate Johnson** was born in Vail. She won a silver medal in rowing (eights-with-coxswain) at the 2004 (Athens) Summer Games.
- **Todd Lodwick** was born in Steamboat Springs and still lives there. Lodwick has the distinction of competing in more Olympic events (13) than any person who was born in Colorado and lived in Colorado during his time as an Olympic athlete. Lodwick competed in the Nordic combined–individual and the Nordic combined–team at the 1994 Winter Games (Lillehammer); the Nordic combined–individual and the Nordic combined–team at the 1998 (Nagano) Winter Games; the Nordic combined–

individual, the Nordic combined–sprint, and the Nordic combined–team at the 2002 Winter Games (Salt Lake City); and the Nordic combined–individual, the Nordic combined–sprint, and the Nordic combined–team at the 2006 Winter Games (Turin). At the 2010 Winter Games in Vancouver, Lodwick's astounding career reached a crescendo when he earned a silver medal in the Nordic combined–men's team 4x5k and placed fourth in the Nordic combined–individual normal hill 10k and thirteenth in the Nordic combined–individual long hill 10k.

- Boulder-born **Davis Phinney** won a bronze medal in the 100k time trial road-biking event at the 1984 Summer Games (Los Angeles) while he called Boulder home. He still calls Boulder home.
- **John M. Spillane** was born in Steamboat Springs and lived there when he competed in 10 separate events spread out over four Olympiads. Spillane competed in the Nordic combined–individual at the 1998 Winter Games (Nagano); the Nordic combined–individual and the Nordic combined–team at the 2002 Winter Games (Salt Lake City); and the Nordic combined–individual, the Nordic combined–individual sprint, and the Nordic combined–team at the 2006 Winter Games (Turin). At the 2010 Vancouver Winter Games, Spillane put forth the best Nordic combined effort in American Olympic skiing history, as he took silvers in the Nordic combined–individual normal hill 10k, the Nordic combined–team 4x5k, and the Nordic combined–individual long hill 10k. He still lives in Steamboat Springs.
- **Rebecca Ward** was born in Grand Junction. She won two bronze medals in fencing at the 2008 Summer Games in Beijing—one in individual saber, the other in team saber.

## OTHER OLYMPIC ATHLETES BORN IN COLORADO MOUNTAIN TOWNS ARE:

- **Jeremy Abbott:** Born in Aspen and living in Aspen when he finished ninth in men's figure skating at the 2010 Vancouver Winter Games.
- **Landis Stevens Arnold:** Born in Boulder and living in Longmont when he competed in the 70m individual ski-jumping event at the 1984 Winter Games (Sarajevo).
- **Lanny L. Barnes:** Born in Durango and lived in Durango when he competed in the 15k individual biathlon and the 4x6k biathlon relay at the 2006 Winter Games (Turin).
- **Lanny Barnes:** Born in Durango and lived in Durango when she finished 17th in the women's biathlon 15k mass start, 23rd in the women's biathlon 15k individual, and 78th in the women's biathlon 7.5k sprint at the 2010 Vancouver Games.

- **Tracy Barnes (Lanny Barnes' twin):** Born in Durango and lived in Durango when she competed at the 2006 Winter Games (Turin) in three biathlon events: the 15k individual, the 7.5k sprint, and the 4x6k relay.
- **John Ray Burrett:** Born in Cedaredge and lived in Hotchkiss when he competed in the 20k biathlon at the 1960 Winter Games (Squaw Valley).
- **Matthew F. Dayton:** Born in Fairplay and lived in Breckenridge when he competed in the Nordic combined–individual, the Nordic combined–individual sprint, and the Nordic combined–team events at the 2002 Winter Games (Salt Lake City).
- **Elva Dryer (Martinez):** Born in Durango and lived in Gunnison when she competed at the 2000 Summer Games (Sydney) in the 10,000m swimming event and at the 2004 Summer Games (Athens) in the 5,000m swimming event.
- **Jere L. Elliot:** Born in Steamboat Springs and lived in Monument when he competed at the 1968 Winter Games (Grenoble) in alpine skiing.
- **Michael L. Elliott:** Born in Durango and competed in a total of nine events spread out over three Olympiads: the 15k and 30k individual cross-country ski races and the 4x10k classical relay at the 1964 Winter Games (Innsbruck); in the 15k, 30k, and 50k individual cross-country events at the 1968 Winter Games (Grenoble); and the 30k individual and 4x10k relay at the 1972 Winter Games (Sapporo).
- **Taylor Fletcher:** Born in Steamboat Springs and a resident there. He placed 45th in the men's Nordic combined–individual long hill 10k at the 2010 Winter Games (Vancouver).
- **Scott David Gorsuch:** Born in Climax and competed at the 1960 Winter Games (Squaw Valley) in alpine downhill and giant slalom.
- **Sasha Gros:** Born in Glenwood Springs and competed at the 1998 Winter Games (Calgary) in giant slalom.
- **Simon Hamilton:** Born in Aspen and was living in Aspen when he finished 29th in the men's cross-country skiing individual sprint classic and 64th in the men's cross-country skiing 15k free at the 2010 (Vancouver) Winter Games.
- **James Brian Hitchborn:** Born in Grand Junction and competed at the 1960 Summer Games (Rome) in eights-with-coxswain (rowing).
- **Anne S. Kakela:** Born in Steamboat Springs and competed at the 1996 Summer Games (Atlanta) in eights-with-coxswain (rowing).
- **Nina M. Kemppel:** Born in Boulder and gained the distinction of competing in more Olympic events—14 total—than any other person born in Colorado. Kemppel competed in the Nordic combined pursuit and the 5k classical cross-country ski events at the 1992 Winter Games (Albertville); the 5k classical, the 10k

freestyle pursuit, the 15k freestyle, the 30k classical, and the 4x5k mixed relay at the 1994 Winter Games (Lillehammer); the 5k classical, the 10k freestyle pursuit, and the 15k classical at the 1998 Winter Games (Nagano); and the 5k freestyle pursuit, the 10k classical, the 15k freestyle mass start, and the 30k classical at the 2002 Winter Games (Salt Lake City). The best finish in Kemppel's illustrious Olympic career was 10th in the 4x5k mixed relay in 1994.

- **Wendy Koenig Knudsen:** Born in Boulder and competed at the 1972 (Munich) and the 1976 (Montreal) Summer Games in the 800m run.
- **Andrew Todd Leroy:** Born in Steamboat Springs and lived there when he competed at the 1998 Winter Games (Nagano) in alpine slalom.
- **William Charles Marolt:** Born in Aspen and competed at the 1964 Winter Games (Innsbruck) in giant slalom.
- **Clark Arvo Matis:** Born in Durango and competed at both the 1968 Winter Games (Grenoble) and the 1972 Winter Games (Sapporo) in the 30k classical cross-country ski race.
- **Alice McKennis:** Born in Glenwood Springs and was living there when she competed in women's alpine downhill skiing at the 2010 (Vancouver) Winter Games.
- **Beth Madsen McNichol:** Born in Aspen and competed at the 1988 Winter Games (Calgary) in alpine combined and slalom.
- **Ricky L. Mewborn:** Born in Steamboat Springs and lived there when he competed in the 70m individual ski-jumping at the 1988 Winter Games (Calgary).
- **Jack Miller:** Born in Boulder and lived in Golden when he competed in alpine slalom and giant slalom at the 1988 Winter Games (Calgary).
- **Richard Norman Mize:** Born in Gilman and competed in the 2k biathlon event at the 1960 Winter Games (Squaw Valley).
- **Katie Leathem Monahan:** Born in Aspen and competed in the alpine combined, the alpine downhill, and the Super-G at the 1998 Winter Games (Nagano) and the Super-G in the 2002 Winter Games (Salt Lake City).
- **John Nunn:** Born in Durango and competed in the 20k walk at the 2004 Summer Games (Athens).
- **Colby W. Pearce:** Born in Boulder and lived there when he competed in the cycling points race at the 2004 Summer Games (Athens).
- **Monique Gia Pelletier:** Born in Aspen and competed in the alpine slalom at the 1992 Winter Games (Albertville) and the alpine combined and alpine slalom at the 1994 Winter Games (Lillehammer).

- **Taylor Phinney:** Born in Boulder and lived there when he competed in the individual pursuit bicycling event at the 2008 Summer Games (Beijing).
- **Casey Puckett:** Born in Boulder and lived in Aspen when he came in 23rd in men's ski cross at the 2010 Vancouver Winter Games.
- **Christophe C. Puckett:** Born in Boulder and lived in Steamboat Springs when he competed in the alpine giant slalom at the 1992 Winter Games (Albertville).
- **Paul Casey Puckett:** Born in Boulder and lived in Aspen during a career that saw him competing in six different events spread over four separate Olympic games. He competed in the alpine slalom and giant slalom at the 1992 Winter Games (Albertville), the alpine slalom and the giant slalom at the 1994 Winter Games (Lillehammer), the giant slalom at the 1998 Winter Games Nagano), and the alpine combined at the 2002 Winter Games (Salt Lake City).
- **Sarah K. Schleper:** Born in Glenwood Springs and lived in Vail when she competed in eight different Olympic events spread out over four Olympiads. She competed in both the alpine slalom and giant slalom at the 1998 (Nagano), 2002 (Salt Lake City), 2006 (Turin), and 2010 Winter Games, finishing 14th in giant slalom and 16th in slalom at the Vancouver (2010) Games.
- **Tommy Schwall:** Born in Steamboat Springs and lived there when he competed in the 120m individual and team ski-jumping events at the 2002 Winter Games (Salt Lake City) and in the 120m team ski-jumping event at the 2006 Winter Games (Turin).
- **Alexandra Shaffer:** Born in Aspen and competed in the alpine combined and the giant slalom at the 1998 Winter Games (Nagano) and the giant slalom at the 2002 Winter Games (Salt Lake City).
- **Jason R. Smith:** Born in Aspen and lived in Basalt when he competed in the snowboard-cross at the 2006 Winter Games (Turin).
- **Katie Uhlaender:** Born in Vail and lived in Breckenridge when she competed in the skeleton at both the 2006 (Turin) and 2010 Winter Games (Vancouver), where she finished 11th.
- **Raymond A. (Randy) Weber:** Born in Steamboat Springs and lived in Morrison when he competed in the 90m, the 120m individual, and the 120m team ski-jumping events at both the 1994 (Lillehammer) and 1998 (Nagano) Winter Games.
- **Ronald Paul Yeager:** Born in Durango and lived there when he competed in the 15k classical cross-country ski race at the 1972 Winter Games (Sapporo) and in the 15k classical and the 4x10k classical relay at the 1976 Winter Games (Innsbruck).

- **Jake Zamansky:** Born in Aspen and still lived there when he took 31st in men's alpine skiing giant slalom at the 2010 Vancouver Winter Games.

Of the 284 athletes listed by the U.S. Olympic Committee as living in Colorado during the time they were competing in the Olympics, 113 lived in mountain towns. Twenty-one of those were Olympic medalists. In addition to Todd Lodwick, Davis Phinney, and Johnny Spillane (listed above), those medalists are:

- **Deirdre Demet Barry** lived in Boulder when she won a silver medal in the individual time-trial bicycle race at the 2004 Summer Games (Athens). She also competed in the individual road race at the 2004 Summer Games.
- **Gretchen Bleiler** lived in Aspen when she won a silver medal in snowboarding halfpipe at the 2006 Winter Games (Turin). She also competed in halfpipe at the 2010 Vancouver Winter Games.
- **Susan Marie De Mattei** lived in Gunnison when she won a bronze medal in cross-country mountain-biking at the 1996 Summer Games (Atlanta).
- **Martha Hill Gaskill** lived in Golden when she won a bronze medal in exhibition/disabled modified giant slalom at the 1988 Winter Games (Calgary).
- **Tyler Hamilton** lived in Boulder when he won a gold medal in the individual time-trial bicycling event at the 2004 Summer Games (Athens). Hamilton also competed in the individual road race at the 2004 Summer Games, as well as in the same two events at the 2000 Summer Games (Sydney).
- **Jimmy Huega** lived in Avon when he won a bronze medal in alpine slalom at the 1964 Winter Games (Innsbruck). He also competed in the giant slalom that same year, as well as in the same two events at the 1968 Winter Games (Grenoble).
- **William W. (Billy) Kidd** lived in Steamboat Springs when he won a silver medal in alpine slalom at the 1964 Winter Games (Innsbruck), in which he also competed in alpine downhill and giant slalom. He also competed in those same three events in the 1968 Winter Games (Grenoble).
- **Chris Klug,** born in Denver, lived in Aspen when he won a bronze medal in the snowboard parallel giant slalom at the 2002 Winter Games (Salt Lake City). He also competed in that same event at the 2008 Winter Games (Nagano), as well as at the 2010 Vancouver Winter Games.
- **Greg A. Mannino** lived in Eagle when he won a bronze medal in exhibition/disabled modified giant slalom at the 1988 Winter Games (Calgary).

## ▲
# AGGREGATED OLYMPIC STATISTICS FROM COLORADO'S MOUNTAIN TOWNS

- Number of Olympic athletes born in the Colorado mountains (by town or county): Boulder (12), Aspen (9), Durango and Steamboat Springs (8 each), Glenwood Springs (4), Eagle County (3), and Grand Junction (2)
- Total number of Olympic events participated in by people born in the Colorado mountains (by town or county): Boulder (36), Durango (28), Steamboat Springs (27), Aspen (21), Glenwood Springs (10), Eagle County (4), Grand Junction and Rangely (3 each)
- Number of Olympic medals won by people born in the Colorado mountains (by town): Steamboat Springs (4), Rangely (3), Boulder and Vail (1 each)
- Number of athletes living in the Colorado mountains at the time they participated in the Olympics (by town or county): Boulder (26), Steamboat Springs (20), Aspen (14), Durango (11), Eagle County (8), Summit County and Gunnison County (6 each)
- Total number of Olympic events participated in by people living in the Colorado mountains at the time they participated in the Olympics (by town or county): Steamboat Springs (66), Boulder (46), Eagle County (33), Durango (25), Aspen (21), Gunnison County (15), Summit County (11)
- Total number of medals won by people living in the Colorado mountains at the time they participated in the Olympics (by town or county): Boulder, Steamboat Springs, and Eagle County (5 each); Aspen, Golden, and Pagosa Springs (2 each); Grand County, Durango, Steamboat Springs, and Gunnison County (1 each)

---

- **Elizabeth G. (Liz) McIntyre** lived in Granby when she won a silver medal in freestyle moguls at the 1994 Winter Games (Lillehammer). She also competed in that same event at the 1992 (Albertville), 1998 (Nagano), and 2002 (Salt Lake City) Winter Games.
- **Cynthia Lee (Cindy) Nelson** lived in Vail when she won a bronze medal in downhill skiing at the 1976 Winter Games (Innsbruck). Nelson also competed in alpine slalom and giant slalom at the 1976 games (Innsbruck); in the alpine downhill, the slalom, and the giant slalom at the 1980 Winter Games (Lake Placid); and the giant slalom at the 1984 Winter Games (Sarajevo).
- **Connie Carpenter Phinney** lived in Boulder when she won a gold medal in individual road-race bicycling at the 1984 Summer Games (Los Angeles). She also competed in the 1,500m long-track ice-skating event at the 1972 Winter Games (Sapporo)—

making her one of the few Colorado athletes ever to compete in both a Summer and Winter Olympics.

- **Fred Schmidt** lived in Pagosa Springs when he won a gold medal in the 4x100m swimming relay, in addition to a bronze medal in the 200m butterfly at the 1964 Summer Games (Tokyo).
- **Frank Charles Shorter** lived in Boulder when he won a gold medal in the marathon at the 1972 Summer Games (Munich) and a silver medal in the marathon at the 1976 Summer Games (Montreal). He also competed in the 10,000m run at the 1972 Summer Games.
- **Jarrett (JJ) Thomas** lived in Golden when he won a bronze medal in snowboarding halfpipe at the 2002 Winter Games (Salt Lake City).
- **Lindsey Vonn** lived in Vail when she won a gold medal in women's alpine downhill skiing and a bronze medal in women's alpine skiing super-G at the 2010 Vancouver Winter Games.
- **Richard Jaydes Warwick** lived in Monument when he won a bronze medal in the welterweight division of the demonstration sport of tae kwon do at the 1988 Summer Games (Seoul).
- **Elaine C. Youngs** lived in Durango when she won a bronze medal in beach volleyball at the 2004 Summer Games (Athens). She also competed in volleyball at the 1996 Summer Games (Atlanta) and in beach volleyball at the 2008 Summer Games (Beijing).

OTHER ATHLETES WHO LIVED IN COLORADO
MOUNTAIN TOWNS WHEN THEY COMPETED IN THE
OLYMPICS (EXCLUDING THOSE ALREADY LISTED) ARE:

- **Patrick Lee Ahern** lived in Ridgway when he competed in Nordic combined at the 1984 Winter Games (Sarajevo).
- **Robert Matthew Aldighieri** lived in Steamboat Springs when he competed in freestyle moguls at the 1992 Winter Games (Albertville).
- **Allen E. Francis** lived in South Fork when he competed in the 10m running target (shooting) at the 1992 Summer Games (Barcelona).
- **Jennifer Barringer** lived in Boulder when she competed in the 3,000m steeplechase at the 2008 Summer Games (Beijing).
- **James Michael Barrows** lived in Steamboat Springs when he competed in the alpine downhill at the 1968 Winter Games (Grenoble).
- **William Scott Berry** lived in Steamboat Springs when he competed in the 70m and 90m individual ski-jumping events in the 1972 Winter Games (Sapporo).
- **Jeremy Bloom** lived in Keystone when he competed in freestyle moguls at both the 2002 (Salt Lake City) and 2006 Winter Games (Turin).

- Ambassador **David Bolen** lived in Boulder when he ran in the 400m sprint at the 1948 Summer Games (London).
- **Elizabeth Bradley** lived in Boulder when she competed in fours-with-coxswain (rowing) at the 1988 Summer Games (Seoul).
- **Robert Clayton Brayton** lived in Golden when he served as an alternate to the U.S. rowing team at the 1968 Summer Games (Mexico City).
- **Travis Brown** lived in Durango when he competed in the mountain-bike cross-country event at the 2000 Summer Games (Sydney).
- **Ingrid Jean Butts** lived in Gunnison when she served as an alternate to the U.S. women's cross-country ski team at the 1988 Winter Games (Calgary). She competed in the Nordic combined, the 5k classical, and 4x5k mixed relay at the 1992 Winter Games (Albertville) and in the 5k classical and 5k classical/10k freestyle pursuit at the 1994 Winter Games (Lillehammer).
- **Patricia A. Byrnes** lived in Aspen when she competed in the snowboarding halfpipe at the 2002 Winter Games (Salt Lake City).
- **John Freeman Callahan** lived in Aspen when he competed in the 30k classical cross-country ski race at the 1992 Winter Games (Albertville).
- Ex–U.S. Senator **Ben Nighthorse Campbell** lived in Ignacio when he competed in judo at the 1964 Summer Games (Tokyo).
- **Susan Hall Charlesworth** lived in Boulder when she competed in the single luge at the 1980 Winter Games (Lake Placid).
- **Sean Padraic Colgan** lived in Steamboat Springs when he competed in eights-with-coxswain (rowing) at the 1980 Summer Games (Moscow).
- **Jennifer Walker Corbet** lived in Golden when she competed in fours-with-coxswain (rowing) at the 1988 Summer Games (Seoul).
- **Gary Crawford** lived in Steamboat Springs when he competed in the Nordic combined–individual at both the 1980 (Lake Placid) and 1988 (Calgary) Winter Games.
- **David Henry Currier** lived in Boulder when he competed in the alpine downhill and the giant slalom at the 1972 Winter Games (Sapporo).
- **Jeffrey Logan Davis** lived in Mesa when he competed in the 70m and the 90m individual ski-jumping at the 1980 Winter Games (Lake Placid).
- **Colleen De Reuck** lived in Boulder when she competed in the marathon at the 2004 Summer Games (Athens).
- **Lincoln DeWitt** lived in Boulder when he competed in the skeleton at the 2002 Winter Games (Salt Lake City).
- **Brendan C. Doran** lived in Steamboat Springs when he competed in the 90m and 120m individual ski-jumping events at both the 1998 (Nagano) and 2002 Winter Games (Salt Lake City).

- **Benji Ray Durden** lived in Boulder when he competed in the marathon at the 1980 Summer Games (Moscow).
- **Rebecca Dussault** lived in Gunnison when she competed in the 30k freestyle mass start, the 7.5k classical/7.5k freestyle, and the 4x5k mixed relay cross-country ski races at the 2006 Winter Games (Turin).
- **Jakob Paul Fiala** lived in Frisco when he competed in the alpine combined and the alpine downhill at the 2002 Winter Games (Salt Lake City).
- **Wendy Fisher** lived in Crested Butte when she competed in the alpine combined at the 1992 Winter Games (Albertville).
- **Chad L. Fleischer** lived in Steamboat Springs when he competed in the alpine combined and the Super-G at both the 1994 (Lillehammer) and 1998 (Nagano) Winter Games.
- **Sidney A. Freudenstein** lived in Boulder when he competed in rings, pommel horse, parallel bars, long horse vault, horizontal bar, floor exercise, team combined exercise, and artistic individual all-around gymnastics in the 1968 Summer Games (Mexico City). This marked the most events participated in by a Colorado mountain-town resident in any one Olympiad.
- **Jean Kay Gaertner** lived in Crested Butte when she competed in high jump at the 1960 Summer Games (Rome) and volleyball at the 1964 Summer Games (Tokyo).
- **Jeanne Marie Golay** lived in Glenwood Springs when she competed in the individual road bicycling race at the 1992 Summer Games (Barcelona) and in the individual time trial, the points race, and the individual road race at the 1996 Summer Games (Atlanta).
- **Amy M. Guras** lived in Breckenridge when she competed in the speed-skiing demonstration sport at the 1992 Winter Games (Albertville).
- **Katherine Ann Hearn** lived in Durango when she competed in the K-1 kayak single event at both the 1992 (Barcelona) and 1996 (Atlanta) Summer Games.
- **Robert Muir Holme** lived in Fraser when he competed in the 90m and 120m individual and the 120-meter team ski-jumping events at the 1992 Winter Games (Albertville), as well as in the 90m and 120m events at the 1994 Winter Games (Lillehammer).
- **Jeremy C. Horgan-Kobelski** lived in Boulder when he competed in mountain-biking cross-country at the 2004 Summer Games in Athens.
- **William M. James, Jr.,** lived in Steamboat Springs when he served as an alternate for the individual three-day equestrian event at the 1952 Summer Games (Helsinki).
- **David L. Jameson** lived in Tabernash when he competed in the modified giant slalom at the 1988 Winter Games (Calgary).

- **Tyler Jewell** lived in Steamboat Springs when he finished 13th in the men's snowboard parallel giant slalom at the 2010 Vancouver Winter Games.
- **Kristina L. Koznik** lived in Edwards when she competed in the alpine slalom at the 1998 Winter Games (Nagano), the alpine slalom and the giant slalom at the 2002 Winter Games (Salt Lake City), and the alpine slalom at the 2006 Winter Games (Turin).
- **Caroline Lalive** lived in Steamboat Springs when she competed in the alpine combined and the giant slalom at the 1998 Winter Games (Nagano) and the alpine combined, the downhill, and the Super-G at the 2002 Winter Games (Salt Lake City).
- **Gregory Gray Lyman** lived in Durango when he competed in the long-track 500m speed-skating event at the 1972 Winter Games (Sapporo).
- **Kerry Joel Lynch** lived in Steamboat Springs when he competed in the Nordic combined–individual at both the 1980 (Lake Placid) and 1984 Winter Games (Sarajevo).
- **Charles F. Martin** lived in Boulder when he competed in freestyle moguls at the 1992 Winter Games (Albertville).
- **Scott Roger Mercier** lived in Grand Junction when he competed in the 100k team time trial bicycle race at the 1992 Summer Games (Barcelona).
- **Erin Veenstra Mirabella** lived in Woodland Park when she competed in the 3,000m individual pursuit and the points bicycle race at both the 2000 (Sydney) and 2004 (Athens) Summer Games.
- **Jim Page** lived in Manitou Springs when he competed in the Nordic combined at the 1964 Winter Games (Tokyo). He also served as a coach and administrator with the U.S. Olympic Committee at the 1980 (Lake Placid), 1984 (Sarajevo), 1992 (Albertville), and 1994 Winter Games (Lillehammer).
- **Daniel Edward Patterson** lived in Aspen when he competed in volleyball at the 1968 Summer Games (Mexico City).
- **Catherine Patti (Gentile)** lived in Leadville when she competed in the demonstration disabled modified giant slalom at the 1988 Winter Games (Calgary).
- **Jo Anne Quirling** lived in Westcliffe when she competed in judo at the 1992 Summer Games (Barcelona).
- **Matthew Reed** lived in Boulder when he competed in the triathlon at the 2008 Summer Games (Beijing).
- **John W. Ruger** lived in Boulder when he competed in the 20k individual cross-country ski race at the 1980 Winter Games (Lake Placid).

- **Laura Coenen Ryan** lived in Manitou Springs when she competed in team handball at the 1988 (Seoul), 1992 (Barcelona), and 1996 (Atlanta) Summer Games.
- **Jerome Francis Siebert** lived in Boulder when he competed in the 800m run at both the 1960 (Rome) and 1964 (Tokyo) Summer Games.
- **Jason R. Smith** lived in Basalt when he competed in the snowboard-cross at the 2006 Winter Games (Turin).
- **Larry Ray Stafford** lived in Cortez when he competed in trap (clay pigeon) at the 1968 Summer Games (Mexico City).
- **Ryan St. Onge** lived in Winter Park when he finished fourth in men's freestyle aerials at the 2010 Vancouver Winter Games.
- **Dale Emery Statina** lived in Boulder when he competed in the two-man bobsled at the 1998 Winter Games (Nagano) and four-man bobsled at the 2002 Winter Games (Salt Lake City).
- **Jorge Torres** lived in Boulder when he competed in the 10,000m run at the 2008 Summer Games (Beijing).
- **Ann Trombley** lived in Boulder when she competed in the mountain-bike cross-country event at the 2000 Summer Games (Sydney).
- **Craig C. Ward** lived in Aspen when he competed in the disabled 5k cross-country ski race at the 1980 Winter Games (Lake Placid).
- **Todd Raymond Wells** lived in Durango when he competed in the mountain-bike cross-country event at both the 2004 (Athens) and 2008 (Beijing) Summer Games.
- **Debra Anne Wilcox** lived in Edwards when she competed in artistic individual all-around gymnastics and team-combined exercises at the 1976 Summer Games (Montreal).
- **Todd Rowe Wilson** lived in Steamboat Springs when he competed in the Nordic combined–individual and the Nordic combined–team at the 1988 Winter Games (Calgary) and the Nordic combined–individual at the 1992 Winter Games (Albertville).
- **Dale Womack** lived in Durango when he competed in the speed-skiing demonstration sport at the 1992 Winter Games (Albertville).
- **Ronald Paul Yeager** lived in Durango when he competed in the 15k classical cross-country ski race at the 1972 Winter Games (Sapporo) and in the 15k classical and the 4x10k classical relays at the 1976 Winter Games (Innsbruck).
- **Joanna Zeiger** lived in Boulder when she competed in the triathlon at the 2000 Summer Games (Sydney).

# THE LONG-LOST DENVER OLYMPICS

It is fairly common knowledge that Denver is the only city in history to be awarded the Olympics by the IOC and to turn them down. Well, that's not exactly 100 percent true, as we will see here in a moment, but it's 99 percent mostly technically true.

Actually, even though Denver was awarded the 1976 Winter Olympics, it was the voters of Colorado who decided that the games were not welcome in the Centennial State.

The games were originally awarded to Denver in May 1970. The Mile-High City beat out Sion, Switzerland; Tampere, Finland; and Vancouver–Garibaldi–Whistler, British Columbia. Only Sion presented a real challenge during the bidding process. When it was announced that the Olympics were coming to Colorado, the Denver Organizing Committee was greeted with a brass band and a motorcade through downtown.

Then a group of state politicians, lead by then–Colorado State Representative (and later three-term Governor) Dick Lamm, started eyeballing the potential impacts—fiscal, environmental, and social—that the Winter Games would bring to Colorado. With Lamm's backing, a ballot measure was placed before state voters asking if the taxpayers of Colorado would be willing to issue a $5 million bond to guarantee financing of the Olympics—a contingency upon which the IOC insisted when it awarded the games to Denver.

On November 7, 1972, the voters overwhelmingly rejected the issuance of the bond—514,228 to 350,964. That amounts to 60 percent against funding the Olympics with a state-backed $5 million bond and 40 percent in favor.

The anti-Olympic lobby brought to the argumentative forefront concerns about potential environmental impacts associated with the construction and expansion of new facilities and infrastructure. There were concerns that the Olympics would generate so much publicity that everyone and their dog would immediately want to move to Colorado. And there were also issues raised about the distances between venues. With many of the events scheduled to take place in Denver, and others scheduled to take place at various mountain resorts (including ski jumping, which would have been held in Steamboat Springs, 177 miles from Denver), Colorado voters could simply not be convinced to fiscally back the games—especially when they were informed that, on average, final expenditures associated with hosting the Olympics were typically 300 percent higher than original estimates[3].

The IOC was shocked at the decision rendered by Colorado voters and had to then scramble to find another venue. The U.S. Olympic Committee tried to steer the games to Salt Lake City but were rebuffed by the very miffed IOC. The IOC then focused on Vancouver–Garibaldi–Whistler, B.C., which had originally bid on the 1976 games but which had been eliminated from consideration after the first ballot in 1970.

Vancouver–Garibaldi–Whistler said thanks but no thanks, partially because British Columbia had just had an election that resulted in a major change of government and partially because of time constraints. (Thus, Denver is not technically the only place to have turned down the games; it is the only city to have turned them down after being officially named host city through the normal IOC host-city selection process.) In frustration, the IOC awarded the 1976 Winter Games to Innsbruck, Austria, which had just hosted the Winter Games in 1964 and, therefore, still had the necessary infrastructure in place.

That was not Colorado's first brush with trying to host the Olympics. In 1954, Colorado Springs and Aspen jointly bid for the 1960 Winter Games, which were awarded to Squaw Valley, California. Denver also made a bid for the 2002 Winter Games, which were awarded to Salt Lake City. Denver has been posturing itself to make a bid to host the 2018 Winter Games. That bid, confirmed by ex–Colorado Governor Bill Ritter in March 2009, was to be contingent upon Chicago failing in its bid to host the 2016 Summer Games (which were eventually awarded to Rio de Janeiro), as the IOC would not award consecutive Summer and Winter Games to the same country. As well, the U.S. Olympic Committee has emphatically stated that it will not be bidding to host the 2018 Winter Games in Denver or anywhere else.

---

NOTES

1. Those "sports-specific facilities" cover the gamut from the single-track mountain-biking trails near Durango to the vibrant road-biking community in Boulder to the groomed cross-country ski tracks of Grand County to the downhill ski and snowboard facilities in Aspen, Vail, Winter Park, and Summit County (most of which now have terrain parks). But there is one facility, Howelsen Hill Ski Area—home to Colorado's only Olympic-size ski jump—that has perhaps attracted more Olympic-caliber athletes than any other, with the obvious exception of the Olympic Training Center in Colorado Springs. Howelsen Hill, located in Steamboat Springs, has the distinction of being the oldest ski area in the state in continuous use (first opening in 1914, it is the only Colorado ski area listed on the National Register of Historic Places), and it boasts having the largest and most complete natural ski-jumping complex in North America. Howelsen Hill has been the training ground for more than 64 Olympians making more than 90 individual Olympic appearances. Fifteen members of the Colorado Ski Hall of Fame and six members of the National Ski Hall of Fame also trained at Howelsen Hill.

2. The U.S. Olympic Complex in Colorado Springs, which also serves as the headquarters for the U.S. Olympic Committee, is one of 14 training facilities operated by the USOC nationwide. Opened in August 1977, the Olympic complex came into being as a result of a 1976 directive issued by the President's Commission on Olympic Sports, established by President Gerald Ford (who maintained a residence in Beaver Creek, Colorado, for many years after he left office) in the

aftermath of problems for U.S. athletes at the 1976 Montreal Summer Olympic Games. There had been an ongoing squabble between the National Collegiate Athletic Association (NCAA) and the Amateur Athletic Union (AAU) related to athlete selection and rights to compete (remember, in those days, only supposedly non-professional athletes could compete in the Olympics). The U.S. Olympic Committee decided to establish a series of training facilities under its auspices throughout the country. At that time, it also opted to move the USOC headquarters from its long-time digs in Manhattan to the relative hinterlands of Colorado Springs. The Olympic complex is now home to the governing bodies of 20 individual sports. It has 13 resident programs, 241 dorm rooms, and an average of 175 resident athletes on site at any one time. An average of 700 international athletes visit the facility every year, and, on average, 11,000 total athletes visit the facility every year. The facility is also home to the U.S. Olympic Hall of Fame.

3. The 2002 Salt Lake City Winter Olympics cost about $1.5 billion. The 2006 Winter Games in Turin, Italy, cost $1.58 billion. The 2010 Winter Games in Vancouver, British Columbia, had budget of $1.6 billion, not counting publicly funded infrastructure improvements, such as a $600 million highway construction project between Vancouver and Whistler. The 2012 Summer Games in London have a budget of $17.4 billion.

## SOURCES

The U.S. Olympic Committee in Colorado Springs; the *Rocky Mountain News* (RIP); the *Deseret News;* Wikipedia; the Town of Steamboat Springs.

# COLORADO: KING OF THE SKI INDUSTRY

When it comes to almost every ski/snowboard-industry-related statistic, there's Colorado, and then there's every other state. Colorado literally dominates skiing in America.

Of the 37 states with operating ski areas, New York actually leads with 50 areas operating, followed by Michigan (38 areas), Wisconsin (34), and California and Pennsylvania (32 each). So, in this regard, Colorado, with 26 operating ski areas, does not lead the nation. But when it comes to skier numbers, Colorado reigns supreme.

Ski areas measure visitation by "skier days" (or "skier visits"), which is yet another example of how difficult it is to come up with a single term that includes all forms of downhill recreational movement on snow. ("Snowslider days" just doesn't cut it, although it has been tried.) Meaning no insult to snowboarders, a "skier" day is one ski-area customer buying one one-day lift ticket, or two ski-area customers buying a half-day lift ticket each.[1]

Of the 59.79 million skier days recorded in the United States during the 2009–2010 ski season (a 4.2 percent increase over the previous winter), 20,377,710 took place in the Rocky Mountain Region, which includes Colorado, Montana, New Mexico, Idaho, and Utah. Of that number, 11.9 million took place in Colorado. This means that Colorado boasted more skier days in 2009–2010 than Utah, New Mexico, Montana, Idaho, and Wyoming combined. (Utah comes in at number two in the Rocky Mountain Region, with 4 million skier days.)

Colorado alone had more skier days than the entire Pacific West Region, the Midwest Region, and, not surprisingly, the Southeast Region.

The state with the second highest number of skier visits in 2009–2010 was California, with 7.5 million, or just less than two-thirds of the skier days recorded in Colorado.

Other superlative statistics that grace Colorado's ski industry are:

- Breckenridge was the single busiest ski area in the nation during the 2009–2010 ski season, with 1,614,000 million skier visits, or more than the entire skier-day numbers in Maine, Montana, Wyoming, New Mexico, Nevada, Arizona, and Alaska.
- Vail is the biggest lift-serviced ski area in the country, with about 5,200 acres of lift-accessed terrain. Powder Mountain, Utah, advertises itself as the biggest single ski area in the country, with more than 5,700 acres within its permit boundaries, but only 2,800 of those acres are accessed via lifts.
- Breckenridge boasts the highest lift in North America. The impressively named  Imperial Express SuperChair tops out at 12,840 feet.
- Based upon the fact that, in 2007, the town of Winter Park annexed the entire Winter Park Ski Area, Winter Park is now the highest incorporated municipality in the country, as the ski area tops out at 12,060 feet.
- Keystone operates one of the largest night-skiing and snowmaking operations in the country.
- Wolf Creek has the highest average annual snowfall of any Colorado ski resort—465 inches.
- Monarch boasts the highest base elevation, at 10,790 feet, with Arapahoe Basin, at 10,780 feet, and Loveland, at 10,600 feet, not far behind.
- The highest inbounds ski-area summit elevation in the state is found at Silverton Mountain. That would be a nosebleed-inducing 13,487 feet, but skiers must hike to that lofty elevation.
- The biggest vertical drop is 4,606 feet, at Snowmass Mountain.
- Vail has 32 lifts, followed by Breckenridge's 28 and Steamboat's 25.

- The newest ski area in Colorado is Echo Mountain, which opened in 2005 on the site of the old Squaw Pass Ski Area, just west of Evergreen.
- The most recent Colorado ski area to close was Berthoud Pass, which bit the bullet in 2001 after a long time on life support. Berthoud had the highest base elevation of any ski area in the state, at 11,022 feet.
- Steamboat Ski Area advertises that it has produced more Winter Olympians than any other Colorado ski town, with 66.
- Eldora advertises that it is the only ski area in Colorado that covers 100 percent of its groomed terrain with snowmaking.
- Summit County has seen the most people charged with violations of the Colorado Skier Safety Act (561) since it became law in 1979.

Skier-day numbers for Colorado's resorts during the 2008–2009 and 2009–2010 seasons are listed below, with the 2008–2009 numbers listed first and the 2009–2010 numbers in parentheses.

- Arapahoe Basin: 409,810 (356,849)
- Aspen Highlands: 199,430 (Did not return phone calls seeking update)
- Aspen Mountain: 304,052 (Did not return phone calls seeking update)
- Beaver Creek: 931,000 (927,000)
- Breckenridge: 1,528,000 (1,614,000)
- Buttermilk: 126,976 (Did not return phone calls seeking update)
- Copper Mountain: 873,039 (Refused to release numbers for 2009–2010)
- Crested Butte: 358,735 (341,260)
- Durango: 239,845 (255,048)
- Echo Mountain: 30,208 (Refused to release numbers for 2009–2010)
- Eldora: 255,119 (287,000)
- Howelsen Hill: 14,680 (13,405)
- Keystone: 981,000 (981,000)
- Loveland: 313,564 (317,790)
- Monarch: 165,724 (184,725)
- Powderhorn: 69,760 (78,132)
- Silverton Mountain: 6,101 ("Don't know, but not many")
- Ski Cooper: 54,998 (Refused to release numbers for 2009–2010)
- Snowmass: 733,597 (Refused to release numbers for 2009–2010)
- SolVista: 63,540 (64,035)
- Steamboat: 959,603 (Refused to release numbers for 2009–2010)
- Sunlight: 69,393 (75,000)
- Telluride: 419,476 (Did not return phone calls seeking update)

- Vail: 1,622,000 (1,559,000)
- Winter Park: 947,331 (Refused to release numbers for 2009–2010)
- Wolf Creek: 178,517 (198,602)

## NOTES

1. Starting with the 2009–2010 ski season, Colorado Ski Country USA (CS-CUSA) stopped releasing skier-day numbers for its individual member resorts (Vail, Beaver Creek, Keystone, and Breckenridge are not members of CSCUSA), preferring to let the individual resorts determine on their own whether to release those numbers. The official reason for the change in the long-held policy focuses on the notion of protecting proprietary information, but there is little doubt that the difficulty of measuring skier-day visits played a large role. The problem is especially poignant when it comes to tracking visitors who hold season passes. Counting season-pass users can be done in numerous ways, including scanning all pass holders in line, estimating season-pass usage, and issuing paper tickets to season-pass holders. Ergo: Counting those numbers is often a case of mixing apples with oranges when it comes to aggregating accurate information. Additionally, several of those ski areas that are willing to release skier-day numbers for the 2009–2010 ski season have obviously resorted to rounding off their numbers.

## SOURCES

Individual ski-area Web sites and media relations departments; Colorado Ski Country USA; National Ski Areas Association.

# COLORADO'S EARLY SKI HISTORY: HIGHLIGHTS

- **1903:** The word "ski" or "skee," rarely used before 1900, is in common usage after the turn of the century. In mid-winter 1903, the *Steamboat Pilot* headlines a story, "Winter Sport on the Treacherous and Speedy Skee." The story reads in part: "Skees are swift but mighty treacherous. The learning of the art of skeeing is the most exciting, dangerous, exasperating, yet satisfying of experiences."
- **1909:** Carl Howelsen, the great Norwegian ski champion, arrives in Denver to pursue his trade as a stonemason. In 1905, he immigrated to the United States due to poor economic conditions at home. Settling first in Chicago, he signed on with Barnum & Bailey's circus, where he was billed as "The Flying Norseman." His ski-jumping act became a star attraction. Eventually, he tired of the circus, longed for the outdoors and mountains, and headed west.
- **1910:** Peter Prestrud contours a small jumping hill from a mine dump at the mouth of Ten Mile Canyon in Summit County, near

Frisco, and uses it for recreational jumping. Later, he and Eyvin Flood build the big jumping hill at Dillon, where Anders Haugen breaks a world distance record in 1919.

- **1911:** Carl Howelsen and Angell Schmidt get off the train at the summit of Rollins Pass and ski down the western slope 44 miles into Hot Sulphur Springs. There they find a winter carnival in progress. They hastily improvise a small jumping ramp, and Howelsen soars off the ramp, flying 79 feet through the air. He astounds the townspeople, who immediately plan a jumping tournament for February 1912.
- **1912:** Hot Sulphur Springs hosts the first official winter sports carnival in Colorado to include a ski-jumping tournament. A special train is run from Denver. The Denver press reports on the sensational new sport, and the ski-sport is born in Colorado.
- **1913:** The big snow of 1913 goes down in the record books as one of the worst storms of the century. The five-day blizzard paralyzes Denver, the Front Range, and the mountain communities as far west as Breckenridge. But skiers glide easily over the snowy streets. George Cranmer watches Carl Howelsen and other skiers sliding down Capitol Hill and stops to inquire about the long runners. Cranmer will later take up skiing himself, become manager of the Denver Parks System, and be the moving force behind the development of Winter Park Ski Area.
- **1914:** It is probable that Carl Howelsen first visited Steamboat Springs after the 1913 Hot Sulphur Springs ski tournament at the urging of Marjorie Perry, a sportswoman who owned property there. On February 12, 1914, the first Steamboat Springs Winter Carnival gets underway with Howelsen and Peter Prestrud making a twin jump. Steamboaters are so taken with the new sport that they decide to make their winter carnival an annual event and feature ski jumping—a tradition that has lasted more than 90 years.
- **1915:** In Steamboat Springs, a new jumping hill is contoured under the watchful eye of Carl Howelsen and is christened "Howelsen Hill" in his honor. The new facility is recognized as being extremely fast. In 1916, Ragnar Omtvedt sets a new national distance record on the hill with a jump of 192 feet, 9 inches (16 feet better than the old record). The following year, Henry Hall breaks the 200-foot distance barrier with a jump of 203 feet.
- **1919:** On March 8 and 9, 1919, the Dillon Winter Sports Club holds a jumping tournament on a new hill built under the direction of Peter Prestrud and Eyvin Flood. The hill is designed to be one of the fastest in the world and Anders Haugen sets a new world record distance jump of 213 feet.

- **1920:** Denver's Rocky Mountain Ski Club dedicates its new Genesee facilities in February with a ski-jumping tournament that brings rave reviews from some of the top jumpers in the country.
- **1921:** Breckenridge's first winter sports carnival is held in March. A 90-foot-long trestle is built on Shock Hill. But the weather is warm, the snow is sticky, the in-run is slow, and the jumps are unspectacular.
- **1922:** It is probable that the first ski hill in Allenspark was contoured by Lars Haugen circa 1917. However, several injuries are reported there, and so the new Willow Creek Ski Hill takes shape in 1922, again laid out by Lars Haugen. Allenspark becomes part of the jumping circuit in Colorado for almost 20 years. The last tournament is held in 1940.
- **1923:** The Rocky Mountain National Park Ski Club of Estes Park clears a jumping course on Old Man Mountain just outside of town. Meanwhile, Cesar Tschudin, a Swiss ski instructor, has been hired by the club to teach classes on ski riding on Davis Hill in the center of town. The hill is the first lighted ski area in Colorado.
- **1924:** The first Winter Olympics (Nordic events only) is held at Chamonix, France. Anders Haugen, who had broken a world distance record on the Dillon, Colorado, hill in 1919, is captain of the U.S. Olympic team. Although he out-jumps the Olympic gold medal winner, Haugen is marked down in style points and officially comes in fourth. Almost 50 years later, an error in the scoring is discovered that indicates he actually won third place. Although the International Olympic Committee (IOC) does not recognize petitions to change its records, Haugen is awarded a bronze medal at a special ceremony in Oslo, Norway, 50 years later at the age of 86.
- **1925:** The first tournament of the newly organized Colorado State Ski Association is held at the Genesee course on January 18.
- **1927:** The Moffat railroad tunnel under the Continental Divide is finished during the summer of 1927, bypassing the treacherous Rollins Pass route. The superb alpine ski country adjacent to the West Portal of the tunnel becomes accessible. Graeme McGowan finds his ski paradise there.
- **1928:** Austrian Rudolph Lettner invents steel edges, but they aren't considered a necessity in Colorado's powder snow until the late 1930s, when ski trails start to get packed out.
- **1929:** Graeme McGowan, Garrett Van Wagenen, and Merriam Berger organize the Colorado Arlberg Club in April to emphasize the sport of ski running as opposed to ski jumping. McGowan

has acquired the old construction buildings at West Portal and converts one into a clubhouse, which the Arlberg Club leases.

- **1930:** On April 6, at Jim Creek Ridge, West Portal, the Arlberg Club sponsors the first downhill race in Colorado in which individuals race separately against time.
- **1931:** Thor C. Groswold begins manufacturing skis in Denver. In 1939, he is licensed to manufacture Splitkein skis and becomes one of three manufacturers to supply skis to the 10th Mountain Division troops during World War II.
- **1934:** In March, Estes Park hosts the National Ski Championships. The second annual national downhill is run on a newly cut trail in Hidden Valley, Rocky Mountain National Park. Junior Duncan of Estes Park wins over the formidable skiers from the Dartmouth College team. Donald Munson wins the national cross-country on the Bear Lake course. Glen Armstrong of Estes Park wins the jumping event on Old Man Mountain.
- **1935:** In Austria, Hannes Schneider makes high-speed turning possible with the Arlberg method. One of his instructors is Friedl Pfeifer, who will later fight with the U.S. 10th Mountain Division in World War II and return to Colorado after the war to develop Aspen Mountain.
- **1936:** Aspen's Tom Flynn, Ted Ryan, and Billy Fiske bring in Andre Roch of Switzerland to look over the Roaring Fork Valley for prime ski sites. Roch lays out a difficult run on Aspen Mountain—Roch Run.
- **1937:** In February, Berthoud Pass installs an 878-foot-long rope tow.
- **1937:** The Climax Molybdenum Company develops a ski area on Chalk Mountain on Fremont Pass. A rope tow is put in and floodlights line the 1,500-foot slope for night skiing. The Climax Ski Area closes in 1960.
- **1937:** In Durango, a run is cleared on Calico Hill and a rope tow is installed. The area is improved in the 1950s and the name is changed to Chapman Hill.
- **1938:** The newly cut Roch Run on Ajax Mountain in Aspen is completed in time for the 1938 Rocky Mountain Ski Association Championships. The meet is the first-ever run in the region in accordance with International Ski Federation (FIS) Rules and Computations. Jarvis Schauffler of Sun Valley comes in first; Barney McLean wraps up the slalom.
- **1938:** After being closed two years for improvements, the Loveland Pass Road opens, and skiers find excellent open terrain on both sides of the pass. Thor C. Groswold and J. C. Blickensderfer set up a portable tow on the east side of Loveland Pass. Mean-

while, Allen Bennett starts Loveland Basin at the east foot of Loveland Pass, where he installs one rope tow.

- **1938:** In the fall, the U.S. Forest Service and the Civilian Conservation Corps construct a shelter house for skiers on the summit of Wolf Creek Pass. The January 31, 1938, *Alamosa Daily Courier* reports that more than 50 automobiles are parked on top of the pass. Four times that many skiers are demonstrating the "telemark, Christiania, backslide, and snows-dive."

- **1939:** The Salida Winter Sports Club applies to the U.S. Forest Service to build a shelter and ski tow on Monarch Pass. By the end of the year, Gunbarrel Run has been cut, a rope tow installed, and the "Inn Ferno" day lodge constructed.

- **1940:** Winter Park, formerly known as West Portal, is dedicated on January 28 and becomes the crown jewel of Denver's Mountain Park System.

- **1941:** Aspen hosts the National Alpine Championships. Toni Matt wins the downhill held on Roch Run. Dick Durrance takes second. The National Ski Championships establish Aspen's reputation in alpine-racing circles and put Roch Run and Colorado on the ski map.

- **1942:** In April, construction starts on Camp Hale at Pando, between Leadville and Red Cliff. The ski troops move into quarters in November. The army constructs the "world's longest T-bar"—6,000 feet—at Cooper Hill on Tennessee Pass, where the recruits learn to ski. The 99th Infantry Battalion, composed of Norwegian nationals, trains with the U.S. ski troops at Camp Hale from December 1942 until August 1943. The unit takes part in the European campaigns and after the war disarms the German garrison in Norway.

- **1942–1943:** The National Ski Patrol serves as part of the Home Defense System in 1942—specifically, search and rescue and firefighting. The Southern Rocky Mountain Ski Association establishes a system of aircraft crash rescue groups. Practice missions originate from Lowry Field in Denver under Art Kidder's direction.

- **1944:** Steamboat Springs holds its 31st annual Winter Sports Carnival in conjunction with the Fourth War Loan drive of Routt County. The event nets $110,000 in War Bond subscriptions. Torger Tokle (10th Mountain Division) wins the jumping competition. He is later killed in the Italian campaign.

- **1945:** The 10th Mountain Division is deployed to Italy, where it becomes a part of the 5th Army under the command of General Mark Clark. On January 26, troops move into the Apennine Mountains. The assault on Riva Ridge takes place on February

18; Mount Belvedere is taken shortly after, and by May 2, the war in Italy is over.

- **1945:** Friedl Pfeifer returns to Aspen. He teams up with Walter Paepcke, who is interested in establishing a cultural center for business executives. They form the Aspen Skiing Company. Pfeifer begins the development of Aspen Mountain and starts a ski school.

- **1945–1946:** Arapahoe Basin, Inc., on the western slope of Loveland Pass, is incorporated by Larry Jump, Sandy Schauffler, and Dick Durrance. They team up with Max Dercum, who owns property along the Snake River, plus several mining claims in the area.

- **1946:** In Aspen, the "longest chairlift in the world" (a single) begins operating on December 14 on Ajax Mountain. The first annual Roch Cup is run and Barney McLean wins. The Aspen Skiing Company buys a downtown block from the D&RG Railroad for $50.

- **1946:** Heron Engineering Company of Denver, in business since 1911 manufacturing aerial trams used in mining operations, starts designing and installing ski lifts in Colorado. Brothers Robert and Webb Heron install Aspen's two single-chair lifts. Heron will go on to design Berthoud's double chair in 1947 and Arapahoe Basin's two T-bar tows. In 1952, they are licensed to make the T-bar tows patented by Ernest Constam of Switzerland.

- **1947:** Arapahoe Basin opens its first official season of 1946–1947 with a rope tow. Two single chairlifts are installed the following year. The official dedication of the area is held on February 15.

- **1947:** An Associated Press article describes Steamboat Springs as "Ski Town USA" and the label sticks. In 1987, the Steamboat Springs Winter Sports Club registers it as a trade name.

- **1947:** Klaus Obermeyer, a popular Aspen ski instructor, founds America's largest skiwear manufacturing firm.

- **1948:** Willie Schaeffler arrives in this country from Bavaria and goes to work at Arapahoe Basin teaching the Austrian technique. Eventually he becomes director of A-Basin's ski school and also coach of the Denver University Ski Team. In 1972, Schaeffler serves as head coach of the U.S. Olympic Ski Team.

- **1948:** Billy Mahoney and other skiers in Telluride purchase an old car engine and build a rope tow up the slopes of the Ball Park Ski Area. In 1953, the tow is moved to the Grizzly Gulch area. Mahoney will go on to play a decisive role in the development and operation of the present Telluride Ski complex.

- **1949:** Winter Park gets flushing toilets and new emergency phone service.

- **1950:** Aspen brings the FIS alpine world championships to the United States for the first time. Dick Durrance, general manager of Aspen Skiing Company, is responsible. The event puts Aspen and Colorado on the international ski map.
- **1951:** Duane Vandenbusche and Duane Smith report in *A Land Alone* that only four ski areas in Colorado operate daily: Arapahoe Basin, Winter Park, Aspen Mountain, and Loveland Basin. He says that 175,000 lift tickets are sold statewide.
- **1951:** The Berry family buys Monarch Ski Area for $100. The town of Salida originally held the lease. In 1954, Roman Fischer takes over and the Berrys return in 1956.
- **1951:** Steve Bradley, director of Winter Park, starts experimenting with his packer/grader. It will eventually evolve into the mechanized grooming cats of today.
- **1953:** The first Pomalift in the United States is installed at Arapahoe Basin by Larry Jump. He forms Pomalift, Inc. in June 1954, a wholly owned subsidiary of Arapahoe Basin, Inc. The corporation eventually sells 465 surface lifts, Pomagalski chairlifts, and three passenger gondolas to more than 400 ski areas. That original Poma surface lift was still in service in 2001 at the Lake City Ski Hill.
- **1953:** In Telluride, the rope tow at the Ball Park is moved to the steeper slope of Grizzly Gulch—now the lower part of the Plunge. The Ski Hi Ski Club is organized.
- **1954:** The Hidden Valley Ski Area in Rocky Mountain National Park needs upgrading, but allotting funds for the improvements requires an Act of Congress. George Peck, president of Estes Park Winter Sports Club, and Fred Clatworthy, Jr., mount a successful write-in campaign to get funding. The improved area opens on December 18, 1955, with two surface lifts and a new lodge.
- **1955:** Wolf Creek Pass Ski Area moves its facilities from the summit of the pass to its present location on the eastern slope. Stock is sold in the Wolf Creek Ski Development Corporation. Ed Sharp of Monte Vista serves as first president of the development company until 1969 and as unpaid manager of the ski area from 1955 through 1960 and again from 1963 through 1965.
- **1957:** Earl Eaton takes Pete Seibert to see Vail Mountain (unnamed at the time). Seibert is stunned by the extensive back bowls. They purchase the 500-acre Hanson Ranch at the base of the mountain for approximately $110 per acre.
- **1958:** Buddy Werner of Steamboat Springs wins the Lauberhorn Combined at Wengen, Switzerland. He becomes the first American male to win major downhill races in Europe, including the Hahnenkaam at Kitzbuhel (1954, 1956, and 1962).

- **1958:** James Temple breaks ground for the new Storm Mountain Ski Area in Steamboat Springs. Between 1958 and 1961, he secures options to buy 827 acres of meadowland at the base of the mountain. "Champagne powder" is the descriptive phrase used to promote the area. Temple gives credit to a Kremmling rancher, Joe McElroy, who said that the fluffy dry snow was "lighter than champagne bubbles."
- **1958:** Buttermilk-at-Aspen formally opens in December with Friedl Pfeifer serving as president of the Buttermilk Mountain Skiing Corporation.
- **1958:** Magic Mountain Ski Area, operated by Foothills Skiing Corporation, Inc., opens near Golden. Although it operates just one season, it is noteworthy for introducing the first snowmaking equipment in Colorado. It sells the snowmaking equipment to the new Broadmoor Ski Area. When it closes, the tows are sold to the new Indianhead (Geneva Basin) Ski Area.
- **1959:** Aspen Highlands, developed by Whipple (Whip) Jones, who owns the base property, is dedicated on January 17. Pete Seibert and Earl Eaton from Loveland Basin have laid out trails and lift-line corridors.
- **1959:** Vail Corporation, under the direction of Pete Seibert, is formed to plan and develop Vail Mountain. The U.S. Forest Service approves the site in September, allowing construction to start in 1961. Stockholders form a general partnership for acquisition and disposition of real estate under the name of "The Transmontane Company."
- **1960:** Ski Broadmoor in Colorado Springs is dedicated and becomes the first area in the state to show the value of artificial snow. The area buys snowmaking equipment from the defunct Magic Mountain. A new Larchmont snowmaker is dubbed "The Phenomenal Snowman."
- **1961:** Crested Butte opens on Thanksgiving Day, with a 2,300-foot Doppelmayr T-bar and a rope tow on the northern flank of Mount Crested Butte.
- **1961:** Indianhead Mountain Ski Area, later named Geneva Basin, opens in mid-December after two years of preparation.
- **1961:** The Summit County Development Corporation opens Peak Eight at Breckenridge on December 15. The new area has one Heron double chairlift, a short T-bar, and a base shelter.
- **1961:** Steamboat Springs Corporation organizes with partners John Fetcher, Marvin Crawford, Gerald Groswold, Bud Werner, William Sayre, and Sam Huddleston to develop Storm Mountain as a major downhill ski area. Common stock is sold. The area opens on December 22 with one lift—a beginner's Poma. John

Fetcher spearheads the Steamboat Partnership, which is responsible for refinancing the plan. The new expanded ski area officially opens in 1963.

- **1962:** Vail Mountain opens December 15 with a Bell gondola lift—the first gondola in Colorado.
- **1963:** Snowmass-at-Aspen opens with guided ski touring. "Trackmaster" snowcats take skiers to the 12,000-foot elevation.
- **1963:** Storm Mountain at Steamboat Springs officially opens with one chairlift.
- **1963:** The National Ski Jumping Championships are held at Howelsen Hill. Gene Kotlarek breaks the national jumping records twice with jumps of 318 and 322 feet. ABC's *Wide World of Sports* televises the event.
- **1963:** Lake Eldora opens.
- **1963:** Telluride explores the feasibility of a ski-lift project on a shady mountainside just south of the city.
- **1963:** Aspen Ski Corporation acquires Buttermilk Mountain by exchange of stock.
- **1963:** Colorado Ski Country USA is formed. It uncorks the "Ski Country USA" ad campaign.
- **1964:** The Kendall Ski Hill in the town of Silverton opens with a 1,000-foot rope tow from Camp Hale. Called the Bingle Tow, it would be replaced in 1998 with a Tramway Board–approved Handle Tow.
- **1965:** President of the Durango Ski Corporation, Raymond T. Duncan, announces the first phase of the multi-million-dollar ski development of Purgatory, to be completed by December.
- **1965:** In February, the name of Storm Mountain at Steamboat Springs is officially changed to Mount Werner in memory of Buddy Werner.
- **1966:** On May 17, a special-use permit is issued to Sunlight Ski Corporation by the U.S. Forest Service. John Higgs of Chicago, along with 23 stockholders, own the operation. Higgs had bought land in the area, including the small Holiday Hills Ski Area dating from the 1940s. The Vanderhoof family is actively involved in the development of Sunlight. The new ski area formally opens on December 16.
- **1966:** The new Powderhorn Ski Area opens on Thanksgiving with a double chairlift, two Pomas, and a two-story lodge. The area is 45 miles east of Grand Junction, set in a bowl on the north side of Grand Mesa.
- **1966:** The small ski area of Hesperus, west of Durango, has a T-bar and two rope tows. Hesperus Ski Area extends its cross-country run to accommodate the U.S. National X-C Championships.

- **1967:** The U.S. Forest Service issues a special-use permit to Ski Valley USA, Inc. (Keystone). Max Dercum, his son Rolf, and Bill and Jane Bergman are the principals.
- **1967:** Denver is the U.S. Olympic Committee's choice for the Winter Olympics of 1976.
- **1967:** Snowmass-at-Aspen officially opens on December 17. Bill Janss is the developer. Approximately $10 million is invested in the West Village. In October 1968, Janss's Investment Corporation sells to American Cement Corp (ACC owned 50 percent of the stock).
- **1968:** In December, Joe Zoline arrives in Telluride to investigate the possibility of developing a major ski area.
- **1968:** Arapahoe Basin Ski Area inaugurates ski instruction for amputees in January, along with a pilot project for disabled children from Children's Hospital in Denver. Willy Schaeffler offers free skiing and instruction. The children's program is switched to Winter Park the following year.
- **1969:** Ralston Purina forms Keystone International, Inc., merging with and acquiring all of the outstanding stock of Ski Valley USA. The firm draws up a comprehensive master plan for Keystone Ski Area.
- **1969:** Vail Associates, Ltd., becomes Vail Associates, Inc. The resort begins a $3 million expansion of Lionshead, including installation of a six-passenger Bell gondola. At the dedication, Simba the lion adds a lively spark to the ceremony.
- **1970:** The handicapped ski program that originated at Arapahoe Basin in 1968 finds a home at Winter Park. Under the directorship of Hal O'Leary, it becomes the largest and most successful such program in the United States.
- **1970:** Aspen Skiing Corporation buys out the Breckenridge Ski Corporation by purchase of stock and launches a major expansion plan on the slopes and at the base of the mountain.
- **1970:** Max Dercum's dream mountain, Keystone, opens on November 21 under the financial umbrella of Ralston Purina Company. Dercum becomes ski school director. The area boasts two chairlifts and one Poma lift, plus mountain and base shelters.
- **1970:** The IOC picks Denver as host city for the 1976 Winter Olympics. Governor John Love and industry leaders are responsible for the coup.
- **1972:** Telluride officially opens in December with five lifts.
- **1972:** In November, a referendum on the Colorado state and Denver ballots is passed that prohibits Colorado or the City of Denver from funding the 1976 Olympic winter games. Beaver Creek, the designated alpine site for the Denver Olympics, be-

comes the focus of struggle between development proponents and environmentalists.

- **1972:** Copper Mountain opens on November 15 with four double chairs, one of which is Colorado's first enclosed bubble.
- **1973:** The north bore of the Eisenhower Memorial Tunnel opens.
- **1973:** The Colorado Avalanche Information Center, funded under the direction of the U.S. Forest Service, begins to issue statewide warnings of high avalanche danger. In 1983, the center becomes part of the Colorado Department of Natural Resources. Funds are secured from a consortium of public and private sponsors.
- **1974:** Crested Butte launches one of the first telemarking races in the country with the tough Al Johnson Uphill and Downhill Memorial Race. The event is named for Al Johnson, a mail carrier of the last century who traversed the Elk Mountains on skis.
- **1974:** The first World Super Hot Dog Classic is held on See Me at Steamboat Springs during Winter Carnival. The event was part of the pro circuit at the time.
- **1975:** In January, the Colorado Land Use Commission recommends to Governor Vanderhoof on his last day in office that he endorse plans for the development of Beaver Creek. When Governor Richard Lamm takes office, he immediately files a complaint on grounds that the environmental data are incomplete. Final plans for Beaver Creek are considerably altered.
- **1975:** A ski streaker disrupts the Thundermug free-for-all race at Steamboat Springs, traditionally held (since 1964) on the last day of the season. Streakers pop up at other ski areas as well.
- **1976:** The Mary Jane area at Winter Park is formally dedicated. The new runs add 80 percent more skiing terrain to the Winter Park complex.
- **1976:** To celebrate America's Bicentennial, several skiers at Vail found the Colorado Ski Museum. A formal dedication is held in 1977 with the first Hall of Fame members inducted.
- **1976:** In March, an accident with the Bell gondola at Vail results in four fatalities and eight injuries. Nevertheless, skier visits at Vail soar over the one million mark—a first for a Colorado ski area.
- **1976:** Rocky Mountain National Park buys the Hidden Valley Ski Area from Ted James of Denver. Hidden Valley Ski Area is also known as Ski Estes Park.
- **1976:** Kingsberry Pitcher buys into the Wolf Creek Ski Corporation. In 1978, he buys the entire company. The Pitcher family still owns Wolf Creek.
- **1977:** On July 28, a groundbreaking ceremony takes place on the site of Beaver Creek Village. President Gerald Ford takes part in the ceremonies.

- **1977:** A snow drought in the Rockies is the worst in 40 years. Colorado ski areas lose $78 million and post a 36.6 percent decline in skier days with a 50 percent drop in business. Areas on the Front Range fare best. Steamboat, Telluride, and Geneva Basin close for the season in February. Keystone stays open because of greater snowmaking capability and posts a 5.81 percent gain.
- **1978:** Howelsen Hill, destroyed by fire in 1972, has been rebuilt and is dedicated on January 28. The construction cost $1.1 million and took five years. The Winter Sports Club was unable to finance the area and transferred title of Howelsen Hill's facilities and equipment to the City of Steamboat Springs in 1977.
- **1978:** Ralston–Purina, owner of Keystone Resort, buys Arapahoe Basin in a stock deal.
- **1978:** Summit County launches the Summit Telemark Series. The series affiliates with USSA in 1984 and eventually becomes known as the Rocky Mountain Telemark Series.
- **1979:** The Skier Safety Act is passed by the Colorado General Assembly. The bill establishes reasonable safety standards for the operation of ski areas and defines the duties and rights of skiers using the areas.

## SOURCES

Most of this information was taken from www.coloradoskihistory.com, which is comprised of information compiled by Patricia Pfeiffer, Chair, Colorado Ski Museum History Committee. This Web site is the absolute best one in the world for those who are interested in the Colorado ski industry. The fact that it is affiliated with the Colorado Ski Museum, located in the heart of Vail Village, makes the site and the information contained therein all the more appealing and important.

# MOUNTAINSPEAK: SKIING LEXICON

- **Air Force:** Old-school kudos for any act of skiing or après that speaks to a level of irreverence. As in, "That's so Air Force." Inspired by the legendary Jackson Hole–based ski fraternity.
- **Ape:** Snowboarder. Derogatory term that refers to dragging one's knuckles and riding in a crunched-down style.
- **Arc:** To make a turn. Specifically, to make long, round turns by riding the edge of the ski. "Nice arc."
- **A-Star:** A small helicopter common to smaller heli-ski operations and/or hut or backcountry lodge drops.
- **Bash:** To look for fresh snow in the trees.

- **Beater:** A bad fall often resulting in bruises and/or loss or damage to your gear. Also used in reference to a bad skier, such as tourists on older gear. "I took a beater when that beater crossed my track."
- **Beeper:** Slang for an avalanche transceiver.
- **Bird:** A helicopter.
- **Blow:** To suck.
- **Blower:** Especially deep snow. Usually reserved in reference to the deep snow that you ski in the middle of a storm. "It was blower up there."
- **Bluebird:** A cloudless day. Big in heli-operations. "Tomorrow is supposed to be bluebird."
- **Boilerplate:** Hard, frozen snow conditions. Blue ice.
- **Bomber:** Hard snow in bounds, but off-piste refers to snow that is deemed so stable it is unlikely to avalanche.
- **Boot-out:** To carve so tightly into a turn that your boot hits the snow and ejects you from your bindings.
- **Bootpack (Bootpacking):** The act of hiking for turns or to reach a pre-determined summit. "We've got to bootpack to the top." Also used to refer to the stepped staircase set by previous skiers. "The bootpack was already set."
- **Boot-top:** A universally accepted level for measuring snow depth and particularly powder depth.
- **Brah (or bra):** Weird term for "Bro" predominately used by East Coast or West Coast transplants trying to interweave both their new and old area codes at the same time.
- **Braille:** How you ski during a whiteout, when the wind is high and the snow at your feet is blowing back up.
- **Bro:** Your best ski buddy.
- **Bro-Brah:** Any subset of male friends at any given mountain (or collection thereof) that smacks of certain tribal/fraternal/homoskirotic tendencies, including lots of extended handshakes, unintelligible slang and hugs. Also used to reference certain gatherings of the same: "It was totally bro-brah in there."
- **Broke:** In reference to anything at all—skis, runs, bars, lovers, chairlifts—that no longer work for you or for the general populace. "She got married, so that, for you, is broke."
- **Burn:** To smoke pot.
- **Camber:** The designed rise in the flex of the ski that reaches its apex beneath your boot/foot.
- **Camp:** To sleep on a friend's couch or any other rent-free, enclosed space.
- **Carve:** See "Arc."
- **Catapult:** To jump a cliff at the lip to obtain loft.

- **Choke:** So much powder it affects your ability to breathe—always said with mock distress.
- **Clean:** An untracked line or slope.
- **Cliff Out:** To reach a point, almost always off-piste, where the line you are skiing suddenly ends in a sheer expanse of rock and your only option is to fly or hike out.
- **Cold Lampin':** Smoking dope in cold conditions. Also, recently, hiking early in the morning for turns before the sun is up.
- **Coral Reef:** Hard, frozen snow conditions, typically in reference to snow that has melted and re-frozen off-piste.
- **Corn:** Soft, spring snow melted like butter by the sun.
- **Crap Out:** Traveling for better conditions and finding your same local crud.
- **Critter:** Anything that shares your bed in the cold months—be that your dog, significant other, family of mice, or porcupine moved indoors. "It's cold—we need more critters in here."
- **Crud:** Heavy snow of mixed and uneven conditions. Hard to ski—the antithesis to powder.
- **Daffy:** An old hotdog ski term from the 1960s meaning a type of air when the skis are crossed and the body is extended in an arch. It's not really used much today.
- **Deck Surfing:** Spending productive recreational time pondering the greater cosmos on the decks of bars located at or close to the base of a ski area. Usually includes appropriate beverages.
- **Deep:** As in the snow, the forest, or your buzz the previous night. "How deep did you take it?"
- **Dick:** Your least favorite ski patroller, the guy who's dating your old girlfriend, or the guy blasting rap in the parking lot.
- **Ding:** A top-of-the-ski or side-of-the-edge nick.
- **Dirt:** As in weed, snow, or cheap rent. "It's dirt."
- **Divot:** A hole taken out of the bottom of your ski, most often by a rock.
- **Dog:** A skier's favorite companion.
- **Dog's Breakfast:** A mixed and often hastily compiled list of bad options. "It was a dog's breakfast trying to pick my way down that chute."
- **Driver:** People who like to steer their skis in lots of quick, short turns, typically a slalom racer or East Coast edgehead. Often paired with aggressive, overtly theatrical hand movements.
- **Drive-by-Duding:** Getting passed by a posse of young skiers and/or snowboarders.
- **Edge:** To control your speed, especially in steeps, by standing hard on the skis. "At the top of that couloir, I really had to stand on my edge."

- **Edgehead:** A ski racer or Eastern skier who is especially proficient or fond of using the edges of his or her skis to tightly control the turns.
- **Face Plant:** Indentation left in the snow after a face-first fall that looks remarkably like, well, your visage. Also used in mountain biking and snowboarding.
- **Face Shot:** The cold, fresh slap of powder blasting up around your cheeks—the basic end-all of top ski experiences when the snow is so deep it threatens your sight and breath.
- **Fag Bag:** A one-piece ski suit.
- **Fart Catcher:** Also a one-piece ski suit.
- **Figure Eights (or "Figure-8s"):** Tracks left in fresh powder by a pair of skiers, each forming half of the figure eight as the second skier crosses the ribbon left by the first. Powder etiquette encourages skiers to ski fresh powder fields in figure eights, as close to the previous set as possible.
- **File Monkey:** A ski tech.
- **Fin:** A rock just below the snow's surface.
- **Flippy-Flopper:** A New School skier, or twin-tip ski-infatuated half-pipe aficionado who spends his or her day skiing "The Park."
- **Freak:** The local skier who car- and/or snow-camps and always seems to be five chairs ahead of you on a powder day and 20 yards up the trail from you on the pass. Always the first guy in line when the happy hour nachos come out. Often labeled as a "freak" out of a grudging sense of respect. "I wish I got as many turns as the freak." Answer: "Yeah, but then you'd be broke."
- **Freezer:** January skiing anywhere in the Rocky Mountain West.
- **Freshies:** New snow.
- **Gnar:** Really good snow conditions. "It's the gnar."
- **Go Large:** To achieve significant height while skiing, snowboarding, or biking off of a cliff (or, in the case of kayaking, a waterfall). Stunningly, the overwhelming majority of the times one goes large are actually intentional, much to the dismay of many, many parents.
- **Gramp-Amp:** Old(er) guys trying to perform tricks in the half-pipe and/or terrain park.
- **Greenies:** Imported or micro-beer, typically exchanged with friendly ski techs for ultra-fast repair service.
- **Grind:** A ski shop edge-sharpening technique. Also, a new-school edge-against-rail sliding technique.
- **Grip:** To get scared or choke at the crux of a shot.
- **Guns:** Skis. Especially big skis.
- **Heavy:** Wet snow conditions, moisture-laden and hard to negotiate.

- **Hero:** Any seemingly significant other seen alongside any especially attractive member of the opposite sex. An obvious detriment to any forthcoming interaction: "Well, her hero can tell her that."
- **Hippie Sticks:** Telemark skis.
- **Hoar:** Derogatory term—both slang and scientific—for the dehydrated snow produced by dry, cold temperatures that can be instrumental in forming the weak layer of snowpack that can cause an avalanche.
- **Ho Chi Minh:** Any somewhat clandestine bootpack leading to a little-used in-bounds line or, more often, an out-of-bounds shot.
- **Holding:** Street-to-snow-to-chairlift slang for finding out who has the bag of pot. "Who's holding?" Often asked as soon as the lift has left the base.
- **Hospital Air:** Launching a jump so big that there is really only one option if you don't land it.
- **Hot:** Bad news for a mountain range, weather pattern, or time of season that causes certain aspects to avalanche a lot.
- **Huck:** Go large in the air, usually on skis or a snowboard, but also on a mountain bike.
- **Kook:** Exactly that, but in a good way—like the old hippie who always gets you high just before the day's last run.
- **Laps:** Typically a term for ski areas with a tram—like Jackson Hole and Snowbird—where you can successively ski from summit to base on one lift. Also, making laps.
- **Line:** The path you choose to take down the slope. Also, what some alpine aesthetes would argue is the obvious path.
- **Lung:** Someone who hikes for their turns a lot—especially a fit, ridge-hopping, Lycra-advertising, body-fat-less creature with blonde teeth.
- **Mach:** Go really fast.
- **Make It:** Land the jump.
- **Maze Rage:** Losing your temper while waiting in line at the base of a ski lift, especially when someone cuts in front of you while you weren't paying attention because you were in a safety meeting. (*See* "Safety Meeting.")
- **Mechanic:** Ski tech.
- **Mo:** Short for moron, but also for Mormon in Jackson and Salt Lake.
- **Mork:** Any strain of long-talking, male, slightly unusual Boulderites.
- **New:** A reference to fresh snow depth.
- **Non-stop:** To ski without stopping from summit to base.
- **Nuke:** To snow very hard for a very long time.

- **Out-of-bounds:** Parts of ski mountains that are not groomed, maintained, or controlled for avalanches. Usually delineated with a big warning sign. A place you are generally not supposed to go.
- **Park Rat:** Kid addicted to skiing half-pipes and terrain parks.
- **Pinner or Pinhead:** Telemarker.
- **Poach:** Skiing around and in front of a person and then skiing down that person's intended line in the powder. Also, jumping into a field of powder ahead of someone else who has been patiently waiting his or her turn. Also, the act of crossing a boundary or closure rope to ski an uncontrolled run or slope. Also, when someone else skis through your powder stash before you get to it. All in all, considered bad form and reason in and of itself for social ostracization.
- **Pow:** Powder. The life-giving, face-freezing, soul-crystal-lighting Holy Grail at the center of the sport.
- **Powder Clause:** The provision in an employment agreement—implicit or otherwise—allowing an employee of a ski-town business to take the morning off and ski on powder days. Also previously applied to businesses themselves that would close for the morning on powder days, back when most ski-town businesses were owned by locals who actually skied.
- **Powder Eights (also "Powder 8s"):** The name of a type of choreographed skiing competition wherein pairs of skiers try to leave behind the most perfect figure-eight tracks possible.
- **Powder Hour:** The now-more-common reality of what was once known as a "Powder Day." (*See* "Powder Clause.")
- **Powder Stash:** An undisclosed location where untracked powder can still be found long after most other runs have been tracked-up on a powder day.
- **Racer Chaser:** Ski race groupie.
- **Randonee:** Alpine touring skis that can be used in a free-heel state to ascend and traverse. With heel locked into the binding, can be used to downhill ski. According to some bumperstickers, randonee is French for "can't tele."
- **Rider:** The opposite of a driver. Someone who "rides" his or her skis, often in long, looping, non-sequential turns. Often identified by a stand-up surfer style—low, still hands, and yet a seemingly set rate of speed.
- **Rip:** To ski hard and well, but also used as reference for an avalanche that moves quickly off of a cornice or peak.
- **Rocker:** Reverse camber ski construction, with an upward bend toward the shovel of the ski so that it can float in the soft snow and still carve on the hard stuff.
- **Rocket Scientist:** Ski designer or product manager, fond of showing you graphs of flex tests and core schematics.

- **Safety Meeting:** What outdoor people like to call getting high together, typically at the end—or beginning—of a long day.
- **Shot:** The line you want to ski (often involving powder) or the jump you want to take. Also used as a reference to certain topographical features on a given mountain: "I hit that shot just to the left of the peak."
- **Shovel:** The forward length of your ski, from the front of your boot/binding to the very tip.
- **Shred:** To carve well, especially in difficult terrain.
- **Six-inch Rule:** *See* "Powder Clause."
- **Skid:** A ski bum with hardly a place to sleep, no cash, and new skis in the garage. Skid is in reference to the stain on his underwear or the skidmark stain of his life, like the black evidence of a car heading off the road.
- **Skin:** The act of ascent when using climbing skins.
- **Slapper:** A bad skier incapable of edging to control his or her turns.
- **Slippers:** Ski boots.
- **Slough:** A natural slide or settling of fresh snow.
- **Smoke:** Get high.
- **Spancered (also, "Sponsored"):** Anyone who is receiving skis, jackets, free lift tickets, or—GASP!—actual cash money from a manufacturer/resort/sticker company for their skiing skills. In general reference, refers to who's buying the drinks.
- **Splat:** To fall hard, usually by moving from a tilted slope to a sudden flat spot, like a catwalk.
- **Stick:** To ski a technical line well, or to ride a tough section on your mountain bike with aplomb.
- **Sticks:** Skis.
- **Stomp:** To land a jump or cliff drop authoritatively. "Dude, you stomped that landing."
- **Sucker Track:** Following someone else's seemingly knowledgeable line through unfamiliar terrain, and, just like they did, you suddenly almost ski into a tree or a rock. This is a sucker track. And by adding your own track to the path, you can be assured it will also happen to someone else.
- **Sufficient Nexus:** Act of launching hospital air so that when the photographer takes your picture, the name of your sponsor is clearly visible on the base of your skis in the shot.
- **Surf:** To sleep on someone's couch.
- **Surfy:** New snow that is moisture laden and well packed, often referred to as being more akin to "a Maritime climate." Fancy talk for especially wet white.
- **Sweep:** Ski patrol's last descent of the day, when they sweep up whatever carnage might be spread about the slopes.

- **Systems:** Binding/ski interfaces with the binding built into the ski. The opposite, more popular old-school method whereby skis and bindings are sold separately is called "flat" or "a la carte."
- **Tapped:** In reference to a keg, ski shot, or pipe that is out of fresh stock.
- **Tater:** To fall, especially in Idaho.
- **Telechick:** Cute mountain mama on telemark skis (*see also* "Hippie Sticks"). Inevitably with a braided ponytail.
- **Tour:** To hike or ski beyond the ski-area boundaries, often in search of fresh powder and unskied chutes.
- **Tracks:** What you make in the powder and turn back to stare at.
- **Twig Pig:** Any member of the U.S. Forest Service charged with the duties of law enforcement.
- **Uncle Sam's Ski Team:** Someone skiing on a severance package or on unemployment.
- **Utah Fluff:** A trademark—the dry, light, continental snow conditions that occur most frequently in the Beehive State.
- **Utarhd:** Someone whose total learnings are limited to a very small range of experiences and very regional travel in the Beehive State. From difficulty understanding how to accept an alcoholic drink order to any surreal-bordering-on-vague-schizophrenia-inducing conversations involving baked goods, this term can be used to describe a variety of experiences based in and around the greater Salt Lake City area.
- **Warp:** A high rate of speed, particularly in dangerous conditions where your only chance is to ski your way out. "When that cornice let loose, I just hit warp."
- **Weld:** Fixing a divot in your ski with high-end P-tex wax.
- **Zipper Line:** Tightly carved turns. Usually performed by competition bumps (moguls) skiers with their knees locked together. Also a symmetrical line through the bumps that offers an opportunity to ski in this fashion.
- **Z-Track:** Diagonal ski tracks stepped or cut by ski patrollers across an avalanche-prone slope. This is done to help separate the snow sheet to keep it from sliding en masse.

SOURCES:

Peter Kray, former editorial director for *Ski Press* magazine, publisher of *The Gear Institute* and author of *American Snow*; Devon O'Neil, ex–sports editor, *Summit Daily News* and columnist for ESPN.com; long-time Aspen-area resident and wordsmith Malcolm McMichael.

# THE NAMING OF COLORADO'S SKI RUNS

Colorado's ski areas boast a total of 2,315 named runs. That's more names than the total number of streets in the south Denver suburbs. Each ski area has its own philosophy for naming its runs, but, since Vail has the most named ski runs (193, to second-place Steamboat's 165), it's worth examining how some of the myriad runs at the state's largest ski resort garnered their appellations.

## NORTHEAST BOWL

Since this part of Vail Mountain, first opened to skiers in 1967, was the site of a sawmill and heavy timbering operations, the resort went with a lumber theme.

- **Blue Ox:** Named after famed lumberjack Paul Bunyon's equally famed Ox, Babe, who turned blue during the "Winter of the Blue Snow."
- **Boomer:** A boomer was a device that tightened the chains around logs that had been loaded for transport.
- **Choker Cutoff:** Chokers were the hauling cables wrapped around the ends of fallen trees in order to skid them out.
- **Flapjack:** A run almost as flat as a pancake on top and named for the loggers' favorite breakfast.
- **Highline:** A pulley rigged to the top of a tree, from which a cable was hooked to a steam-engine donkey to haul trees out of the woods.

## GOLDEN PEAK

Named by Vail's first marketing man, Bob Parker, for its glorious autumn display of aspen gold, this was the site of Vail's first major expansion in 1967.

- **Afterthought:** This steeply pitched run, above and to the east of the Golden Peak lift, was literally added as an afterthought and is now simply a portion of the Golden Peak racecourse.
- **Boo Boo:** The topmost section of the Golden Peak racecourse, named for the straight slash through the trees above it where a cut was made for a chairlift that was never built.
- **Ruder's Route:** Golden Peak's main trail, named after Leonard Ruder, the son of Gore Creek pioneers. He was responsible for the construction of some of Vail's first runs.

## MID-VAIL

Mid-Vail has been a focal point of Vail skiers since 1962, when only a gondola out of Vail Village served the area and a double chairlift took skiers to the top of the mountain from there. Today, Mid-Vail has two quad chairs and three restaurants.

- **Cappuccino:** Named to match its neighboring run, Espresso, cappuccino is espresso mixed with milk or cream.
- **Christmas:** The beautifully shaped evergreens along this run remind skiers of Christmas trees.
- **Compromise:** A catwalk off of Riva Ridge allowing skiers to bypass the steep face of Tourist Trap.
- **Ramshorn:** A story goes that the horns of a bighorn sheep were found when this run was first surveyed. Viewed from a distance, the curve of the run itself resembles a ram's horn.
- **The Skipper:** Named for George Knox, nicknamed "The Skipper," who, at age 62, came to Vail and began publication of the now-defunct *Vail Trail* newspaper. This run was named for Knox after his death in 1975.
- **Tourist Trap:** The steepest pitch on Riva Ridge, named by Rod Slifer, former mayor of Vail, who, when he saw the run being cut, remarked that it would be "a real tourist trap."

## THE CENTRAL MOUNTAIN
These runs connect Mid-Vail with Lionshead.

- **Avanti:** Doubtless suggested by members of the famed 10th Mountain Division, whose troops fought in Italy during World War II. "Avanti" means "forward" or "let's go."
- **Bear Free:** Named for an aspen tree at the run's edge that bore the black, curved lines of bear claws, indicating a spot where a mother bear taught her cub to climb. That particular tree was accidentally cut down in the late 1970s, but sections of its trunk were rescued and placed in the Colorado Ski Museum.
- **Chicken Legs:** A section of catwalk on the lower mountain for beginning skiers leading from Mill Creek Road to Lionshead Catwalk.
- **Giants Steps:** Literally a series of giant steps increasing in steepness as they descend to the bottom of Vail Mountain.

## LIONSHEAD
The Lionshead area opened for the 1969–1970 ski season and included not only ski terrain on the front of the mountain but a new gondola and village as well. At the top of the mountain, Lionshead Ridge extends to the west, ending in a rock formation that, viewed from the town of Minturn, resembles the head of a lion. Thus, the African theme of Lionshead's runs.

- **Born Free:** Born Free commemorates the book and movie of the same name, which relates the story of Elsa, an orphan lion cub, who was raised by humans and later set free. The sharp pitch at the top of the run is named Elsa's Face.
- **Cheetah:** Africa's speedy, speckled cat and the world's fastest land animal. Also a play on the word to poke good-natured

fun at those who opt to cheat by taking the easy way around the steepest face of the Simba run.

- **Simba:** Swahili for "lion." The name was applied (for just that day) to the lion that rode the gondola on Lionshead's dedication day. The lion's real name was Frazier. (The bar at the bottom of Lionshead was once named Frazier's.) The upper portion of Simba marks the western boundary of Vail's ski terrain.

Some other interesting names for ski runs from non-Vail resorts in Colorado include:

- In **Beaver Creek's** Larkspur Bowl, many of the runs take their names, like the bowl itself, from the myriad species of wildflowers that grace the Colorado high country—Van-Gogh-painting-like—every summer. Runs in Larkspur Bowl include Bluebell, Lupine, Paintbrush, Shootingstar, and Yarrow.
- **Winter Park** has many runs named for men who played an important role in the development of this ski area. But one noteworthy run was named for a lady. Members of the Colorado Ahlberg Club began clearing the first man-made ski trail in the western part of the United States in the early 1930s. That trail now bears the name of the same lady of the night after whom the entire Mary Jane part of Winter Park was named. Mary Jane, according to legend, acquired the land upon which the Mary Jane Trail now lies as payment for her services in lieu of cash from railroad workers and miners. As part of the naming process for the trails in the Eagle Wind area (June 2007), Winter Park Resort officials worked with current leaders of the Northern Arapaho Tribe to decide on eight names belonging to historic tribe leaders, symbols, and areas. The former name of an Arapaho area, Eagle Wind, was decided upon as the name for the backside's new triple chairlift, while the seven trails were named Left Hand, Little Raven, Sharp Nose, Medicine Man, Black Coal, and Thunderbird.
- **Steamboat,** like Vail, has so many runs that serious imagination is needed to name them all creatively. Steamboat's beginners' area near Gondola Square nods it head toward the area's western history, with names like Wrangler, Desperado, Sundance, and Buckeroo. Higher on the mountain, off of the Sundance Express, are trails named with a time theme: Noon, One O'Clock, Two O'Clock, and Rolex. Rolex was thus named because of its premium location in the time-themed area. Rolex gave permission in 1985 for its name to be used. The runs off Morningside have a western-heritage breakfast theme: Frying Pan, Cowboy Coffee, and Hot Cakes. Just below Storm Peak are runs with weather-themed names: Tornado, Twister, Hurricane, and Rainbow.
- **Crested Butte** has a wide and wild array of ski-run names. Predator and Total Recall, as well as the out-of-bounds Terminator

Chutes, are all named after Arnold Schwarzenegger flicks. Dead Bob's and Body Bag were named after the late Bob Gillen, who was quoted as saying when the runs first opened, "This is so steep, ski patrol will be waiting at the bottom with a body bag." Redden's Switchback is named after Paulie Redden, who rolled a bulldozer while cutting this trail in. Sock-It-To-Me Ridge, Slot, Toilet Bowl, Rosy Lane, Cesspool, and Phaser are all named after famous rapids on rivers like the Taylor River, Westwater Canyon of the Colorado River, and the South Fork of the American River.

- In addition to several runs named after area mining claims, such as Gold Hill and Mountain Quail, **Telluride** has numerous trails named after people with local ties. Teddy's Way was named after Teddy Ebersol, the son of Dick Ebersol and Susan St. James, who died in a car accident. Andy's Gold was named after Andy Hanley, mayor of Telluride Mountain Village, who died of a heart attack at age 42 in the early 2000s. Gorrono Ranch was the original Basque name for the sheepherding ranch that once operated on Telluride Mountain. See Forever and Happy Thought need no further explanation.

- **Silverton Mountain** has a run named after the late Dolores LaChapelle, long-time Silverton resident whose groundbreaking books include *Sacred Land, Sacred Sex: Rapture of the Deep: Concerning Deep Ecology and Celebrating Life* and *Deep Powder Snow: Forty Years of Ecstatic Skiing, Avalanches and Earth Wisdom*.

## SOURCES

Media relations departments at Vail, Beaver Creek, Steamboat, Crested Butte, Telluride, and Silverton Mountain ski areas.

# COLORADO'S "LOST" SKI AREAS

By any standard, the fact that Colorado is now home to 26 operating ski areas is pretty impressive, especially when one considers the scale of those areas. Perhaps even more stunning is the fact that, depending on how one defines them—some consisted of only one rope tow, some were nothing more than a few short runs cleared through the trees, while others were only open a short time—at least 168 other "ski areas" that are now closed once operated in Colorado. These are usually referred to as Colorado's "lost" ski areas.

Here is a smattering of them:

- **Arapahoe East** stood beside Interstate 70 for two decades but only operated for about half that time. Larry Jump, founder of the area, actually made money one year but had to rely too heavily on snowmaking, which had its limits. Alternative proposals for grass skiing and an alpine slide failed to gain traction. The end came in 1984. Its one chairlift came from another lost ski area—Meadow Mountain, near Minturn.

- When **Berthoud Pass Ski Area** closed in 2001, many Colorado skiers were stunned. Considered one of the state's true extreme areas, Berthoud operated sporadically starting in 1937. With a base elevation of 11,022 feet and a vertical drop of 993 feet, Berthoud rivaled such better-known natural-snow areas as Arapahoe Basin and Wolf Creek. After not opening for business for several years, the U.S. Forest Service yanked Berthoud's Special Use Permit and demanded that both lifts—a double and a triple—be removed. A cat-skiing operation organized by SolVista Ski Area near Granby, which owned Berthoud during its last few years of operation, failed to generate enough cash to keep the area afloat.

- **Conquistador's** development began in 1974, but it wasn't until 1977 that this area, located outside Westcliffe on the east side of the Sangre de Cristo Range, actually opened. Two pony lifts with a scant 85-foot drop served for five years. Two chairlifts were added in 1982 in a major expansion, accompanied by a major default on loans. The federal Small Business Administration lost millions running Conquistador for six years before finally pulling the plug. A planned re-opening as Mountain Cliffe failed in 1992–1993.

- **Evergreen Basin,** between Evergreen and Conifer, consisted of little more than high hopes and good publicity. It made a big splash when it was announced in 1965. Two chairlifts were supposed to be ready by that winter. A lodge was supposed to be built within 90 days, kicking off a development that would have been larger than Winter Park. A few trails were cleared before development stopped entirely. Denver's South High School ski team did train there one winter, drawn uphill by a team of horses.

- **Fun Valley,** near Phillipsburg, was first developed in 1938 as Watson's Ski Hill, with a homemade sled tow that could haul 15 skiers, if they were all standing. Revived in the mid-1960s, it limped along until 1977 by adding an old single chairlift that was procured from Arapahoe Basin, night-lights, and background music. It never overcame its lack of snow, though.

- **Genesee Mountain,** just off of Interstate 70 near the Evergreen exit, was a centerpiece of the national ski-jumping circuit, hosting the 1921 and 1927 National Jumping Championships. The hill had a 700-foot drop and four jumps. Snow, however, was undependable; even so, events continued until the mid-1930s. The University of Denver ski team used the site briefly in the mid-1950s.

- **Geneva Basin,** near Guanella Pass, opened as Indianhead Mountain in 1962, with challenging terrain and often-frigid temperatures. Former Colorado Governor Roy Romer owned the area in the early 1970s. Equipment woes mounted, and, when one empty chair fell from a lift in 1984, that was pretty much the end of the road. An attempt to revive the area as Alpenbach failed in 1986.
- **Magic Mountain,** located beside Heritage Square near Golden, is a lost ski area that is literally gone. The slope, 1,100 feet long and 150 feet high, has been obliterated by a gravel quarry. In 1958–1959, Magic Mountain was the first ski area in Colorado to offer snowmaking. Its first successful season was never repeated. Bankruptcy of an associated amusement park left the entire site padlocked. The snowmaking equipment eventually found a home at Ski Broadmoor in Colorado Springs.
- **Marble** ran a mile-long chairlift from 1971–1974, but that was supposedly only going to be the beginning. A vast development was planned, but opposition mounted. A million-dollar lodge was half completed when spring mudslides demonstrated the geological power of the area. The U.S. Forest Service refused an expansion scheme, and the operation soon went bankrupt.
- **Montezuma Basin,** outside Aspen, had no competition but still managed to have little success. It was open only in late summer when the jeep road to the snowfield beneath Castle Peak, at 13,000 feet, was passable. A portable rope tow operated from August to October 1967, 1968, and 1969. The area was popular with racers in training, but it never found its economic footing.
- **Old Man Mountain's** jumping events, begun in 1931, often had to rely upon snow hauled up the slope in an old ore cart. So, went the thinking, why not hold an event in August, when nearby Estes Park was already full of tourists? In 1951 and 1952, the Estes Park Ski Club had 55 tons of crushed ice delivered and spread on the slopes to make what veteran jumper George Peck called "a great surface, better than snow."
- **Pikes Peak Ski Area** went bust in 1984, its brand-new chairlift being repossessed by its manufacturer. Beginning in 1954, the 500-foot-high slope at Elk Park had claimed skiers who formerly used Glen Cove, a small area a mile uphill that went out of business in the late1940s (and which boasted the state's first "rope escalator," added in 1936). Pikes Peak had two Pomas and a rope tow that serviced three slopes until funding for a major expansion foundered.
- **Pioneer Mountain,** near Crested Butte, opened in late 1939 with Colorado's first chairlift, built from a converted mine tram by local ski club volunteers and workers from the Works Progress Administration (WPA). Initially, nervous U.S. Forest Service officials

demanded that the seats be no more than three feet off the ground. But they later relented. The main Big Dipper Trail, with slopes of 53 degrees, proved a bigger challenge. The area lasted until 1953.

- **Red Mountain's** slopes, in Glenwood Springs, served by one of the nation's longest chairlifts, were considered among the West's best in 1940. But the lift was plagued by defects and failures. The area boomed in the late 1950s, with a new lift rising 1,750 feet. Money woes brought closure in 1959. A higher portion of the same slope operated as the Glenwood Mountain Park, another lost ski area, in 1965–1966.

- **Sharktooth** was the state's most unlikely ski area. This stray hill above the Poudre River near Greeley provided almost 200 vertical feet of what can charitably be described as "plains skiing." It opened in 1971 with one surface lift and operated night and day through 1986. Some of the usual ski-area costs were negligible at Sharktooth, such as avalanche control and ski patrol, but the operator had to plant 1,000 trees in an attempt to block dust blowing in from neighboring ranches.

- **Ski Broadmoor** never matched the permanence or luxury of its namesake Colorado Springs hotel. Begun in 1959 with a 600-foot drop, Ski Broadmoor specialized in night skiing and ski instruction. Colorado Springs took it over in 1986 for one successful season, then suffered through 400-percent cost overruns stemming from renovations in 1987. Vail ran it for two years, then abandoned the aging, balky lift and the too-often-icy trails. The creators of this lost ski area, which can still be seen, included Steve Knowlton, the founder of Colorado Ski Country USA.

- **Ski Sugarite,** otherwise known as Raton Ski Basin, was somewhat elusive. Its slogan, "New Mexico's Only Colorado Ski Area," was part of the image problem. Where was it exactly? Not on the west-facing slopes above Raton Pass, where remnants of a summer-only chairlift can still be seen. Instead, it was 12 miles northeast of Raton, New Mexico, literally feet from the Colorado state line. It ran from 1965 to 1989.

- **Stagecoach,** near Oak Creek, was one of the largest in Colorado ever to go out of business, leaving three chairlifts dangling empty. It opened in 1972 and ran for two seasons. Controversy plagued the development, the plans of which reportedly included condos but not a base lodge for skiers.

## SOURCES

"Colorado's Lost Resorts" map, published in 1999 by Colorado Ski Country USA. This map, which is still for sale at the Colorado Ski Museum in Vail, is an absolute must-have for any true Colorado-phile.

▲

## THE YEARS IN WHICH COLORADO'S
## CURRENT SKI RESORTS OPENED
## FOR BUSINESS

- Arapahoe Basin: 1946
- Aspen Highlands: 1957
- Aspen Mountain: 1946
- Beaver Creek: 1980
- Breckenridge: 1961
- Buttermilk: 1958
- Copper Mountain: 1972
- Crested Butte: 1961
- Durango Mountain Resort
  (Purgatory): 1965
- Echo Mountain: 2006
- Eldora: 1962
- Howelsen Hill: 1915/1974
- Keystone: 1970
- Loveland: 1937
- Monarch: 1939
- Powderhorn: 1966
- Silverton Mountain: 2002
- Ski Cooper: 1942
- Snowmass: 1967
- Steamboat: 1963
- Sunlight: 1966
- Telluride: 1972
- Vail: 1962
- Winter Park: 1940
- Wolf Creek: 1955

SOURCE

Colorado Ski Country USA.

▲

## PROPOSED COLORADO SKI AREAS THAT
## NEVER GOT OFF THE GROUND

- Adam's Rib (Vail)
- Battle Mountain (Vail)
- Catamount (Steamboat)
- Crystal Peak (Colorado Springs)
- East Fork (Pagosa Springs)
- Evergreen Basin (Evergreen)
- Little Annie (Aspen)
- Mount Vernon (Genesee)
- Paradise Valley (Estes Park)
- Putney Gulch/Sentinel Point (Colorado Springs)
- Shadow Mountain (Grand County)
- Wolf Creek Valley (Wolf Creek)
- Quail Mountain (Twin Lakes)

SOURCE

Colorado Ski Museum.

# THE COLORADO SKI SAFETY ACT

First passed in 1979, the Colorado Ski Safety Act has become a mainstay concept for anyone venturing onto the slopes. The act was ostensibly passed to ensure safe on-slope conduct on the part of skiers (and, later, snowboarders), but subsequent judicial and legislative interpretation of the act has also shown that part of its intent was to protect the economic bread and butter of mountain country from civil lawsuits. While the act does not absolve the ski areas from liability resulting from ski or snowboard accidents, it does shift much of the onus of responsibility for mishaps onto the consumers.

The original act stipulated fines as high as $300 per person per incident for violations. In 2006, the maximum fine for violating the act was raised to $1,000 per person per incident.

The impetus for the increase of the penalty came about in 2005, when Summit County Sheriff John Minor began pursuing a change in the law after the Summit Rescue Group helped find an Erie snowboarder who spent three nights in Jones Gulch after illegally leaving Keystone's boundary.

Minor approached Colorado Ski Country USA and local ski resort officials to begin a discussion about establishing a stiffer penalty for breaking the rules of the act.

"We came to the conclusion that we've done all the education we can do, and we're going to continue with education, but the deterrence factor needs to be ramped up a little bit," Minor said in February 2006.

The bill was sponsored by then-representative Gary Lindstrom, D-Breckenridge, who spent 20 years with the Summit County Sheriff's Office.

The wording of the Colorado Ski Safety Act has remained consistent since 1979. Highlights include:

- Do not board a lift unless you feel confident that you have sufficient physical dexterity, ability, and knowledge to use the lift safely. Please follow the instructions of the lift operators.
- Do not throw or expel an object from a lift while you are riding on the lift.
- Your skis must be equipped with a strap or other device capable of stopping your skis if they become unattached while skiing.
- Each skier solely has the responsibility for knowing the range of his or her own ability to negotiate any ski slope or trail and to ski within the limits of such ability.
- It is your responsibility to maintain control of your speed and course at all times and to maintain a proper lookout so as to be

able to avoid objects and other skiers. Careless and reckless skiers will have their skiing privileges revoked.

- It is unlawful for you to ride a lift or use any ski slope or trail when your ability to do so is impaired by the consumption of alcohol or any drug.
- If you are involved in a collision with another skier that results in injury, it is unlawful for you to leave the vicinity of the collision before you have left your name and current address with a member of the ski patrol.
- It is unlawful for you to ski on any slope, land, or trail that has been posted "closed." Closed trails and slopes will be marked. Roped-off areas also designate that area as being closed.
- It is your obligation and responsibility to heed all posted information and other warnings, and to refrain from acting in a manner which may cause or contribute to your injury or the injury of any other skier or person. Please read and heed all posted information and warnings.

The wording and concept of the Colorado Ski Safety Act was based partially on "Your Responsibility Code," which the National Ski Areas Association (NSAA) established in 1966 as a code of ethics for all skiers on the mountain. Today, the code reflects not only skier safety, but snowboarder and lift safety as well. The NSAA "Your Responsibility Code" reads:

- Safety on the slopes is everyone's responsibility. Ski safely—not only for yourself, but for others as well.
- Always stay in control and be able to stop or avoid objects.
- People ahead of you have the right-of-way. It is your responsibility to avoid them.
- Do not stop where you obstruct the trail or are not visible from above.
- Whenever starting downhill or merging into a trail, yield to others.
- Always use devices to help prevent runaway equipment.
- Observe all posted signs and warnings.
- Keep off of closed trails and out of closed areas.
- Prior to using any lift, you must know how to load, ride, and unload safely.

The number of cases charged and convicted of violating the Colorado Ski Safety Act, 1989–2008, by county, with the ski area(s) within those counties, are as follows:

- Boulder (Eldora): 19 citations issued, 9 convictions
- Clear Creek (Loveland): 27 citations issued, 21 convictions
- Eagle (Vail, Beaver Creek, and Arrowhead): 40 citations issued, 13 convictions

- Garfield (Ski Sunlight): 13 citations issued, 7 convictions
- Grand (Winter Park and SolVista): 42 citations issued, 39 convictions
- Gunnison (Crested Butte): 196 citations issued, 145 convictions
- La Plata (Durango Mountain Resort/Purgatory): 5 citations issued, 1 conviction
- Mineral (Wolf Creek): 23 citations issued, 15 convictions
- Pitkin (Aspen Mountain, Buttermilk, Snowmass, and Aspen Highlands): 55 citations issued, 36 convictions
- Routt: (Steamboat and Howelsen Hill): 41 citations issued, 25 convictions
- San Juan (Silverton Mountain): 11 citations issued, 8 convictions
- San Miguel (Telluride): 62 citations issued, 26 convictions
- Summit (Arapahoe Basin, Breckenridge, Copper Mountain, and Keystone): 561 citations issued, 270 convictions

## SOURCES

www.yampavalleyinfo.com; National Ski Areas Association; Planning and Analysis Department of the Colorado State Court Administrator's Office; *Summit Daily News*.

# WORDS FOR SNOW—ESKIMO AND COLORADO

To armchair linguists, especially those who spend significant time in places dominated by snow (read: residents of the Colorado high country), it is one of the most endearing commonly held beliefs: Despite the fact that the exact number changes from telling to telling, the "Eskimos," as we all "know," have "X" number of words for "snow." Well, whatever number of words the Eskimos supposedly have for snow (50, 100, sometimes even 400) is at best an exaggeration and, at worst, according to many frost-covered linguists, a flat-out urban myth.[1] And, truth be told, depending on certain linguistic criteria, English speakers likely have at least as many words for "snow" as the Eskimos.

First things first. It is important to note that linguists have studied many Arctic-dwelling Native American languages. As Geoffrey K. Pullum notes in his book *The Great Eskimo Vocabulary Hoax* (University of Chicago Press, 1991), "There is no single language 'Eskimo,' just as there is no single language 'Indian.' And, like 'Indian,' 'Eskimo' is not a very good name: it lumps together two major cultural groups, the Inuit and Aleut, and ignores major differences (including huge language variation) within each group."

This is no small concern when one is tallying up the number of Eskimo (we'll go with that name as a generic) words for snow. If you have two major cultural groups, both of which have "huge language variation" (as well as, one would guess, much in the way of regional variation within those two major language groups), do you count the words for "snow" that group A has, *in addition* to the words group B has, or do you focus solely on one group, while ignoring the words for "snow" used by the other group?

To wit: You have an Eskimo sitting in his igloo, telling his shivering children, "Down south, the people have many words for 'path.'" Does that Eskimo count the English "path" and the Spanish "sendero" as two separate words? From the Eskimo perspective, there might be very little in the way of cultural and linguistic difference between John the English speaker in Leadville, Colorado, and José the Spanish speaker in Palomas, Chihuahua. Therefore, it would seem perfectly reasonable for the Eskimo to lump all of "our" words into one vocabulary when he's telling his son how many words the warm-country people have for "path."

There is further complication. You have to decide, before you start tallying up the Eskimo words for "snow," exactly what you mean by the word "word."

Steven J. Derose, in his 1999 essay (revised 2005) *Eskimo Words For Snow*, writes, "Just deciding what we mean by 'word' is subtle. How do we count 'go,' 'goes,' and 'went?' How do we count 'dog' as in 'woof woof' versus 'dog' as in 'to follow someone?' What of 'snow' meaning 'to confuse?' How do we count compound words? How do we count 'love' versus 'lovesong,' 'lovebird,' 'lovesick,' and many others? When does a common phrase or idiom become a word?"

Derose continues, "Inuit and Aleut," are agglutinative languages: they tend to assemble large words out of many parts. English is more likely to use multiple 'words' instead: 'new-fallen snow.' This pattern has nothing to do with snow; it's just part of how English, Inuit, and Aleut differ in general."

In other words, by anyone's definition, comparing the number of Eskimo words for "snow" to the number of English words for "snow" is, on numerous levels, like trying to compare linguistic apples and oranges.

Anthony Woodbury, of the University of Texas at Austin, wrote *Counting Eskimo Words for Snow: A Citizens' Guide* in 1991. In the introduction, he examines only one Eskimo language, Central Alaskan Yupik, which is spoken by about 13,000 people from Norton Sound to Bristol Bay.

Woodbury stresses a very important point before jumping head-long into the icy waters of actual snow-word counting. He writes, "This is a list of lexemes rather than words. Roughly, a lexeme can be thought of as an independent vocabulary item or dictionary entry. It's different from a word, since a lexeme can give rise to more than one distinctly inflected word. Thus, English has a single lexeme, 'speak,' which gives rise to inflected forms like 'speaks,' 'spoke,' and 'spoken.' It's especially important to count lexemes rather than words when talking about Eskimo languages. That's because they are inflectionally so complicated that each single noun lexeme may have about 280 distinct inflected forms, while each verb lexeme may have over 1,000! Obviously, that would put the number of snow words through the roof very quickly."

Woodbury counts fifteen different Eskimo lexeme snow meanings, which he places into four distinct categories:

- "Snow particles," which contains the Central Alaskan Yupik lexemes for "snowflake," "frost," "fine snow-rain particles," and "drifting particles."
- "Fallen snow," which includes the lexemes for "fallen snow on the ground," "deep fallen snow on the ground," "crust on fallen snow," "fresh fallen snow on the ground," and "falling snow floating on water."
- "Snow formations," which include "snowbank," "snow block," and "snow cornice."
- "Meteorological events," which include "blizzard/snowstorm" and "severe blizzard."

In 1990, Ken Muldrew, of the University of Calgary, penned a paper, "A Lexicon of Snow," in which he lists 32 Inuit snow lexemes[2], although he does not indicate, as did Woodbury before him, whether these lexemes come from one language or whether he has amalgamated lexemes from various languages and/or dialects.

Derose, who argues that the number of defendable Inuit words for snow hovers somewhere between two and 24, says, when applying the same criteria to English as to Inuit in this context, "Purveyors of the [Eskimo snow word] myth seem bound to include as many faintly snow-related phenomena as possible when deciding which Eskimo words to count, but to require perfect synonymy to 'snow' when deciding about English (this leaving us but one 'word for snow').

"One example of this conveniently inconsistent definition is from a list of 20 ostensibly Eskimo snow-words that came to Pullum: igluqsaq. This is a compound word meaning 'house-building material.' It can mean plywood or brick as well as snow. If we pulled the same trick with English, we could start counting words like 'etiology' (a slip on snow can cause injury), 'projectile' (you can throw snowballs), 'food' (you can eat snow as long as it's white), and so on. Hmmm."

Derose goes on to list what he calls "a veritable hail of terms" for "snow" in English: berg, cornice, crevasse, floe, frost, glacier, hail, hardpack, hoarfrost, powder, rime, slush, sleet, avalanche, blizzard, dusting, flurry, and, yes, finally, snow. (Derose points out that he intentionally skips inflected forms of snow, such as snows, snowed, snowing, and snowy, underscoring the difference between a "word" and a "lexeme.")

He adds to his list additional compound words, such as snowball, snowbank, snowcap, snowdrift, snowflake, snowman, and snowstorm, as well as snow-related objects, such as snowboards, snow skis, and snow shovels.

Then he further adds "phrases that have become lexical items through frequent and distinctive use: freezing rain, new-fallen snow, yellow snow, glare ice, purple wax snow, and a host of others skiers can cite. If we were as generous as some are for Eskimo, beyond those, we'd add etiology, construction material, food, weapon, toy, floor, projectile, sculpture, refrigerator, obstruction, and probably dozens more, reaching double the total for Inuit. And we haven't even considered any synonyms for 'snow job' (a quick look in a thesaurus reveals over 100), 'snow' on your TV, and being 'snowed' under."

## NOTES

1. According to Boulder-based freelance medical writer David Mendosa (www.mendosa.com/snow.html), what he calls "The Great Inuit Vocabulary Hoax" apparently started in 1911 when anthropologist Franz Boaz casually mentioned that the Inuit...had four different words for snow. With each succeeding reference in textbooks and the popular press, the number grew to sometimes as many as 400 words, according to Mendosa.

2. Muldrew has put together a list of 120 "English snow and ice lexemes," 60 of which are more snow than ice.

## SOURCES

*Inuit Words for Snow* by David Mendosa; *Eskimo Words for Snow* by Steven J. Derose; *Counting Eskimo Words for Snow* by Anthony C. Woodbury; "A Lexicon of Snow" by Ken Muldrew.

There is a saying among more geo-culturally chauvinistic Coloradans that, if God had meant for Texans to ski, He would have
given them mountains and snow. Well, He did—at least while the
Republic of Texas existed from 1836 to 1845.

The Adams–Onis Treaty of 1819 settled a border dispute between the United States and Spain caused by ambiguities resulting
from the 1803 Louisiana Purchase. In addition to ceding Florida
to the United States, the treaty firmly established the boundary for
U.S. territorial claims through the Rocky Mountains and west to
the Pacific Ocean in exchange for the United States relinquishing
claims on parts of Texas west of the Sabine River and other Spanish
areas under the terms of the Louisiana Purchase.

When Texas declared independence from Mexico in 1836, its
northern boundaries adhered to the terms of the Adams–Onis
Treaty, which meant that a large swath of what is now Colorado
became part of the short-lived Republic of Texas.

The part of what is now Colorado that was part of the Republic
of Texas is basically the Rio Grande from the New Mexico border
upriver to its headwaters near Creede, then north to what is now
the Wyoming border, then east along the Wyoming border to a
point due north of Leadville, then south to the headwaters of the
Arkansas River, very near Leadville, then downriver along the Arkansas to the eastern border of Colorado.

That means the unthinkable: Crested Butte, Aspen Mountain,
Aspen Highlands, Snowmass, Buttermilk, Sunlight Mountain, Vail,
Beaver Creek, Monarch, Ski Cooper, Steamboat, Howelsen Hill, and
Cuchara ski areas are located in what used to be Texas! Yee-haw!

Fortunately for Colorado's self-esteem, when Texas applied for
admission to the United States as the country's twenty-eighth state
in 1845, it wanted to do so as a slave state. But the Compromise of
1820 forbade slavery north of 36 degrees, 30 minutes north latitude. So, Texas had a choice: enter the Union as a non-slave state
or lop off a significant chunk of the northern part of its territory. It
chose the latter, relinquishing all of its land north of 36-30 to the
U.S. government.

SOURCE

"How the States Got Their Shapes" by Mark Stein.

# MOUNTAINSPEAK:
# CROSS-COUNTRY SKIING LEXICON

- **Angulation:** Arcing the body at the hip, knee, and ankle joints to achieve a higher degree of ski edge.
- **Biathlon:** Competition that combines cross-country skiing with, of all things, target shooting, usually with a rifle. Most Americans forget this sport even exists, until the Winter Olympics, when we all get to watch biathletes from Europe, where apparently biathlon is Big, sweep the medals yet again.
- **Brown Klister:** Euphemism for doggie deposits that have been made right in the middle of the ski tracks. Sometimes, these deposits are covered by new snow—meaning they can't be seen before the skier makes contact—then, the next day, they warm up, thaw out, and result in a one's skis having a particularly unsavory form of "wax" being inadvertently applied to the bottom of them. (*See also* "Klister" and "Waxing.")
- **Christy Turn:** A skiing turn with a skidding phase.
- **Classic Technique (a.k.a. "Diagonal Stride," "Kick and Glide," "Track Skiing"):** When a cross-country skier is moving straight ahead instead of skating, often with the skis inside groomed tracks. Until the advent of skating (also called "skate-skiing"), this is the propulsion technique that everyone on earth thought of when they thought of "cross-country" or "Nordic" skiing. When you see cross-country skiers competing in the Olympics these days, almost all of them are utilizing skating technique. (*See* "Skating.")
- **Cross-Country Skiing (a.k.a. "Nordic Skiing"):** Back in days of yore, this was a simple enough term that described all forms of skiing that were not alpine-style, downhill skiing. Basically, until fairly recently, if you were a skier, you had your downhill skis and your "skinny skis," which were cross-country skis used for everything from kicking and gliding in groomed tracks to making your way through the deepest backcountry. These days, "cross-country" and "Nordic" skiing are, to the non-initiated, catchall terms that include classic technique, skating, ski touring, telemarking and biathlon. Most often, though, "cross-country" and "Nordic" are used to mean skiing that takes place on machine-groomed surfaces—tracks for classic skiers and compacted snow for skaters. (*See* "Grooming.") Cross-country skiing is a highly aerobic activity considered by many to be the single best form of exercise in the world.

- **Double-Poling:** Using both poles at the same time to thrust the body forward as opposed to the alternating, diagonal-stride poling method.
- **Edges:** Metal strips on the outside of skis that people who ought to know better always expect to have on their skinny skis (*see* "Skinny Skis") when they try cross-country skiing, especially when they are frantically trying to turn. This expectation often amounts to a real-life lesson in making assumptions, as most skinny skis do not, in fact, boast metal edges.
- **Fish Scales:** The fundamental technology that allows for waxless skiing. Fish scales are irregularities machined into the bottoms of cross-country skis that allow easy forward progress while simultaneously inhibiting sliding backwards. Adherents of waxless skis consider fish scales to be among the greatest innovations in the history of outdoor recreation, while traditionalists consider them yet another example of the outdoor world gone to hell in a handbasket.
- **Flask:** Essential piece of cross-country ski gear back when people still wore wool. Has lost cachet in recent years, as more and more cross-country skiers have come to think of themselves as "outdoor athletes" rather than as "outdoor recreationists."
- **Grooming:** Lets you glide on top of a solid, consistent base that's been prepared by snowcats or snowmobiles pulling special attachments. Groomed trails are used by both classic skiers and skaters.
- **Hard Wax:** Wax used to negotiate newer, fine-grained, and colder snow.
- **Herringbone:** Moving forward on cross-country skis in a stepping mode with the ski tips farther apart than the tails, forming a herringbone pattern in the snow. Most often used on steep uphills.
- **Inclination:** (1) Leaning of the body in the direction of the turn to engage ski edges and resist centrifugal forces from the turn. (2) A desire to cut the ski day short in order to hit happy hour.
- **Kick Turn:** A way of turning to the opposite direction of travel by kicking one ski outward to as much as 180 degrees, followed by the other ski (hopefully). Not recommended for those who recently had hip-replacement surgery (or who need to).
- **Kilometers:** How cross-country ski trail lengths are measured, even if those measurements take place in rural Utah. A kilometer (km or k) is a little more than half a mile. Skiers get more of a kick out of saying, "Hey, I skied 10 kilometers today!" than, "Well, I skied about six miles."
- **Klister:** A type of wax designed primarily for older, coarser, and warmer snow. Klister comes in a squeeze tube and is rather nasty stuff because it is very sticky and, no matter how hard one tries,

it gets on everything—hands, clothes, car, lunch, dog. A standard bromide for determining whether to use klister or hard wax (see "Hard Wax") is, "If there's snow in the trees, leave the klister be." Many people would argue that you ought to just use waxless skis. (*See* "Fish Scales.")

- **Knickers:** Fashion statement that once dominated cross-country ski trails. Consists of pants that looked far more at home on the lower bodies of Munchkins than on skiers. Mostly made of wool. Rarely seen nowadays, as they have been replaced by equally hideous Lycra and Spandex garments. No one ever said that cross-country skiers set any high marks for fashion standards.
- **Parallel Skiing:** Skiing with the skis, well, parallel. Skis can be either together or apart.
- **Parking Lot Plant:** The extremely embarrassing act of taking a hard fall between the time you attach your skis in the parking lot and the time you actually start skiing. Buttocks are often the recipient of these mishaps, which, given the fact that many parking lots are paved, can be stunningly impactful.
- **Side Step:** Moving laterally in small steps on cross-country skis. Usually used as a form of ascent.
- **Skating:** A relatively new cross-country ski technique involving an ice-skating-like motion of arms and legs, thrusting out to the side. It's dynamic and uses a lot of energy.
- **Ski Joring:** Being pulled while skiing by a dog, horse, reindeer, snowcat, snowmobile, or VW Bug. Many mountain-town winter carnivals offer ski-joring events, which often boast much in the way of good-natured carnage.
- **Skinny Skis:** Once referred to all types of cross-country skis. Now used mainly to refer to skis that are designed for use at groomed Nordic areas.
- **Ski Touring:** Skiing on ungroomed snow, whether it's playing in your backyard or doing daylong treks in the mountains.
- **Snowshoes:** Extremely practical modes of traveling on snow that, in the past 20 years, have cut significantly into the sales of all forms of cross-country ski gear, at least partially because very little skiing ability is necessary to navigate and propel snowshoes. Often, snowshoers and cross-country skiers find themselves at odds because snowshoes obliterate ski tracks. Many areas are now asking snowshoers to travel on one side of the trail and skiers on the other.
- **Straight Run:** Traveling straight down a hill with the skis parallel and the body on the skis in balance.
- **Telemarking:** The earliest known form of skiing. Originating in the Telemark region of Norway at least 4,000 years ago, telemark-

ing is an elegant and practical descent and turning technique often favored by hippie vegetarians who drive older Subarus.

- **Track Skiing:** For classic skiers (*see* "Classic Technique"), this means skiing in machine-compressed grooves that guide your skis, with snow compacted on both sides of the track for planting your poles.
- **Traverse:** Method of going up hills where the skier zigzags up the side of the mountain.
- **Waxing:** Applying a coating to the bottom of the skis to reduce friction.
- **Wedge Turn (a.k.a. the "Snowplow Turn"):** An elementary turn with the skis in a wedge position where the tips of the skis are closer than the tails. Often accompanied by desperate-looking facial expressions.

## SOURCES

Jonathan Wiesel, author of *Cross Country Ski Getaways: A Guide to Great Resorts, Lodges, and Groomed Trails in North America;* J.D. Downing, National Director/Editor, American Cross Country Skiers.

# MOUNTAINSPEAK: SNOWBOARDING LEXICON

- **Air:** Any time the snowboard leaves the snow. Examples: credit-card air or ozone air, or a type of grab during air. (Grabs named by riders who were hungry at the time: Canadian bacon, roast beef, stale fish, eggplant, chicken salad, Swiss cheese.)
- **Betty:** A hottie female rider.
- **Bone:** To stylize a trick to the max (a.k.a. tweak).
- **Bone Out:** To straighten out the legs during a grab or trick to "a stiffy."
- **Bullet-proof:** Very icy snow conditions.
- **Bust:** To do, but in a more enthusiastic manner. "I busted a Five on that kicker!"
- **Cockroach:** To borrow without any intention of returning it. "Who cockroached my Red Bull?"
- **Dope:** The best, the coolest; or it could mean marijuana. "That dope was really *dope!*"
- **Duct Tape:** A ski bum's sewing machine. "If you can't duct it, f*** it!"
- **Fakie (or Switch Stance):** Riding with the back foot in front (backwards to a rider's normal stance).

- **Fall Line:** The path that a beginner snowboarder will take before learning to turn and stop.
- **Five:** A 540-degree rotation during air (a "three" is a 360; a "seven" is a 720).
- **Flyswatter:** The kind of fall caused by catching a downhill edge (a.k.a. slam).
- **Fruitbooters:** People who use shortie skis.
- **Gap:** A space between two jumps or features. Also: a new space between teeth that is created when a rider or skier misses a gap jump.
- **Gays on Trays:** One of the many derogative terms skiers call snowboarders.
- **Ghetto:** Lower class, lame. "The base lodge is kind of ghetto, but at least they have Dillon Dam Brewery beer on tap in the bar!"
- **Goofy:** Riding stance with the right foot in front.
- **Hammer:** To ride as hard as possible.
- **Hammered:** Drunk. (It is not advisable to hammer a steep run when you're hammered.)
- **Huck:** To go for huge air without any concern for the consequences of gravity.
- **Huckfest:** A peer-driven session of big air.
- **Inchworming:** Traveling up a slope with the board attached.
- **Lawnchair Air:** Huge air followed by a total collapse of the body.
- **Leash:** A useless cord invented by skiers that is supposed to keep a rider attached to his board should he or she crash so hard that the bindings rip off.
- **Ollie:** A verb or noun that means to jump over something when there is no takeoff/jump by springloading the tail of the board and pulling the knees up. A Nollie is the same thing but using the nose of the board to spring from.
- **Park Rats:** People who hang out exclusively in terrain parks (a.k.a. rail monkeys).
- **Rail:** A handrail that is used as a park feature that a rider or skier slides down as a trick; or to make hard-carving turns at mach speed.
- **Ride, to:** To snowboard. Can also refer to a vehicle, but only if it runs.
- **Session:** A period of time devoted to certain jumps or rails.
- **Shred, to:** To snowboard.
- **Shreddin' the Gnar-Gnar:** Carving up particularly difficult terrain.
- **Slope Nazis:** Guys who secretly wanted to be cops all of their lives but decided to be slope speed enforcers instead (a.k.a. snow pigs).
- **Spinal Tap:** A fall that ends up with a rider's entire back hitting the ground at once, followed by whiplash and, often, colorful language.

- **Steez:** Really cheesy style. "He really showed some steez during that rail sesh."
- **Vultures:** The crowds that gather at dangerous spots in a course or park.

## SOURCES

Cindy Kleh, author of *Snowboarding Skills: The Back-to-Basics Essentials for All Levels*, national age-group boardercross champion and a serious Betty.

# MOST COMMON MOUNTAIN RECREATIONAL INJURIES

In a part of the country defined by outdoor recreation, it comes as no surprise that many people suffer injuries while skiing, snowboarding, and bike riding. Here are some injury breakdowns.

- A significant percentage of all ski injuries serious enough to require the intervention of an orthopaedist are centered on the knee. About 30 percent of all knee injuries caused by skiing accidents involve trauma specifically to the anterior cruciate ligament—the dreaded ACL.
- Upper-extremity injuries account for about 45 percent of all snowboarding injuries serious enough to require the intervention of an orthopaedist. About 23 percent of all snowboarding injuries serious enough to involve the intervention of an orthopaedist are to the wrist, with another 16 percent being fractures of the distal radius (forearm). Twenty-eight percent of all injuries to beginning snowboarders are distal radius fractures, and a beginner female is at the highest risk. About a third of all upper-extremity snowboarding injuries are to the shoulders and clavicles. Ankle injuries in snowboarders are more inclined to suffer talus fractures to the front/outside portion of the ankle.
- More than half of all mountain-biking injuries serious enough to require the intervention of an orthopaedist take the form of concussions and clavicle and shoulder injuries, mostly to the rotator cuff, caused by riders going over the handlebars.

## SOURCE

Dr. Peter Janes, a 22-year orthopaedist working for the famed Vail–Summit Orthopedics.

# HIGH COUNTRY EMERGENCY ROOM ADMISSION STATISTICS

In 2008, 1,578 people arrived in the emergency room of the Aspen Valley Hospital via ambulance. Of those:

- 544 were involved in "some sort" of "recreational-type" activity, the majority of which were of the skiing/snowboarding variety.
- 82 were involved in motor-vehicle accidents.
- 81 were involved in domestic accidents, which can include falling off of a ladder or cutting oneself with a kitchen knife.
- 49 were involved in some sort of industrial/workplace accident.
- 41 were involved in bicycling accidents.
- 2 were hit by lightning.
- 2 were involved in accidents involving animal-drawn vehicles.
- 1 was suffering from a hornet, wasp, or bee sting.
- 1 was involved in a parachuting accident.

In 2009, the Aspen Valley Hospital had a total of 7,361 visits to its emergency room, 857 of which arrived by ambulance. The top five emergency room diagnoses in 2009 were upper respiratory infections, abdominal pain, vomiting, fever, and contusion on the face/scalp. The more unusual diagnoses were one case of Super Glue in the eye, one case of a bicyclist/coyote collision, and one person bitten by a fox.

In 2008, 970 people were admitted to the emergency room of the Kremmling Memorial Hospital District (which has a satellite facility in Granby). Of those:

- 70 were admitted for lacerations.
- 51 were admitted as a result of motor-vehicle accidents, not involving motorcycles, snowmobiles, or all-terrain vehicles (ATVs).
- 36 were admitted because of falls.
- 10 were involved in motorcycle accidents.
- 9 had received some sort of insect bite.
- 9 were involved in ATV mishaps.
- 8 were admitted because of negative fishhook interactions.
- 8 had a hand impaled.
- 3 were involved in horse accidents.
- 2 were involved in snowmobile accidents.
- 0 people were admitted as a result of frostbite or hypothermia.

In 2009, there were 1,091 total admissions to the emergency room at the Kremmling Memorial Hospital. Of those:
- 98 were admitted for abdominal pain.

- 91 were admitted for injuries to the extremities.
- 86 were pediatric injuries.
- 53 were for chest pain/cardiac issues.
- 48 were from injuries sustained in car accidents.
- 33 were for injuries sustained during falls.
- 16 were for bicycle or ATV accidents.
- 10 were for injuries sustained from negative horse-related interactions.
- 7 were from burns.
- 7 were from insect bites/stings.
- 4 were from snowmobiling-related injuries.

October was the busiest month in 2009 for in the Kremmling emergency room, with 121 admissions, followed by July (108 admissions) and September (98 admissions).

From December 2007 through December 2008, 2,248 people were treated in the emergency room of St. Anthony Summit Medical Center in Frisco. Of those:

- 743 were involved in some sort of skiing accident.
- 620 were involved in some sort of snowboarding accident.
- 295 were involved in some sort of "fall"—which can include everything from slipping on ice to falling off of a ladder or falling while climbing.
- 174 were involved in some sort of vehicular accident.
- 125 were involved in some sort of biking accident.

SOURCES:

Public information offices, Aspen Valley Hospital, Kremmling Memorial Hospital District, and St. Anthony Summit Medical Center.

# COLORADO MOUNTAIN PATHOGENS

In a world where dengue fever, cholera, malaria, and ebola are found, Colorado is pretty chilled on the funky pathogen front. But, even in Mountain Country, some nasty little bugs occasionally make their way into the here-and-now of people otherwise going about their vertical business. It should be stressed, though, that just because someone was diagnosed with a certain disease in a certain mountain county does not mean the malady was contracted in that place. It could have been brought in by an infected tourist, or it could have been contracted elsewhere and brought back home, like a microscopic souvenir.

The listings here include the disease, followed by the mountain counties where people were diagnosed in 2008 and 2009 with that disease and the number of cases of that disease diagnosed in that county.

## DISEASES, COUNTIES, CASES DIAGNOSED: 2008

- **Giardia:** Boulder, 62; Chaffee: 3; Clear Creek, 2; Conejos, 1; Eagle, 4; Fremont, 1; Garfield, 4; Grand, 2; Jefferson, 35; La Plata, 2; Mesa, 12; Montezuma, 4; Montrose, 4; Ouray, 1; Pitkin, 3; Rio Blanco, 4; Rio Grande, 1; Routt, 11; Saguache, 1; San Miguel, 1; Summit, 8; Teller, 1. **Total cases in Colorado: 562.**
- **Hantavirus:** Delta, 1; Dolores, 1; Fremont, 1. **Total cases in Colorado: 6.** *Note:* There were a total of 67 hantavirus cases in Colorado from 1993–2008, 25 of which were fatal.
- **Lyme Disease:** Lake, 1. **Total cases in Colorado: 3.**
- **Plague:** Although no cases of human plague were reported in Colorado in 2008 or 2009, 49 human cases have been reported in Colorado since 1975.
- **West Nile Virus:** Boulder, 13; Delta, 1; Gunnison, 1; Jefferson, 3. **Total cases in Colorado: 71.**

## DISEASES, COUNTIES, CASES DIAGNOSED: 2009

- **Giardia:** Boulder, 66; Chaffee, 1; Custer, 5; Eagle, 7; Fremont, 10; Garfield, 3; Gilpin, 1; Grand, 3; Gunnison, 5; Huerfano, 1; Jefferson, 45; La Plata, 13; Lake, 7; Mesa, 14; Moffat, 1; Montezuma, 2; Montrose, 5; Park, 3; Pitkin, 12; Rio Blanco, 4; Routt, 4; Saguache, 3; San Miguel, 1; Summit, 3. **Total cases in Colorado: 219.**
- **Hantavirus:** Chaffee, 1. Total cases in Colorado: 1.
- **Lyme Disease:** The only verified reported case of Lyme disease in Colorado in 2009 occurred in El Paso County.
- **West Nile Virus:** No cases of West Nile were reported in Colorado in 2009.

## SOURCES

Weld County Department of Public Health and Environment, July 8, 2009; Zoonoses Newsletter; http://www.cdphe.state.co.us/dc/codiseasestatistics/Statistics_08/Diag_County_2008.pdf; http://www.cdphe.state.co.us/dc/zoonosis/wnv/HUMAN_WNV_09.HTML; http://www.cdphe.state.co.us/dc/zoonosis/hanta/Hanta_stats.pdf.

# NATIVE AMERICANS IN COLORADO

When people think in terms of Native American culture in Colorado, their mental images will invariably include Hollywood Western–inspired portrayals of tepees and wagon trains under attack. Some might think in terms of the long-abandoned cliff dwellings of Mesa Verde. But both of those images stem from relatively recent Native American culture.

The area that is now Colorado has been inhabited for at least 12,500 years and maybe even 15,000 years, as evidenced by the Clovis-era site found at Dent, near present-day Greeley.

The first Native Americans to have permanently inhabited the Colorado mountains were the Utes, the official tribe of the high country. While other Colorado tribes seem better known via Hollywood—the Arapaho, Cheyenne, Kiowa, Comanche, and Apache—it was (and remains) the Utes who called the Colorado Rockies home. The other tribes were mainly based upon the Plains, and, certainly, they ventured up high to hunt in the summer. However, like the snowbirds who now drive their motorhomes to Arizona when the aspens change, those Native Americans apparently had little stomach for six-month-long winters.

Scholars do not generally agree as to when the Utes entered what is now Colorado, or where they came from. The Utes themselves say they have been in Colorado since the beginning, which may not be too far off, as it is quite possible that they are direct descendents of the Fremont Culture (400–1200 A.D.). Some think that their lineage might even go back to late Plano or early Archaic culture, which means that the tribes we now lump together as Utes might have been living in what is now Colorado for 10,000 years. Lineage aside, the Utes were assuredly the dominant Native American culture in the Colorado Rockies when Spanish explorer Don Diego de Vargas arrived on the scene in 1694. This we know because Vargas actually skirmished with the Utes as he made his way up the Rio Grande and into the San Luis Valley.

The Utes speak one of the Shoshonean languages, quite similar to the tongues of the Shoshone, Comanche, Bannock, and Paiute—which indicates that the Utes have a linguistic and therefore likely historic connection to the Great Basin Native American tradition. More distantly related languages are spoken by the Hopi, some of the California tribes, and even the Aztecs of Mexico.

Utes have long inhabited all of the mountainous parts of Colorado, from the Yampa River near present-day Steamboat Springs to the San Juan River in the Four Corners region, and from the slopes of the Front Range to the present-day Utah border.

Their way of life was hunting and gathering. Only rarely did they plant crops of maize or beans. They spent the summer months moving as family groups through their customary hunting territories, often high in the mountains. In winter, they moved into semipermanent settlements in the mountain valleys.

In historic times, seven bands of Utes lived in Colorado:

- The Capote band lived in the San Luis Valley and the upper Rio Grande.
- The Mouache band ranged south along the Sangre de Cristo Mountains into New Mexico.
- The Weminuche band occupied the San Juan drainage.
- The Tabeguache (Uncompahgre) band lived in the Gunnison and Uncompahgre watersheds.
- The Grand River (Parianuc) band occupied the Colorado River area.
- The Yampa band lived near the river that took their name.
- The Uintah band, actually more of a Utah group, sometimes entered western Colorado.
- Other bands of Utes lived in Utah.

The Utes hunted buffalo, deer, elk, bighorn sheep, and antelope and, unlike the Plains Indians, depended to a great degree on smaller animals, particularly jackrabbits. Their plant foods included the brown-skinned roots and tubers of the yampa family, yucca, camas bulbs, and piñon nuts. Because they were nomadic, they early on began utilizing tepees, like their Plains brethren. The Utes' boundaries shifted from time to time as other tribes moved into the periphery of Ute territory. In the late 1700s, for instance, the Jicarilla Apaches moved into the San Luis Valley.

But it was the incursions by whites that forever altered the Ute way of life. After 1848, U.S. Indian policy in Colorado was directed first and foremost toward protecting the transcontinental wagon routes to Oregon, California, and Santa Fe; safeguarding settlers; and, consequently, restricting the natives to certain areas. The first treaty between the U.S. government and a Colorado tribe was concluded with the Utes in 1849. This treaty set no boundaries but required the Utes, who were represented by Principal Chief Quiziachigiate and 27 other lesser chiefs, to recognize U.S. law and sovereignty. The Utes were allowed to stay in their "accustomed territory."

Things went to hell in a handbasket for the Utes, as well as the other tribes living on the Plains, when the Pikes Peak Gold Rush kicked off in 1858. When thousands of prospectors started flooding into what is now Colorado, the Utes' days of hunting and gathering throughout their "accustomed territory" were numbered. By 1868, the Utes had "agreed" to move to a large reservation that covered a significant portion of the western part of the state. Then, in 1873, just before the big gold and silver booms in the San Juans, the Utes were forced into the San Juan Cession, which chopped off most of the southern third of the Ute Reservation.

Then came the Meeker Massacre (September 29, 1879). Nathan Meeker, the White River Ute Indian agent, had been trying in vain to get the Utes to change their nomadic ways and decided that one way to achieve his goal was, inexplicably, to plow up parts of one of the Utes' horse-racing tracks. After engaging in a fistfight with the man whose track he had just destroyed, Meeker thought it would be a good idea to wire for reinforcements, claiming he had been assaulted by an Indian, driven from his home, and beaten severely. The government responded by sending 200 troops, led by Major Thomas Tipton Thornburg.

When the troops were about 50 miles from the agency, a group of Utes rode out to meet them, saying they wished to have a peace conference with Meeker and that only Thornburg and five soldiers would be allowed to come. Remembering the 1864 Sand Creek Massacre, which took place in eastern Colorado, the Utes wanted the main body of the soldiers to stay 50 miles away on a hill designated by the Indians. Thornburg ignored this demand and continued onto Ute land. At Milk Creek, the soldiers were ambushed. In the first few minutes of fighting, Thornburg and all of his soldiers above the rank of captain were killed. The Utes then attacked the Indian agency, killing eight men, including Meeker, and taking several women, including Meeker's wife and daughter, captive to ensure their own safety as they fled.

This did not endear the Utes to Colorado's burgeoning white population. The Ute Removal of 1881 relieved the Utes of most of their remaining lands and left the tribe with only the two relatively small parcels in the southwestern part of the state that they occupy to this day.

Of the seven bands that once roamed Colorado's mountain country, only the Weminuche, Capote, and Mouache bands remain in Colorado, on the Ute Mountain and Southern Ute reservations. The Uintah, Tabeguache, Grand River, and Yampa bands were moved to the Uintah Reservation in northeastern Utah.

The last remaining Plains Indians that once called Colorado home—the Cheyenne and Arapaho—were removed to reservations in Oklahoma and Wyoming, far from their native lands. The Jicarilla Apaches, who once moved into the San Luis Valley, have a reservation in northern New Mexico.

## CHIEF OURAY

South Dakota has Sitting Bull and probably Crazy Horse, Oregon has Chief Joseph, New Mexico has Geronimo, and Arizona has Cochise—all people who have transcended one-time historic infamy to rise in the eyes of people worldwide to become recognized not just as great Native Americans but as great human beings.

Colorado has Ouray (1833?–1880). Born in what is now New Mexico, Ouray was a leader of the Uncompahgre band of the Utes. According to oral history passed down by Ute elders, Ouray sprang forth on the gloriously clear night of November 13, 1833, as the magnificent display of the annual Leonid meteor shower streaked across the winter sky. The elders believed it was a sign that portended great things for Ouray. (It should be noted that some accounts state that he might have been born as early as 1820.) Ouray was the son of a Jicarilla Apache father adopted by the Utes and a Tabeguache Ute mother. He learned Spanish, English, Ute, and Apache, which was very helpful in negotiating treaties later in life.

When he was about 18, Ouray came to modern-day Colorado to join his mother's band, where his father was already a leader. He spent much of his youth working for Mexican sheepherders and fought both the Kiowas and the Sioux while living with the Tabeguache. When his father died in 1860, Ouray became chief of his band.

Ouray was actually considered a coward by more militant Utes, who derisively called him "the white man's friend" as he lobbied for reconciliation between the Indians and the newcomers, understanding that war with the whites would surely spell doom for the Utes. President Rutherford B. Hayes, whom Ouray met in 1880, called Ouray "the most intellectual man I've ever conversed with." Ouray also met President Ulysses S. Grant.

After the 1879 Meeker Massacre, which did not even involve the Tabeguache Utes, Ouray sent word to his fellow tribesmen to cease and desist fighting. But the damage had been done. To white settlers incensed by the massacre, a Ute was a Ute. Despite Ouray's attempt to calm things down, his people were all sent to a reservation in Utah. He died shortly thereafter.

Ouray never cut off his long, Ute-fashioned hair, but he often dressed in white man's garb. He was secretly buried near Ignacio, Colorado. Forty-five years later, he was reburied close to the Los Pinos Indian Agency in a marked grave.

Chief Ouray's obituary in the *Denver Post* read: "In the death of Ouray, one of the historical characters passes away. He has figured for many years as the greatest Indian of his time, and during his life has figured quite prominently. Ouray is in many respects a remarkable Indian with pure instincts and a keen perception. A friend to the white man and the Indians alike." That's about as high a compliment as a newspaper ever paid a Native American in those days.

Ouray County and its county seat, the town of Ouray, are named after Colorado's most famous chief. Two different mountains also bear his name, Mount Ouray, one of the southernmost peaks in the Sawatch Range, and Ouray Peak in Chaffee County.

## A UTE LEGEND: PORCUPINE HUNTS BUFFALO

In olden days, when mostly animals roamed this earth, a Porcupine set out to track some buffalo. He asked the buffalo chips, "How long have you been here on this trail?" He kept asking until one finally answered, "Only lately have I been here."

From there, the Porcupine followed the same path. The farther he went, the fresher the tracks. He continued until he came to a river; there he saw a buffalo herd that had crossed the ford onto the other side.

"What shall I do now?" thought the Porcupine as he sat down. He called out, "Carry me across!"

One of the buffalo replied, "Do you mean me?"

Porcupine called again, "No, I want a different buffalo." Thus he rejected each member of the herd, one after another, as each asked, "Do you mean me?"

Finally, the last and the best one in the herd said, "I will carry you across the river." The buffalo crossed the river and said to the Porcupine, "Climb on my back."

Porcupine said, "No, I'm afraid I will fall off into the water."

Buffalo said, "Then climb up and ride between my horns."

"No," replied the Porcupine. "I'm sure I'll slide off into the river."

Buffalo suggested many other ways to carry him, but Porcupine protested. "Perhaps you'd rather ride inside of me?" offered the buffalo.

"Yes," said the Porcupine and let himself be swallowed by the buffalo.

"Where are we now?" asked the porcupine.

"In the middle of the river," said the buffalo.

After a little while, the Porcupine asked again.

"We have nearly crossed," said the buffalo. "Now we have emerged from the water; come out of me."

Porcupine said, "No, I want to go a little farther."

Soon the buffalo stopped and said, "We have gone far enough, so come out."

Then Porcupine hit the buffalo's heart with his heavy tail. The buffalo started to run, but fell down and died right there. Porcupine had killed him. Others in the herd tried to hook Porcupine, but he sat under the buffalo's ribs, where he could not be hooked. Soon the herd tired and ran on their way.

Porcupine came out and said aloud, "I wish I had something to butcher this nice big buffalo with."

Now, Coyote was sleeping nearby and woke up and heard him. Coyote went to Porcupine and said, "Here is my knife for butchering." So they went together to the side of the buffalo.

"Let him butcher who can jump over it," said Coyote. Porcupine ran and jumped, but only partway over the buffalo. Coyote jumped over it without even touching the dead animal, so he began to butcher, cutting up the buffalo.

After a little time, he handed the paunch to Porcupine and said, "Go wash it in the river, but don't eat it yet."

Porcupine took the paunch to the river and washed it, then he bit off a piece. When Coyote saw what porcupine had done, he became very angry with him and went after him. "I told you not to eat any of the paunch."

Coyote picked up a club and killed Porcupine and placed him beside the buffalo and went to his home. "I have killed a buffalo and I have killed a porcupine. Let us go and carry them home."

Before Porcupine had come out of the buffalo, he had said magic words: "Let a red pine grow here fast." Then at once a red pine had begun to grow under the meat and under Porcupine. It grew very tall and fast. All of the meat and Porcupine rested at the top of the red pine tree, high in the air, Porcupine magically coming to life again.

Coyote and his family arrived and were surprised that all of the meat was gone. They began to hunt for it.

"I wish they would look up," said Porcupine. Then, the smallest child looked up and said, "Oh!" The family looked up and saw Porcupine sitting on top of the meat in the tall red pine tree.

Coyote said, "Throw down a piece of the neck. We are very hungry."

"Yes," said Porcupine. "Place that youngest child a little farther away."

"Yes," they responded and took him to one side.

"Now make a ring and all hold hands upward," said Porcupine. So the family joined hands and held them up. Porcupine threw down several pieces of the buffalo meat, killing Coyote and those in the ring. Porcupine threw down the rest of the meat and climbed down the tree.

He took charge of the young coyote and fed him all the meat he desired. Porcupine took all the meat he could carry to his home. He and the young coyote became good friends and helped each other hunt buffalo together for a long, long time.

## SOURCES

*American Indians in Colorado* by Professor J. Donald Hughes, augmented by a personal phone interview with Dr. Hughes; *Historical Atlas of Colorado* by Thomas J. Noel, Paul F. Mahoney, and Richard E. Stevens; www.firstpeople.us; Wikipedia.

# COLORADO GEOLOGY: THE LARAMIDE OROGENY

The Rocky Mountains pretty much came into being because of the forces of one particular geologic event called the Laramide Orogeny, which was named after the Laramie Mountains between Cheyenne and Laramie, Wyoming, just north of the Colorado border. "Orogeny" is geologist-speak for a process in which a section of the Earth's crust is folded and deformed by lateral compression of tectonic plates to form a mountain range. Think of the Earth's crust as a series of broken ice shards floating on a pond surface. The "pond" upon which the shards—the tectonic plates—float is called the lithosphere. When those "shards" collide, whole continents are shaped by the plates driving into one another until one finally yields and slides beneath the dominant shard—a process known as "subduction."

As the "defeated" plate slides under the "victorious" plate, the land of the upper plate is pushed higher and higher and the raw forms of mountains begin to appear.

The Laramide Orogeny, which began about 80 million years ago and continued for 40 million years, give or take, occurred as the North American Tectonic Plate slid westward and eventually got into a shard duel with the Pacific Plate. The dominant North American Plate began to slide over the Pacific Plate, pushing it down. Slowly, the Pacific Plate slid between the North American Plate and the mantle, the last solid layer before the Earth's molten core. That single geologic event resulted in land growing increasingly higher from Mexico all the way north to Alaska.

As the plates settled, cracks—faults—occurred, and through these cracks, high-pressure volcanic magma was released. These delayed eruptions, which took place millions of years after the Laramide Orogeny, resulted in major flows that helped form both the San Juan and Sawatch ranges. Eventually, the North American and Pacific plates locked into place, pretty much sealing the magma beneath the Earth's surface. With the exception of occasional releases that heat the odd hot spring, for the past 30 million years or so, the spawn of the Laramide Orogeny—the Rocky Mountains—has been free to evolve through the process of erosion into the beautiful peaks we all now know, love, and ski upon.

## SOURCES

This text came almost verbatim, with permission, from one of the best guidebooks to the Colorado Mountains ever written and published: *Best Summit Hikes of Colorado: An Opinionated Guide to 50-Plus Ascents and Little Known Peaks From 8,144 to 14,433 Feet* by James Dziezynski (Wilderness Press). The introduction of this book alone is worth the cover price.

# COLORADO GEOLOGY: THE RIO GRANDE RIFT VALLEY

Casual observers would likely be of the opinion that the most prominent geological features in the Colorado mountains would be, well, the mountains themselves. And while that would certainly be a hard contention to dispute, there is another geologic feature that has defined a significant percentage of the state's topography.

Although it pales by comparison to the 3,700-mile East African Rift Valley, the 640-mile Rio Grande Rift Valley is one of only a handful of active continental rift valleys on the planet. (Others include the Lake Baikal Rift Valley in the Russian Federation and the West Antarctic Rift Valley, the study of which is still in its nascent stages.)

A continental rift valley is one in which tectonic plates actually are pulling themselves apart. Most rift valleys are found in the ocean depths. Ocean rifts are most often caused by actual divergence of submerged tectonic plates. Continental rifts, such as the Rio Grande, are known as "extensional rifts," which, unlike their ocean rift counterparts, are caused by the buoyancy of rocks deep below.

The Rio Grande Rift Valley runs from its oldest section in northern Chihuahua, Mexico, to its newest extension near Leadville. Despite its name, it was not formed by the Rio Grande, or, for that matter, the upper Arkansas River, which flows through the Rio Grande Rift Valley from its source near Leadville to a point where it exits the rift proper near Salida. Both of those major rivers take advantage of the path of least resistance provided by the rift rather than having caused the valleys through which they flow via erosion.

The Rio Grande Rift Valley, which began forming between 29 and 35 million years ago, is considered "tectonically quiescent," meaning that it goes about the business of rifting (think in terms of a geologic-scale zipper being slowly pulled apart) at a small and slow rate of between 0.5 and 2 millimeters a year. (The East Africa Rift Valley, otherwise known as the Great Rift Valley, by comparison, is pulling itself apart at the geologically rapid pace of about 6 millimeters a year.)

Although it is impossible to predict what course a rift valley will eventually take, geologists guess that the Rio Grande Rift Valley will continue its northern march past Leadville toward Copper Mountain. It is also possible, geologists concede, that it might just stop dead in its tracks pretty much directly below the Cloud City.

The question many people have, of course, is: Is there a risk of volcanoes and/or earthquakes along the rift?

Seismic activity associated with earthquakes along the rift is now considered to be low to moderate in Colorado in general, with a slightly higher risk along the Rift Valley. But there are still many unknowns about the rift. Geologic evidence indicates that large earthquakes (magnitude 7.0–7.3 on the Richter Scale) have occurred in south-central Colorado within the past 5,000 to 15,000 years—well into the era of human habitation. While statistically less likely to have large-scale seismic activity than, say, the San Andreas Fault in California, there is little doubt that, at some point, a large earthquake will occur along the Rio Grande Rift.

As for the potential for volcanoes, as recently as 1.2 million years ago (a matter of moments in geologic time), Valle Caldera, New Mexico, one of the world's largest and newest calderas, was created right in the heart of the Rio Grande Rift. Presently, though, geologists consider the Rio Grande Fault to be volcanically dormant (but not extinct).

Although the tallest mountains that border the Rio Grande Rift—the Sawatch and the Sangre de Cristo[1] ranges—will continue to be lowered by the forces of erosion, chances are that their vertical rise above the San Luis Valley and the Arkansas River Valley will actually increase, because, as geologic forces continue pulling, the bottom of the rift will sink faster than the proximate mountains erode.

In the meantime, scientists from the University of Colorado and the University of New Mexico, with funding from the National Science Foundation's Earthscope Program, are now using a series of Global Positioning Systems that are fixed to geologic features in a grid system that runs from the central Colorado Rockies into southern New Mexico to try to ascertain how much the Rio Grande Rift is actually moving. The goal is to assess the potential seismic hazard presented by the Rio Grande Rift, as well as to determine how wide the rift actually is and how far north it has moved.

## NOTES

1. Unlike the Sawatch and San Juan ranges, which are primarily volcanic in origin (see the "Laramide Orogeny" section), the Sangre de Cristos are fault-block mountains that were pushed up by tectonic activity about 27 million years ago, pretty much as one big chunk of rock.

## SOURCES

Cooperative Institute for Research in Environmental Studies; personal interviews with Robert Fillmore, Ph.D., Professor of Geology at Western State College in Gunnison, Colorado; www.sangres.com.

# COLORADO GEOLOGY: THE ASPEN ANOMALY

It was a simple enough question that only a geologist would think of, much less try to answer: Given the age of Colorado's highest mountains—the northern end of the Sawatch Range between Leadville and Aspen—why have peaks such as Mount Elbert and Mount Massive remained so high? After all, since the Terminator-like forces of erosion have been working their mountain-killing magic for more than 50 million years, those peaks ought to be less altitudinous.

It ends up that at the northern end of the Rio Grande Rift—extending from Leadville to Paonia and down to Aspen—lies a geologic oddity called the "Aspen Anomaly."

The Aspen Anomaly is basically a large area of anomalously hot and thin mantle about 50 kilometers below the crust that is being pushed up by the Earth's molten core at about the same rate as the northern Sawatch Mountains are eroding.

From a geologic perspective, mountains are like icebergs insofar as they have roots, and only a small percentage of their mass appears above the Earth's surface. No matter their mass, they still basically float atop the warm upper mantle, which, while not liquid, is still viscous. Thus—and this is a hard one to grasp when you're eyeballing Mount Massive—all mountains have a degree of buoyancy. This means that they can be pushed upward by almost inconceivable forces many miles beneath the Earth's surface.

The Aspen Anomaly was only discovered about 10 years ago, and geologists are studying it intensely even as we speak. But, already, those few members of the public who have even heard about it are wondering aloud if the Aspen Anomaly has the same degree of super-volcano potential as does the infamous Yellowstone Anomaly.

Time (geologic time, that is) will tell.

In the meantime, Leadville, at this moment of geologic history, finds itself sitting at the epicenter of two world-class geologic phenomena: one of the world's longest active continental rift valleys and a bubble of viscosity large and strong enough to lift the state's highest mountains even higher.

## SOURCES

Personal interviews with Dr. Karl Karlstrom, Ph.D., Professor of Geology at the University of New Mexico in Albuquerque (the man credited with discovering the Aspen Anomaly), and Dr. Robert Fillmore, Ph.D., Professor of Geology at Western State College in Gunnison.

# COLORADO GEOLOGY: COLORADO'S HIGHEST-EVER MOUNTAINS

In an elevation-crazy state like Colorado, almost everyone knows that the state's highest peaks are the famed Fourteeners, with 14,433-foot Mount Elbert, outside of Leadville, being the highest. But what was the highest mountain in the geologic history of Colorado?

No one knows exactly, but there is zero in the way of doubt that, at one time, there were prominences in Colorado that were significantly higher than the lofty peaks that verily define the high country today.

West Elk Peak, at 13,035 feet, the highest point in the 176,000-acre West Elk Wilderness (located basically between Gunnison and Paonia), is a stratovolcano—a tall, conical volcano with many layers of lava, tephra, and volcanic ash—that was active about 30 million years ago. Stratovolcanoes are characterized by steep profiles, and the lava that flows and hardens from these types of volcanoes tends to be extremely viscous; it cools and hardens before spreading far. Stratovolcanoes (Mount Fuji in Japan and Mount Hood in Oregon are classic examples) have pretty much the same geometry, steepness of slopes, and flanks that flatten out gradually, all of which allow geologists to calculate their probable height while they were still spouting lava toward the heavens.

Using calculations based on the consistent profiles of stratovolcanoes, geologists have concluded that West Elk Peak was once more than 17,000 feet tall. (Using those same types of lava-dispersal calculations, geologists have determined that 14,411-foot Mount

Rainier, the highest mountain in Washington State, was once about 16,000 feet high, while 12,637-foot Humphrey's Peak, the highest point in Arizona, was once at least 15,000 feet high.)

Thing is, there are other stratovolcanoes in Colorado, primarily in the San Juan Mountains, that are significantly higher than West Elk Peak. One, 14,309-foot Uncompahgre Peak, is the sixth highest mountain in the state. Although a peak-specific study has never been performed, if the same types of calculations used to determine how high West Elk Peak, Humphrey's Peak, and Mount Rainier used to be were applied to Uncompahgre Peak, it is estimated that, between 24 and 30 million years ago, it likely achieved a maximum elevation of about 20,000 feet. The same could likely be said about numerous other stratovolcanoes in the San Juan Mountains.

## SOURCES

Personal interviews with Robert Fillmore, Ph.D., Professor of Geology at Western State College in Gunnison, Colorado; Wikipedia; www.peakbagger.com.

# THE NAMING OF GEOGRAPHIC FEATURES

By 1885, there were electric streetlights in downtown Denver and phone lines connecting Denver with Pueblo. Yet, in 1890, a mere 13 years before Wilbur and Orville Wright took their first flight at Kitty Hawk, and a mere 13 years before the Ford Motor Company was founded, there was still no institutionalized means in the United States by which places and geographic features were given formal, universally accepted names. And, even if there was, no central repository for that information existed.

That situation was remedied in 1890, when President Benjamin Harrison signed an executive order establishing the Board on Geographic Names (BGN) and giving it authority to resolve the many unsettled and disputed geographic name questions that were then vexing Manifest Destiny.

The original program of name standardization addressed the complex issues of domestic geographic feature names during the surge of exploration, mining, and settlement of western territories after the Civil War. Inconsistencies and contradictions among many names, spellings, and applications became a serious problem to surveyors, mapmakers, scientists, and speculators who required uniform, non-conflicting geographic appellations.

OK, simple enough. However, after 121 years, you'd think there would be little these days for the members of the BGN to do, save maybe talking about the good old days. You know—by now, everything worth naming would have already been named. Stunningly, nothing could be further from the truth. On average, the BGN entertains more than 200 formal naming requests every year. Those requests cover the gamut: formalizing informal names, changing culturally offensive names, giving names to unnamed geographic features (of which there are still surprisingly many), choosing between conflicting names, and correcting grammatical and spelling errors for mountains, rivers, valleys, and even towns.

The process of changing, giving, or clarifying the names of geographic features is almost always externally driven. Proponents go through a formal application process. Standards are tough, and only a small percentage of applications are accepted. Burden of proof lies entirely with the applicant. Whenever the BGN accepts an application, it becomes almost pharaoh-edict-like, insofar as it enters the realm of, "So let it be written; so let it be done." That decision becomes codified on all federal maps and in all federal literature. New trail signs reflect that decision.

In September 2002, the BGN began posting its Quarterly Review Lists online. Between then and November 2010, the BGN has entertained 42 applications from Colorado requesting formal name changes and/or clarifications. The applications range from the ridiculous to the sublime. For the most part, however, they are fairly blasé. Here is a sampling of the applications received by the BGN from Colorado's mountain country in the past decade. Unless otherwise stated, decisions had yet to be rendered by the BGN on these applications by the time this book went to press.

- In 2010, a Cascade man proposed renaming an unofficially named 13,384-foot peak in the Sangre de Cristo Mountains in Saguache County as "Deadman Peak." The name reflects the summit's proximity to Deadman Lakes. According to the proponent, there are four unnamed peaks higher than 13,000 feet in the area, with this being the most prominent and least accessible (hence the appropriateness of the proposed name). The proposed name was posted on summitpost.org and pikespeakphoto.com, but one other source applies the name to a completely different peak. The fall 2008 issue of Colorado Bird Atlas Quarterly applies "the unofficial name Deadman Peak" to another nearby summit—one that the same Cascade man has proposed naming "Golden Lotus Mountain" (which is actually closer to Deadman Lakes). The proponent suggests that the proposals are warranted in order to eliminate confusion between names that have come into use within the mountain-climbing community and to aid search-and-rescue efforts.

- In 2009, an Arvada man proposed that an unnamed 13,626-foot mountain 1.9 miles west of Mount Princeton in Chaffee County be named "Frontier Visions Peak," in recognition of the contributions of the artists and photographers of the American West. These include the more well-known Charles M. Russell, Frederic Remington, Albert Bierstadt, Thomas Moran, William H. Jackson, and Ansel Adams, as well as the less-recognized Samuel Seymour and Titian Peale, the latter two of which, according to the proponent, produced the first drawings of the Rocky Mountains in 1819.

- In 2009, that same Arvada man proposed naming an unnamed peak located on the boundary of the San Isabel and Rio Grande national forests as "Padre Peak," in honor of the priests who accompanied the Spanish explorers of early America, such as Francisco Coronado, Joao Cabrillo, and Juan Bautista de Anza.

- In 2008, a Carbondale man proposed that a small, unnamed lake located close to an unnamed tributary of Avalanche Creek in the White River National Forest be named "Ranger Pond." The proponent reported that, while researching the local wildlife habitat, he noticed the lake on Google Earth and had proposed to name it "for all the wildlife and forest rangers that have hiked in the area and apparently missed this feature." The proponent suggested that the Colorado Division of Wildlife and the U.S. Forest Service would appreciate the irony of the name.

- In summer 2006, the BGN ended a six-year nomenclatural war of attrition by agreeing to name an unnamed 11,282-foot peak in the southern part of the Sawatch Range "Mount KIA/MIA." While this may sound like some sort of linguistic homage to Native Americans, it is, in fact, a compound acronym honoring U.S. military personnel "Killed in Action" and "Missing in Action."

  The proposal was put forth by a retired air force master sergeant who lives in New Mexico. It marked the man's third attempt to get a peak thusly named. In 2003, he applied to the BGN to get Sheep Mountain, outside Telluride, renamed "Mount Kiamia." His request was based at least partially on the fact that there are 29 Colorado mountains officially named "Sheep," and, therefore, at least one could be spared as homage to the country's KIAs and MIAs. The BGN gave the applicant a thumbs-down on this one because of the opposition of local residents who wanted to keep the old name.

So, the man went searching for an unnamed peak. He found one in the Sawatch Range. He submitted another proposal to the BGN in 2005, asking that it name the unnamed peak "Mount Kiamia." The BGN turned him down again, this time because the word "Kiamia" too closely resembled a Ute word for "departed warriors," which, you would think, given the nature of the man's request, would have been a very contextual coincidental cognate.

Finally, in 2007, the man applied yet again, for the same unnamed peak in the Sawatch. This time, though, he went with the spliced-together double acronym. And this time his request was approved.

- In spring 2008, a resident of Crestone, Colorado, petitioned the BGN to clear up some serious nomenclatural confusion involving one of Colorado's famed Fourteeners in the Sangre de Cristo Range. The applicant asked that 14,165-foot Kit Carson Mountain be renamed Mount Crestone. According to the applicant, residents of the town of Crestone feel that the existing name is confusing, because most of them already refer to Kit Carson Mountain as Crestone Peak, while the name "Kit Carson Mountain," they contend, refers to an entirely different summit "behind Crestone Peak." According to the applicant, the names were screwed up years ago by the U.S. Geological Survey, and locals refuse to call them by their official names. The confusion apparently causes all manner of directional discombobulation for tourists trying to get oriented in a part of the state where disorientation can have serious ramifications on the mortality front.

  This was further complicated by the fact that there has already been significant BGN action on this same mountain. The mountain in question was called "Frustrum Peak" by the Wheeler Survey in 1878. It was officially named "Kit Carson Peak" by the BGN in 1906. In 1970, the BGN changed the name to "Kit Carson Mountain."

  Locals have stressed to the BGN that the new name ought to be Mount Crestone, rather than Crestone Peak, because that name already applies to a summit just one mile to the southeast, which combines with Crestone Needle to make up the Crestone Peaks.

  Then, to add even more confusion to this situation in the Sangres, the same applicant has asked the BGN to name the highest point on Kit Carson Mountain—the very same mountain that the applicant hopes to get changed to "Mount Crestone"—"Tranquility Peak," which, the BGN is told in the application, is appropriate, as it describes "the tranquility found in the citizens of the town of Crestone"—unless, of course, they find themselves getting worked up over the confusion regarding the names of their local mountains!

- A resident of Glenwood Springs has petitioned the BGN to name an unnamed 13-acre lake "Gallagher Lake" after his grandfather, who had a cabin in the area in the 1930s.
- In 2008, the BGN was petitioned to name an unnamed 13,087-foot peak outside of Silverton "Spencer Mountain" after the late Dr. Donald Spencer, who, the applicant states, "is recognized as the inventor of the theory of deformation of complex structures, which has had enormous influence in geometry and mathematical physics." After his retirement, Dr. Spencer returned to Colorado, where he became an ardent hiker and environmentalist.
- Morefield Canyon, Morefield Ridge, and Morefield Village, located in the Mesa Verde area, had been misspelled on maps as "Morfield" since the early 1900s. Oops. A USGS geologist hopes to get this remedied.
- Another whoops: Agnes Vaille Falls in Chaffee County had long been misspelled as Agnes Vail Falls.
- The BGN was petitioned in 2006 to change the unofficial name of 13,799-foot "Obstruction Peak," in the Sangre de Cristo Range, to "Galaxy Peak," which is appropriate, according to the applicants, because of its proximity to Columbia Point and Challenger Point, both of which were named after space shuttles.
- Also in 2006, the BGN received an application to name an unnamed 13,513-foot peak in the San Isabel National Forest "Maltese Peak," because the Maltese Cross is a symbol of firefighters. The same applicant, at the same time, petitioned to have another unnamed peak in the same area named "Triage Point," in honor of those working in the Emergency Medical Services industry.
- Those are not the only examples of the BGN receiving a petition to honor people who deal with emergency situations. In the 1990s, in Summit County's Tenmile Range, members of the Red, White, and Blue Fire Protection District petitioned the BGN to have an officially unnamed 13,841-foot peak above Breckenridge formally named "Red, White, and Blue Peak." On the surface, this was an easy one, because the Red, White, and Blue Fire Protection District had long maintained an exemplary local reputation. It wasn't like anyone was going to say that the local fire department was not deserving of having an unnamed mountain named after it. But the peak had long been informally known as "Atlantic Peak" because of its proximity to Pacific Peak, and, if there's any demographic that stands on tradition for tradition's sake, it's peak baggers, who united in opposition against the fire department's request.

A surprisingly intense battle waged for several years, during which time there were actually two registers on the summit of "Atlantic" Peak. One register was for those who believed the mountain should be renamed to "Red, White, and Blue Peak;" the other was for those who believe it ought to be formally named "Atlantic Peak." The "Atlantic Peak" register held three times as many entries, many of which were, shall we say, stunningly emphatic.

In 2001, the BGN decided to formally name that mountain Atlantic Peak. It contended that Red, White, and Blue Peak was too long and cumbersome. As well, it cited "local tradition."

- In 2006, the BGN was asked to name an unnamed five-acre alpine lake just below Pacific Peak as "Pacific Tarn." This request actually had national implications because, at 13,420 feet, this little body of water would become the highest named lake in the country, displacing 13,020-foot Lake Waiau in Hawaii.

- The most amusing attempt to name an unnamed mountain in Colorado comes from Tracy Ross, a writer for *Backpacker* magazine, who was given the assignment by her editors to "find, climb, and name her own peak." She found, climbed, and *tried* to name a 13,038-foot mountain near the famed Collegiate Peaks and petitioned the BGN to have it named "Rejection Peak," in honor of, Ross's application states, "...those who chose a less conventional and more adventurous path in life."

Her request was eventually turned down by the BGN, at least partially, Ross suspects, because the BGN people read her subsequent *Backpacker* story. The irony is that, as part of the BGN's vetting process, it routinely takes into account whether or not a proposed name has appeared in print.

# BUREAU OF GEOGRAPHIC NAMES ACTION IN OTHER WESTERN STATES
between 2002 and July 16, 2010

- Montana, with 112, actually leads the West in proposed BGN name changes/clarifications since 2002. Twenty-five of those requests were submitted in 2007 by the Confederated Salish and Kootenai tribes in hopes of replacing a whole slew of culturally offensive names with traditional Native American names. Most of the requested name changes centered upon geographic features containing the word "squaw," including one prominence known as "Squaw's Tit."

- California comes in second in the West, with 86 applications to the BGN, including one 2006 application to name an unnamed creek "Stream of Consciousness."

- The BGN received 79 applications from Wyoming. Fifty-six of those were from one applicant in 2006 seeking to clarify a whole slew of names in the Popo Agie Wilderness.

- It should come as no surprise that Alaska has the most unnamed geographic features in the country. Thus, the BGN received 69 applications between 2002 and July 16, 2010.
- Utah produced 47 BGN applications between 2002 and July 16, 2010. Two stand out. In 2003, there was an application to change the name of Lake Powell to "Glen Canyon Reservoir." The application was based on the fact that there was already a lake in Grand County, Colorado, near the headwaters of the Colorado River, named after John Wesley Powell, the first man to successfully traverse the Grand Canyon in a boat. The main reason for the application, however, was to pressure the BGN to make it a policy for all reservoirs, which is what "Lake" Powell is, to be accurately named. Had the BGN accepted this application, which it didn't, it may very well have established a national naming precedent that would apply to all reservoirs in the country. In Colorado, this would have opened the door for renaming applications for bodies of water such as "Lake" Dillon, "Lake" Granby, and Blue Mesa "Lake," all of which are actually reservoirs.

    In 2004, the BGN received an application from Utah to name a side canyon of Glen Canyon "Not Annie's Canyon," because it is close to, and often confused with, "Annie's Canyon," which, by golly, it is not!
- Only three applications to the BGN came out of New Mexico—by far the least of any western state—between 2002 and July 16, 2010.

SOURCE

The Bureau on Geographic Names.

# GORGES VERSUS CANYONS

Royal GORGE. Black CANYON. What's the difference?

There is some disagreement as to whether the words "canyon" (sometimes spelled in its Spanish form, cañon) and "gorge" are synonyms. Some would argue that the major difference is that "canyon" traces its lexicographic roots back to Spanish, while "gorge" evolved from French.

Wikipedia, for instance, says: "A canyon or gorge is a deep valley between cliffs often carved from the landscape by a river. Most canyons were formed by a process of long-time erosion from a plateau level." This definition not only treats the terms as interchangeable but manages to simultaneously treat the word "valley" as a synonym of both.

Traditionally, though, canyons are geomorphologic events that are wider than they are deep, while gorges are deeper than they are wide.

Colorado is home to a wide array of noteworthy canyons, gorges, and, yes, even valleys, which are generally considered wider and more gentle than gorges or canyons, and which often were formed by the actions of glaciers as well as erosion, or, in the case of the Rio Grande Rift Valley, tectonic plates pulling apart.

Unlike mountains, though, attempts to statistically quantify canyons and gorges are thwarted by the reality that there is no accepted means by which depth is measured. Often, in an attempt to gain superlatives, they are measured from the highest point on an adjacent rim to the river level. Some argue, however, that canyons and gorges ought to be measured from an average rim height to the river, while others still argue that overall displacement ought to be used, that is to say: How much dirt would it take to fill the entire canyon or gorge up to rim level? The displacement argument, therefore, takes into account not only the depth of a canyon or gorge but the length and width as well.

Given its mountainous nature, it is not surprising that Colorado is home to numerous noteworthy canyons, gorges, and, yes, valleys.

- The deepest canyon in the state actually fits the definition of a gorge. The **Black Canyon of the Gunnison** reaches a depth of 2,000 vertical feet while, in some places, the distance from rim to rim is only 1,150 feet. At its narrowest point, the canyon is only 40 feet across at river level. In 1999, the Black Canyon was upgraded in status from a national monument to a national park. The Gunnison River through the Black Canyon drops an average of 43 feet per mile through the entire canyon, making it one of the steepest mountain descents in North America. In comparison, the Colorado River through the Grand Canyon drops an average of 7.5 feet per mile. The greatest descent of the Gunnison River occurs at Chasm View, where it drops 240 feet per mile.
- The **Royal Gorge,** located near Cañon City, is probably Colorado's best-known canyon, or, well, gorge. Carved by the Arkansas River, the Royal Gorge is about 10 miles long, 1,200 feet deep, and, at places, only 200 feet across. The Royal Gorge is home to the world's highest suspension bridge over water. Built in 1929 solely to serve as a draw for tourists, the Royal Gorge Bridge is 1,053 feet above river level. The bridge has served as the launching point for BASE jumping, bungee jumping, and, sadly, about 20 suicides.
- The **San Luis Valley** is advertised by area marketing mavens as being the largest alpine valley in the world. It covers approximately 8,000 square miles (122 miles long by 74 miles at its wid-

est point). Home to the Great Sand Dunes National Park, the San Luis Valley has gained international notoriety in the recent past for its plethora of unexplained phenomena. The valley is famous for its multitude of UFO sightings, Bigfoot sightings, cattle mutilations, weird noises, apparitions, and unusual military activity.

- **Byers Canyon** is a short gorge on the Upper Colorado River in Grand County. It is eight miles long and perhaps is best known for having on its upper end the voluminous Hot Sulphur Springs.

- **Big Thompson Canyon** drops from a source elevation of 11,310 feet to a mouth elevation of 4,670 feet along its 78-mile length on the east side of the Rockies near Loveland. Big Thompson Canyon will forever be known as the site of one of Colorado's biggest natural disasters. On July 31, 1976, during the celebration of the state's centennial, a series of flash floods swept down the canyon, killing 143 people. The flood was triggered by a near-stationary thunderstorm near the upper section of the canyon that dumped 12–14 inches of rain in less than four hours, which amounted to almost three-quarters of the area's annual rainfall average. Very little rain fell over the lower section of the canyon, where most of the victims were located. Around 9 P.M., a wall of water more than 20 feet tall raced down the canyon at 14 miles per hour. That wall destroyed 400 cars, 418 houses, and 52 businesses. Six bodies were never recovered.

- **Clear Creek Canyon,** a tributary of the South Platte River, is about 40 miles long and was home to some of the most intense early mining activity in the Gold Rush of 1859. Clear Creek Canyon now provides access to a high percentage of traffic heading up from Denver to the gambling casinos of Central City and Black Hawk. Clear Creek itself is famous for providing the water utilized by Coors to make its world-famous beer.

- Three-mile-long **Gore Canyon** is home to the wildest commercially viable whitewater in Colorado. Located near Kremmling, this 1,000-foot-deep canyon is not accessible by road and is home to the annual Gore Canyon Whitewater River Festival, held the third Saturday of August. Gore Canyon boasts many Class 5 and Class 6 rapids and has been the site of several whitewater fatalities.

- **Platte Canyon** is a narrow gorge on the South Platte River near Denver. Part of this canyon includes eight-mile-long Waterton Canyon, which is about 1,000 feet deep. The easternmost section of the Colorado Trail passes through Waterton Canyon on its way toward—or from—Durango.

- **Poudre Canyon,** near Fort Collins, is 40 miles long. Its name notwithstanding, it is actually a glacier-formed valley through the foothills of the Front Range.

- **Rattlesnake Canyon,** accessed primarily through Colorado National Monument near Grand Junction, is home to nine natural arches, the second highest concentration of arches in the United States, after the much better-known Arches National Park in Utah. The entry road is known for being treacherous. According to the Bureau of Land Management, at least four vehicles were stranded trying to get to Rattlesnake Canyon in 2006 alone due to unexpected rains that made the road impassable.
- **Unaweep Canyon** is a geologically distinct canyon that cuts across the Uncompahgre Plateau in western Colorado. There is much dispute among geologists as to how this canyon came to cut across a plateau. Some argue that the Dolores River once flowed through Unaweep Canyon. Some argue that it was the Gunnison River that once flowed through the canyon. Still others argue that the canyon was actually formed by glaciation.

SOURCE

Wikipedia.

# THE FOURTEENERS

Colorado's mountain country is dominated literally and increasingly figuratively by all of those lofty summits higher than 14,000 feet in elevation. The process of standing atop the Fourteeners has evolved in recent years to both a craze and a bonafide tangible outdoor-recreation industry. More than 500,000 people attempt to climb the state's Fourteeners every year.[1] On summer weekends, hundreds of people can be found making their way toward the summits of each of the state's loftiest peaks. Numerous small mountain towns, like Lake City and Alma, now rely fairly heavily upon Fourteener traffic to augment their local business coffers.

An entire industry of Fourteener-based merchandise has sprung up: water bottles adorned with Fourteener profiles; a series of collectible lapel pins bearing the visages of all the Fourteeners that people ostensibly purchase and display on their packs after having successfully ascended the corresponding Fourteeners; T-shirts dedicated to individual Fourteeners; T-shirts bearing check-off lists, upon which people can show via their attire which of the mountains they have climbed; T-shirts that utilize the ski-run difficulty rating system by listing Fourteeners as green, blue, black, or double-black; posters; solid bronze summit markers; Fourteener-specific journals, calendars, and "passport" books; at least four different guidebooks; numerous coffee-table books; several varieties of "Don't trust anyone under 14,000 feet" pins; videos; DVDs; a Fourteener-inspired New Age music CD—Robbie Deaton's *XIV: Colorado Elysium;* a National Basketball Association Development League Team once based in Broomfield called the "Colorado 14ers"; and even a brand of vodka named Colorado 14, which sports on the bottle's front a profile of 14,017-foot Wilson Peak.

With all the attention Colorado's Fourteeners have garnered in the past decade, one would think that almost every bit of Fourteener-based information would be catalogued, codified, and writ in

▲

## COLORADO FOURTEENERS INITIATIVE

The Colorado Fourteeners Initiative (CFI) is a Golden-based organization incorporated in 1994 "to protect and preserve the natural integrity of Colorado's 14,000-foot peaks through active stewardship and public education." It first formed as a partnership between the U.S. Forest Service, the Colorado Mountain Club, Outward Bound West, Volunteers for Outdoor Colorado, Rocky Mountain Field Institute, and Leave No Trace Center for Outdoor Ethics.

Although its mandate covers a large swath of ground, including aggressive educational programs, much of CFI's effort has been focused over the years on building durable trails to the summits of all but a few Fourteeners. When CFI first formed, it was estimated that at least seven Fourteeners were suffering environmental degradation as a result of not having durable trails upon which the burgeoning numbers of Fourteener aficionados could access the summits in orderly and environmentally benign fashion. CFI has built and/or restored trails on more than 20 Fourteeners with more projects ongoing. For more information on the Colorado Fourteeners Initiative, go to www.14ers.org.

---

stone long ago. But, truth be told, even in these Fourteener-dense times, there is still no consensus regarding the most fundamental Fourteener question: Just how many Fourteeners are there?

Most sources contend that there are 54 Fourteeners in Colorado. This is the number the Colorado Fourteeners Initiative uses. It's also the number used most frequently in the various Fourteener guidebooks.

But that number derives to a large extent from purely subjective sentiments expressed in *Trail & Timberline,* the official magazine of the Colorado Mountain Club. In 1968, William Graves wrote that, in order for a peak, Fourteener or not, to be considered distinct, it should be separated from a neighboring peak by a saddle that is at least 300 feet lower than the summit of the lower peak. This observation has morphed from one man's opinion—albeit a reasonable one made by a well-respected man of the mountains—to a veritable "rule."

Thing is, at the time Graves posited this "rule," modern topographic surveys had yet to be completed in the Colorado Rockies. When those surveys were finished in the 1970s, it was discovered that North Maroon Peak and El Diente, both of which had long been considered legitimate Fourteeners, failed to meet Graves's 300-foot criterion. That aside, out of respect for tradition, those two peaks continued to be listed among the elite, bringing the number of Fourteeners in Colorado to 54[2].

However, in the tenth edition of the *Guide to the Colorado Mountains,* published by the Colorado Mountain Club, El Diente and North Maroon were left off the Fourteeners list, while another mountain, 14,081-foot Challenger Point, located on the northwest shoulder of another Fourteener, 14,165-foot Kit Carson Peak in the Sangre de Cristo Range, was added. Thing is, Challenger Point, much to the chagrin of traditionalists, did not even receive its current name until 1987. Thus, the current Fourteeners list espoused by the Colorado Mountain Club stands at 53 peaks.

It is obvious that the true number of Fourteeners will always be in the eye of the list maker. And confusion, as well as contention, will likely always reign supreme. Wikipedia, for instance, lists 53 Fourteeners in its "Fourteener" entry. But, it also lists Longs Peak as "one of 58 Fourteeners in the Rocky Mountains of Colorado." Wikipedia further lists Kit Carson Peak as "one of Colorado's 51 Fourteeners."

Peakbagger.com goes with 53 Fourteeners, including Challenger Point but, once again, eliminating both El Diente and North Maroon.

Gerry Roach, author of *Colorado's Fourteeners: From Hikes to Climbs,* covers his bases by including El Diente and North Maroon, as well as Challenger Point, making his list 55 peaks long.

Fourteenerworld.com lists 59 Fourteeners, including five "named but unranked" peaks (Conundrum Peak, North Maroon, Mount Cameron, El Diente, and North Eolus) and one "soft" peak (North Massive).

Listsofjohn.com lists the increasingly common "53" (the traditional 54 list, minus El Diente and North Maroon, plus Challenger Point)—plus, for reference purposes, 14 additional peaks (North Maroon, El Diente, Mount Cameron, North Massive, Massive Green, Northeast Crestone, West Evans, South Elbert, South Massive, South Wilson, West Wilson, Conundrum Peak, Southeast

Longs, and North Eolus) that are based upon a 100-foot-drop criterion, rather than Graves's traditional 300-foot criteria.

## NOTES

1. The roots of this 500,000 figure remain elusive. In the November 2007 issue of *Mountain Gazette*, Brendan Leonard quotes T.J. Rapaport, ex–executive director of the Colorado Fourteeners Initiative in his story, "Private property at 14,000 feet": "The use numbers are an estimate, and they're based on some data points that were collected in 1984, 1994, and the late-'90s that showed an increase of at least 10 percent per year. We think it's quite a bit higher than [500,000]. So, those data points, plotted on a graph, take you up to around 690,000 this year. So, to stay conservative and make sure we don't overshoot, we have been saying a half-million, so it could be easily a half-million, and probably more accurately closer to three-quarters of a million. I don't ever say three-quarter million in print or in an interview, because I don't want to overshoot when the numbers finally come in. You could say something like, the Colorado Fourteeners Initiative conservatively estimates—or the U.S. Forest Service conservatively estimates—500,000, and that would be quite accurate."

2. Some people granted El Diente what amounts to a style-points exemption to Graves's 300-foot edict by invoking what amounts to the "scary traverse rule," wherein some slack was cut because, in order to get from the summit of nearby 14,246-foot Mount Wilson to the 14,159-foot summit of El Diente, one needs to traverse one of the gnarliest ridges in all of Colorado. Those style points are at least somewhat mitigated, and often ignored entirely, by the fact that one does not need to traverse that gnarly ridge in order to summit El Diente, because it can be accessed directly from either Kilpacker Creek or Navajo Basin.

## SOURCES

The Colorado Mountain Club; the Colorado Fourteeners Initiative; fourteenerworld.com; peakbagger.com; listsofjohn.com; Wikipedia; Gerry Roach's *Colorado's Fourteeners, From Hikes To Climbs;* and 25 years of personal experience making my way to the tops of a whole slew of Fourteeners.

# COLORADO FOURTEENER RECORDS

The history of speed records on the Colorado Fourteeners goes back almost 50 years, when Cleve McCarty climbed all 52 of the then-recognized Fourteeners in 52 days.

Since the mid-1970s, attempts to lower the record have become fairly commonplace.

Two issues dominate the Fourteener-record discussion: Determining how many Fourteeners there are and determining whether the 3,000-foot Colorado rule will be enforced, and, if so, to what degree.

Generally, those attempting to break the speed record for the Fourteeners in the past 20 years have listed 55 Fourteeners and sub-scribed to the 3,000-foot rule, with the caveat that a climber needs to gain 3,000 vertical feet (up and down) only once when climbing and descending Fourteener groups or clusters. Thus, for instance, a climber going for the Fourteener speed record would only need to gain 3,000 vertical feet while laying claim to the summits of closely grouped Eolus, Sunlight, and Windom, located in the San Juan Range, and Blanca, Lindsey, Ellingwood, and Little Bear in the Sangre de Cristo Range.

McCarty's 52-day record for climbing all of the Fourteeners stood for 14 years. Other climbing statistics are as follows:

- 1974: The "Climbing Smiths"—father George Smith and sons Flint, Quade, Cody, and Tyle—climbed the by-then-accepted 54 Fourteeners in 33 days. They then continued on to California and Washington and climbed the then-accepted 68 Fourteeners in the Lower 48 in 48 days, a record that still stands.
- 1976: Steve Boyer climbed all 54 Fourteeners in 22 days.
- 1980: Dick Walker finally beat the 20-day barrier, climbing the 54 Fourteeners in 18 days, 15 hours, 40 minutes.
- 1990: Quade and Tyle Smith, of the 1974 "Climbing Smiths," us-ing knowledge gained from their 1974 trip, regained their speed record with a 16-day, 21-hour, 35-minute effort. Except for ar-ranging for others to transfer their truck from the start to the end of five specific traverses, the Smith brothers were essentially self-reliant. This was the last record set sans support crew.
- 1992: Runners began getting involved in the Fourteener-record quest. Ultra-marathoner Adrian Crane ran on the trails and low-ered the record to 15 days, 17 hours, 19 minutes.
- 1993: Jeff Wagener was the first record holder to include Chal-lenger Point, upping the number of Fourteeners to 55. Despite the added peak, he still lowered the record to 14 days, 3 hours.
- 1995: Mountain runners Rick Trujillo of Ouray and Ricky Den-esik of Telluride, because of numerous route-finding errors and generally bad weather, failed to break the record, coming in at 15 days, 9 hours, 55 minutes. But the two runners kept meticulous track of their trip statistics. They covered 337 miles and gained 156,130 vertical feet.
- 1997: Trujillo and Denesik tried again. Although Trujillo dropped out on Peak Number 39 (Grays) in a raging sleet/snow-storm that was characteristic of that summer's stronger-than-normal El Niño–enhanced monsoon season, Denesik soldiered on and set a new record of 14 days, 16 minutes. Were it not for an ill-timed snowstorm on Longs Peak, Denesik would have been

the first person to break the 14-day barrier. Better planning resulting from his unsuccessful 1995 effort resulted in a streamlined itinerary that still boasted 153,215 vertical feet gained and 314 miles on the trail.

- 1999: Andrew Hamilton of Boulder finished all 55 Fourteeners in 13 days, 22 hours, 48 minutes. He achieved 18 of the summits in total darkness. He also had to descend many of the trails backwards because of severe knee pain. Hamilton gained extra credit/style points because, without stopping his clock, he helped a mountain rescue helicopter locate a dead mountain climber whom he found on Mount Eolus.

- 2000: The most momentous year for Fourteener records. Ricky Denesik was back at it and lowered the record to 12 days, 15 hours, 35 minutes. That same summer, Danelle Ballengee proceeded to set the first woman's record: 14 days, 14 hours, 49 minutes. Denesik's record barely lasted a month. Ted E. Keizer, aka Cave Dog, after two-and-a-half years of meticulous planning, scouting, and training, set the current record of 10 days, 20 hours, 26 minutes. Keizer experienced strong winds on 12 peaks, lightning on three, falling snow on four, snow on the ground on 12 and five summits coated with ice. He spent 29 percent of his time on the trail at night and spent 67 percent of those 10 days, 20 hours, and 26 minutes actually hiking and climbing. Aided by a five-person support crew, he enjoyed a total of 138,558 feet of vertical gain on the trip.

- 2003: Hamilton was back at it. He walked out his front door, hopped onto his bike, and completed the first "self-powered Fourteener record." He returned home 19 days, 10 hours, 40 minutes later, having ridden his bike the entire distance, with no vehicular support. His record contains an asterisk because he was unable to summit Culebra Peak, which is located on private property, due to access issues.

## SOURCES

www.TheDogTeam.com; www.thecavedog.com.

# PEAK PROMINENCE AND ISOLATION

For most people, a mountain's elevation above mean sea level (MSL) is all they need to know, statistically speaking. Others—mostly those with an interest in making their way toward a distant summit—are often additionally curious about vertical-gain information.

However, while measurements of vertical gain might be useful when eyeballing a route from the trailhead to the summit, they do little to measure mountains in a geophysical sense. Neither does a close relative of vertical gain: base-to-summit measurement, which fails in the minds of many topographers because there is generally no universally accepted base for most mountains.

Take Colorado's highest peak, for instance. Mount Elbert, at 14,433 feet above mean sea level, dominates the western horizon of the Arkansas River Valley between Leadville and Granite. Yet, what exactly is its base-to-summit measurement? Would you begin that measurement, say, in the middle of Leadville? Or would you begin, say, in the Arkansas River immediately east of Elbert's summit? What about taking a measurement from the higher western side, in the heart of the Sawatch Mountain Range?

Two relatively new forms of topographic measurement—clean prominence and peak isolation—have recently gained traction among climbers, geographers, and mathematicians, who believe that such measurements are better indicators of a mountain's "significance" than are pure elevation or the ambiguous base-to-summit measurement. Prominence rewards the highest points of major mountain ranges and free-standing peaks.

"Clean prominence" is the vertical distance a given summit rises above the lowest col (synonyms: gap, saddle, pass, or notch) connecting it to a higher summit. In other words, prominence is a measurement of a mountain relative to its surrounding terrain. It is the elevation one must descend before re-ascending to a higher summit. To calculate a peak's prominence, you must know the elevation of its summit and the elevation of its "key col"—the lowest col connecting it to a higher peak.

The prominence of Mount Elbert is 9,093 feet, which seems highly unlikely, given the fact that the Arkansas River at the base of Elbert is at about 10,000 feet. The answer, believe it or not, lies in California's Sierra Nevada. Mount Whitney, California's highest peak at 14,505 feet, is the closest mountain—669.98 miles away—to Mount Elbert that is *higher than* Mount Elbert. So, Mount Elbert's prominence is actually measured from a point near the California–Nevada state line that lies at 5,360 feet above MSL. That's the amount of vertical distance you would have to descend before you start re-ascending to a higher peak.

Obviously, prominence loses its palpability somewhat when you're talking about the very highest peak in a given area. Mount Massive, at 14,421 feet, is Colorado's second-highest peak. Yet, because it is so close to Mount Elbert, its prominence doesn't even rank in the top 80 of Colorado's mountains.

Isolation, often used in conjunction with prominence, is simply the distance between a summit and the nearest higher land. Compared to prominence, isolation rewards peaks that may be low but that dominate a large area. A significant isolation measurement makes, for instance, Eagle Mountain, Minnesota, and Magazine Mountain, Arkansas, seem much more impressive than their prominence ever would.

Another of these kinds of measurements is called "nearest topographic higher peak," which is the closest higher peak to a given summit following ridgelines past the key col.

## COLORADO PEAKS WITH THE MOST PROMINENCE

- Mount Elbert (elevation 14,433 feet; Sawatch Range): 9,073 feet of prominence
- Pikes Peak (elevation 14,110 feet; Front Range): 5,510 feet of prominence
- Blanca Peak (elevation 14,345 feet; Sangre de Cristo Range): 5,326 feet of prominence
- Culebra Peak (elevation 14,047 feet; Sangre de Cristo Range): 4,807 feet of prominence
- Crestone Peak (elevation 14,294 feet; Sangre De Cristo Range): 4,534 feet of prominence
- Uncompahgre Peak (elevation 14,309 feet; San Juan Range): 4,277 feet of prominence
- Flat Top Mountain (elevation 12,354 feet; Flat Tops area): 4,054 feet of prominence
- Mount Wilson (elevation 14,246 feet; San Juan Range): 4,024 feet of prominence
- Ute Peak (elevation 9,979 feet; Southeast Colorado Plateau): 4,019 feet of prominence
- Mount Lincoln (elevation 14,286 feet; Mosquito Range): 3,862 feet of prominence

## COLORADO'S MOST ISOLATED PEAKS

- Mount Elbert (elevation 14,433 feet; highest peak in Colorado; 9,093 feet of prominence[1]; Sawatch Range): 669.98 miles. Proximate parent: Mount Whitney, California

- Blanca Peak (elevation 14,345 feet; 4th highest mountain in Colorado; 5,326 feet of prominence; Sangre de Cristo Range): 103.61 miles. Proximate parent: Mount Harvard, Sawatch Range
- Uncompahgre Peak (elevation 14,309 feet; 6th highest mountain in Colorado; 4,242 feet of prominence; San Juan Range): 85.16 miles. Proximate parent: La Plata Peak, Sawatch Range
- Pikes Peak (elevation 14,110 feet; 30th highest mountain in Colorado; 5,530 feet of prominence; Front Range): 60.88 miles. Proximate parent: Mount Evans A, Front Range
- Unnamed Point 5575 (elevation 5,575 feet; 4,338th highest mountain in Colorado; 310 feet of prominence; Great Plains in Weld County): 55.41 miles. Proximate parent: Unnamed Point 6740B, Great Plains
- Longs Peak (elevation 14,225 feet; 15th highest mountain in Colorado; 2,940 feet of prominence; Front Range): 43.71 miles. Proximate parent: Torreys Peak, Front Range
- Summit Peak (elevation 13,300 feet; 392nd highest mountain in Colorado; 2,760 feet of prominence; South San Juan Range): 41.56 miles. Proximate parent: Phoenix Peak, San Juan Range[2]
- Two Buttes (elevation 4,711 feet; 4,359th highest mountain in Colorado; 356 feet of prominence; Great Plains): 40.95 miles. Proximate parent: Lone Mesa B, Great Plains
- Flat Top Mountain A (elevation 12,354 feet; 1,104th highest mountain in Colorado; 4,054 feet of prominence; Flat Tops Range): 40.8 miles. Proximate parent: Meridian Peak, Gore Range
- 9060 A (elevation 9,060 feet; 2,893rd highest mountain in Colorado; 880 feet of prominence; Roan Cliffs area): 39.4 miles. Proximate parent: Monument Peak, near Rio Blanco

## NOTES

1. Because of the inexact science of defining and measuring key cols, many of which have to be extrapolated because exact elevations are often not marked on U.S. Geographical Survey maps, prominence figures will often vary from one source to another.

2. Also known as Creede Crest and Gwynedd Mountain, 13,895-foot Phoenix Peak, located near Creede, is the highest mountain in Colorado without an official name.

## SOURCES

peakbagger.com; peaklist.org; listsofjohn.com; summitpost.org.

# THE MOST DANGEROUS FOURTEENERS

It is difficult to classify one Fourteener as "more dangerous" than another for two reasons. First is the fact that accident reports are based as much upon a mountain's popularity as they are upon the objective danger presented by a particular mountain. In other words, the more people who visit a given mountain, the more the likelihood of accidents. Second, bad weather can turn even easy, walk-up Fourteeners into difficult ascents.

Still, the Fourteeners are often subjectively ranked. Those rankings can be based upon distance from the trailhead to the summit, the amount of exposure, and the risk of loose rock.

This is a reasonable aggregation of Fourteeners ranked by difficulty based upon the easiest, or standard, route to the summit:

**Easier:**
Grays Peak, Torreys Peak, Handies Peak, Mount Sherman, Mount Democrat, Mount Bross, Mount Lincoln, Quandary Peak, Mount Evans, Mount Bierstadt, Mount Elbert, Mount Massive, Mount Antero, Pikes Peak, Mount Princeton, Culebra Peak, San Luis Peak, Huron Peak, La Plata Peak

**Moderate:**
Mount Belford, Mount Oxford, Humboldt Peak, Redcloud Peak, Sunshine Peak, Mount Columbia, Uncompahgre Peak, Mount Shavano, Tabeguache Mountain, Blanca Peak, Castle

## ▲ FOURTEENERS TIDBITS

- Mount Massive, at 14,421 feet, Colorado's second-highest peak, has more area above 14,000 than any other mountain in the Lower 48, edging out Washington State's Mount Rainer. Mount Massive boasts a total of five peaks above 14,000 feet along its three-mile-long summit ridge.
- 14,259-foot Longs Peak, in Rocky Mountain National Park, is the only one of Colorado's Fourteeners located north of Interstate 70.
- California has 12 Fourteeners and Washington State has two, although Liberty Cap, a subsidiary summit of Mount Rainier, at 14,112, is not often listed as a separate Fourteener, even though it boasts 492 feet of prominence.
- Alaska is home to the country's 15 highest peaks. Twelve of those peaks are higher than 15,000 feet. Since all things are bigger in the Last Frontier, Alaska uses a 500-foot rule to define separate peaks.

Peak, Mount Yale, Missouri Mountain, Mount of the Holy Cross, Ellingwood Point (or Peak), Mount Lindsey

**Difficult:**

Longs Peak, Wetterhorn Peak, Mount Sneffels, Kit Carson Peak, Snowmass Mountain, Mount Eolus, Windom Peak, El Diente Peak, South Maroon Peak, Sunlight Peak, Wilson Peak

**Very Difficult:**

Capitol Peak, North Maroon Peak, Crestone Needle, Little Bear Peak, Mount Wilson, Pyramid Peak

---

### Eldorado Canyon

Although Longs Peak is Colorado's best-known mountaineering destination, Eldorado Canyon State Park, outside Boulder, is the state's best-known climbing destination. Its proximity to Metro Denver means that lots of people, from raw beginners to world-class rock jocks, test their mettle at Eldorado Canyon. Therefore, Eldorado Canyon has seen more than its fair share of carnage. Since 1988, there have been 53 reported climbing accidents and 14 reported climbing fatalities on Eldorado Canyon's cliffs, making it statistically one of the most dangerous places in the state.

---

## DEATH ON THE FOURTEENERS

Based on statistics alone, 14,255-foot Longs Peak, located in Rocky Mountain National Park, is not only the most dangerous Fourteener but the most dangerous mountain in Colorado. More than 50 fatalities have been recorded on Longs Peak, although this statistic is slightly skewed. Unlike most Fourteeners, Longs Peak is a destination for serious mountaineers. Its East Face, otherwise known as "The Diamond," is considered a classic route by international standards. Many of the fatalities on Longs Peak have taken place on technical routes like The Diamond.

The lists in this section are both inconsistent and incomplete, because available records for some of the Fourteeners go back only to 2005, while others go back to 2008. There is no comprehensive, up-to-date list of all of the mishaps that have transpired on Colorado's Fourteeners, so these lists should be used for comparison purposes only.

# DEATH FIGURES FOR COLORADO'S FOURTEENERS

- Longs Peak: 51
- Maroon Peak: 12
- Pikes Peak: 10
- North Maroon Peak: 9
- Little Bear Peak: 8
- Quandary Peak: 7
- Crestone Needle: 6
- Capitol Peak: 5
- Mount Evans: 5
- La Plata Peak: 5
- Crestone Peak: 5
- El Diente Peak: 5
- Snowmass Mountain: 4
- Kit Carson Mountain: 4
- Ellingwood Point (or Peak): 4
- Pyramid Peak: 3
- Mount Sneffels: 3
- Mount Eolus: 3
- Mount Wilson: 3
- Blanca Peak: 3
- Missouri Mountain: 2
- Mount of the Holy Cross: 2
- Huron Peak: 3
- Sunlight Peak: 1
- Sunshine Peak: 1
- Mount Lincoln: 1
- Mount Bross: 1
- Mount Massive: 1
- Mount Harvard: 1
- Mount Antero: 1
- Mount Shavano: 1
- Mount Belford: 1
- Mount Princeton: 1
- Tabeguache Peak: 1
- Challenger Point: 1
- Humboldt Peak: 1
- Mount Lindsey: 1

# ACCIDENT FIGURES FOR COLORADO'S FOURTEENERS, INCLUDING DEATHS

- Longs Peak: 116
- Maroon Peak: 20
- Crestone Needle: 18
- Pikes Peak: 15
- Quandary Pk: 14:
- Mount Evans: 14
- Mount of the Holy Cross: 11
- North Maroon Peak: 10
- Little Bear Peak: 10
- Capitol Peak: 10
- Torreys Peak: 10
- Mount Sneffels: 9
- Crestone Peak: 8
- El Diente Peak: 7
- Mount Bierstadt: 7
- Mount Wilson: 6
- Blanca Peak: 5
- Huron Peak: 5
- Snowmass Mtn.: 4
- Kit Carson Peak: 4
- La Plata Peak: 4
- Ellingwood Point: 4
- Mount Eolus: 4
- Mount Princeton: 3
- Pyramid Peak 3
- Castle Peak: 3
- Missouri Mtn.: 2
- Mount Lincoln: 2
- Mount Democrat: 2
- Mount Shavano: 2
- Sunlight Peak: 2
- Sunshine Peak: 1
- Mount Yale: 1
- Wilson Peak: 1
- Tabeguache Peak: 1
- Mount Sherman: 1
- Mount Lindsey: 1
- Humboldt Peak: 1
- Mount Antero: 1
- Mount Belford: 1
- Challenger Point: 1
- Grays Peak: 1
- Mount Harvard: 1
- Handies Peak: 1

*Note:* These figures reflect only reported accidents, of course.

## MOST DANGEROUS FOURTEENERS BY MOUNTAIN RANGE

- Front Range: Total reported accidents: 164; deaths: 66
- Sangre de Cristos: Total reported accidents: 51; deaths: 33
- Elk Mountains: Total reported accidents: 50; deaths: 32
- Sawatch Range: Total reported accidents: 32; deaths: 19
- San Juans: Total reported accidents: 30; deaths: 16
- Tenmile and Mosquito ranges: Total reported accidents: 20; deaths: 9

## MOST COMMON CAUSES OF FATALITIES ON COLORADO'S FOURTEENERS

- Falls: 110
- Lightning: 14
- Avalanches: 14
- Rockfall: 8
- Natural causes: 8
- Exposure: 7
- Unknown: 7
- Helicopter crash: 2
- Gunshot: 1
- Suicide: 1

## A SAMPLING OF FOURTEENER ACCIDENT NARRATIVES

- September 8, 1962: Susan Greene was practicing self-arrests on a snowfield (on Castle Peak) when the adze of her ice axe struck her in the head. The ice axe struck while being attached to a leash after she lost her grip.
- July 26, 1986: Greg Mace, president of the Mountain Rescue Association, while on a mountain rescue training exercise with three others, was testing the snow on the Bell Cord Couloir (on Maroon Peak) when he lost his ice axe. He slid 700 feet down into boulders feet first, breaking all of the ribs on his left side and puncturing his left lung, which preceded his death.
- August 18, 2001: Sharon Jones slipped while descending North Maroon Peak, the final Fourteener on her list, and twisted her ankle. She fell and came to a rest at the edge of an overhang at the 11,500-foot level. Her party descended and summoned help, which arrived for her rescue the following day.
- July 31, 1989: Paul Hammond and Carl Steger were ascending the Lambs Slide (on Longs Peak) when Hammond fell while dodging rockfall. Hammond slid 200 feet down before self-arresting, causing Steger to follow downward on the rope before Steger was stopped by the rope after sliding 400 feet. Hammond injured his ankle in the fall and Steger suffered rope burns on his neck.
- April 20, 1991: Joe Massari was climbing up toward Broadway (on Longs Peak) when he slipped and fell 1,500 feet to Mills Glacier, where he was covered by an avalanche and died of his injuries.

- August 30, 1992: Lathe Strang fell 20 feet while climbing The Diamond (on Longs Peak), fracturing his ankle when his foot impacted the rock. His partner lowered him 800 feet down the East Face.
- February 3, 1993: Carl Siegel and Derek Hersey were descending the Cable Route after completing The Diamond when Siegel fell from a patch of snow and lost his ice axe. He fell a total of 500 feet to his death. Hersey attempted to rescue Siegel to no avail. Hersey himself died in a climbing accident in Yosemite three months later.
- June 12, 2005: Cory Justice and Dan Welle hiked up Mount Evans from Summit Lake to attempt the Sawtooth Traverse when poor weather forced them to retreat. The two took shelter in the summit restroom facility and were found returning down the Mount Evans Road the following morning.
- September 4, 1995: A mountain biker was resting near the 16 Golden Stairs on Pikes Peak when he lost his balance and fell 100 feet and slid a farther distance. He suffered head injuries, broken bones, and several bruises. He was rescued.
- March 8, 1997: Dan Fenaughty, a news anchor, was on the north side of Pikes Peak digging a trench to evaluate snow stability when the wind blew his pack a short distance away. He reached around for it and fell 1,000 feet down the Little Italy Chute. He remained in critical condition from head injuries for a month before his eventual recovery.
- August 9, 1998: John Wang, a well-respected assistant astronomy professor, was descending La Plata Peak on the newly built trail when his partner suggested he turn back because a thunderstorm was approaching. Wang chose to continue, fell down a gully on his ascent, and died before rescuers arrived.
- July 9, 1994: Sandy Sigman, a flight nurse, and Gary McCall, pilot, were ironically killed in a helicopter crash near the 12,000-foot level of Huron Peak while attempting to rescue a woman who had injured her ankle. This marked the first Flight for Life accident in its 22 years of existence. The injured hiker eventually hiked out under her own power.
- July 26, 2003: A Slovakian couple had ascended Kit Carson Peak and were descending via the lower switchbacks of the Willow Creek Trail about a mile from the trailhead in deteriorating weather. They were both struck by lightning. The man was conscious and waited for rescue to arrive to assist his wife, but flash flooding created access problems and rescue could not arrive in time.
- September 30, 2000: David Syring slipped and fell 800 feet to his death in a rockslide while descending Mount Lindsey. Jon Sher-

man was also descending and fell on ice. He gained control only a few feet from Syring, whom he had seen descending earlier. Body recovery efforts were called due to the unstable nature of the slope.

- August 21, 2001: Sean Spinney fell while descending Mount Sneffels and was rescued in part by members of an anti–Yankee Boy Basin fee protest group. He suffered multiple cuts and bruises, as well as a collapsed lung and a broken pelvis. Spinney died while backpacking near Conejos, Colorado, in June 2003.

## SOURCES

Colorado State Parks; www.listsofjohn.com; www.fourteeners.org.

# MOUNTAINSPEAK: CLIMBING LEXICON

- **Alpine Style:** A fast and light form of mountaineering that lessens dependency on quantity of gear and puts an emphasis on getting up and down a mountain quickly.
- **Bail:** To retreat from a route due to inclement weather, approaching darkness, or an inadequate set of stones. Originally a nautical term and signifies a sinking ship.
- **Beer 30, Beer-Thirty:** The conclusion of the actual climbing capped by the enjoyment of adult beverages. This mutable working-day standard allows for satiation of desire no matter the time. Say, for instance, a climb goes particularly slow, forcing a cold, sleepless night and morning return to the car. (*See* "bail.") Beer-thirty marks the end of a day even if it comes in the A.M.
- **Belayer:** Person who holds the rope for the climber and will arrest the climber's fall, should it come to that. Relies not just upon acumen of the belayer but a variety of technical devices with names like "gri-gris" and "reversos."
- **Belay Slave:** A poor soul who is talked into belaying for long periods of time without receiving appropriate compensation (*see* "Belayer").
- **Beta:** (1) The subtle and sometimes-not-so-subtle information or advice passed from climber to climber. With the rise of the Internet, several Web sites have jockeyed to be the central hub for the dissemination of beta. One day so much beta will be available online, climbers will no longer have to complete the route. (2) Any type of information in the mountain world. The name of a good mechanic might be considered "beta."

- **Big Ditch, the:** Yosemite. Also the Black Canyon of the Gunnison, Colorado.
- **Bivouac:** An overnight experience that can be planned (meaning intentionally spending the night with a minimum of gear) or unplanned (generally meaning that the climbers did not make it either to the summit or back down to their gear before darkness fell). Often combined with the word "epic" (*see* "Epic").
- **Bomber:** A good hold or gear placement. Also used as a generic to mean anything that is strong and dependable.
- **Bong:** (Not what you think.) A big piton used for wide cracks in the 1950s and 1960s.
- **Bootie:** Gear, often left on a route by an inexperienced climber, which is later scarfed off a route by another party.
- **Bouldering:** (1) The popular act of ascending small pieces of stone via the most difficult, contrived path. Viewed by many as the poetry of the sport. (2) Practice for climbing.
- **Bullet:** Good, hard, quality rock.
- **Camp Out:** Hang out on a hold for awhile.
- **Carabiners:** Aluminum, semi-oval-shaped pieces of hardware with gates that open and close, allowing them to be clipped onto bolt hangers, harnesses, or the rope. Also known as "'biners." Particularly popular with non-climbers who use them as keychains and jewelry and to attach water bottles onto day packs.
- **Chalk:** Literally ground-up chalk used to dry the hands while climbing, carried in a small pouch called a "chalk bag."
- **Choss:** Bad rock; also, vegetation, loose rock, and other stuff often found on rarely climbed or new routes. (*See also* "Munge.")
- **Crash Pad/Mat:** Foam pad placed under a bouldering route to protect the falling boulderer from uneven ground or rocks.
- **Decking or Deck:** The act of hitting the ground due to inadequate protection, mental snafus, or bad belaying. The term can also be applied to life's inevitable screwups, such as, say, striking out with a girl, screwing up a job interview, etc.
- **Delhi Belly:** Intestinal distress that often accompanies trips to foreign locales (*see also* "Mexican Gravyleg").
- **Dialed:** To be able to do every move or the whole problem very well.
- **Dirt Burglar:** Boulder problem that starts so low that dirt has to be removed for the climber to fit.
- **Dirt Me:** Command for your partner to lower you to the ground.
- **Elvis Leg/Sewing Machine Leg:** When a climber's leg is shaking a lot due to muscle fatigue or fear. Looks like the bob on a sewing machine or like the "Elvis leg shake."

- **Epic:** Long, trying experience. Perhaps the second most over-used word in the mountain lexicon, after "dude." Now used to mean anything from a medium-length drive along perfectly dry highways in the light of day to a long haul in a bar.
- **Evac:** Evacuate. Often meaning that something went Seriously Wrong.
- **FecoFile (a.k.a. "Shit Tube"):** A big plastic tube that you use as a portable restroom when you are many thousands of feet up a big wall and don't want to ruin the experience of the climbers below you.
- **Flapper:** A big, loose piece of skin that's been mostly, but not entirely, ripped off.
- **Gardening:** Cleaning the dirt and vegetation out of cracks on a dirty chunk of rock; often done mostly during the first ascent.
- **Gaston:** Small, square-cut hold.
- **Gearhead:** A climber obsessed with gear and capable of scaring away an entire campfire of women with endless discussion of weights, fabrics, and alloys.
- **Gerry Rail:** A very big hold.
- **Gobi:** Big, open wound on the back of the fingers and hands where the rock has rubbed away the skin.
- **Goomba:** Novice climber; novice anything.
- **Grounder:** A fall; when your climbing ambitions (and some-times life) are cut short because you fell and hit the ground.
- **Gumby:** An inexperienced or bumbling climber.
- **Jingus:** Crappy; could apply to a hold, a route, or a person.
- **Jug:** A large hold. "I clung to the jugs like my life depended on it."
- **Jug Haul:** An enjoyable, fun route that consists of nothing but large holds.
- **Manky:** Typically used to describe crappy, "fixed" gear (a bolt, a fixed piton, etc.).
- **Mexican Gravyleg:** *See* "Delhi Belly."
- **Monkey:** A climber (particularly a Yosemite climber).
- **Munge:** *See* "Choss."
- **Nuts:** Metal wedges slotted into cracks for protection. Also: parts of the male human anatomy required for serious climbing.
- **Onsight:** To climb a route on the first try with no previous knowledge of the route.
- **Party Ledge:** A ledge big enough for cocktail hour.
- **Pig:** A haul bag, taken on longer climbs to carry anything and ev-erything from extra gear, clothing, food, water, and bivouac gear.
- **Pimp, to:** Not quite a dynamic move (a leap from one set of holds to another), but not quite a static move.
- **Pre-excusing:** Making excuses before even trying to climb.

- **Protection:** Gear, passive and active (nuts, chocks, hexes, cams), that hopefully protects climbers when they fall.
- **Rack:** (Not what your think.) One's climbing gear.
- **Rig:** Quickdraws (two carabiners connected by a sling) pre-placed on bolts on a cliff (for extremely difficult climbs).
- **Screamer:** A type of protection that you place when you're un-sure of the ability of your gear to hold a fall. The screamer rips when you fall and thus reduces the force put on a piece of protec-tion to which it is clipped, reducing the chances of said protec-tion pulling out.
- **Send:** To complete a route. To claim a send, you must climb the route bottom up without falling.
- **Sewn-up:** A pitch in which the leader has placed tons of gear for protection.
- **Sharp End:** The end of the rope attached to the lead climber. A very metaphoric term with many uses outside the climbing world.
- **Smearing:** To rely solely on the friction of your rubber-climbing-shoe-coated foot against the rock for a foothold.
- **Spooning:** The act of staying warm by cuddling up to your climb-ing partner(s), usually during unplanned bivouacs (*see* "Biv-ouac"). Only to be implemented when cold finally represses any angst about holding another man for prolonged periods of time. May lead to awkward moments once the sun rises. Also known as "manwich" or "mancuddle." Women climbers seem to harbor less unease about this highly practical way of keeping warm.
- **Spot:** To help catch your partner if he or she falls while boulder-ing and guiding the person toward the crash pad that hopefully you have placed in the right spot.
- **Spray:** (1) The act of unabashed self-promotion. Often used, un-successfully, to attract female climbers. (2) To spew. "The climber sprayed unwanted beta. We finally had to kill him after he chased all the women away."
- **Sprayathon:** People talking about how great they are or how great people they know are.
- **Spraylord:** A climber who constantly talks about him- or herself or belittles others regardless of skills. Often done from the safety of an Internet chat room.
- **Superbomber:** A very good hold or gear placement.
- **Tomato Paste:** A hapless climber who is bound to screw up and hit the ground. "That guy is tomato paste."
- **Tool:** (1) An individual who does the bidding of The Man. (2) To make a bust. Traditional Yosemite dialect.
- **Tourist Meat:** Non-climbers you've brought along.
- **Trucker:** A very solid anchor

- **Whipper:** A very long fall, wherein the hapless faller is saved, sometimes at the very last moment, by his or her gear and the good work of the belayer.
- **Woodie:** (Not what you think.) A wooden climbing wall, often found in your basement.
- **Yabo:** A sit-start when bouldering. Named for John Yablonski, a Southern Cal climber.

## SOURCES

Cameron Burns, author of many books, including *Postcards from the Trailer Park: The Secret Lives of Climbers* and *Kilimanjaro and Mount Kenya: A Climbing and Trekking Guide*; Fitz Cahall, producer of *The Dirtbag Diaries* (www.dirtbagdiaries.com); Boulder climber Jackie Hueftle.

# THE 3,000-FOOT "RULE"

Almost as ubiquitous, as well as ambiguous, as William Graves's 300-foot rule for determining whether an individual peak is indeed an individual peak, is the so-called "Colorado 3,000-foot rule," which helps climbers ascertain whether they can truly claim to have summited a mountain.

Simply stated, the 3,000-foot rule mandates that folks should gain at least 3,000 vertical feet in order to ethically claim that they have "climbed" a peak.

Although the historic roots of the 3,000-foot rule are cloudy, the concept of a minimum vertical gain to claim a summit certainly has merit. After all, it is possible to drive to the summits of two of Colorado's highest peaks, 14,264-foot Mount Evans and 14,109-foot Pikes Peak. Though many climbers will argue that such things ought to be left to the value systems of individual climbers, few would agree that a person driving to within a quarter mile of the top of Mount Evans or Pikes Peak, then getting out and walking the rest of the way, had truly "climbed" those mountains.

The 3,000-foot rule supposedly applies to all mountains within the state but evolved as a direct result of the Fourteener-bagging craze. Adherents point out that 3,000 vertical feet is plus or minus about the distance between tree line and the summits of most Fourteeners, although many people correctly point out that tree line can easily go as high as 12,000 feet.

Purists contend that one cannot in good conscience add a Fourteener to his or her summit list if he or she gains less than 3,000 vertical feet while achieving that summit. But there are problems with that purism on at least two levels.

First, many of the "classic route" trailheads for the Fourteeners are high enough that they do not allow for 3,000 feet of vertical gain between the trailhead and the summit. For instance, the Blue Lake Trailhead, which accesses 14,265-foot Quandary Peak, is located "only" 2,600 feet below the summit.

And the Kite Lake Trailhead, which accesses 14,286-foot Mount Lincoln, 14,238-foot Mount Cameron, 14,172-foot Mount Bross, and 14,148-foot Mount Democrat, is located at 12,000 feet. Thus, climbers who subscribe to the 3,000-foot rule are faced with either having to park several miles away and walk along a dirt road in order to gain those 3,000 feet or else modifying their perspective toward that rule.

Second, the 3,000-foot rule does not adequately address the issue of gaining multiple summits with one vertical gain. It is common for people to summit Lincoln, Cameron, Bross, and Democrat in one fell swoop. Ditto Shavano and Tabeguache, Redcloud and Sunshine, Grays and Torreys, Belford and Oxford, and a host of other Fourteener clusters. Subscribing religiously to the 3,000-foot rule would necessitate a descent from, say, Belford and a re-ascent of Oxford in order to lay clear-conscience claim to both summits.

Understanding the impracticality of manifesting such a purist philosophy into one's climbing consciousness, most reasonable climbers caveat the 3,000-foot rule to allow for summit claims when aggregating proximate summits. Those striving for purity, but who still allow reasonable loopholes into their climbing consciousness, will argue that multiple summits can be claimed without re-ascending close-at-hand summits only if the summits are connected by one of the state's notorious gnarly traverses, such as the traverse that connects Evans and Bierstadt or the one that connects Mount Wilson with El Diente.

Fourteener junkies will generally define successful summit bids as those beginning at the generally accepted class-route trailheads, and they count multiple summits gained after one ascent.

It is considered good form, when laying claim to any Fourteener records, to acknowledge how one integrated the 3,000-foot rule into one's philosophy.

## SOURCES

*Colorado's Fourteeners: From Hikes to Climbs* by Gerry Roach; 14ers.com; Eskimo.com.

# COLORADO'S STEEPEST POINTS

1. **Chimney Rock** (Hinsdale and Ouray counties): Average angle: 61.40 degrees; average drop: 602 feet; elevation: 11,781 feet; prominence: 401 feet; rank among western contiguous states: 13
2. **The Sharkstooth** (Larimer County): Average angle: 60.90 degrees; average drop: 589 feet; elevation: 12,630 feet; prominence: 490 feet; rank among western contiguous states: 16
3. **Elephant Head Rock** (Archuleta County): Average angle: 58.10 degrees; average drop: 527 feet; elevation: 9,963 feet; prominence: 463 feet; rank among western contiguous states: 38
4. **Curecanti Needle** (Gunnison County): Average angle: 56.89 degrees; average drop: 503 feet; elevation: 7,856 feet; prominence: 396 feet; rank among western contiguous states: 59
5. **Chimney Rock** (Montezuma County): Average angle: 54.94 degrees; average drop: 467 feet; elevation: 6,110 feet; prominence: 690 feet; rank among western contiguous states: 86
6. **East Toe** (Montezuma County): Average angle: 54.89 degrees; average drop: 467 feet; elevation: 7,765 feet; prominence: 345 feet; rank among western contiguous states: 87
7. **Turret Ridge** (Hinsdale County): Average angle: 54.57 degrees; average drop: 461 feet; elevation: 12,260 feet; prominence: 680 feet; rank among western contiguous states: 90
8. **Unnamed point 6,719** (Mesa County): Average angle: 53.43 degrees; average drop: 442 feet; elevation: 6,719 feet; prominence: 509 feet; rank among western contiguous states: 122
9. **Lizard Head** (Dolores and San Miguel counties): Average angle: 53.24 degrees; average drop: 439 feet; elevation: 13,113 feet; prominence: 1,133 feet; rank among western contiguous states: 126
10. **Independence Monument** (Mesa County): Average angle: 53.14 degrees; average drop: 437 feet; elevation: 5,739 feet; prominence: 389 feet; rank among western contiguous states: 129

SOURCE

listsofjohn.com.

# THE PEAKS OF MARTIN LUTHER KING'S "I HAVE A DREAM" SPEECH

On August 28, 1963, the Reverend Martin Luther King delivered what has come to be known as his "I Have A Dream" speech[1], justifiably considered one of the greatest examples of oration in American history.

The speech was delivered to an estimated 250,000 people at the Lincoln Memorial in Washington, D.C., during the March on Jobs and Freedom, one of the largest gatherings during the entire Civil Rights Movement.

Dr. King went vertical as the speech reached its glorious crescendo:

> So let freedom ring from the prodigious hilltops of New Hampshire. Let freedom ring from the mighty mountains of New York. Let freedom ring from the heightening Alleghenies of Pennsylvania. Let freedom ring from the snowcapped Rockies of Colorado. Let freedom ring from the curvaceous slopes of California. But not only that—Let freedom ring from Stone Mountain of Georgia. Let freedom ring from Lookout Mountain of Tennessee. Let freedom ring from every hill and mole hill of Mississippi. From every mountainside, let freedom ring!

The rank of the mountains referenced directly or indirectly in Dr. King's "I Have A Dream" speech are:

1. Mount Whitney, California: 14,495 feet
2. Mount Elbert, Colorado: 14,433 feet
3. Mount Washington, New Hampshire: 6,288 feet
4. Mount Marcy, New York: 5,344 feet
5. Mount Davis, Pennsylvania: 3,213 feet
6. Lookout Mountain, Tennessee: 2,146 feet
7. Stone Mountain, Georgia: 1,680 feet
8. Woodall Mountain, Mississippi: 806 feet

## NOTES

1. Segments of the "I Have A Dream" speech, part of which was prepared and part of which was extemporaneous, were given a test drive by Dr. King in June 1963, when he delivered a speech incorporating some of the same sections in Detroit, where he marched on Woodward Avenue with Walter Reuther and the Reverend C.L. Franklin. He had reportedly rehearsed other segments of the speech previously.

The "I Have A Dream" speech was embroiled in controversy on two occasions.

First, there were allegations that King had plagiarized at least 20 percent of the speech—most of the last two minutes—from a speech delivered at the 1952 Republican National Convention by the Reverend Archibald Cary, Jr.

Second, because King had distributed copies of his speech prior to its delivery at the Lincoln Memorial, its copyright status was in dispute for 36 years! In 1999, the civil case, Estate of Martin Luther King, Jr., Inc. versus CBS, Inc., was settled out of court with the understanding that the King estate owned the copyright for the speech.

## SOURCES

The idea for this section, as well as much of the information, came from peakbagger.com. The details of the speech came from Wikipedia.

# HEADWATERS HILL AND COLORADO'S CLOSED BASINS

When it comes to mountains, Colorado is generally all about the superlative numbers: How high is a given peak? Mostly, this question pertains to the state's obsession with its Fourteeners, but other manifestations include preoccupations with the High Thirteeners, the state's Hundred Highest Peaks, and, in many cases, a focus on the highest points within an artificial political construct, like a given county, wilderness area, or national park.

Rarely do the myriad peaks of lesser elevation—especially those less than 12,000 feet—gain so much as a cursory nod from those focused on keeping ascent lists.

But there is one "little" mountain, the summit elevation of which is still higher than the highest point in 38 states, which stands among only a few similar peaks in the entire country as far as stature.

In Colorado's little-visited Cochetopa Hills can be found what by state standards is a very minor mountain, 11,683-foot Headwaters Hill, which did not even receive its official appellation until July 2001 (before that, it was, as almost all non-officially named mountains are, known merely by its elevation: Peak 11,683).

Headwaters Hill is one of only five "triple-divide peaks" in the Lower 48. A "triple-divide peak" is a mountain that drains into three different major watersheds. Many mountains along the Continental Divide in Colorado drain into Atlantic- and Pacific-bound watersheds. But Headwaters Hill, a few miles from Marshall Pass (just off of the Colorado Trail, where Saguache, Gunnison, and Chaffee counties come together), sends from its sides waters that flow into three drainages: From the flanks of Headwaters Hill, rainwater and snowmelt flow into the Arkansas, Colorado, and Rio Grande drainages[1], where those waters do not again meet up until they find their way to the ocean.

There is one other Colorado mountain, 13,852-foot McNamee Peak, in the Mosquito Range just east of Climax and Fremont Pass, which also services three drainages—the South Platte, the Arkansas, and the Colorado. But McNamee loses critical stature in the triple-divide-peak club because the waters of two of those rivers—the Arkansas and the South Platte—join back up in the Mississippi before they reach saltwater. That's a penalty flag that cannot be overlooked in this rarefied club.

Even though the three-drainage runoff from Headwaters Hill does not meet again until it reaches the sea, there is one asterisk next to its triple-divide-peak claim. Purists maintain that a true triple-divide peak is a place where two Continental Divides meet—meaning that runoff from those mountains eventually flows into three distinct bodies of saltwater.

Triple Divide Peak in Glacier National Park, Montana, marks the intersection of the Northern Divide and what Rocky Mountain dwellers call the Continental Divide[2]. Waters diverted from Triple Divide Peak drain into the Pacific-bound Columbia River Basin, the Gulf-of-Mexico-bound Missouri Basin, and the Hudson-Bay-bound Saskatchewan and Nelson River drainages.

The Hill of Three Waters, Minnesota, near Hibbing, is where the Saint Lawrence Seaway Divide intersects the Northern Divide. Waters from this point flow north to the Hudson Bay, south to the Gulf of Mexico, and east to the Gulf of Saint Lawrence.

Another triple-divide peak, an unnamed point near Gold, Pennsylvania, separates water into the Mississippi (Gulf of Mexico), the Great Lakes (Saint Lawrence), and the Susquehanna River (Atlantic) drainages.

Three Waters Mountain, in western Wyoming, is also considered a triple-divide peak, although, like Headwaters Hill, it does not lie at the junction of two of the Continental Divides. Water from Three Waters Mountain flows into the Columbia, Colorado, and Missouri–Mississippi river systems. But, like Headwaters Hill, Three Waters Mountain has an asterisk, because two of those rivers, the Columbia and the Colorado, both flow into the Pacific Ocean, although the Colorado, of course, enters the Pacific by way of the Sea of Cortez/Gulf of California. Or at least it did before over-allocation of the Colorado caused the river to dry up before entering saltwater.

## NOTES

1. There is debate about whether it is truly accurate to state that the water from the south side of Headwaters Hill actually "flows" into the Rio Grande (at least naturally), because the water goes—mostly underground, traceable only via riparian vegetation—into the Middle Creek drainage and, after that, into a geo-

physically unique part of the San Luis Valley: the Closed Basin (one of Colorado's three significant examples of what geologists call endorheic drainage basins). This large area in the northern part of the San Luis Valley covers about 2,900 square miles and is separated from the rest of the valley (i.e., those parts of the valley that unequivocally flow into the Rio Grande) by a low alluvial fan. There is no drainage from the Closed Basin, and much of the water that flows into it is lost through evapotranspiration. Water that is not lost thusly eventually flows into San Luis Lakes on the periphery of the San Luis Valley. Therefore, following the definition of a closed basin (see below), that water—much of it originating on the flanks of Headwaters Hill—has either seeped into the ground or evaporated since time immemorial. Since the entire San Luis Valley is considered part of the Rio Grande drainage, however, Headwaters Hill maintains its tenuous triple-divide status via that reality. That tenuous status, though, has been mitigated somewhat by the fact that the waters flowing from its south side, although they may never actually reach the Gulf of Mexico naturally, now do so artificially, as the federal Bureau of Reclamation pumps water from the Closed Basin into the Rio Grande to help meet the state's legal obligation at the border. It's a piece of the bureau's San Luis Valley Project, which went on line in May 1952.

The largest closed (endorheic) basin in the United States is the 200,000-square-mile Great Basin, an intermontane plateau that covers most of Nevada and more than half of Utah, as well as parts of California, Idaho, Oregon, and Wyoming. The Great Basin is not a single basin but rather a series of contiguous watersheds bounded on the west by the Sacramento/San Joaquin and Klamath rivers, on the north by the watershed of the Columbia/Snake, and on the south and east by the watershed of the Colorado/Green. A major example of a closed basin with a Colorado connection is Wyoming's 3,959-square-mile Great Divide Basin, around which the Continental Divide passes. When you look at a map of the divide as it goes north from Colorado into Wyoming, you will notice a split. The Continental Divide Trail, of which more than 800 miles traverse Colorado, passes right through the heart of the Great Divide Basin, which was formed by a geologic anticline. Other major examples of closed basins include Nevada's Black Rock Desert, where the annual Burning Man gathering takes place every year; Utah's Great Salt Lake; California's Mono Lake; South America's Lago Titicaca—the world's highest navigable body of water; the Caspian Sea in Asia—the world's largest lake; and, perhaps most famous, the Dead Sea, which straddles the border of Israel and Jordan and which, at 1,378 feet below sea level, is the lowest surface point on earth. Colorado is home to two other closed basins besides the one in the San Luis Valley: Bear Creek Basin in the southwestern part of the state and White Woman Basin, spanning the Colorado–Kansas border south and north of the Arkansas River.

2. What we call the "Continental Divide" in Colorado is known as the "Great Divide" to geographic sticklers who are prone to note that all four of North America's major divides—the Great, the Northern, the Eastern, and the Saint Lawrence Seaway Divide—are "continental" in nature and scope, despite the fact that none of those other three divides contain peaks that reach 14,000 feet (not by a long shot!).

## SOURCES

Ed Quillen / *Denver Post*; George Sibley / *Colorado Central Magazine*; Ed Quillen / *ColoradoCentral Magazine*; www.geocities.com/mapguygk07/3RP/articles/index.htm; www.western.edu/headwaters/headwatershill.html; www.atlas.usgs.gov/articles/geology/a_continentalDiv.html.

# THE NAMING OF
# CHALLENGER POINT

It seems a bit strange that a new Fourteener was born out of thin air—literally—in 1987. But that's exactly what happened with Challenger Point, a 14,080-foot (or 14,081-foot, depending on your source[1]) sub-peak of Kit Carson Mountain, in the Sangre de Cristo Range.

The name "Challenger Point" was approved by the U.S. Board on Geographic Names (BGN) on April 9, 1987. The naming proposal had been submitted by a resident of Colorado Springs immediately following the January 1986 loss of the space shuttle Challenger, but at that time, the BGN responded that it would defer any decision until after one year had passed. This was done in accordance with the BGN's Commemorative Naming Policy, which required that the intended honoree(s) of a new name must have been deceased at least one year. (The waiting period has since been extended to five years.)

Over the course of the next year, the BGN received numerous letters of support for the Challenger Point naming proposal, including from the Saguache County commissioners and several other elected officials. The BGN discussed concerns that the unnamed point was not an identifiable feature separate from the larger Kit Carson Mountain. The U.S. Forest Service suggested it could be confusing to "name a secondary peak on an [already] named mountain," and the question of whether or not to apply a name to a separate point "should depend on its distance from the actual summit."

Nonetheless, the BGN regarded it as a new name for an unnamed feature, and not a name change. The BGN has long recognized that "sub-peaks" of larger summits (massifs) can and often are given individual names, "much as the individual lakes that make up the Great Lakes have their own names." The BGN also does not attempt to classify a "sub-peak" (i.e., the amount of local relief and/or distance between two adjacent peaks is not a factor in whether or not one or both should or should not be named).

A colleague of the naming proponent responded to the U.S. Forest Service's comments by asserting that, in Colorado, there are about 60 additional high points above 14,000 feet on topographic maps at 40-foot vertical resolution. It was further asserted that only four of those additional high points now have official names — meaning there are at least 56 points in Colorado marked as being above 14,000 feet on USGS topographical maps that are not yet named. Challenger Point is a high point on a long ridge at 37-58-49 north, 105-36-21 west, or about 0.22 mile WNW of the main summit of Kit Carson Mountain. It is separated from the main peak by a steep-walled, 320-foot-deep cut, the deepest saddle drop of any Colorado Fourteener sub-peak. That amount of drop qualifies Challenger Point as a separate peak under William Graves's 300-vertical-foot separation rule.

Despite the concerns, the BGN continued to receive overwhelming support for the naming effort and approved the name in April 1987. Over the weekend of July 17, 1987, a bronze memorial plaque was placed on the newly named point by a group of mountain climbers and colleagues of the proponent. The plaque states: "CHALLENGER POINT, 14,080+. In memory of the Crew of the Shuttle Challenger Seven who died accepting the risk, expanding Mankind's horizons. January 28, 1986. Ad Astra Per Aspera." (The Latin phrase translates as "To the stars through adversity."

The Geographic Names Information System[2] entry notes specifically that Challenger Point is named for the members of the *Challenger* crew:

> *Named as a memorial to the men and women, Francis (Dick) Scobee, Michael Smith, Gregory Jarvis, Ronald McNair, Ellison Onizuka, Judith Resnick, and Christa McAuliffe, who died in the NASA* Challenger *space shuttle accident on January 28, 1986 at the John F. Kennedy Space Center, Florida.*

## NOTES

1. Both Wikipedia and Gerry Roach, in his book, *Colorado's Fourteeners, from Hikes to Climbs,* state that Challenger Point has an elevation of 14,081 feet. The Colorado Mountain Club's "Challenger Point Memorial Plaque Trip Report" (July 22, 1987), states that the elevation is 14,080 feet.

2. The official U.S. government repository for two-million-plus place names and their locations; http://geonames.usgs.gov.

## SOURCES

The bulk of the naming information process comes from Jennifer Runyon, research staff, U.S. Board on Geographic Names, U.S. Geological Survey, Geographic Names Office, via e-mail.

# SOME NOTEWORTHY COLORADO UPHILLS

- The biggest single vertical gain in the state—and one of the biggest in the Lower 48—is the Barr Trail, which climbs 7,500 feet in 12 miles from Manitou Springs to the summit of Pikes Peak.
- 12,965-foot West Sopris, which dominates the horizon as you're making your way from Carbondale to Aspen, offers up a 6,250-foot vertical gain in a mere 2.5 miles. The Sopris Trail, which starts near Dinkle Lake, offers a 4,300-foot vertical ascent in 12 miles.
- The biggest vertical gain as you move from Denver to Durango on the 483-mile Colorado Trail is Hope Pass, near Twin Lakes, which gains 3,181 feet in 4 miles.
- The biggest single vertical gain as you make your way from Durango to Denver on the Colorado Trail is 5,220 feet, from the trail's southern terminus at Junction Creek, outside Durango, to Kennebec Pass. This elevation is spread out over almost 20 miles and includes a 4-mile descent.
- The journey to the summit of Colorado's highest peak, 14,433 Mount Elbert, gains 4,400 feet in 3.8 miles, starting at the Mount Elbert Trailhead near Halfmoon Creek.

## SOURCES

Colorado Trail Foundation maps; various USGS topographical maps.

# COLORADO'S LONG HIKING TRAILS AND THE NATIONAL SCENIC TRAILS

Colorado is without a doubt the long-distance hiking trail capital of the country.

Three world-famous long-distance trails traverse Colorado: the 483-mile **Colorado Trail (CT)**, the 3,100-mile **Continental Divide National Scenic Trail (CDT)**, and the 6,800-mile **American Discovery Trail (ADT)**.

The National Scenic Trail system was authorized under the National Scenic Trails Act of 1968. That year, Congress established the first two National Scenic Trails: The 2,174-mile **Appalachian Trail (AT)**, which goes from Springer Mountain, Georgia, to Mount Katahdin, Maine, and the 2,638-mile **Pacific Crest Trail (PCT)**, which zigzags from Mexico to Canada via California, Oregon, and Washington. Although it was not designated as a National Scenic Trail until 1968, the AT, which was first conceived in 1921, was actually dedicated in 1937, making it one of the oldest, marked, long-distance hiking trails in the world. Work began on the PCT in the 1930s, but it was not designated a National Scenic Trail until 1968, and it was not officially dedicated until 1993. At that time, the PCT displaced the AT as the world's longest continually marked hiking trail.

There have been numerous subsequent updates to the National Scenic Trails Act. One of those modifications, in 1978, legally established the CDT, except that, all these years later, the CDT is still far from actually being completed. However, substantial progress is made every year, mainly through volunteer trail crews. The other National Scenic Trails in the United States are:

- North Country Trail: 3,200 miles (established 1980)
- Ice Age Trail: 1,000 miles (established 1980)
- Florida Trail: 1,300 miles (established 1983)
- Potomac Heritage Trail: 700 miles (established 1983)
- Natchez Trace: 695 miles (established 1983)
- Arizona Trail: 807 miles (established 2009)
- Pacific Northwest Trail: 1,200 miles (2009)
- New England Trail: 220 miles (established 2009)

## COLORADO'S LONG TRAILS

All told, there are at least 2,391 marked, long-distance trail miles in Colorado[1,2].

### Colorado Trail

Connecting Waterton Canyon, just outside Denver, with Durango, the 483-mile CT passes through eight major mountain ranges, seven national forests, and six wilderness areas. The estimated total vertical gain for the CT—the high point of which is 13,334-foot Coney Summit (near Lake City)—is about 75,000 feet.

### Continental Divide Trail

About 800 of the CDT's total miles pass through Colorado, including the high point of the entire trail—the summit of 14,270-foot Grays Peak. The southern terminus of the CDT is found on the Mexican border in New Mexico's remote Bootheel area (the closest "dot on the map" being the border crossing of Antelope Wells, New Mexico[3]. The northern terminus is on the Canadian border in Glacier National Park, Montana. The CDT enters Colorado (depending on which direction you are traveling) just south of Cumbres Pass, near Chama, New Mexico, and leaves the state at the Wyoming border in the remote Sierra Madre Range, north of Steamboat Springs.

## American Discovery Trail

This is the country's only coast-to-coast long-distance hiking trail, connecting Cape Henlopen, Delaware, with Limantour Beach, California. The official length of the ADT is 6,800 miles, although this is not entirely accurate, as the trail splits into two routes — Northern and Southern — between Denver and Ohio. Those hiking coast-to-coast can expect to cover about 5,000 miles, much of which follows roads through parts of the country that are not home to significant quantities of public land. The ADT, which, on its sea-to-shining-sea meander, passes through 14 national parks and 16 national forests, enters Colorado near Lomas and leaves the state near Holly (Southern ADT route) and Julesburg (Northern ADT route). All told, there are 1,153 ADT miles in Colorado. The ADT's high point is 13,206-foot Argentine Pass, between Summit and Clear Creek counties. Its low point is actually 17 feet below sea level, between Isleton and Antioch, California.

## NOTES

1. This is admittedly a stretch on several levels. First, most of the 1,153 miles of the ADT through Colorado follow paved and dirt roads, and likely always will, given the lack of public land upon which to build "real" trail on the overwhelmingly private land through which the ADT route passes. Second, the CDT and CT are one in the same for about 200 miles. As well, 133 miles of the ADT in Colorado are contiguous with the CT, the CDT, or both. In fact, Colorado is the only state in the country where you can hike on three major trails—at the same time: The 80-mile stretch of tread from Georgia Pass (between Summit and Park counties) to Turquoise Lake (near Leadville), and the 13-mile stretch from Halfmoon Campground (which serves double duty as the main trailhead to the summit of both Mount Elbert and Mount Massive, Colorado's two highest peaks) to the Clear Creek Road, are home to the CT, the CDT, and the ADT. Much of the CT/CDT/ADT route between Halfmoon Creek and Clear Creek Road also serves as the route for the famous Leadville Trail 100 Race Across the Sky ultra-marathon.

2. California, home to 1,697 miles of the PCT, is second, with about 1,908 marked long-distance trail miles within its borders, although, with 1,697 miles of the PCT, the Golden State is certainly tops when it comes to miles of National Scenic Trail within its borders. Washington State, with 876 miles of the Pacific Northwest National Scenic Trail and 508 miles of the PCT, has a total of 1,384 national scenic trail miles within its borders.

3. Unlike the other trails listed in this segment, the CDT actually has a weird organizational dynamic at work. Matter of fact, the trail really has two distinct routes. In 1978, one man and one man only, Jim Wolf, testified before Congress when the National Scenic Trails Act was modified to include the CDT. Wolf, president of the Baltimore, Maryland–based Continental Divide Trail Society (CDTS), had spent many years splicing together a route that he laid before Congress. For the first 15 years of the CDT's official existence, Wolf and his cohorts

spearheaded the slow process of actually turning a proposed 3,100-mile route (much of which, admittedly, was set to follow existing paths) through the heart of some of the roughest territory in the United States into an actual National Scenic Trail. Then, in the mid-1990s, a second CDT-oriented group sprang up. In 1994, the U.S. Forest Service, the lead governmental agency for the CDT, hooked up, through the non-profit National Forest Foundation, with a man named Steve Fausel (a part-time Summit County, Colorado resident), president of the Fausel Foundation, in hopes of establishing a public–private partnership that would jumpstart the CDT. The result of that effort became the Golden, Colorado–based Continental Divide Trail *Alliance* (CDTA), which incorporated as a non-profit entity in 1995. Thing is, Wolf's group did not go away. At this point, both the CDTA and the CDTS operate separately. Wolf's route, now called by many the "traditional route" or the "Wolf Route," and the CDTA route, which is now considered the "official route," are contiguous in many places. There are significant divergences, especially in New Mexico. Unofficial and unverifiable estimates are that about half of all CDT through-hikers—those intending to hike from Mexico to Canada (or vice-versa) in one fell swoop—follow the traditional route, while the other half follow the official route.

SOURCES:

The Colorado Trail Foundation; the Continental Divide Trail Alliance; the Continental Divide Trail Society; www.discoverytrail.org; Pacific Northwest Trail Association; Pacific Crest Trail Association.

# MOUNTAINSPEAK: HIKING AND BACKPACKING LEXICON

- **Access Trail:** A trail that connects the main trail to a road or another trail system. Often traverses private property via the good graces of the property owner.
- **Backcountry:** Area where there are no maintained roads or permanent buildings; only primitive roads and trails exist.
- **Backpacking:** A hike that extends to at least one overnight stay where the essentials (food, shelter, clothing, etc.) for that stay are packed.
- **Billy-Goat:** To either run up a huge mountain fast or to hop from rock to rock down a hairy ski line. "He billy-goated that ascent." Or, "Dude, you billy-goated that gnarly section like, well, a billy-goat." Also refers to a person who billy-goats.
- **Bivouac (Bivy):** An overnight stay with little or no shelter, usually unplanned and almost always used as fodder for long-winded post-trip stories.
- **Bivouac Sack (Bivy Sack):** A lightweight and waterproof bag that covers a sleeping bag; almost always used instead of a tent.

- **Blazes:** Trail markers. Usually in the form of a 2-inch-wide by 6-inch-high section of bark chipped from a tree and often painted.
- **Blister:** A physiological aberration that causes many hikers to wonder aloud, often with invectives intertwined, how something so small can cause so much pain. Caused by a combination of prolonged friction resulting from pressure and/or repeated movement along the skin. In an effort to protect itself, the body reacts to this friction by moving blood serum (plasma) under the first layer of skin in an attempt to prevent further injury to the epidural layer. The other means by which the body reacts to blisters is to make them extremely painful in hopes that the hiker will have the good sense to get off of his or her feet until the blister heals. This is often not possible when the hiker is, say, four days from the trailhead. Blisters can and often do get infected.
- **Bluff:** A steep headland, riverbank, or cliff.
- **Bridleway (Bridle Path):** Trail designed and maintained primarily for equestrian use.
- **Bunched Sock:** When a hiking sock is not stretched evenly around the foot. Common as a sock gets distended by use and/or saturated with dirt and sweat during a long hike. If not addressed, can result in hot spots and blisters (*see* "Hot Spots" and "Blisters").
- **Cache:** A supply of food, tools, etc., usually buried or hidden.
- **Cairn:** A constructed mound of rock located adjacent to a trail used to mark the trail route. Especially useful along little-used trails.
- **Canyoneering (a.k.a. "Canyoning"):** Traveling in canyons using a variety of techniques that may include walking, scrambling, climbing, jumping, rappelling, and/or swimming.
- **Cathole:** Term appropriated from litter boxes to refer to the holes dug in the woods into which one makes number-two.
- **Causeway:** Elevated section of trail contained by rock, usually in permanent or seasonally wet areas.
- **CDT:** Continental Divide National Scenic Trail, which runs 3,100 miles from the Mexican border near Antelope Wells, New Mexico, to the Canadian border in Glacier National Park, Montana. Approximately 800 miles of the CDT pass through Colorado, with about 200 of those miles being contiguous with the Colorado Trail.
- **Cherry Stem Loop:** A loop hike accessed by an access trail on which you both hike in and out.
- **Cirque:** An amphitheater-like valley formed at the head of a glacier by erosion.

- **Compass:** A device used to indicate direction. In the age of Global Positioning Systems (GPS), compasses and the knowledge of how to use them is waning rapidly.
- **Contour Lines:** Lines on a topographical map indicating elevation and steepness.
- **Creeking:** The process of attempting to follow a creek from its mouth to its source by walking entirely in the creek bed itself. Considered contrived and potentially environmentally impactful by many outdoorspeople.
- **CT:** Colorado Trail, a 483-mile trail that runs from Denver to Durango.
- **Ecosystem:** A natural system consisting of all plants, animals, and microorganisms in an area functioning together with all of the physical factors of the environment. A unit of interdependent organisms that share the same habitat. Term has been co-opted to apply to any number of decidedly non-natural environments, like "social ecosystems" or "workplace ecosystems."
- **Extra Protein:** Any sort of insect or unidentifiable detritus that falls into the food or beverage of backpackers who have been in the woods for so long that whatever civilized tendencies they might once have harbored are so far gone that they scarcely flinch while deadpanning, "Extra protein," after which they simply continue eating and drinking, as if nothing out of the ordinary had happened on the culinary front.
- **False Summit:** A deceptive piece of geology that disguises itself as the top of the mountain you have been slogging up for hours, only to reveal at the most discouraging moment that you still have a considerable distance left to ascend before you get to the actual summit, which might very well also be false. This can go on for a long enough time that many people often wonder if they have been somehow caught in the middle of an alpine M.C. Escher painting. False summits are often accompanied by outbursts of colorful language.
- **Fastpacking:** Carrying the least weight possible while backpacking, the idea being that, with less weight, you can cover significantly longer distances in shorter periods of time. Especially appealing to 10k runners who are tiring of pavement.
- **Footpath:** A right-of-way in which the public has access by foot only.
- **Front Country:** Planner-ese for territory that is close enough to populated areas that it needs to be managed in such a way as to accommodate significant visitor numbers, yet is far enough from those populated areas that it still maintains some backcountry characteristics. Part of a public-land-management

progression that goes from (most used to least used): urban parklands, open space, urban/wildlife interface, front country, backcountry, wilderness.

- **Geocaching:** Outdoor "treasure"-hunting game in which the participants use a Global Positioning System (GPS) receiver to hide and seek containers, called "geocaches," anywhere in the world. A typical cache is a small waterproof container, such as Tupperware or an ammo can, containing a logbook and "treasure"—usually trinkets of little value. Geocaches can now be found in more than 100 countries. There are almost one million active geocaching sites throughout the world. Geocaching owes its roots to "letterboxing," a 150-year-old game that uses clues and references to landmarks embedded in stories. Geocaching was imagined shortly after the removal of Selective Availability from GPS on May 1, 2000, because the improved accuracy of the system then allowed for small containers to be specifically placed, marked, and located. The first documented placement of a GPS-located geocache took place on May 3, 2000, by Dave Ulmer of Beaver Creek, Oregon. The location was posted on the Usenet newsgroup sci.geo.satellite as 45°17.460'N 122°24.800'W. By May 6, 2000, it had been found twice and logged once (by Mike Teague of Vancouver, Washington). According to Ulmer's message, the original stash was a black plastic bucket buried most of the way into the ground, which contained software, videos, books, money, food, and a slingshot. Geocaching is not without controversy, especially when it is practiced in legally designated wilderness areas, because many people consider the leaving behind of items in the woods to be littering, whether it is part of a game or not.
- *Giardia Lamblia:* Protozoan parasite that colonizes and reproduces in the small intestine, causing giardiasis. Causes a degree of intestinal illness that is often stunningly extreme. Often called "beaver fever," it is spread by urine and feces of warm-blooded animals. Often ingested in cyst form via drinking untreated backcountry water. Use of filters or purification systems is always recommended when drinking from natural water sources in the high country.
- **GORP:** "Good Ol' Raisins and Peanuts." A trail snack made with fruit, nuts, chocolate, etc. Has become a generic to indicate any concoction of fruits, nuts, and candy.
- **Habitat:** An area that supports a plant or animal population because it supplies that organism's basic requirements of food, water, shelter, living space, and security.
- **Hike:** A walk lasting one day or less.

- **Hiking Staff (or Stick):** Long considered *de rigueur* trail equipment, now generally relegated to the arena of fuddy-duddy-ness. Hiking staffs have now generally been replaced on the trail by trekking poles, which are modified cross-country ski poles used to aid balance and thrust, as well as to mitigate impacts to the body. Trekking poles can also cost upwards of $100, whereas most hiking sticks are free—though a hiking-staff cottage industry has grown in the past couple decades, with decorative sticks often costing almost as much as trekking poles.
- **Hot Spot:** A point on one's foot that is starting to get rubbed enough that it hurts, but not yet rubbed enough that a blister has been formed. Often aided and abetted by wet feet.
- **Junction:** Site where one trail meets another. Often perfect places to lose your hiking buddies if you have become strung out along the trail. Good places to have a snack while everyone catches up.
- **Leave No Trace Center for Outdoor Ethics (LNT):** Educational program founded in 1994 and headquartered in Boulder, Colorado, designed to instill behaviors in the outdoors that leave minimum impact of human activities. Its core tenets are: Plan ahead and prepare, travel and camp on durable surfaces, dispose of waste properly, leave what you find, minimize campfire impacts, respect wildlife, and be considerate of other visitors.
- **Lost:** Term often misused to mean not knowing where one is (disoriented), when in actuality it means not knowing where you are and simultaneously not being able to follow one's footsteps back out the way you came.
- **Lug Sole:** Thick sole, with deep indentations, found on hiking boots. The tread pattern varies from V-shaped to diamond-shaped indentations. Lug soles are somewhat controversial because many people blame them for causing erosion on trails.
- **Magnetic Declination:** The angle between the local magnetic field (i.e., the direction the compass needle is pointing wherever on Earth you are) and true north. Almost all maps will have magnetic declination shown. It is necessary to factor magnetic declination into any direction-based decisions. It is also important to note that, because the North Magnetic Pole gradually moves, magnetic declination figures change.
- **Moleskin:** Heavy cotton fabric woven and then sheared to create a short pile on one side. Moleskin can be coated with an adhesive backing and used to prevent or treat blisters by cutting an "O" shape into the middle of a piece of the fabric so that the fabric itself does not contact or adhere to the blister. The thickness of the rest of the surrounding moleskin then protects the blister from further friction or impact.

- **Moraine:** A ridge or pile of boulders, stones, and other debris carried along and deposited by a glacier.
- **Orienteering:** Using a map and compass to navigate between points along an unfamiliar course. Often used to mean a competition that combines map-and-compass skills with trail running.
- **Orienting:** Basically, getting your bearings based upon a combination of factors that can include map, compass, and/or a visual surveying of your surroundings. Also the process of using a compass and/or surrounding terrain to move a map so that it aligns with both the North Pole (true north) and physical reality.
- **Out-and-Back Hike:** A hike that goes to a set turnaround point, then follows the same route back out again.
- **Outcrop:** A rock formation that protrudes through the level of the surrounding soil.
- **Pain Gorp:** A combination of several varieties of painkillers/anti-inflammatories that are taken together to relieve a limping hiker of having to worry about whether Advil or aspirin is best for blisters or whether Tylenol or Aleve is best for knee pain. Probably not a real popular concept with physicians.
- **Pass:** A geographic term to indicate a named low point where generally are found trails and roads that cross ridgelines. Historically, passes are a combination of a geographic feature and a historic use—footpath, wagon-train road, railroad bed—that crossed the geographic feature.
- **Peak Bagging:** A term used by people who often summit mountains with the intent of adding summits to a list or outdoor-based CV. Popular with people attempting to summit all of Colorado's Fourteeners, or the state's hundred highest peaks, or the high points in each of the states. Many people consider the term to be disrespectful of individual mountains.
- **Personal Hydration Systems:** What used to be called "canteens" or "water bottles."
- **Responsible Party:** The person with whom you leave your trip itinerary in case you do not return when you're supposed to. It is usually suggested that you let this person know beforehand that he or she now bears this title.
- **Scale:** The ratio of a single unit of distance on a map to the corresponding distance on the ground. The larger the area covered by a map, the larger its scale. The 7.5-minute quads published by the U.S. Geological Survey cover, as their name would indicate, 7.5 minutes of latitudinally measured distance. They have a scale of 1:24,000—meaning that one inch on the map represents 24,000 inches (or about 2,000 feet). A map covering an entire national forest may have a scale as big as 1:250,000, which is generally

considered the largest scale upon which on-ground decisions can be reasonably made.

- **Scree (a.k.a "Talus"):** An accumulation of broken rock fragments at the base of mountain cliffs or valley shoulders.
- **Shortcut:** Term used by people who, hours later, often regret the fact that they ever even heard that seemingly innocuous word.
- **Shuttle Hike:** Point A to Point B hike requiring either the pre-placement of a shuttle at the destination or having someone pick you up.
- **Sierra Cups:** Made of metal, with a heat-resistant handle, these once ubiquitous cups could be used to cook in. The handle could be looped over your belt. They were often used as bowls, candle-holders, and ashtrays. Have been relegated to the realm of fuddy-duddy-dom.
- **Slackpacking:** Backpacking term coined by long-distance hiker O.d. Coyote in the late-1970s to indicate a thru-hiking mentality (*see* "Through Hiker") centered around carrying a lot of stuff to maximize camping comfort. Often included were musical instruments, bottles of alcoholic beverages, and lots of good food. The term further applied to the fact that, by carrying a lot of weight, backpackers would, of course, take a more languid perspective toward the amount of miles they hiked per day. The opposite of fastpacking (*see* "Fastpacking"). The term has been co-opted to now mean hiring someone to carry your backpack ahead to the next road crossing—meaning you can hike a trail without having to carry a pack. Considered by many backpackers to be cheating.
- **Social Trail:** A trail that has come into being by people hiking on it, rather than by a land-management agency going in and building it. Usually not included on maps and often known only by word-of-mouth.
- **Switchback:** A sharp turn in a trail to reverse the direction of travel and to gain elevation with the intent of preventing or slowing erosion.
- **System Trail:** A trail designed and constructed by a land-management agency. Usually included on maps.
- **Tarn:** Mountain lake or pool formed in a cirque (*see* "Cirque"). Most often contains water that is a bit on the brisk side.
- **Ten Essentials:** A list of items that are recommended for safe travel in the backcountry, mostly by companies that either make or sell those items. The Ten Essentials were first described in the 1930s by The Mountaineers, a Seattle-based hiking and climbing club formed in 1906 and now boasting more than 15,000 members. According to *Mountaineering: The Freedom of the Hills* (one of the most important and best-selling outdoor books of all time

and first published in 1934; now in its 8th edition), the Ten Essentials are: (1) map, (2) compass, (3) sunglasses and sunscreen, (4) extra food and water, (5) extra clothes, (6) headlamp or flashlight, (7) first-aid kit, (8) fire starter, (9) matches, and (10) knife. Many people add personal "essentials"—such as tobacco, alcohol, reading material, toilet paper, and fishing poles—to their owns lists.

- **Through-Hiker:** A hiker whose intent is to complete one of the long-distance hiking trails, such as the Colorado Trail or the Continental Divide Trail, in one fell swoop.
- **Topographical Map:** A map showing the shape and elevation of a given area via contour lines. Also has representations of trails, streets, buildings, streams, woods, etc.
- **TP Blossom:** Those nice little wads of used toilet paper we all find stashed behind boulders and trees throughout the mountains.
- **Trail Handle:** A nom de guerre invented by through-hikers while they are on the trail. Often, these names are self-generated and represent a hiker's self-perception (e.g., "Trail Stud" or "Windwalker"). Often, they are given to hikers by other hikers (e.g., "Slowpoke" or "The Blabber"). It is considered especially lame if a hiker takes his or her handle off of the trail and back into the real world once the hike is over.
- **Trailhead:** An access point to a trail often accompanied by various public facilities.
- **Trek:** A long-distance hike.
- **Waffle Stompers:** Generic term used to define any boots that leave waffle-like prints. Also the name of a specific boot product produced by Dunham Boots.
- **Wilderness:** Any piece of land that is legally protected under the Wilderness Act of 1964 from development and motorized vehicles. Almost always more than 5,000 acres in size. Most wilderness acreage in the United States is found on land administered by the U.S. Forest Service, the National Park Service, the Bureau of Land Management, and the U.S. Fish & Wildlife Service. Also used as a generic term, mostly by city dwellers, to describe any basically remote area that is generally uninhabited and undeveloped. Generally, legally designated Wilderness is spelled with a capital "W," while de facto wilderness has a small "w."
- **Wildland/Urban Interface:** Term used most often by firefighters and land-management agencies to describe the zone where populated areas transition into less-populated wildlands.

## SOURCES

Wikipedia.com; a wide variety of friends, books, magazines, and experience.

# MOUNTAINSPEAK: MOUNTAIN BIKING LEXICON

- **Auger:** To involuntarily take samples of the local geology, usually with one's face, during a crash. (*See* "Endo" and "Face Plant.")
- **Bail:** To jump off of one's bike in order to avoid an imminent crash.
- **Betty:** A woman who rides a bike. Men sometimes try to use this term derogatorily, but women keep appropriating it and making it their own.
- **Biff:** A crash. Synonym: wipeout.
- **Blood Donor:** An injured rider.
- **Cashed:** Too tired to continue riding.
- **Clean:** To negotiate a trail successfully without crashing. "I cleaned that last section like the stud I am!"
- **Clear:** Ride a technical line well, or to ride a tough section on your mountain bike with aplomb. The mountain-biking equivalent of "to stick" (*see* the section "Mountainspeak: Skiing Lexicon").
- **Corndog:** To become covered in silt, usually after a fall.
- **Dab:** Putting your foot down on a technical section of a ride.
- **Death Cookies:** Fist-sized rocks that knock your bike in every direction except the one in which you want to go.
- **Derby:** To ride around in a circle with a beer in one hand, steering with the other, trying to knock your friends off of their bikes.
- **Endo:** Going posterior-over-teacups (or, more accurately, face over handlebars). Often results in a face plant. Short for end-over-end.
- **Face Plant:** When a rider biffs (*see* "Biff") in such a way as to land nose-first in the dirt. In particularly egregious/amusing instances, the rider's face imprint will be left in the mud.
- **Foot Fault:** When a rider can't disengage his or her cleats from the pedals before falling over.
- **Gravity Check:** A fall.
- **Gutter Bunny:** A bicycle commuter.
- **Hammer:** To ride fast and hard.
- **Man Trap:** A hole covered with autumn leaves, resembling terra firma, and effective at eating the front wheel of an unsuspecting rider. (*See* "Face Plant" and "Endo.")
- **Mo:** Momentum.
- **Over-the-Bar Blood Donor:** A rider who is injured during an endo.
- **Potato Chip:** Bending your wheel during a crash.

- **Prune:** To use your helmet to remove leaves and branches from the area next to the trail. Usually unintentional.
- **Quag:** Slimy green mud that flies off of your rear wheel.
- **Skid Lid:** Helmet.
- **Sky:** To jump extremely high.
- **Soil Sample:** A face plant.
- **Spring Planting:** Face plant.
- **Stack:** Crash.
- **Superman:** A rider who flies over the handlebars but doesn't hit the ground for a long time. This may result in an injury (*see* "Blood Donor" and "Over-the-Bar Blood Donor"), but, when it doesn't, is generally very funny for everyone else.
- **Taco:** Folding your wheel entirely over during a crash.
- **Three-Hour Tour:** A ride that before the fact looks like a piece of cake but turns out to be a 12-hour death march. Taken from the theme song for the TV show *Gilligan's Island.*
- **Wild Pigs:** Poorly adjusted brake pads that squeal when used.
- **Wipe Out:** Crash.
- **Wonky:** Not functioning properly. "I bailed, and now my wheel is all wonky, and all I hear are wild pigs."
- **The Zone:** A state of mind experienced while riding wherein you don't think, you just do. A truly mystical experience that can't be fully explained, but, when you get there, you'll know, and from that point on, you'll strive to get there again often.
- **Zone Out:** A state of mind where you think you've reached The Zone, but you really just stopped paying attention to what you're doing. Usually used as an excuse for a particularly embarrassing biff.

SOURCES

www.librarythinkquest.org; www.wombats.org.

# PUBLIC AND/OR PROTECTED LAND IN COLORADO

Of the approximately 66,604,124 acres[1] of land in Colorado, 29.9 million acres—almost 45 percent of the state's total area—are public and/or protected[2] to one degree or another by:
- The federal government (23,455,115 total acres)[3]. Four different federal agencies manage public land in Colorado: the U.S. Forest Service (14.5 million acres), which is part of the Department of Agriculture, and the National Park Service (673,264 acres), the

U.S. Fish & Wildlife Service (180,000 acres), and the Bureau of Land Management (8.3 million acres), which are part of the Department of the Interior.

- The Colorado state government, mainly through the state parks system (246,000 acres) and state trust lands (3 million acres).
- The myriad city, town, and county open space and mountain parks systems (cumulative acreage unknown).
- Private conservation organizations (such as The Nature Conservancy, which alone owns 437,000 acres in Colorado).
- Conservation easements on private land (at least 30,000 acres).

## NOTES

1. This acreage exceeds the total area of 19 states: Connecticut, Delaware, Hawaii, Indiana, Kentucky, Louisiana, Maine, Maryland, Massachusetts, New Hampshire, New Jersey, Ohio, Pennsylvania, Rhode Island, South Carolina, Tennessee, Vermont, Virginia, and West Virginia. The area of both New York and Mississippi are only slightly larger than the total amount of public and/or protected land in Colorado.

2. It may sound at least a bit disingenuous to keep using the spliced-together compound adjective "public and/or protected." But it is actually the most accurate representation of land-management reality in Colorado, because the various land-stewardship entities go about the business of managing their holdings in very different ways. For example, the extensive Bureau of Land Management lands, upon which are now found literally thousands of oil and natural gas wells, are undeniably "public," but there are many people who would rationally argue that the presence of thumper trucks, newly constructed access roads, and oil wells does not serve as poster-child denotation for the word "protected." As well, conservation easements located on privately owned ranches and land owned by The Nature Conservancy are, by most people's definition, very well "protected," but they are certainly not "public." Most of the land described in this book falls somewhere in the middle: It is pretty much accessible to the public but is also pretty much protected from development.

3. Federal lands in Colorado alone cover more total area than 13 states: Connecticut, Delaware, Hawaii, Indiana, Maryland, Maine, Massachusetts, New Hampshire, New Jersey, Rhode Island, South Carolina, Vermont, and West Virginia.

## SOURCES

"44% of state land is open space," by Bill McKeown, April 17, 2007, edition of the *Colorado Springs Gazette,* citing figures provided by Colorado State University's Natural Resource Ecology Lab and Southpaw Consulting; National Park Service; Bureau of Land Management; U.S. Fish & Wildlife Service; U.S. Forest Service; Colorado State Parks; The Nature Conservancy; www.coloradoconservationtrust.org.

# COLORADO'S WILDERNESS

People venturing into Colorado from points east and south might be forgiven for thinking that a significant percentage of the state is "wilderness" in the traditional, conceptual sense: "Any unsettled, uncultivated region left in its natural condition" *(American Heritage Dictionary of the English Language).*

However, in Colorado, as in all western states, "wilderness" has a legal meaning that generally gets translated to an uppercase "Wilderness." "Wilderness" is land designated and protected by the federal Wilderness Act of 1964, the original draft of which was actually written by Howard Zahniser of The Wilderness Society in 1956. (Zahniser passed away four months before President Lyndon Johnson signed the Wilderness Act into law.) Whereas traditional definitions of "wilderness" often put forth a sense of desolation and foreboding, "Wilderness" in Colorado puts forth a sense of beauty, spiritual regeneration, and even economic development.[1]

The world-famous introduction to the Wilderness Act says it all: "A Wilderness, in contrast with those areas where man and his own works dominate the landscape, is hereby recognized as an area where the earth and community of life are untrammeled by man, where man himself is a visitor who does not remain."

When the Wilderness Act was signed into law, the entire national system consisted of 34 areas covering 9.1 million acres. Today, the National Wilderness Preservation System includes 756 designated areas covering 109,494,428 acres in every state except Connecticut, Delaware, Iowa, Kansas, Maryland, and Rhode Island.

Five Wilderness areas, totaling 719,150 acres, were created in Colorado when the Wilderness Act was passed in 1964: Maroon Bells–Snowmass, La Garita, Mount Zirkel, Rawah, and West Elk.

Today, Colorado boasts 41 legally designated Wilderness areas.[2] Colorado therefore ranks fifth in the nation behind California (138), Arizona (90), Nevada (68), and Alaska (48).

In terms of actual acres designated as Wilderness, Colorado, with 3.7 million acres, ranks eighth behind Alaska (57.4 million acres), California (15 million acres), Arizona and Idaho (4.5 million acres each), Washington (4.4 million acres), Nevada (3.45 million acres), and Montana (3.44 million acres).

Legally designated Wilderness covers about 5.11 percent of Colorado's total area, which places the state sixth behind Alaska (15.73 percent), California (14.36 percent), Washington (10.38 percent), Idaho (7.56 percent), and Arizona (6.23 percent).

Colorado's legally designated Wilderness areas are as follows:

- **Black Canyon of the Gunnison:** Established 1976; 15,599 acres; high point: Green Mountain, 8,563 feet
- **Black Ridge Canyons:** Established 2000; 75,438 acres, 70,319 of which are in Colorado; the remaining 5,119 acres are in Utah; high point: Unnamed, 6,800 feet
- **Buffalo Peaks:** Established 1993; 43,410 acres; high point: West Buffalo Peak, 13,326 feet
- **Byers Peak:** Established 1993; 8,913 acres; highest point: Byers Peak, 12,804 feet
- **Cache la Poudre:** Established 1980; 9,238 acres; highest point: Unnamed, 8,634 feet
- **Collegiate Peaks:** Established 1980; 166,938 acres; highest point: Mount Harvard, 14,420 feet
- **Comanche Peak:** Established 1980; 66,791 acres; highest point: Comanche Peak, 12,702 feet
- **Dominguez Canyon:** Established 2009; 66,280 acres; highest point: Information not available
- **Eagles Nest:** Established 1978; 132,906 acres; highest point: Mount Powell, 13,560 feet
- **Flat Tops:** Established 1975; 235,035 acres; highest point: Flat Top Mountain, 12,354 feet
- **Fossil Ridge:** Established 1993; 31,534 acres; highest point: Henry Mountain, 12,254 feet
- **Great Sand Dunes:** Established 1976; 33,450 acres; highest point: Unnamed, 10,520 feet
- **Greenhorn Mountain:** Established 1993; 22,040 acres; highest point: Greenhorn Mountain, 12,347 feet
- **Gunnison Gorge:** Established 1999; 17,700 acres; highest point: Side of Green Mountain, 8,442 feet
- **Holy Cross:** Established 1980; 122,797 acres; highest point: Mount of the Holy Cross, 14,005 feet
- **Hunter–Fryingpan:** Established 1980; expanded 1993; 81,866 acres; highest point: Far northwest peak of Mount Massive, 14,169 feet
- **Indian Peaks:** Established 1978; expanded 1980; 73,291 acres; highest point: North Arapaho Peak, 13,502 feet
- **James Peak:** Established 2002; 14,000 acres; highest point: James Peak, 13,294 feet
- **La Garita:** Established 1964; expanded 1980 and 1993; 128,858 acres; highest point: San Luis Peak, 14,014 feet
- **Lizard Head:** Established 1980; 41,193 acres; highest point: Mount Wilson, 14,246 feet

- **Lost Creek:** Established 1980; expanded 1993; 119,790 acres; highest point: Bison Peak, 12,431 feet
- **Maroon Bells–Snowmass:** Established 1964; expanded 1980; 181,117 acres; highest point: Castle Peak, 14,265 feet
- **Mesa Verde:** Established 1976; 8,500 acres; highest point: Morefield Point, 8,393 feet; note that this Wilderness area, Colorado's smallest legally designated Wilderness area, is closed to visitors due to the sensitive nature of the archeological features
- **Mount Evans:** Established 1980; 74,401 acres; highest point: Mount Evans, 14,264 feet
- **Mount Massive:** Established 1980; 30,540 acres; highest point: Mount Massive, 14,421 feet, the highest point in any Colorado Wilderness area
- **Mount Sneffels:** Established 1980; 16,565 acres; highest point: Mount Sneffels, 14,150 feet
- **Mount Zirkel:** Established 1964; expanded 1980 and 1993; 159,935 acres; highest point: Mount Zirkel, 12,180 feet
- **Neota:** Established 1980; 9,924 acres; highest point: Thunder Mountain, 12,040 feet
- **Never Summer:** Established 1980; expanded 1993; 20,747 acres; highest point: Howard Mountain, 12,810 feet
- **Platte River:** Established 1984; 22,749 acres, only 743 of which are in Colorado; the remaining 22,006 acres are in Wyoming; highest point in Colorado that is part of the Wilderness: Unnamed, 8,500 feet
- **Powderhorn:** Established 1993; 61,510 acres; highest point: Unnamed, 12,405 feet
- **Ptarmigan Peak:** Established 1993; 12,594 acres; highest point: Coon Hill, 12,757 feet
- **Raggeds:** Established 1980; expanded 1993; 64,992 acres; highest point: Treasure Mountain, 12,528 feet
- **Rawah:** Established 1964; expanded 1980; 73,068 acres; highest point: Clark Peak, 12,951 feet
- **Rocky Mountain National Park Wilderness:** Established 2009; 250,000 acres; highest point: Longs Peak, 14,259 feet
- **Sangre de Cristo:** Established 1993; 226,420 acres; highest point: Crestone Peak, 14,294 feet
- **Sarvis Creek:** Established 1993; 47,190 acres; highest point: Unnamed, 10,778 feet
- **South San Juan:** Established 1980; expanded 1993; 158,790 acres; highest point: Summit Peak, 13,300 feet
- **Spanish Peaks:** Established 2000; 17,855 acres; highest point: West Spanish Peak, 13,626 feet
- **Uncompahgre:** Established 1980 as the Big Blue Wilderness; expanded and name changed in 1993; 102,721 acres; highest point: Uncompahgre Peak, 14,309 feet

# MORE WILDERNESS THAN WILDERNESS

Most people mistakenly believe that, once an area is designated as Wilderness, an administrative barrier is erected, a few trails are built and maintained, and primitive bridges are repaired. Besides that, Mother Nature is then left to her own devices. Such is hardly the case. The U.S. Forest Service actually has three different "management prescriptions" for Wilderness areas:

- 1.11: Pristine
- 1.12: Primitive
- 1.13: Semi-primitive

Each of these three designations has specific descriptions, but they differ slightly in application from national forest to national forest.

In general, "pristine" is managed to have little or no use, no system trails, and no outfitter or guide camps. As well, the U.S. Forest Service is inclined to let naturally caused wildfires burn their course unless those fires threaten structures or the fire conditions are extreme.

"Primitive Wilderness" prescriptions have evidence of some human use but generally have low to moderate use levels. There are some maintained system trails, and some outfitter and guide camps are permitted. The management inclination is to let naturally occurring wildfires to burn their course unless those fires threaten structures and/or the wildfire conditions are extreme.

"Semi-primitive" areas are more heavily used portals and transition zones that have significant system trails and campsites. Outfitter and guide camps are generally located in semi-primitive areas. Naturally occurring wildfires are more aggressively managed in semi-primitive areas.

About 30 percent of all U.S. Forest Service–administered Wilderness is managed as pristine, about 30 percent is managed as primitive, and the remaining 40 percent is managed as semi-primitive. Those averages vary from forest to forest and from Wilderness area to Wilderness area.

---

- **Vasquez:** Established 1993; 12,986 acres; highest point: Vasquez Peak: 12,947 feet
- **Weminuche:** Established 1975; expanded in 1980 and 1993; 492,418 acres; highest point: Mount Eolus, 14,083 feet; Colorado's largest Wilderness area
- **West Elk:** Established 1964; expanded 1980; 176,172 acres; highest point: West Elk Peak, 13,035 feet

The National Wilderness Preservation System is very fluid, with additional Wilderness designations occurring almost every year since the Wilderness Act was passed in 1964. New Wilderness areas are generally proposed for designation by one or more members of the congressional and/or senatorial delegations in the state where the new designations are proposed. Most often, numerous proposed Wilderness designations are lumped together into one bill. Proposed new Wilderness areas come to the attention of congressmen, congresswomen, and senators via a variety of means, including input from land-management agencies, organizations, and individual citizens.

The first step in the new Wilderness designation process is to determine which lands actually retain Wilderness qualities, which are usually described as areas without roads or other significant evidence of human impacts that are at least 5,000 acres in size unless they border an already-established Wilderness area.

The process of completing an inventory of lands that fit those criteria began in earnest in the 1970s, when Congress directed the U.S. Forest Service, which administers the overwhelming majority of Wilderness acres, to begin its Roadless Area Review and Evaluation (RARE) process. In 2001, the process was expanded under the Roadless Area Conservation Rule (RACR), which tasked the U.S. Forest Service with completing a more detailed analysis of roadless areas. Under RACR, inventories of roadless areas were categorized one of three ways: (1) roadless areas recommended for Wilderness designation, (2) roadless areas where new road construction or reconstruction was prohibited but Wilderness designation was not recommended, and (3) areas where new road construction and reconstruction were allowed, thus effectively eliminating the area from future Wilderness consideration.

Since 2001, the U.S. Forest Service, as well as various citizens' groups, has undertaken intense reviews of roadless areas throughout Colorado. There have been legal battles galore. Those legal battles reached a crescendo in 2005, when what has become known as the "Colorado Rule" replaced RACR (in Colorado only; in other states, the provisions of RACR remained). The Colorado Rule does two things: (1) it establishes Colorado roadless areas by accurately identifying areas with roadless character, and (2) it provides prohibitions on road construction and tree cutting in those roadless areas. The main means by which the U.S. Forest Service meets those conditions is by soliciting public input regarding Colorado's roadless area inventory and integrating that input into its roadless-area management decisions. By October 23, 2008, the U.S. Forest Service had received approximately 105,000 responses to its Colorado Roadless Area Management Draft Environmental Impact Statement.

All told, there are about four million inventoried roadless acres on U.S. Forest Service land in Colorado out of about 14.5 million total national forest acres. Those acres are spread across 363 inventoried roadless areas within all 11 national forests in Colorado.

To add to the Wilderness-designation confusion, there are also parcels known as "Wilderness Study Areas," which are basically roadless areas administered by the Bureau of Land Management (BLM). There are 55 Wilderness Study Areas in Colorado covering a total of 623,021 acres. Wilderness Study Areas are exempt from the Colorado Rule and the future management strategies for those parcels will be made by the BLM through its normal decision-making process.

## CITIZENS' GROUP–INITIATED WILDERNESS PROPOSALS

Environmental groups statewide are constantly trying to get more roadless areas designated as Wilderness. Among the more noteworthy active Wilderness proposals being floated or recently floated by citizens' groups in Colorado:

- **Hidden Gems.** Focusing mainly on the White River and Gunnison national forests, the White River Wilderness Coalition proposed 44 new Wilderness designations/additions covering a total of 342,000 acres in Gunnison, Eagle, Pitkin, Garfield, and Summit counties. The original Hidden Gems proposal covered 612,000 acres, but that total was slashed via an often acrimonious, ongoing public-input process. In October 2010, Congressman Jared Polis introduced a bill that would designate 88,000 of the proposed Hidden Gems acres as Wilderness, with another 78,000 being designated as special-management areas, which would have greater protection than many public lands but less protection than designated Wilderness areas.
- **Colorado's Canyon Country.** This Wilderness proposal is spearheaded by the Colorado Wilderness Network, established in 1975, which has as member organizations the Colorado Environmental Coalition, the Colorado Mountain Club, the Sierra Club, the Western Colorado Congress, and the Wilderness Society, among others. This proposal consists of 62 areas and just more than 1,650,000 acres, mostly located on BLM turf in the western part of the state.

# A NEW DESIGNATION

Opposition to the establishment of new Wilderness areas is often predictable. Motorized recreation groups usually oppose new designations because motorized vehicles are not allowed in Wilderness areas. The extractive and development industries also generally oppose new designations because mining, timbering, dam building, and real-estate operations are likewise disallowed in Wilderness areas. Even ski areas sometimes oppose new designations because they can't expand their ski runs onto Wilderness lands. Some hunters favor new designations because Wilderness provides for the best circumstances for healthy game populations, but hunters who prefer motorized access often oppose Wilderness areas.

In the past couple of decades, however, opposition to new Wilderness designations has come from a new source: mountain bikers, who often see some of their favorite trails suddenly off limits because mountain bikes are considered mechanized transport under a 1984 amendment to the Wilderness Act and, therefore, are not allowed in Wilderness areas.

When negotiations were ongoing to establish the Sangre de Cristo Wilderness in the early 1990s, the proposed boundaries had to be changed so that the Rainbow Trail—popular with mountain bikers—fell outside of the Wilderness. In 2002, establishment of the James Peak Wilderness was in doubt because mountain bikers around Winter Park had long used the trails in the proposed new Wilderness area for recreation.

Several of the proposed Hidden Gems Wilderness areas in Summit County are being opposed by the local mountain-bike community because those areas have long been open to riding.

Mountain bikers and mountain-bike groups throughout Colorado and the nation are pushing for the establishment of a new type of hyper-protected roadless designation that would allow mountain biking while still disallowing motorized recreation and the extractive industries.

Proposed names for this new type of designation, which is opposed by most pro-Wilderness groups, run the gamut from "national conservation areas" to "national scenic areas" to "special-management areas" (see "Citizens' Group-Initiated Wilderness Proposals" in this chapter).

Pro-Wilderness groups are also battling some of the more radical elements of the mountain-biking community, who are working to overturn the 1984 amendment to the Wilderness Act that specifically prohibits bikes in Wilderness areas.

- **Wild 10.** The Central Colorado Wilderness Coalition is a group of citizens in the Pikes Peak region who are proposing Wilderness designation for parcels totaling 276,500 acres. Despite its name, Wild 10 now has 11 proposed Wilderness areas on its list.
- **San Juan Mountain Wilderness Act.** This act was proposed by Colorado Congressman John Salazar in the summer of 2009. The bill, which was presented by the Sheep Mountain Alliance in partnership with the San Juan Citizens Alliance and the Colorado Wilderness Network, calls for the establishment of four new Wilderness areas in the San Juan Mountains totaling 33,390 acres. The wording of the bill calls for two other designations: 21,697 acres would be designated as the Sheep Mountain Special Management Area (see "A New Designation" sidebar), where heli-skiing—which is prohibited in Wilderness Areas—would still be allowed, but no new roads or other development would be permitted. In addition, 6,595 acres would be withdrawn from eligibility for mineral leasing in Naturita Canyon.

## NOTES

1. Despite anti-Wilderness protestations to the contrary, designated Wilderness pays large and growing economic dividends to local communities. Protected public lands increase the property values of surrounding private lands and contribute to a high quality of life that attracts new businesses and residents. Research confirms that Wilderness has a positive influence on local economies and that counties containing a higher percentage of Wilderness have higher total income, employment, and per-capita income growth rates than counties without Wilderness. Total employment in Wilderness counties grew 65 percent faster than total employment in non-Wilderness counties, in part because businesses move to counties with Wilderness because of the quality of life it offers employees. In a survey sponsored by the National Science Foundation of 2,670 people who live in counties with Wilderness, 53 percent cited Wilderness as an important reason why they located there, and 45 percent as the reason why they do not move elsewhere (Colorado Environmental Coalition).

2. Although it has never been legally designated as a Wilderness area, 136,413 acres of the Colorado portion of Dinosaur National Monument (which also extends into Utah) have been managed as Wilderness since 1974. If that is added to the state's total, then Colorado passes both Nevada and Montana with 3.47 million acres of Wilderness. The highest point of the Colorado part of Dinosaur National Monument that is managed as Wilderness is 9,006-foot Zenobia Peak.

## SOURCES

www.wilderness.net; www.canyoncountrywilderness.org; Colorado Environmental Coalition; U.S. Forest Service; Bureau of Land Management; www.coloradowilderness.com; www.roadless.net; www.ccwcwilderness.org; www.sheepmountainalliance.org; www.sanjuancitizens.org; www.whiteriverwild.org; *Summit Daily News*; personal interview with Ralph Swain, Wilderness Program Manager, Region 2, U.S. Forest Service, http://wilderness.org/content/wilderness-act-1964.

# COLORADO: BIRTHPLACE OF MAJOR RIVERS

What Colorado lacks in large lakes, it more than makes up for in rivers. Colorado is the mother of major rivers for the entire country, as no other state gives birth to as many substantial waterways. The fact that, while most of those rivers wind their way through Colorado, they are little more than modest mountain streams does not diminish the fact that they were born and raised among the frosty peaks of the Colorado Rockies.

Depending on your source (and there is much more statistical variation than you would think on this subject), Colorado gives birth to the country's fourth, sixth, seventh, fourteenth, and sixteenth longest rivers. Sure, there are other ways to define a given river's grandiosity other than simple length (discharge volume and size of drainage basin among them), but there's no denying that distance from source to mouth holds its own in any superlative-based discourse.

**The longest rivers, the sources of which lie in Colorado, are the following:**

1. **The Rio Grande.** Known as the Rio Bravo del Norte in Mexico, the Rio Grande is 3,034 miles long. It begins in the mountains near Creede like all Colorado rivers: as a small trickle. It drains a total area of 176,555 square miles. Despite its length, by the time it empties into the Gulf of Mexico (as one of only two Colorado-born rivers that travel all the way from mountains to saltwater—the other being the Colorado), its terminal discharge averages only 160 cubic feet per second (cfs). (For purposes of comparison, by the time the Montana-born Missouri River reaches its junction with the Mississippi, it carries an average discharge of 87,950 cfs.) *Note:* If you want to avoid looking like a rube, never, ever call it the "Rio Grande River," which, translated, would mean the "Great River River."

2. **The Arkansas.** At 1,460 miles in length, the Arkansas, the main source of which is located north of Leadville, near Fremont Pass, is the country's sixth longest river. It empties into the Mississippi River in Desha County, Arkansas.

3. **The Colorado**[1]. At 1,440 miles in length, the Colorado, which begins at La Poudre Pass Lake in Rocky Mountain National Park, is the country's seventh longest river. But, in actuality, because of the serious over-allocation of its flow for everything from agriculture to golf courses in Phoenix and decorative fountains in Las Vegas, the Colorado now rarely reaches its official mouth, the Sea of Cortez/Gulf of California between the Mexican states

of Sonora and Baja California. The Colorado's drainage basin is 271,481 square miles, an area larger than Texas. Its average discharge now hovers somewhere between 0 and about 600 cfs.

4. **The Platte.** Officially, the Platte River, at 990 miles, is the country's 14th longest river. That figure assumes the source of the Platte as the 618-mile North Platte, which rises from the mountains of North Park, near Walden. The South Platte, at 450 miles, is therefore considered a tributary. Both forks of the Platte come together at North Platte, Nebraska. The unified Platte River then travels to its junction with the Missouri River just south of Omaha. The North Platte drains an area of 80,755 square miles, while the South Platte drains 62,738 square miles.

5. **The Canadian.** This river traverses Colorado for only 1.5 of its 906-mile total length, but its source lies on the east side of the Sangre de Cristo Mountains near Trinidad. The Canadian, which drains a total of 47,375 square miles, is the largest tributary of the Arkansas River, which it joins in Robert S. Kerr Reservoir in eastern Oklahoma.

**The rivers with the most river miles actually within Colorado are:**

1. The South Platte (South Platte drainage): 450 river miles within the state
2. The Arkansas (Arkansas drainage): 315 river miles
3. The Colorado (Colorado drainage): 225 river miles
4. (Tie) The Dolores (Colorado drainage): 180 river miles and The Rio Grande (Rio Grande drainage): 180 river miles
6. The Yampa (Colorado drainage): 175 river miles
7. The Purgatoire (Arkansas drainage): 157 river miles
8. The Gunnison (Colorado drainage): 140 river miles
9. (Tie) The Little Snake (Colorado drainage, by way of the Yampa): 120 river miles and The Arikaree (Republican drainage): 120 river miles

**The longest rivers that are totally within Colorado are:**

1. The Yampa (Colorado drainage): 175 river miles within the state
2. The Purgatoire (Arkansas drainage): 157 river miles
3. The Gunnison (Colorado drainage): 140 river miles
4. (Tie) The Apishapa (Arkansas drainage): 100 river miles and The Conejos (Rio Grande drainage): 100 river miles
6. The Huerfano (Arkansas drainage): 90 river miles
7. The San Miguel (Colorado drainage): 83 river miles
8. The Cache la Poudre (South Platte drainage): 75 river miles
9. The Eagle (Colorado drainage): 70 river miles

10. (Tie) The Big Thompson (South Platte drainage): 65 river miles and
    The Blue (Colorado drainage): 65 river miles

**The largest river drainage basins within Colorado are:**

1. The Colorado: 38,686 square miles drained within the state (out of a total drainage area of 271,481 square miles)
2. The Arkansas: 27,036 (184,750)
3. The South Platte: 18,899 (24,223)
4. The Green: 10,556 (44,750)
5. The Gunnison: 8,051 (8,051)
6. The Yampa: 5,903 (8,404)
7. The San Juan: 5,859 (24,927)
8. The Rio Grande: 4,660 (176,555)
9. The North Fork of the Republican: 4,449 (5,086)
10. The Dolores: 4,100 (4,633)

# CONTINENTAL COMPARISONS TO ROCKY MOUNTAIN–BORN RIVERS

- At 2,294 miles in length, the Volga, which lies entirely within the boundaries of the Russian Federation, is the longest river in Europe. This means that the Volga is exactly as long as the Missouri—as long as you add the entire length of the 175-mile Colorado-born Yampa River onto the Volga's length, plus the entire length of the 57-mile Roaring Fork.
- At 1,777 miles in length, the Danube is the longest river in Europe that does not traverse country that was once part of the USSR. Even with that restrictive caveat, it is still the second longest river in all of Europe. This means that the longest river in Western Europe is the same length as the Colorado-born Rio Grande, as long as you add the 140-mile, Colorado-born Gunnison River onto the Danube's length.
- The second and third longest rivers in Western Europe, the 820-mile Rhine and the 678-mile Elbe, added together are only 40 miles longer than the Colorado-born Arkansas.
- The 482-mile Seine, France's second longest river (after the 629-mile Loire), is justifiably one of the most famous rivers in the entire world, passing as it does through the heart of Paris. It is slightly longer than the Colorado-born South Platte River, which runs through the heart of Denver.
- The River Thames, the best-known river in the United Kingdom (it is not the United Kingdom's longest river; that honor goes to the 220-mile Severn), is 215 miles long, or 15 miles shorter than the 230-mile Colorado-born Dolores River.

# NOTES

1. Colorado's namesake river has had several monikers since Spaniard Melchior Diaz, on his third expedition in 1540, named what is now the Colorado River, the "Rio del Tizon"—the River of Embers or Firebrand River (based upon the practice used by the natives for warming themselves). It is not clear when or why the name "Colorado" first replaced Tizon. Every use of "Colorado" from 1540 to 1720 was applied to a tributary of the Gila River that seems best to correspond to what is known today as Arizona's Verde River. The earliest-known map that replaces "Tizon" directly with "Colorado" (which, by the way, translates from Spanish as "colored," not "red," as many sources would have us believe) was printed in 1743. In 1836, a map by Henry Schenct Tanner used the name "Grand River" as far as its confluence with the Green. Here things get dicey on the nomenclatural front, as a mere three years later, a map by David H. Burr shows the "Colorado River of the West" flowing from the headwaters of the Green River, which begins in the Wind River Mountains in what is now Wyoming, all the way to the Sea of Cortez/Gulf of California. On that map, the "Grand River" is marked as a tributary of the "Green" that intersects the Green River in what is now Canyonlands National Park, near present-day Moab, Utah. (Note: Because the Colorado River was called the Grand River for more than 100 years, it left in its wake much in the way of seemingly inexplicable nomenclatural baggage, including Grand Lake, Colorado [both the actual lake and the town on the lake's shores], Grand Valley, Grand Junction, and Grand County [one in Utah, one in Colorado].)

In 1921, however, U.S. Representative Edward T. Taylor, a Democrat from Glenwood Springs, Colorado—through which the Colorado River flows—petitioned the Congressional Committee on Interstate and Foreign Commerce to rename the Grand River as the Colorado River. On July 25, 1921, the name change was made official in House Joint Resolution 460 of the 66th Congress, over the vigorous objections of representatives from lesser-populated Wyoming and Utah, as well as the U.S. Geological Survey, which noted that the drainage basin of the Green River was 70 percent more extensive than that of the Grand River, although the Grand carried a slightly higher volume of water at its confluence with the Green. Politics won by taking advantage of the fact that there are no set criteria by which rivers retain or lose their name when a significant confluence occurs. (Note: Taylor's other claim to legislative fame was the Taylor Grazing Act of 1934, which regulates grazing on federal lands and thus has significant land-management impact on the Colorado mountains. During the Herbert Hoover Administration, it became clear that federal regulation of public land use was necessary. Since large tracts of public land were used for livestock grazing, the importance of range management was a large part of that debate. Congressman Don B. Colton of Utah introduced a bill to create grazing districts, but the bill failed to pass the U.S. Senate. In 1933, Congressman Taylor re-introduced the Colton Bill as the Taylor Bill. The bill created the Grazing Service in the Department of the Interior to administer the rangelands. The Grazing Service was merged with the General Land Office in 1946 to form the Bureau of Land Management. So, in the course of 12 years, Taylor had not only stolen the name of a river from Utah but had absconded with a piece of legislation from a Utah senator that ended up being one of the most important land-use laws in U.S. history.)

# SOURCES

Wikipedia; www.waterknowledge.coloradostate.edu; U.S. Geographic Survey; www.media.utah.edu.

# MOUNTAINSPEAK:
# FISHING LEXICON

- **Action:** The bend/flex of a rod.
- **Bait Fishermen:** Those who hunt fish by using worms, grass-hoppers, other fish, or even liverwurst. Held in utter disdain by people who consider Norman Maclean's *A River Runs Through It* to be Gospel.
- **Banker's Hours Cast:** The neophyte technique of interpreting fly casting between "10 and 1 o'clock" to mean somewhere between 8:30 and 4.
- **Bush God:** The deity to which you pray for release of fly and line when your cast errantly lands in waterside trees or bushes. To be effective, you must vocalize, "Bush God!" which doesn't necessarily guarantee release, but often helps.
- **Cast and Blast:** When fishing and hunting are combined in one trip.
- **Catch and Release:** Dominant ethical belief system held, and advertised mightily, by fly fisherpeople. Meaning that a fish is caught, reeled in, and fondled while being held in the water and deep, philosophical, Norman Maclean-esque thoughts are being pondered, before being set back out in the current to be caught and released by the next fly fisherperson. Many are the fish in the more popular rivers, like Colorado's Roaring Fork, that have been down this road so often, they roll over while being held so that the fisherperson can more easily admire their underbellies. Bait fishermen (*see* "Bait Fishermen") are often not as enamored of catch and release as are fly fishermen.
- **"Doing the African Queen":** Having to jump out and walk your boat back upstream after taking a side channel that closes out. Often accompanied by colorful invectives.
- **Dredging the Bottom:** A term used exclusively when nymphing to refer to getting the fly down to the bottom of the water column in a stream. "You're not dredging the bottom—put on a couple more split shots." (With kudos to Rob Laverty—the Dredge Master.)
- **Eggs and Bacon:** Salmon eggs threaded on a hook followed with a strip of pork rind.
- **Gobbaworms:** Large ball of night crawlers on the hook.
- **Honey Hole:** Secret fishing spot.
- **Hot Pocket:** The bouquet released when waders are peeled off after several hours of fishing in the hot sun that followed starting the morning with a beer and a breakfast burrito.

- **"It's Not About the Catching":** Quite possibly the most inane and annoying phrase in the angling lexicon (with "Tight Lines" running a close second; *see* "Tight Lines"). Basically used as a Zen-like response when a fisherman who has just been skunked is asked how the fishing was.
- **Long Release (or Long-Line Release or Long-Distance Release):** Intended to mean that you ethically allowed a fish to slip off of your hook unharmed and unfatigued on purpose. Considered a more ethical version of catch and release. Also used as an excuse when the fish simply gets away.
- **Nantucket Sleigh Ride:** Float tube/kayak/canoe fisherman who, while fishing for trout, hooks a large pike and gets dragged all over the lake. Old whaling term where whalers would harpoon a whale and get dragged around in their boats until the whale died of exhaustion.
- **Nobody Home:** Used in the case when a fly is presented to what appears to be prime fish-holding water and no fish takes the offering. "I can't believe there's nobody home in that hole."
- **"No-Questions-Asked" Rod Warranties:** About the only thing (besides the cheap, tasty fried chicken at Albertson's) that keeps fly-fishing guides in the black.
- **Nymphs:** The life stage of a bug, not (necessarily) the young ladies frolicking in the kayaks out in the middle of the river.
- **Polish Wading:** To fly fish wearing sport sandals rather than traditional wading gear. Otherwise known as "wet wading."
- **Pounding the Hole:** Excessive fishing of a hole or run of water, which typically results in spooking fish more than catching them. "Let's move upstream; you've pounded that hole."
- **River Dance:** Refers to wader boot lack of traction on slippery, algae-covered rocks. Also referred to as the "tailwater two-step."
- **Rocky Mountain Bonefish:** The much-maligned whitefish that has saved many a day of guiding.
- **San Juan Shuffle:** When a fisherman in a stream purposefully dislodges the river bottom to release nymphs and other food material to attract fish downstream of the fisherman. The fisherman will then fish downstream of where he is standing, oftentimes with positive results. The term is interchangeable with whatever stream is being fished, but San Juan is generally used as the referred body of water.
- **Thinking Like a Fish:** The consumption of alcohol or other mind-altering substances to shift the fisherman to a different mental level. "It's no wonder you're not catching anything... you're not thinking like a fish."

- **"Tight Lines":** A cheesy and overused salutation that fly fishermen often (over)use.
- **Tip-to-Tail:** Refers to hooking large fish that cause the rod to double over. "That son of a bitch was so big, it had my rod bent tip-to-tail."
- **Water Weenie:** A tuber/kayaker who drifts right into your casting line.
- **Weed Bass:** Any form of sunken vegetation or like material caught on the fly that causes the fisherman to mistakenly think that he or she has a fish on the line. The term is not necessarily specific to fly fishing, but is applicable to all fishing forms. Often accompanied by the liberal use of colorful invectives.
- **Wet a Line:** Go fishing.
- **"What Are They Biting On?":** Most common question asked of fishing guides by beginners. Immediately tells those guides that the person asking the question is a rube.
- **Window Shopping:** When a fish approaches your dry fly, creating anticipatory anxiety on the part of the fisherman, and then takes a pass on the offering. "It was a perfect cast, but that cutthroat was just window shopping..."

## SOURCES

Carbondale, Colorado–based writer/fisherman Malcolm McMichael; Peter Sutcliffe, a sales executive, entrepreneur, and avid fly fisherman who lives in Lyons, Colorado; Bruce Smithhammer, a writer and fishing guide employed by High Country Flies in Jackson, Wyoming.

# COLORADO'S ENDANGERED RIVERS

Since 1986, American Rivers, a 65,000-member environmental organization based in Washington, D.C., has released its "America's Most Endangered Rivers" report. Every year, American Rivers solicits nominations for inclusion on the endangered rivers list from river groups, environmental organizations, outdoor clubs, local governments, and taxpayer watchdog groups. The report highlights the rivers facing the most uncertain futures rather than those suffering from the worst chronic problems and then presents alternatives to the threats it outlines, identifies those who make the crucial decisions, and points out opportunities for the public to take action on behalf of each listed river. Sadly, the word "Colorado" has appeared on the endangered rivers list 37 times since 1986, a total exceeded in the West only by California's 51 times. That said, some caveats are necessary.

First, all state names through which an endangered river flows appear on the list, even though the actual threats to that river might occur in a different state upriver or downriver.

Second, certain endangered rivers appear on the list in consecutive years. This does not diminish the threats to the individual rivers (truth be told, multiple listings actually underscore the threats), but it does result in individual states getting named in subsequent years.

And, last, it must be stressed that American Rivers goes out of its way to list a geographic mix of rivers; therefore, while not diminishing the threats to those rivers making the endangered rivers list, there is no doubt that the entire process is somewhat manipulated to cover all parts of the country.

## Number of Total Listings for Western States on American Rivers's Endangered River Lists, 1986–2009

- California: 51
- Colorado: 37
- Oregon: 26
- Washington: 25
- Wyoming: 23
- Arizona: 21
- Montana: 20
- Idaho: 18
- New Mexico: 13
- Utah: 11
- Nevada: 8

From 1986 to 1988, American Rivers released a list that included only the 10 most endangered rivers. In 1989, the group added an additional 10 "threatened" rivers. From 1990 until 1993, the "threatened" part of the list was expanded to include 15 rivers. From 1994 to 1997, that "threatened" part of the list was expanded to include 20 rivers. In 1998, the "endangered" and "threatened" lists were combined into one "endangered" list, which included 20 rivers. In 1999, the list took its current form, which has since included only the 10 most endangered rivers. The following Colorado-specific list includes rivers appearing as either "endangered" or "threatened" by American Rivers since 1986.

- **1986:** No Colorado rivers were listed.
- **1987:** The Platte River, through Colorado, Wyoming, and Nebraska, was listed as the country's eighth most endangered river.
- **1988:** The South Platte River in Colorado was listed as the country's most endangered river as a result of the proposed Two Forks Reservoir. Also in 1988, Colorado's Animas River was listed as the ninth most endangered river; the reason was a "proposed irrigation project." That would be the infamous Animas–La Plata Reservoir Project.
- **1989:** The Platte River through Colorado and Nebraska was moved up to the top spot on the endangered list. Once again,

Two Forks Dam was the reason. The Animas River was listed again, this time at the number 10 spot. The Yampa River was listed as the country's third most threatened river because of "proposed water projects."

- **1990:** The South Platte came in as the country's second most threatened river, once again, because of Two Forks. The Animas was listed as the country's most threatened river, while the Yampa was listed as the fifteenth most threatened river.

- **1991:** Colorado scored big, as the Colorado River was listed as the country's most endangered river, although the main threat listed was Glen Canyon Dam, which is in Arizona. The Gunnison River, all of which lies in Colorado, was listed as the country's eighth most endangered river because of a "proposed hydro and diversion project." The Animas was listed as the country's most threatened river (Animas–La Plata once again), and, right behind it, the Arkansas made its debut on the threatened list, coming in second place because "water projects would flood area."

- **1992:** The Animas was listed as the second most threatened river, while the Gunnison was listed as the fourth most threatened river in the country.

- **1993:** The Colorado-born Rio Grande was listed as the country's most endangered river even though the main threat listed—"sewage and industrial pollution"—was occurring primarily downriver in New Mexico and Texas. The Animas was once again listed, this year as the country's most threatened river.

- **1994:** The Rio Grande was listed as the country's eighth most endangered river, but, once again, the main culprits were in New Mexico and Texas. The Animas River came in as the seventh most threatened river, while Snowmass Creek was listed as the eleventh most threatened river because of "snow making."

- **1995:** The Animas River made the leap up from the threatened list to the fourth most endangered river.

- **1996:** The Animas was once again listed, this time making it the tenth most endangered river. La Poudre Pass Creek was listed as the seventh most threatened river because of a proposed water-development project, while the Rio Grande was listed as the fourteenth most threatened river.

- **1997:** The Animas River was listed as the country's most threatened river.

- **1998:** No Colorado rivers made the list.

- **1999:** No Colorado rivers made the list.

- **2000:** The Rio Grande was listed as the country's seventh most endangered river. The Green River, which passes through Colorado for only a short distance, came in at number 11.

- **2001:** The Animas River was listed as the country's ninth most endangered river due to the Animas–La Plata Reservoir Project yet again.
- **2002:** No Colorado rivers made the list.
- **2003:** The Gunnison River was listed as the country's fourth most endangered river, followed by the Rio Grande at number 5 and the Platte at number 7. Again, the main threats listed for the Rio Grande and the Platte system occurred downriver from Colorado.
- **2004:** The Colorado was listed as the most endangered river in the country because of "three major pollution sources," all of which were found in Arizona, Nevada, and California. In 2005, the Department of Energy announced its plans to relocate one of those three pollution sources—a 120-million-ton pile of radioactive waste—away from a flood-prone location on the bank of the Colorado.
- **2005:** The Fraser River was listed as the country's third most endangered river because of water-diversion threats from Denver. Less than two weeks after the Fraser's listing, Representative Mark Udall (now Senator Mark Udall) met with the head of the Denver Water Board, and, as a result, those diversion threats were delayed indefinitely.
- **2006:** No Colorado rivers were listed.
- **2007:** No Colorado rivers were listed.
- **2008:** The Cache la Poudre River was listed as the third most endangered river in the country because of a proposed water-diversion project known as Glade Reservoir.
- **2009:** No Colorado rivers were listed.
- **2010:** The Upper Colorado River was listed as the country's sixth most endangered river because of two new proposed major water diversions.

SOURCE

www.americanrivers.org.

# WILD AND SCENIC RIVERS

The National Wild & Scenic Rivers Act was an outgrowth of the recommendations of the Outdoor Recreation Resources Review Presidential Commission. It was sponsored by Senator Frank Church (D-Idaho) and signed into law by President Lyndon Johnson in 1968 with the specific intent of preserving certain rivers with outstanding natural, cultural, and recreational values in a free-flowing condition for the enjoyment of present and future generations.

The benefits of a river being given wild and scenic status are numerous, but most noteworthy is the "free-flowing" component of the original congressional act. Once a river is designated as wild and scenic, it becomes much harder for proposed dams to be built—a thought that makes water developers see red.[1] Wild and Scenic designation also can result in potentially damaging riverside mining claims being withdrawn, and governmental scrutiny of potentially river-impacting issues such as agricultural runoff and grazing activities may be intensified.

Wild and Scenic rivers are not afforded the same degree of preservation as national parks or legally designated wilderness areas. Numerous wild and scenic rivers, however, do have segments that overlap with parks and wilderness areas. Wild and scenic rivers are managed by whichever federal agency through whose lands the river flows. Federal agencies that have Wild & Scenic Rivers passing through their jurisdictional turf include the National Park Service, the U.S. Forest Service, the Bureau of Land Management, the U.S. Fish & Wildlife Service, and the Army Corps of Engineers.

Rivers are nominated for inclusion in the Wild & Scenic Rivers system on the state level—either by members of a state's congressional delegation or by federal land-management agencies located within a given state. Actual designation requires either a specific act of Congress (which often includes multiple rivers simultaneously being designated within a state) or a decree from the Secretary of the Interior.

In its 40-plus-year history, the National Wild & Scenic Rivers system has come to include 252 rivers, covering a total of more than 12,000 river miles. National wild and scenic rivers can be found in 39 states, plus Puerto Rico.

Oregon leads the way as of 2009 with 48 wild and scenic rivers, followed by Alaska with 25, Michigan with 16, and California with 15. Arkansas has 8; Idaho and Pennsylvania have 6 each; North Carolina and New Jersey have 5 each; New Mexico and Wisconsin have 4 each; and Minnesota, Ohio, Nebraska, and Puerto Rico have 3 each. Even diminutive Connecticut and Massachusetts each have two Wild and Scenic rivers. Colorado, which is home to the headwaters of numerous of the great rivers of the Western Hemisphere has...one: the 126-mile Cache la Poudre River, which flows from the northernmost reaches of Rocky Mountain National Park through Fort Collins and ultimately to its union with the South Platte near Greeley.[2]

It's not as though there have not been plenty of attempts to get additional Colorado rivers listed as wild and scenic. It's just that none have made it all the way through the process.

There have been at least 57 Colorado-based nominations for Wild and Scenic status since 1968, with several rivers having different sections nominated for inclusion within the system. (When a river is nominated for inclusion in the Wild & Scenic system but does not get designated, it can be inferred that the state's congressional delegation did not enthusiastically support its inclusion for any number of reasons.)[3]

All of the following Colorado rivers have been nominated for inclusion in the Wild & Scenic Rivers system, but, stunningly, none have made the cut.

- **Animas:** 57 miles from Animas City to Mineral Creek (1982)
- **Arikaree:** 48 miles from the Nebraska/Kansas state line to Alder Creek (1982)
- **Arkansas:** Eight different nominations covering a total of 265 sometimes overlapping miles (1982–1993)
- **Badger Creek:** 25 miles from the source to its junction with the Arkansas River (1982)
- **Beaver Creek:** 20 miles from Skagway Reservoir to the east side of State Refuge (1993)
- **Big Thompson:** 14 miles covering the entire segment of the river within Rocky Mountain National Park (1993)
- **North Fork of the Big Thompson:** Entire 9-mile segment within Rocky Mountain National Park (1993)
- **Blue Creek:** 2-mile section from the Curecanti National Recreation Area to Morrow Point Reservoir (1993)
- **North Fork of the Cache la Poudre:** 31-mile section from Source to Dale Creek (1982)
- **Chacuaco Canyon:** 37-mile section from U.S. Highway 160 to the Purgatoire River (1982)
- **Coal Creek:** Section, less than a mile long, from Curecanti National Recreation Area to Blue Mesa Reservoir (1993)
- **Colorado:** 23-mile section from the Blue River to State Bridge (1982)
- **Colorado:** Entire 21-mile section within Rocky Mountain National Park (1993)
- **Conejos:** 57-mile section from the sources of the North, Middle, and El Rito Azul forks to the junction with the South Fork (1993)
- **Crystal:** 45-mile section from the source of the North and South forks to the White River National Forest boundary (1982)
- **Crystal:** 40-mile segment from the source of the North and South forks to Sweet Jessep Headgate (1992)
- **Curecanti Creek:** 1-mile section from Curecanti National Recreation Area to Morrow Point Reservoir (1993)

- **Dolores:** 105-mile section from just below McPhee Dam downstream to 1 mile above the Colorado Highway 90 bridge near Bedrock (1993)
- **East:** 20-mile section from the source to its confluence with the Gunnison River
- **Elk:** 29-mile section from the junction of the North and South forks to the confluence with Gilpin and Gold creeks (1993)
- **Encampment:** 20-mile section from Wyoming state line to the headwaters at West Fork Lake (1993)
- **Fall:** 10-mile section from its headwaters to Fan Lake, in Rocky Mountain National Park (1993)
- **Gunnison:** Entire 12-mile section within Black Canyon of the Gunnison National Park (nee: the Black Canyon of the Gunnison National Monument) (1993)
- **Lake Fork of the Gunnison:** 1-mile section from Curecanti National Recreation Area to Blue Mesa Reservoir (1993)
- **Lake Fork of the Gunnison:** 13-mile section from Sloan Lake to Wager Gulch (1993)
- **Huerfano:** 9-mile section from the Huerfano–Cucharas Ditch to the Cucharas River (1982)
- **Los Pinos:** 54-mile section from the confluence of the North Fork to the northern boundary of Granite Peak Ranch (1993)
- **North St. Vrain Creek:** 19-mile section from the source to Ralph Price Reservoir (1982)
- **North Fork of St. Vrain Creek:** Entire 8-mile section within Rocky Mountain National Park (1993)
- **Piedra:** 32-mile section from the headwaters to the confluence with Indian Creek (1993)
- **Purgatoire:** 75-mile section from Trinchera Creek to Smith Canyon (1982)
- **Purgatoire:** 42-mile section from Smith Canyon to the Arkansas River (1982)
- **Rio Grande:** Four sections totaling 49 miles from the Alamosa Wildlife Refuge to the New Mexico state line (1982–1993)
- **San Juan:** 50-mile section from the sources of the East and West forks to Fourmile Creek (1982)
- **South Platte:** Four sections totaling 51 miles from Lake George to Cheeseman Reservoir (1982–1993)
- **South Fork St. Vrain:** 11-mile section from the Rocky Mountain National Park boundary to Ralph Price Reservoir (1993)
- **Taylor:** 21-mile section from its source to Illinois Creek (1982)
- **West Elk Creek:** Section less than a mile long from Curecanti National Recreation Area to Blue Mesa Reservoir (1993)

- **North Fork of the White River:** 25-mile section from the source to the junction with the South Fork of the White River (1982)
- **South Fork of the White River:** 35-mile section from the source to the junction with the North Fork of the White River (1982)
- **South Fork of the White River:** 38-mile section from the source to just below the junction with the North Fork of the White River (1993)
- **Yampa:** Short segment within the boundaries of Dinosaur National Monument (1982 and 1995)
- **Yampa:** 83-mile section from the Williams Fork to the Little Snake River (1982)

## RECOMMENDED

In 2009, the Bureau of Land Management (BLM) recommended 20 segments on 15 different Colorado rivers for inclusion in the Wild & Scenic Rivers system. The Grand Junction BLM field office culled these recommendations from 117 total sections of streams and rivers that were examined for suitability. The proposed designations stem from a federal mandate requiring that, every time the BLM updates its management plans, it is required to make Wild & Scenic Rivers recommendations.

By the end of the year, very little progress had been made on those recommendations, but there was a bit of good news. The BLM's Little Snake field office had recommended that a 22-mile section of the Yampa be designated Colorado's second wild and scenic river. As well, the BLM has recommended that sections of two other rivers, the Dolores and the Colorado, be established as national conservation areas.

Rivers on the BLM's 2009 Wild & Scenic River recommendation list include:

- Colorado River (3 segments)
- Dolores River
- Yampa River
- North Fork Mesa River
- Blue Creek
- Dominguez Canyons and Little Dominguez (4 segments)
- Gunnison River (2 segments)
- Little Dolores River
- Roan Creek and Carr Creek
- Rough Canyon River
- Unaweep Canyon River
- East Creek
- West Creek
- North Fork West Creek
- Ute Creek

1. Colorado is the only state that uses an adjudicative (court) system rather than a permit (administrative agency) system to administer its water-rights system. To have a new water right recognized or to change the use of a water right in Colorado, you have to go to water court. In other states, you get a permit from a state agency. Permits are typically for limited periods and, especially when a permit must be renewed, your rights are always subject to revision by the state. In contrast, a water right in Colorado is considered a real property interest. It is inheritable, just like land, and the constitutional protections for private property are stronger for a real property interest than they are for a permit. Thus, water rights holders in Colorado tend to take this subject very seriously.

2. Colorado is certainly not the only western state that is woefully underrepresented in the Wild & Scenic Rivers system. Washington only has three wild and scenic rivers—the Klickitat, the Skagit, and the White Salmon. Montana has but two—the Flathead and the Missouri. Arizona has one—the Verde. Wyoming has one—the Clark Fork of the Yellowstone. Utah and Nevada have none.

3. Other reasons why Congress can opt to not designate a nominated river as wild and scenic can include the fact that, if a river is located within a national park or wilderness area, it already receives a degree of protection that exceeds that which is provided by inclusion in the Wild & Scenic Rivers system.

## SOURCES

www.rivers.gov; www.nps.gov/ncrc/programs/rtca/nri/states/co.html; Mark Haas, Wild & Scenic Rivers Specialist, U.S. Fish & Wildlife Service; Jackie Diedrich, Wild & Scenic Rivers Specialist, U.S. Forest Service; personal interview, Joseph B. Dischinger, Attorney-at-Law.


# COLORADO'S HIGHEST ROADS

- The highest road in the country (actually, according to mountevans.com, it is the highest paved road in the world) is the **Mount Evans Road,** which begins in Idaho Springs and ends a few feet below the summit of Mount Evans at 14,240 feet above sea level.
- **Pikes Peak Road** (14,115 feet), which is a well-maintained dirt road, comes in a close second.
- The highest through-road is the very rough 13,186-foot **Mosquito Pass Road,** which connects Alma with Leadville.
- The highest paved through-road in the country is **Trail Ridge Road** (U.S. Highway 34), which transects Rocky Mountain National Park and reaches a high point of 12,183 feet.
- All of the above-listed roads are closed in winter. The highest road that is kept open year-round is **U.S. Highway 6 over Loveland Pass,** between Arapahoe Basin Ski Area and Interstate 70, at an altitude of 11,990 feet.

## SOURCES

Rand-McNally; Colorado Department of Transportation.

# MOUNTAINSPEAK:
## ROAD BIKING LEXICON

- **Abandon:** When a rider quits during a ride or race. Pronounced in the French manner: "ah-ban-dohn," even if it's being uttered in Texas.
- **Big-Ringing It:** When a rider has his or her chain in the largest gears on the bike (the big chain ring in the front and the small sprocket in the rear), allowing him or her to go especially fast but also using considerable effort. Typically used on downhill or flat terrain. Also used to describe a macho move in finance or business—he's "big ringing it" means that one is out in front regardless of the head winds, be they actual or literal.
- **Bonk:** To run out of energy or grow exhausted during a ride, sometimes to the point of having to drop out. "I bonked so early today, it was humiliating." Now widely used in other sports.
- **Breakaway:** One or more riders who sprint away from the peloton in an effort to build a lead. Competing riders in a breakaway will often form uneasy alliances, working together and drafting to increase or maintain their lead. Those alliances break down, though, as they approach the finish. A team leader in a breakaway with multiple teammates has a decided advantage over a rider who has no support. Widely used in popular culture.
- **Breaking the Wind:** To be at the front of a pace line with riders behind you in your slipstream (*see* "Slipstream"). Used in popular culture to describe someone out in front who is being noble and doing all of the work.
- **Bridge:** A rider or riders who sprint away from the main group of riders, or peloton, and catch the breakaway. Now widely used in popular vernacular: "Vietnam is attempting to bridge the gap to the Chinese and Koreans"—implying that they are attempting to jump from third-world to first-world status.
- **Broom Wagon:** The vehicle that follows the race, picking up racers who have to abandon the race. This is an embarrassing moment. There have been quite a few recent references to the U.S. government being the "broom wagon" for AIG, Bear-Stearns, Fannie Mae, etc. *See* "Sag Wagon."
- **Cat 4 Mark:** Grease stain from a bicycle chain on your leg, arm, or jersey. A derogatory term used mostly in reference to newbie cyclists who are so clueless they let their own bike get them dirty.

- **Chain Suck:** When the chain travels inside of its typical line and gets caught underneath the crank arm. Often followed by many expletives.
- **Col:** A mountain or climb, such as "Col du Tourmalet."
- **Corncob:** The rear gears, or cassette. Specifically, a cassette with a range of gears that have one-tooth increments.
- **Criterium:** A multi-lap, one-day race on a closed, short course, typically one mile or less. Often, the route goes through the middle of a town, making it one of the most spectator-friendly bike race events, especially for devotees of carnage.
- **Derailleur:** A mechanism for moving the chain from one sprocket to another to change gears on a multi-speed bicycle.
- **Disc Wheel:** A bicycle wheel with covers or a solid disc, rather than open spokes. Disc wheels are very aerodynamic but heavy and can turn into a sail in a strong crosswind.
- **DNF:** Short for "Did Not Finish." "He DNF'd" is the popular usage, often accompanied by a sad shaking of the head.
- **Domestique:** A team rider who will sacrifice his or her individual performance to help a designated teammate during a race. Duties can include giving up one's bike for another rider whose wheels have malfunctioned and supplying refreshments to teammates. French for "servant."
- **Drafting:** One or more riders ride single file behind another rider, taking advantage of that rider's slipstream. By doing so, the rider behind has less of a head wind and gets a breather. In a crosswind, riders may ride in a diagonal line instead. Drafting is the lynchpin of most bicycle racing tactics. *See* "Pace Line." If you are drafting off of someone else (say in a car or in life), you are taking it easy and being smart, because you are conserving energy.
- **Drop/Dropped:** When a rider has been left behind by another rider or group of riders.
- **Echappee:** The cyclist who escapes from the pack. The "escapee."
- **Echelon:** A staggered, long line of riders, each downwind of the rider ahead, allowing them to move considerably faster than a solo rider or small group of riders. In windy sections where there are crosswinds, a large peloton will form into echelons.
- **Equipe:** A cycling team.
- **Feed Zone:** A designated area along the route where riders can grab "musette bags" filled with food and drinks as they ride by. There is an unwritten rule in the peloton that riders should not attack the field while the riders are going through the feed zone.

- **Field Sprint:** A mass sprint at the finish among the main group of riders in a road race.
- **Gap:** The amount of time or distance between a rider or group of riders and another rider or group of riders. Also used as a verb, as in "he'd been gapped" or dropped. "Gap gapped" was a *Financial Times* headline, which says that the clothing retailer has fallen badly out of the lead.
- **General Classification (G.C.):** The overall leader board in the race, representing each rider's total cumulative time in the race. The rider with the lowest time is number one on the G.C.
- **Grand Tour:** Refers to three-week major cycling stage races: Tour de France, Giro d'Italia (Tour of Italy), and Vuelta a España (Tour of Spain).
- **Granny Gear:** Easiest gear for climbing.
- **Gruppetto:** A group of riders that forms at the back of the field on mountain stages and rides at a pace that allows them to finish just inside the time limit. Usually the gruppetto is comprised of sprinters and other riders who are not climbing specialists or race leaders. "Gruppetto" is Italian for "a small group." If you are in the gruppetto, it means that you are taking it easy.
- **Gruppo:** The collection of bike parts, such as the derailleur, that go on the bicycle frame.
- **Hammer:** To ride hard. Also, to "put the hammer down." Also used in popular lingo: "He hammered on that project," which means that he worked swiftly and intensely.
- **Hook:** To suddenly move one's back wheel to slow down to avoid running into the front rider's bike.
- **Jump:** A quick acceleration, which usually develops into a sprint.
- **King of the Mountains:** The KOM is the fastest climber in a bike race.
- **Kitted-out:** A cyclist who is decked out head to toe in full team "kit"—official custom helmet, sunglasses, jersey, shorts, leg warmers, socks, and cycling shoes. Also used in popular culture to describe a man or woman who is very fancily attired in the latest fashions and pays great attention to his or her appearance.
- **Lacher:** To be dropped.
- **LBS:** Local bike shop.
- **Lead Out:** A racer's teammate(s) form a pace line in front of the leader, pulling hard for the finish. The supporting cast pulls off one at a time, leaving the leader rested and fast for the last sprint. Lead outs typically happen right before the finish line or sprint. Also used in popular lexicon: "Howard Dean was John Kerry's lead-out man in 2004," which is to say that Dean broke

the wind for Kerry until Kerry could sprint to the Democratic primary victory.

- **LSD (not acid…):** Long Slow Distance; old-school winter training approach.
- **Mechanical:** Slang for a mechanical problem with the bike. "He had a mechanical."
- **Motorpace:** Ride inches behind a scooter or motorcycle for training. Also, sometimes used for when a rider drafts off of a car (illegally) in a race to rejoin a group.
- **Off the Back:** When a rider or riders cannot keep pace with the main group and lag behind. A derogatory term. Also in the popular lexicon: "He's off the back" means that the guy is clueless.
- **Off the Front:** When a rider takes part in a breakaway.
- **Pace Line:** A formation of two or more riders who are drafting. Typically, racers take turns doing the hard work at the front of the line. Used in popular culture to describe a team of people who operate like a well-oiled machine.
- **Peloton:** The main group of racers. With its dozens of colorful jerseys, maneuvering for position and breakneck speeds, the peloton can be quite a sight. Also called the "pack" or "field."
- **Popped:** Blown; had it; knackered; stuffed: Words used to describe the legs losing all power.
- **Presta:** French valve stem on tire tubes.
- **Prologue:** One type of beginning for a stage race, which is a relatively short time trial.
- **Puncture:** Flat tire. Often accompanied by expletives, often articulated in French.
- **Road Rash:** Skin abrasions resulting from a fall or crash onto the road.
- **Saddle:** The bike seat.
- **Saddle Sores:** Pimply little devils cause by lots of riding time.
- **Sag Wagon:** A vehicle designated to give rides to bike racers and tour riders who need help. Can be caused by a mechanical problem, injury, or lack of fitness. The ultimate humility for road bikers.
- **Shraeder:** Car-style valve stem on tire tubes.
- **Sitting In:** Drafting or sitting closely behind the rider immediately in front.
- **Slipstream:** The area of least wind resistance behind a rider.
- **Sprint:** A quick scramble for the finish line or a mid-race king of the mountain or other competition. A professional road race sprint is fast, furious, and tactical. Watch for riders to jockey for the second or third spot, or to organize lead outs by their teammates.

- **Squirrel:** A small rodent, but also a rider who is erratic and "squirrelly" when riding in a group. Used to describe erratic drivers as well: "He's squirrelly."
- **Stage Race:** A race comprised of multiple one-day races, or stages. The Tour de France is a stage race.
- **Technical:** A descent or other portion of a race that is twisty, steep, or otherwise challenging from the point of view of bike handling.
- **Time Trial:** Often called the Race of Truth, a time trial pits a rider or a team against the clock. Individual time trials are grueling affairs, with each rider expending maximum effort.
- **Train:** A fast-moving pace line of riders.
- **Velo:** French for "bicycle." Often used by people dressed in very brightly colored, tight-fitting clothing.
- **Wheelsucker:** A rider who doesn't take his turn at the front of the pace line to break the wind. A derogatory term, because the person is essentially not sharing in the work; widely used in popular culture to describe someone who is essentially a parasite.

## SOURCES

Felix Magowan, who used to own *VeloNews;* Josh Liberies, who had the honor of racing against Lance Armstrong in the 2009 Tour de Gila in New Mexico.

# COLORADO WILDFIRES

Although Colorado does not have the same reputation for frequent devastating wildfires as does, say, California, the state has surely seen its fair share of major conflagrations.

Here are some of Colorado's more noteworthy wildfires in recent history.

- **1994:** The South Canyon Fire burned[1] 1,856 acres[2]. Although the South Canyon Fire was, by wildfire standards, fairly small in size, it was perhaps Colorado's most infamous wildfire. This fire, which took place on Storm King Mountain near Glenwood Springs and which was caused by lightning, took the lives of 14 firefighters, most of whom were from Oregon. A memorial trail has been built to the site of the tragedy, which was recounted in the book *Fire on the Mountain: The Story of the South Canyon Fire* by John Maclean, son of the late Norman Maclean, who penned *A River Runs Through It*.
- **1996:** The lightning-caused Buffalo Mountain Fire burned 12,000 acres and torched 10 dwellings. A section of the Colorado Trail

had to be closed for several months because of danger posed by trees that had been burned but that had not yet toppled.

- **2000:** The 10,800-acre, lightning-caused High Meadows Fire, which burned near Bailey and Conifer, destroyed 58 homes and cost $5.5 million to fight. Almost $10 million in property was lost.
- **2000:** The lightning-caused Bobcat Fire burned 10,599 acres near Drake. Fifteen structures were lost and more than 1,000 firefighters were involved. The Bobcat Fire burned in the same area that was devastated in 1976 by the Big Thompson Flood, the single worst natural disaster in Colorado history in terms of human life lost.
- **2002:** This was the single worst wildfire year in Colorado history and was when Colorado Governor Bill Owens declared, "All of Colorado is burning," much to the chagrin of tourist-oriented business owners throughout the state. Actually, Owens' "quote" was badly taken out of context. Responding to a question from a reporter after taking a helicopter tour of two of the fires then burning in Colorado, Owens said, "It looks as if all of Colorado is burning today." Within weeks, T-shirts adorned with people sitting in chairlifts and smoking illicit substances came out, along with the truncated version of Owens' quote: "All of Colorado is burning." All told in 2002, Colorado experienced 1,400 wildfires, which affected a total of 379,287 acres.

It was in the summer of 2002 that the Hayman Fire, the largest ever in Colorado, burned 137,760 acres and destroyed 600 structures near Deckers, southwest of Denver. The fire was set by Terry Barton, ironically a U.S. Forest Service employee who claimed she was attempting to burn a letter from her estranged husband in a campfire ring located in an area with an absolute fire ban (which was designated due to extreme drought conditions). The Hayman Fire, which raged across four counties and resulted in thick smoke that covered the Denver Metro area for more than week, caused an estimated $40 million in damage, burned 166 homes, and caused damage to at least 600 additional structures. More than 5,000 people had to be evacuated from their homes.

Worse, five firefighters, all from Oregon, died in a traffic accident on their way to fight the Hayman Fire.

Barton was sentenced to 12 years in prison on state arson charges, and on federal arson charges, she was sentenced to six years in prison and ordered to pay restitution of $14.6 million. The state charges were overturned on appeal on the grounds that the presiding judge had "the appearance of prejudice" because smoke from the Hayman Fire motivated him to voluntarily leave his home for one night. In March 2008, Barton was re-sentenced by a different judge to 15 years of probation and ordered to complete 1,500 hours of community service. She was released from prison in June 2008.

**Also in 2002, the Colorado mountains saw:**

- The 70,785-acre, human-caused Missionary Ridge Fire, north of Durango, which caused an estimated $152 million in damage
- The 33,000-acre Trinidad Complex Fire near Trinidad
- The 31,016-acre Mount Zirkel Complex Fire near Steamboat Springs
- The 17,056-acre Big Fish Fire near Yampa
- The 13,490-acre Spring Creek Complex Fire near Gunnison
- The 12,209-acre Coal Seam Fire near Glenwood Springs

- **2005:** The Mason Gulch Fire, caused by lightning, burned 11,357 acres north of Beulah and cost $5.3 million to subdue.
- **2006:** The 13,820-acre Mato Vega Fire, northeast of Fort Garland, caused the evacuation of 270 homes but burned no structures. The state government used $3 million in emergency funds to battle the blaze.

## NOTES

1. The public is often told, usually by a media that is little inclined to investigate further, that certain acreage within a fire perimeter has been "burned," "scorched," or "destroyed." Ignoring for a moment that wildfire is a perfectly natural component of ecosystem regeneration, those terms are inaccurate, or at least not accurate enough for use by fire scientists. After a wildfire is contained, the U.S. Forest Service, generally the lead federal agency when it comes to fighting wildfires—even if those fires move onto private land or public land administered by other governmental agencies—issues a Burned Area Report. On-ground observations regarding depth and color of ashes, size and amount of live fuels consumed, litter consumption, plant root crowns, and soil crusting are all included in mapping what are called "intensity zones." Areas within a wildfire perimeter are classified as either:

- **Low-intensity fire.** These are areas that are minimally enough impacted by the fire that they usually do not even contribute to what the U.S. Forest Service calls an emergency watershed condition. As a matter of fact, areas of low fire intensity often act as buffers to moderate flood hazards that may originate in more intensively burned areas. Low-intensity wildfires usually occur on rangeland. Within low-intensity wildfire perimeters, duff and debris are only partly burned, soil remains a normal color, hydrophobicity (the soil's inclination to repel water) is low to absent, and standing trees may have some green needles. Land experiencing low-intensity fires can expect that root crowns and surface roots will re-sprout within one year, and water infiltration and erosion potential are not significantly changed from pre-fire conditions.

- **Moderate-intensity fire.** This classification indicates that high-intensity burns are found on less than 40 percent of the affected area. A moderate-intensity rating alerts fire teams that the designated zone is a potential flood source area, as one of the biggest post-wildfire concerns is flooding due to a diminishment of ground cover. Moderate-intensity wildfires primarily occur on steep, lightly timbered slopes with grass, and they often cause some erosion. Within moderate-intensity wildfire perimeters, duff is consumed, burned needles are evident, ash is generally dark colored, hydrophobicity is low to medium on surface soil up to one inch deep, shrub stumps and small fuels are charred, but present and standing trees are blackened but are not charcoal. Land experiencing moderate-intensity wildfires can expect that root crowns will usually re-sprout, roots and rhizomes below one inch will re-sprout, and most perennial grasses will re-sprout. Vegetative recovery in a moderate-intensity wildfire zone is one to five years.
- **High-intensity fire.** This rating indicates that high-intensity fire has occurred on more than 40 percent of the area within the wildfire perimeter. High-intensity wildfires primarily occur in unprotected drainages on steep, timbered, north or east slopes with a dense forest canopy. They are primarily defined by the ominous words: "natural recovery limited." Within high-intensity wildfire zones, the duff is totally consumed; ash is uniformly gray or white; no shrub stumps or small fuels remain; hydrophobicity is up to two inches deep; soil is darkened two to four inches deep and often is reddish in color; the soil is crusted, crystallized, and agglomerated; roots are burned two to four inches deep; and standing trees have been turned to charcoal at least one inch deep (meaning that they are dust from a mortality perspective). Land experiencing high-intensity wildfires can expect that soil productivity will be significantly reduced and that only roots and rhizomes located in deep soil will re-sprout. Vegetative recovery in a high-intensity wildfire zone is 5 to 10 years, and soil erosion is a significant concern.

2. The acreage figures used to describe the size of wildfires are, in reality, areas contained within wildfire perimeters. Wildfire perimeters are calculated using Global Positioning System (GPS) technology combined with observations, mapping, and photography gleaned from aerial overflights and ground-truthing. Fire size is then calculated using Geographic Information Systems (GIS). Thing is, significant areas within a given fire perimeter might not have actually been burned. Depending on the size of the unburned islands within a wildfire perimeter, they are usually counted in the total acreage for the fire. Therefore, fire "sizes" released to the public and regurgitated by the media are often inaccurate.

## SOURCES

Steve Segin, Lead Public Information Officer, Joint Incident Information Center, Rocky Mountain Area Coordination Center, U.S. Forest Service; Craig Cowie, Fire and Vegetation Staff Officer, Gila National Forest; www.wildfireto-day.blogspot.com; Natural Resources Conservation Service; Wikipedia.

# OTHER LARGE WILDFIRES IN
# WESTERN NORTH AMERICA

While not diminishing the impacts of the 137,760-acre Hayman Fire, Colorado's largest, that particular conflagration barely even registers when compared to other wildfires that have swept through parts of the western United States and Canada. Here is a partial list of the largest wildfires in western North American history, along with some of their impacts.

- **1865:** The Silverton Fire burned 1 million acres in Oregon and to this day is the largest single fire in Oregon history.
- **1871:** The Peshtigo Fire burned 1 million acres and killed more than 1,700 people in Wisconsin. It has the dubious distinction of causing the most deaths by fire in U.S. history, even though it was overshadowed by the Great Chicago Fire that occurred on the very same day.
- **1876:** The Bighorn Fire burned 500,000 acres in Wyoming.
- **1910:** The Great Fire of 1910 burned 3 million acres and killed 86 people in Montana and Idaho.
- **1933–1951:** Fire raged through the Tillamook area of Oregon a total of four times, burning more than 600,000 acres.
- **1949:** While the Mann Gulch Fire burned only 4,500 acres in Montana, it caused the deaths of 13 firefighters. The fire was recounted in the book, *Young Men and Fire* by Norman Maclean, best known for his book *A River Runs Through It.*
- **1953:** The Rattlesnake Fire burned only 1,500 acres in California, but 15 firefighters died fighting it. This fire is considered a textbook case that to this day is used to train firefighters.
- **1970:** The Laguna Fire in California burned 175,425 acres, destroyed 383 homes, and killed eight people.
- **1988:** The Yellowstone Fires burned a total of 793,880 acres in Wyoming and Montana.
- **1991:** The Oakland Hills firestorm burned only 1,520 acres but killed 25 and destroyed 3,469 homes in the cities of Oakland and Berkeley, California.
- **2000:** The Cerro Grande Fire in Los Alamos, New Mexico, burned about 420 dwellings and damaged more than 100 buildings at the Los Alamos National Laboratory. With more than $1 billion in damage, it remains the worst fire in New Mexico's history. It was, ironically enough, started by a controlled burn initiated by the National Park Service at nearby Bandelier National Monument. There was significant concern while the Cerro

Grande Fire was burning that it might make its way to the special nuclear material stored at Los Alamos.

- **2002:** The 467,066-acre Rodeo–Chediski Fire was at the time the largest in Arizona history. Several communities, including Show Low, Pinetop–Lakeside, and Heber–Overgaard, were threatened and had to be totally evacuated. This was actually two fires that merged into one. They were both human caused. The Rodeo Fire began near the Rodeo Fairgrounds on the Fort Apache Indian Reservation. It was intentionally set by Leonard Gregg, a Cibecue resident who worked as a seasonal firefighter for the Fort Apache Tribal Fire Department. He told investigators that he set the fire in hopes of getting hired to fight the very fire he set. He was indeed one of the first to be called to fight the Rodeo Fire. He was eventually sentenced to 10 years in prison. The Chediski Fire was accidentally set by a stranded motorist, Valinda Jo Ellicott, whose car had run out of gas two days earlier. She started a fire to try to signal a news helicopter that was flying overhead. The U.S. attorney's office opted not to charged Ellicott with arson.
- **2003:** The 280,278-acre Cedar Fire was the largest in California history. It burned 2,232 homes and killed 15 in San Diego County. The Cedar Fire burned simultaneously with 15 other fires in Southern California that consumed a total of 721,791 acres, killing a total of 24, displacing 120,000, and destroying 3,640 homes. Damage from the combined fires was estimated at $2 billion.
- **2006:** The Esperanza Fire burned 40,200 acres and killed five firefighters in California.
- **2007:** The 363,052-acre Milford Flat Fire was the largest on record in Utah. Smoke from the fire caused numerous wrecks on Interstate 15, including a five-car pileup and a fatal hit-and-run that killed two motorcyclists from California.
- **2007:** The 240,207-acre Zaca Fire, the second largest single wildfire in California history, was started by sparks from water-pipe repair equipment. Its containment costs exceeded $117 million.
- **2007:** A series of wildfires in California covering a total of 500,000 acres killed nine people, injured 85, including 61 firefighters, and burned at least 1,500 homes from Santa Barbara County to the Mexican border.
- **2007:** The Murphy Complex Fire burned 653,100 acres in southern Idaho and northern Nevada. It was the largest fire in 2007, which is saying a mouthful, as 2007 was the single worst wildfire season in U.S. history.
- **2008:** California experienced yet another catastrophic wildfire season, with more than 1,102,293 acres burned.

- **2011:** The human-caused Wallow Fire replaced the Rodeo–Chediski Fire as the largest in Arizona history, consuming almost 540,000 acres in the Grand Canyon State, as well as almost 16,000 acres in New Mexico. Epicentered in the White Mountains, more than 7,000 people were evacuated from the towns of Eager and Springerville, one of the largest wildfire-caused evacuations in the nation's history. The hamlets of Alpine, Nutrioso, Greer, Sunrise, Alpine, Blue and Luna, New Mexico, also were evacuated. At almost exactly the same time as the Wallow Fire, the human-caused Horseshoe II Fire was burning in Arizona's Chiricahua Mountains. The Horseshoe II Fire eventually consumed 223,000 acres, making it the state's third-largest wildfire in history.

SOURCES

Wikipedia.com; *Wildfire Today.*

# ALL FIREWOOD IS NOT CREATED EQUAL

Part and parcel of the Colorado mountain image and mind-set is the notion of stoking up a monster fire in one's fireplace or wood-stove and kicking back, comfortably warm, with a snifter of brandy and pondering one's good fortune.

But all is not perfectly cozy on the wood-heat front in Colorado. First of all, more and more Colorado counties and towns are prohibiting the installation of wood-burning devices in new and even existing homes (due to issues of smoke-based particulate pollution that is made worse by cold-weather-based air inversions).

And, secondly, the wood available for heating purposes in the Colorado mountains is relatively poor, on a couple of different levels.

The main way that the efficacy of firewood is measured is MMBTUs—millions of British Thermal Units[1]—per cord, which, although imperfect (given such variables as how well cured a given cord of wood is), is the best way for determining the relative value of various woods. In the Colorado mountains, the number of species of trees is low, and all of the tree species found at high altitude—aspen, Douglas fir, blue spruce, and lodgepole pine—rate low when plugged into the MMBTU/cord formula.

An additional measurement of firewood quality, very interrelated with the MMBTU/cord measurement, is weight per cord, which is by default also a measurement of wood density.

Some firewood aficionados will add subjective measurements to the firewood-quality formula, including such categories as ease of burning, ease of splitting, quantity of smoke, and spark factor.

It is not possible to rank all types of firewood, because there are simply too many species. But a look at the extreme MMBTU rankings lets us get a grip on the quality of Colorado mountain-born firewood. Any measurement above 30 MMBTU indicates superlative firewood. Few tree species rank that high, and most are southern hardwoods. Live oak has an MMBTU ranking of 34.4–36.6, while eucalyptus ranks 32.5–34.5. Dogwood ranks 28.6–30.4. The only Western species that ranks above 30 is madrone, a small desert-dwelling tree, which comes in at 29.1–30.9.

Toward the low end, we find balsam fir, with an MMBTU rating of 14.5, which ties it with one of the most-common high-country tree species, aspen, which also has an MMBTU rating of 14.5. It should be noted, however, that just because a given type of firewood has a low MMBTU ranking does not mean you ought to eschew it entirely, as the woods with lower MMBTU ratings often burn faster and hotter during the fire-building stage—meaning they work well getting the denser woods ignited.

## COLORADO MOUNTAIN FIREWOODS AND THEIR RATINGS

- Aspen: Heat output—low; ease of burning—high; ease of splitting—high; smoke factor—medium; spark factor—low; pounds/cord (dry)—2,290; MMBTUs/cord—14.5; overall rating as firewood—fair
- Douglas fir: Heat output—high; ease of burning—high; ease of splitting—high; smoke factor—high; spark factor—high; pounds/cord—2,900; MMBTUs/cord—18.1–21.4; overall rating—good
- Lodgepole pine: Heat output—high; ease of burning—high; ease of splitting—high; smoke factor—high; spark factor—high; pounds/cord—2,000; MMBTUs/cord—19.7–22.3; overall rating—good

Colorado mountain dwellers benefit from the fact that, in every direction, there is lower-elevationed land, which generally offers higher-quality firewood that often makes its way up into the high country. Here are some MMBTU ratings for firewood types that are found a bit lower down but are still accessible.

- Mesquite: Probably overall the best firewood found in the West, with an MMBTU rating of 28, but, given the recent popularity of mesquite-based grilling and smoking, this slow-growing, low-desert-dwelling tree has suffered mightily from over-cutting, and it is highly recommended that people not use it as a fuel source

- Western juniper: 23.4–26.4
- Red or black oak: 21.7–24
- Sycamore: 21.9–23.3
- Juniper: 22.8
- Lodgepole pine: 19.7–22.3
- Western red cedar: 15.4–17.4
- Cottonwood: 12.2 (i.e., don't waste your time)

## NOTES

1. The British Thermal Unit—BTU—is one of those measurements whose days are clearly numbered, mainly because it is a non-metric measurement. Thus, its use is pretty much limited to the United States, and, to a lesser extent, Canada, Australia, and the United Kingdom. One BTU is defined as the amount of heat required to raise the temperature of one pound of liquid water by one degree from 60 degrees to 61 degrees Fahrenheit at a constant pressure of one atmosphere. Although the various manifestations of the BTU are well entrenched in the United States, especially in the heating, air conditioning, and refrigeration industries, most of the world now uses the International System of Units (SI, from the French le Systeme International d'Unites) measurement, joule, which is defined as the mechanical energy that must be expended to raise the temperature of two kilograms of water from 0 degrees to 1 degree Centigrade.

## SOURCES

Oklahoma State University; Wikipedia.com; mb-soft.com/juca/print/firewood.html; thelograck.com; chimneysweeponline.com; consumerenergyreport.com.

# ENDANGERED AND THREATENED SPECIES IN THE COLORADO MOUNTAINS

Colorado is home to 13 species of plants and 18 species of animals listed as endangered[1] or threatened[2] by the federal government under provisions of the Endangered Species Act (ESA) of 1973, which is administered by the U.S. Fish & Wildlife Service (FWS).

Colorado lies toward the back of the national pack in terms of federal endangered and threatened species listings. (Hawaii, with 330, has the most listings, followed by California, with 309, and Alabama, with 117.) It should be noted, however, that endangered and threatened species listings are, sadly, not always a reflection of biological or ecological reality. Politics often play a significant role in whether a species is listed. (*See* "Endangered Species Recovery Tools" in this section.)

# ENDANGERED SPECIES RECOVERY TOOLS

The FWS has two main tools under the ESA with which it can help endangered and threatened species recover.

1. Recovery plans outline the goals, tasks required, likely costs, and estimated time line to recover an endangered species, which means to increase a given species's numbers to the point where it can be removed from the endangered species list—the goal of every listing.

   The ESA does not specify when a recovery plan must be completed. The FWS has an agency policy specifying completion within three years of a species being listed, but the average time to completion is approximately six years. The annual rate of recovery plan completion increased steadily from the Ford Administration (4), through Carter (9), Reagan (30), Bush I (44), and Clinton (72), but declined drastically under Bush II (16).

2. Critical habitats are required to contain "all areas essential to the conservation" of the endangered or threatened species. The FWS has a policy limiting designation to lands and waters within the United States, and the agency can exclude recovery areas deemed essential by wildlife biologists if administrators determine that economic or other costs (read: political) exceed the benefit. Critical habitats can be public or private. All federal agencies are prohibited from authorizing, funding, or carrying out actions that "destroy or adversely modify" critical habitats.

   While the regulatory aspect of critical habitat does not apply directly to private and other non-federal landowners, large-scale development and logging and mining projects on private and state land typically require a federal permit and thus become subject to critical habitat regulations. For this reason, there is often serious opposition from landowners, developers, and the extractive industries to endangered species listings.

   The ESA requires that critical habitat be designated within one year of a species being listed as endangered. In practice, it usually takes several years. Between 1978 and 1986, the FWS regularly designated critical habitat. In 1986, the Reagan Administration issued an executive order limiting the protective status of critical habitat. As a result, few critical habitats were designated between 1986 and the late 1990s. In the late 1990s and early 2000s, a series of court orders invalidated the Reagan regulations and forced the FWS to designate several hundred critical habitats, mostly in the Western states, including Colorado.

   Most provisions of the ESA revolve around preventing extinction. Critical habitat is one of the few that focuses on recovery. Species with critical habitat designations are twice as likely to be recovering as species without critical habitat.

# SUCCESS STORIES FROM
# THE ENDANGERED SPECIES ACT

Since the ESA was passed into law in 1973, a total of 1,375 plant and animal species have been listed as either endangered or threatened. Of those, less than 50 species have been "delisted"—meaning removed from ESA protection. Of those, nine species were delisted because they went extinct prior to or during their listing as endangered. Twenty-one delistings have taken place for the best of reasons: because the species had recovered sufficiently that their survival was no longer contingent upon being listed as endangered or threatened.

Colorado is home to three of those success stories.

- By 1971, only 324 pairs of peregrine falcons were left. The peregrine—the fastest animal in the world—was listed almost as soon as the ESA was enacted into law. By 2000, there were 1,700 pairs and the species, which lives in several parts of Colorado, was delisted.
- The bald eagle, the symbol of the United States, was down to 417 nesting pairs in 1963. Like the peregrine falcon, the bald eagle was listed as an endangered species soon after the ESA was passed. By 2007, there were 11,040 pairs of bald eagles, and the species, which lives throughout the Colorado mountains, was delisted.
- Although the last grizzly bear in Colorado was killed in the southern San Juan Mountains in 1979, it was still listed as endangered in Colorado, at least partially because Colorado formed part of its native home range and at least partially because some people still believe that there are remnant grizzly populations in the southern San Juans and/or in the Sawatch Range. Grizzly populations in the Greater Yellowstone ecosystem increased from 271 to 580 between 1975 and 2005. The grizzly was delisted in 2007.

---

Sixteen of the 19 threatened or endangered animal species in Colorado can be found (hopefully) in the mountainous part of the state,[3] while nine of the plant species claim as part of their native habitat Colorado's altitudinous terrain.

## ENDANGERED OR THREATENED ANIMAL SPECIES
## WHOSE NATIVE RANGE IS FOUND ALL OR IN PART IN
## THE COLORADO ROCKIES

- Uncompahgre fritillary butterfly (Colorado's only legally endangered insect)
- Bonytail chub (fish)

- Humpback chub (fish)
- Whooping crane (bird)
- Black-footed ferret (mammal)
- Southwestern willow flycatcher (bird)
- Canada lynx (mammal)
- Preble's meadow jumping mouse (mammal)
- Mexican spotted owl (bird)
- Pike minnow (a.k.a. squawfish) (fish)
- Piping plover (bird)
- Pawnee montane skipper (butterfly)
- Razorback sucker (fish)
- Least tern (bird)
- Greenback cutthroat trout (fish) (*See* "The Recovery of Colorado's State Fish" in this section.)
- Mexican gray wolf (mammal)[3]
- Eskimo curlew (bird)
- Pallid sturgeon (fish)

## ENDANGERED OR THREATENED PLANT SPECIES WHOSE NATIVE RANGE IS FOUND ALL OR PART IN THE COLORADO ROCKIES
- Dudley Bluffs bladderpod
- Colorado butterfly plant
- Ute ladies' tresses
- Mancos milk-vetch
- Osterhout milk-vetch
- Penland alpine fen mustard
- North Park phacelia
- Dudley Bluffs twinpod
- Penland beardtongue
- Colorado hookless cactus
- Knowlton's cactus
- Mesa Verde cactus
- Clay-loving wild buckwheat

## COLORADO PLANTS AND ANIMALS LISTED AS "CANDIDATE" SPECIES BY THE FWS FOR POSSIBLE INCLUSION AS ENDANGERED OR THREATENED SPECIES
- Western yellow-billed cuckoo (bird)
- Arkansas darter (fish)
- Gunnison's prairie dog (mammal)
- Lesser prairie chicken (bird)
- Rio Grande cutthroat trout (fish)
- Parachute beardtongue (plant)
- White River beardtongue (plant)

- Sleeping Ute milk-vetch (plant)
- DeBeque phacelia (plant)
- Pagosa skyrocket (plant)

# THE RECOVERY OF COLORADO'S STATE FISH

The greenback cutthroat trout is the easternmost sub-species of cutthroat trout. Today, this sub-species, once widespread, occupies less than 1 percent of its historical range. It is currently listed as a threatened species under the ESA.

Since 1994, it also has been Colorado's state fish.

Although the greenback cutthroat trout was common in the late nineteenth century, being found in large numbers along the Front Range from Wyoming to New Mexico, its numbers began to decline when settlers arrived in Colorado. Mining in its native river basins led to sediment and heavy-metals-laden runoff. Water-diversion projects for agriculture and over-fishing also led to the green cutthroat's rapid decline. The introduction of non-native species, such as the brook trout, brown trout, and rainbow trout, did not exactly help matters either. The brook and brown trout competed with the greenback cutthroats for food and habitat, while the rainbows hybridized with it, creating "cutbows."

By 1937, the greenback cutthroat was considered extinct. But, in 1957—miracle of miracles!—a population was discovered in the headwaters of the Big Thompson River in Rocky Mountain National Park. Additional populations were discovered in 1965 and 1970, making it possible for the greenback cutthroat to be listed under the ESA with realistic hopes of a species-wide recovery. Recovery efforts were so successful that the greenback cutthroat was down-listed in 1978 from endangered to threatened, where it remains.

It was recently discovered that, due to insufficient study of the original stock populations, most—if not all—of the fish used to help repopulate the sub-species were actually the similar Colorado River cutthroat trout. It has yet to be determined what effect that discovery will have on future recovery plans for Colorado's state fish, which, when push comes to shove, might not be Colorado's state fish after all.

The greenback cutthroat trout today is found east of the Continental Divide in the clear, cold foothill and mountain waters of the Arkansas and South Platte river basins, where catch-and-release fishing of Colorado's state fish is currently permitted.

## STATE ENDANGERED AND THREATENED SPECIES

The ESA provides funding for the management of endangered and threatened species by state wildlife agencies. Subsequently, lists of endangered and threatened species within their boundaries have been prepared by all 50 states. These state lists often include species that are considered endangered or threatened within a specific state, but not within all states, and which are therefore not included on the national lists of endangered and threatened species. The Colorado Division of Wildlife, which became the Colorado Division of Parks and Wildlife on July 1, 2011, maintains its own endangered (SE) and threatened (ST) species lists, as well as a "special concern" category (SC) that is not an actual statutory category.

## AMPHIBIANS

- Boreal toad (SE)
- Northern cricket frog (SC)
- Great Plains narrowmouth toad (SC)
- Northern leopard frog (SC)
- Wood frog (SC)
- Plains leopard frog (SC)
- Couch's spadefoot (SC)

## BIRDS

- Whooping crane (SE; also listed as a federal endangered species)
- Least tern (SE; also listed as a federal endangered species)
- Southwestern willow flycatcher (SE; also listed as a federal endangered species)
- Plains sharp-tailed grouse (SE)
- Piping plover (ST; also listed as a federal threatened species)
- Bald eagle (ST)
- Mexican spotted owl (ST; also listed as a federal threatened species)
- Burrowing owl (ST)
- Lesser prairie chicken (ST)
- Western yellow-billed cuckoo (SC; also listed as a federal candidate species)
- Greater sandhill crane (SC)
- Ferruginous hawk (SC)
- Gunnison sage grouse (SC; also listed as a federal candidate species)
- American peregrine falcon (SC)
- Greater sage grouse (SC)
- Western snowy plover (SC)
- Mountain plover (SC)
- Long-billed curlew (SC)
- Columbian sharp-tailed grouse (SC)

## FISH

- Bonytailed chub (SE; also listed as a federal endangered species)
- Razorback sucker (SE; also listed as a federal endangered species)
- Humpback chub (ST; also listed as a federal threatened species)
- Colorado pike minnow (ST; also listed as a federal threatened species)
- Greenback cutthroat trout (ST; also listed as a federal threatened species)
- Rio Grande sucker (SE)
- Lake chub (SE)
- Plains minnow (SE)
- Suckermouth minnow (SE)
- Northern redbelly dace (SE)
- Southern redbelly dace (SE)
- Brassy minnow (ST)
- Common shiner (ST)
- Arkansas darter (ST)
- Mountain sucker (SC)
- Plains orange-throat darter (SC)
- Iowa darter (SC)
- Rio Grande chub (SC)
- Colorado roundtail chub (SC)
- Stonecat (SC)
- Colorado River cutthroat trout (SC)
- Rio Grande cutthroat trout (SC; also listed as a federal candidate species)
- Flathead chub (SC)

## MAMMALS

- Gray wolf (SE; also listed as a federal endangered species)
- Black-footed ferret (SE; also listed as a federal endangered species)
- Grizzly bear (SE; also listed as a federal threatened species)
- Preble's meadow jumping mouse (ST; also listed as a federal threatened species)
- Canada lynx (SE; also listed as a federal threatened species)
- Wolverine (SE)
- River otter (ST)
- Kit fox (SE)
- Townsend's big-eared bat (SC)
- Black-tailed prairie dog (SC)
- Botta's pocket gopher (SC)

- Northern pocket gopher (SC)
- Swift fox (SC)

## REPTILES

- Triploid checkered whiptail (SC)
- Midget faded rattlesnake (SC)
- Longnose leopard lizard (SC)
- Yellow mud turtle (SC)
- Common king snake (SC)
- Texas blind snake (SC)
- Texas horned lizard (SC)
- Roundtail horned lizard (SC)
- Massasauga (SC)
- Common garter snake (SC)

## MOLLUSKS

- Rocky Mountain capshell (SC)
- Cylindrical papershell (SC)

## NOTES

1. Endangered species are populations that, unless drastic and immediate preservation measures are undertaken, find themselves at imminent risk of becoming extinct because they are too few in number and/or their habitat is threatened by changing environmental parameters and/or man-made impacts.

2. Threatened species are populations that are deemed vulnerable to extinction in the near future unless drastic preservation measures are taken.

3. Three of the animal species listed as threatened or endangered by the federal government in Colorado do not actually live in Colorado. The Eskimo curlew, one of the world's most endangered bird species, once flew through Colorado on its round-trip migration between Argentina and northern Canada and Alaska. No Eskimo curlews have been spotted in Colorado in decades. The pallid sturgeon is listed as endangered in Colorado because its native habitat is the Mississippi/Missouri drainage, and several Colorado-borne rivers flow into that drainage. Then there's the Mexican gray wolf. Few animals listed under provisions outlined by the ESA have had as rough an administrative ride as the various gray wolf sub-species. The Mexican gray wolf was listed as an endangered subspecies in 1976, then consolidated with other gray wolf subspecies as "endangered gray wolves"—species-level—in 1978. The Mexican gray wolf was listed as an endangered distinct population segment in 2003, and that listing was remanded by court order in a suit concerning wolf policy nationwide in 2005. Today, the Mexican gray wolf is part of the endangered listing for all gray wolves in much of the Continental United States. Although there are currently no stable populations of gray wolves in Colorado, numerous rogue wolves have wandered into the state in the past few years.

## SOURCES

U.S. Fish & Wildlife Service; Colorado Division of Parks and Wildlife; the Tucson-based Center for Biological Diversity; Wikipedia.

# COLORADO MOUNTAIN BIRDS

About 490 different species of birds have been identified in Colorado, making it the country's seventh most bird-species-dense state. Many of the species identified in Colorado are migratory and only visit the state on their way to and from somewhere else. Many are transient, in that they come to Colorado for the summer and head to points south in the winter. And even a few are accidental in that they may have visited Colorado simply because they were disoriented or blown off course.

Colorado has the second most number of bird species of any non-coastal state in the country, after New Mexico. One of the main reasons for that species density stems from the fact that Colorado is home to two prominent migration flyways. The first lies along the Front Range, hugging the easternmost extensions of the Rockies while keeping one toe in the lower elevations of the Great Plains. Then there's the Rocky Mountain Flyway that follows the San Luis and Upper Arkansas River valleys north from New Mexico, into Wyoming, and, for some species, all the way to the Arctic tundra.

## SANDHILL CRANES

No individual species of bird gets more press in Colorado than the greater sandhill crane, which famously stops in the lower San Luis Valley on its way north from New Mexico's Bosque del Apache Wildlife Refuge to its summer digs 850 miles north in the Greater Yellowstone ecosystem.

Almost like clockwork, starting in late February, generally until late March or early April, sandhill cranes begin their annual trek from south to north, stopping off near the Monte Vista National Wildlife Refuge to load up on fuel. For millions of years, the sand-hills have been passing through this altitudinous area (elevation about 7,700 feet), which is bordered by some of Colorado's most pronounced vertical topography—the Sangre de Cristo Mountains to the east and the South San Juan Mountains to the west.

Even the earliest residents of southern Colorado made note of the annual crane migration. High on a rocky cliff face southwest of Monte Vista is a well-protected, six-foot-long, 2,000-year-old petroglyph that is unmistakably of a sandhill crane.

Today, crane watchers come from far and wide to join this celebration at the Monte Vista Crane Festival, held in mid-March. While the festival offers outstanding opportunities for celebrating and understanding cranes and other wildlife, the common denominator that brings visitors back year after year is the 20,000 or so greater sandhill cranes and a few thousand lesser sandhill cranes that put on a show for each other and visitors, too. In addition to the cranes, there are thousands of waterfowl, numerous wintering bald eagles, and other raptors that highlight the wildlife viewing.

The festival hosts wildlife experts, local naturalists, and biologists, who present educational workshops at the Monte Vista Middle School, while flocks of dancing sandhills assemble in the neighboring farm fields, just east of town. Bus tours to the nearby Monte Vista National Wildlife Refuge and adjacent farmlands provide visitors with the opportunity to view this spectacle up close and personal, with knowledgeable local guides. Special tours feature raptor identification, sunset trips to view cranes, and visits to closed areas of the refuge for Crane Fest participants.

A craft fair is held in the Ski-Hi building, which features a prominent crane mural on the outside walls. A dinner with live entertainment, a pancake breakfast, local restaurants, and concessions at the craft fair provide sustenance for happy crane watchers from as far away as Japan. Motels and B&Bs fill up weeks in advance, and the population of Monte Vista nearly doubles during the weekend of Crane Fest.

It is also in the San Luis Valley that the cranes perform their courtship dance, leaping and bowing while raising and lowering their wings, and making a croaking sound to one another. Once a male and female bond, they form a pair for life.

Greater sandhill cranes are about four feet tall with a six-foot wingspan. They weigh around 12 to 13 pounds and are uniformly gray except for a red patch of skin on their forehead.

You may also see similar-looking but much smaller birds in the area. These are lesser sandhill cranes, and about 1,200 of them are part of the Rocky Mountain flock. Most lesser sandhill cranes stay east of the Continental Divide in a flock of 500,000 that makes a well-known migratory stop in the Platte River basin of Nebraska.

From April to August, the flock nests in the Greater Yellowstone area—Idaho, Montana, and Wyoming—with the largest concentration centering on Grays Lake National Wildlife Refuge, a remote, marshy plateau near Pocatello, Idaho. The cranes trumpet back through Colorado from early September through November en route to their wintering grounds in New Mexico's Rio Grande Valley, near Socorro.

What turned placid Monte Vista, population about 4,300, into the cranes' major stopover point? In addition to lying along the species' flyway, in recent times, the attraction is the small grains, mainly wheat and barley, which remain on the ground after harvesting. But fields of waste grain aren't the only lure. The cranes also require sufficient water—the Rio Grande winds through the valley—and close proximity to roost sites such as the ponds that dot the Monte Vista National Wildlife Refuge. The absence of adjacent grain fields is why the Alamosa National Wildlife Refuge, only about 20 miles away, doesn't attract the cranes.

## COLORADO'S MOST ALTITUDINOUS BIRD

The brown-capped rosy-finch (*Leucosticte australis*) is the highest-nesting bird in Colorado. No other North American species north of the Mexican border breeds at as high an elevation, and flocks will stay in these areas even in chilling, –30°F winters as long as the snow does not obscure their food sources. They have a very restricted range that barely extends beyond the high peaks of Colorado.

The brown-capped rosy-finch is a stocky, medium-sized finch. Males are cinnamon-brown overall with rosy-tipped feathers in the rump, belly, tail, and bend of the wing. In contrast to the other two species of North American rosy-finches—the black rosy-finch and the gray-crowned rosy-finch, otherwise known as Hepburn's rosy-finch, both of which live in the Colorado mountains as well—the male brown-capped lacks the gray on the back of the head. In flight, the underwings look silver. The female is similar looking, but both the brown and the red colors are of a much lighter shade.

The brown-capped rosy-finch is found almost exclusively in Colorado. Its range, however, extends from southern Wyoming to north-central New Mexico. In winter, it moves to lower elevations when snow covers its high-altitude food sources. Audubon Colorado has identified Rocky Mountain National Park as an "Important Bird Area" that is thought to support a breeding population of 1,000–2,000 brown-capped rosy-finches. The bird is considered rare in Wyoming and rare to uncommon in New Mexico. Christmas Bird Count data seem to indicate a steady decline over the last 30 years, with average annual total counts of more than a thousand in the 1970s compared to about 500 in the 1990s, but more detailed analysis is needed.

In the breeding season, brown-capped rosy-finches build their nests on cliffs or in caves, rock slides, or old buildings above timberline in areas offering protection from precipitant rocks or weather and predators. They dine on seeds and insects, seeking them on rock slides, the tundra, snowfields, fell fields, and glaciers. In the winter, they eat seeds and can be found in open areas such as the alpine tundra, high parks, meadows, and valleys of grass or shrubland. Males' territoriality is focused on the location of their mates at any one time rather than on a geographic area. Nests are made of grass, stems, rootlets, and mud. After hatching, the young stay in the nest between 14 and 20 days and can feed themselves within two weeks after they fledge. Normally, only one clutch is produced in a season; however, replacement clutches are sometimes laid.

The limited range of the brown-capped rosy-finches and recent drop in population make it a conservation concern. In addition, there have been few systematic studies of this species because of the difficulty of accessing its habitat and nesting sites. Thus, much information is speculative. The species' requirements during the non-breeding season particularly need further study, as little is known about the amount of different habitat types and natural food sources that are needed to sustain healthy populations. Birds may only occasionally need certain "lifesaving" habitats or food under extreme snow-cover conditions, but lack of such habitats or foods may increase mortality in unusual years.

At this point, no conservation actions have been directed at this species. Most high-altitude breeding areas are within protected areas or are largely protected because of their inaccessibility. However, the species is not adequately monitored or studied, and consequently little is known about potential threats and causes for the apparent decline. Actions to protect lower-elevation habitats that are used by the species, especially those in proximity to known breeding areas, are likely to be beneficial.

Audubon's Important Bird Area program is a vital tool for the conservation of brown-capped rosy-finches as well as other species. To learn more about the Important Bird Areas program and how you can help, visit www.audubon.org/bird/iba/, or contact your state Important Bird Areas coordinator at www.audubon.org/bird/iba/state_coords.html to find out if there are sites in your area that are important for brown-capped rosy-finches that need increased protection.

One of the best places to view all three species of rosy-finches that can be found in the Colorado mountains is the Fawnbrooke Inn in Allenspark—elevation 8,505 feet—between Nederland and Estes Park on the Peak-to-Peak Highway in early April.

## COLORADO'S STATE BIRD

The lark bunting was adopted as the official state bird on April 29, 1931. The lark bunting, like many visitors to Colorado, does not winter here. Flocks arrive in April and inhabit the plains regions and mountain–foothills areas up to 8,000 feet in elevation. They fly south again in September.

The male lark bunting is black with snowy white wing patches and edgings, tail coverts, and outer tail feathers. In winter, the male changes to a grayish brown color like the female bird; however, the chin remains black and the black belly feathers retain white edgings.

The female bird is grayish brown in color above and white below with dusky streaks. The male bird is six to seven inches high, and the female is slightly smaller. The male bird performs a spectacular courtship flight during which he warbles and trills a distinctive mating song.

## SOURCES

www.cranefest.com; *Crane Spotting* by Dianne Zuckerman, September 2009 edition of *Front Range Living*; www.about.com; Audubon Society; http://blog.wildsidenaturetours.com.

# FATAL BEAR AND MOUNTAIN LION ATTACKS IN COLORADO

There have been about 86 fatal attacks on humans by bears in the United States and Canada since 1870. Three of those fatal attacks have occurred in Colorado. All three victims were killed by black bears[1] (*Ursus americanus*), the only species of bear now living in Colorado, although brown bears, often generically called "grizzlies" (*Ursus arctos*), once called the state home[2].

- **1971:** John Richardson, 31, was killed by an older male black bear while camping on his honeymoon in Grand County, on the west side of Rocky Mountain National Park. Richardson was dragged out of his tent. Wildlife officials hunted the bear and destroyed it. A necropsy revealed that the bear had badly abscessed teeth and a plastic bucket in its stomach and was therefore probably starving.
- **1993:** Colin McClelland, 24, was killed as result of a crushed skull after a 240-pound male black bear tore open the door of his trailer in Fremont County, between Cañon City and Salida. The bear was later killed by game wardens.
- **2009:** Donna Munson, 74, had reportedly been feeding as many as 11 local bears for more than 10 years at her home near Ouray, even though she had repeatedly been warned by wildlife officials to cease and desist. A larger, older bear came up to her house, where she had enclosed the back porch with a wire fence. She was attempting to scare away the bear when it clubbed her through the screened porch, dragged her off, and killed her. Wildlife officials destroyed the bear.

There have been about 22 mountain lion fatalities in the United States and Canada since 1890. About half of those have occurred since 1991. Two of those fatalities have occurred in Colorado[3].

- **1991:** Scott Lancaster, 18, was killed while jogging just a few hundred yards from his high school in Idaho Springs. The lion dragged the 130-pound boy 200 yards uphill before killing him, evidenced by the uprooted vegetation along the way. The lion was found feeding on his body three days later.

- **1997:** Mark David Miedema, 10, was killed by an 88-pound adult female mountain lion while returning from a hike to Cascade Falls on the North Inlet Trail on the west side of Rocky Mountain National Park, just outside Grand Lake. Mark had raced ahead of his family on the well-traveled trail in order to see if animals had eaten the peanuts he had left on the trail on the way up. Mark was only three to four minutes ahead of his parents, but he was out of their sight; his family arrived to see his feet and legs extending onto the trail from adjacent brush. The cougar attempted to drag him away before fleeing. Mark died from choking on his own vomit, not from his wounds from the attack. Mark had tried to fight the cougar and had scratches on his face and puncture wounds on his face, neck, and scalp.

## NOTES

1. The Colorado Division of Parks and Wildlife estimates that there are between 8,000 and 10,000 black bears living in Colorado.

2. For 27 years, it was thought that the last grizzly bear in Colorado was killed in 1952. Then, in 1979, a hunting outfitter was mauled by a grizzly in the South San Juan Mountains near Blue Lake. (The hunter survived; the bear was killed.) Since then, there have been a few reported sightings of grizzlies without scientific confirmation, mostly in the South San Juans. There are also people who think that there is a small population in the Sawatch Range, west of Leadville.

3. The Colorado Division of Parks and Wildlife estimates that there are between 3,000 and 5,000 mountain lions living in Colorado.

## SOURCES

Colorado Division of Parks and Wildlife; the *High Country News*; *Ghost Grizzlies* by David Peterson; Wikipedia.

# HIGH COUNTRY SNAKES

In the eyes of people visiting or recently moved from snake-infested environs like Dixie, California, and the desert Southwest, one of the best things about Colorado's mountain country is its relative lack of snakes. When you're stepping across logs while hiking in the high country, you don't have to worry about getting bit by a 12-foot timber rattler. When you're crossing a mountain stream, your thoughts need not be dominated by visions of the water moccasin scene in *Lonesome Dove*.

But there are indeed snakes in the high country. As a matter of fact, the highest-dwelling snake in the United States makes its home in the land of snow and ice. The western terrestrial garter snake (*Thamnophis elegans*) counts as its regular habitat territory that goes up to 11,000 feet. This non-venomous snake has actually been found as high as 13,100 feet in San Miguel County. Its range includes literally every mountain county in the state.

Adult western terrestrial garter snakes reach lengths of 24 to 42 inches. They are brown to gray, with gray and light-tan checkerboarding conspicuous in juveniles. They have light stripes down their sides that become less prominent with age. These hearty snakes survive the frigid temperatures of the Colorado Rockies by finding shelter under rocks and in small mammal holes that extend down below freezing zone—actually to a point where the temperature does not go below 50 degrees.

Although it is the most prominent species in the mountains, the western terrestrial garter snake is not the only snake that calls the high country home. Here are some other mountain snake dwellers:

- The night snake *(Hypsiglena torquata)* reaches elevations of 7,900 feet in the southwestern part of Colorado.
- The milk snake *(Lampropeltis triangulum)* reaches 8,000 feet, primarily in the southern part of the state.
- The coachwhip *(Masticophis flagellum)* has been found as high as 7,700 feet in the Wet Mountains of Custer County.
- The striped whipsnake *(Masticophis taeniatus)* has been found as high as 8,100 feet in San Miguel County.
- The smooth green snake *(Opheodrys vernalis)* has been found as high as 9,000 feet in Custer, Eagle, Hinsdale, La Plata, Park, Pitkin, and Routt counties.
- The gopher snake/bullsnake *(Pituophus catenifer)* is found as high as 8,500 feet throughout Colorado.
- The prairie rattlesnake *(Crotalus viridis)* is the only venomous snake to venture into the high country. While uncommon at altitude, the prairie rattlesnake has been found as high as 9,500 feet in Alamosa, Boulder, Chaffee, Clear Creek, Custer, Dolores, El Paso, Garfield, Gilpin, Huerfano, Jefferson, La Plata, Routt, Saguache, and San Miguel counties. This snake can reach 48 inches in length. On second thought, it may be best to check it out before you step over logs while hiking.

## SOURCE

Colorado Herpetological Society.

# THE COLORADO STATE FLOWER:
## WHAT EXACTLY IS IT?

Colorado's state flower, the mountain-dwelling white and lavender columbine *(Aquilegia caerulea)* is commonly known as the Rocky Mountain columbine. Its journey from alpine meadows, creek sides, and parklands to official status began humbly enough in 1891, when Colorado schoolchildren overwhelmingly voted the Rocky Mountain columbine as their favorite flower. The final tally was 14,472 florally inclined schoolchildren in favor of the columbine, with the remaining 7,844 votes being spread out among the remaining members of Colorado's plant kingdom. (An unspecified species of cactus came in second place.)

All was well and good in the land of the columbine until 1899, when the Cripple Creek Women's Club discovered that the Rocky Mountain columbine had never been officially adopted as the state flower! They immediately began working to rectify that significant legislative oversight. On April 4, 1899, Senate Bill 261 declared the white and lavender columbine to be Colorado's official state flower.

Thing is, the state senate bill never made reference to the Latin name for the flower.

A few years later, that oversight caused some taxonomic heartburn. In later legislation declaring it the duty of the citizens of the state to protect the state flower, the white and lavender columbine is referred to as *Aquilegia caerulea*. In fact, *Aquilegia caerulea* is more commonly called the Colorado blue columbine, or simply the Colorado columbine, rather than the white and lavender columbine.

That oversight aside, in 1925, the twenty-fifth session of the Colorado General Assembly approved a bill protecting the state flower, whichever columbine sub-species that flower happened to be. (The law names the white and lavender columbine specifically but also uses *Aquilegia caerulea*.)

Section 24-80-907 of the Colorado Revised Statutes states: "It is unlawful for any person to tear the state flower up by the roots when grown or growing upon any state, school, or other public lands or in any public highway or other public place or to pick or gather upon any such public lands or in any such public highway more than twenty-five stems, buds, or blossoms of such flower in any one day; and it is also unlawful for any person to pick or gather such flower upon private lands without the consent of the owner thereof first had or obtained."

The next section states: "Any person who violates the provision of Section 24-80-907 is guilty of a misdemeanor and, upon conviction thereof, shall be punished by a fine of not less than five nor more than fifty dollars."

SOURCE

http://www.netstate.com/states/symb/flowers/co_columbine.htm.

# THE COLORADO STATE QUARTER

The 50 States Commemorative Coin Program Act (otherwise known as the 50 State Quarters Program) was signed into law by President Bill Clinton on December 1, 1997. The program called for the release of a series of commemorative quarters over the course of 10 years, beginning in 1999. The quarters, released five per year in the exact order in which the states joined the Union, were to depict on the reverse side designs unique to each of the states and determined by special committees formed within each of the states. The program was expanded in 2009 to feature quarters from the District of Columbia, Puerto Rico, American Samoa, Guam, the U.S. Virgin Islands, and the Northern Mariana Islands. Each state or territory is allowed under the program to design its own quarter, but the U.S. Mint reserved the right to reject any design proposals deemed unsuitable.

The program was conceived as a means of creating a new generation of coin collectors, and in that it has succeeded brilliantly, as it has become the most successful numismatic program in history, with roughly half the U.S. population collecting the coins, either in a casual manner or as a serious pursuit. The federal government made almost $5 billion profit from collectors taking the coins out of circulation.[1]

The Colorado Commemorative Quarter Advisory Commission was formed by an executive order issued by then-Governor Bill Owens. Colorado First Lady Frances Owens, obviously using connections that some cynics might argue bordered on nepotistic, served as commission chair. A call was issued to citizens to submit narrative descriptions of proposed designs. More than 1,500 submissions were accepted by the commission. From that stack, five narrative concepts were forwarded to the U.S. Mint. The sculptor/engravers of the Mint, along with artists from the Mint's Artistic Infusion Program, developed the candidate designs from the narratives provided, and the designs were returned to Colorado in May 2005. The final quarter design, which was engraved by long-time Mint employee Norm Nemeth based upon artwork completed by Leonard Buckley, was approved by Governor Owens on May 31, 2005.

Colorado's state quarter, the thirty-eighth issued, was released in 2006. The official mintage consisted of 569,000,000 quarters bearing the visage of what many people assumed was Longs Peak, along with the profound and poetic text "Colorful Colorado." (There are no colors to be colorful on any of the quarters; they're all silver and only silver, except for the little value-diminishing copper strip on the side, so you'll have to use your imagination.)

From the get-go, there were questions regarding Colorado's quarter, and those questions stemmed less from the overall design than they did from the design's ambiguity: No one knows for certain exactly which mountain is depicted on the Colorado quarter.

Understanding that, at least in theory, the Mint's artists and engravers were working only from narrative descriptions, numerous sources state unambiguously that the Colorado quarter depicts the North Face of Longs Peak. Some sources further state that the view is of Longs Peak from Bear Lake, one of the most popular destinations in Rocky Mountain National Park. Another reliable source contends that the view is from the Mills Lake area of Glacier Gorge, in Rocky Mountain National Park, and that the quarter's design, although somewhat generic, clearly shows the Keyboard of the Winds, a prominent ridgeline on Longs Peak, and proximate Pagoda Peak.

But the man who did the actual engraving, Norm Nemeth, has stated, "The resemblance to the north side of Longs Peak, Keyboard of the Winds, and Pagoda Peak, is coincidental. It is the overall look that we were trying to achieve."

Governor Owens himself stated, shortly after the Colorado quarter was released, that the intent was to "represent all of Colorado, rather than focusing on one specific landmark or one particular aspect of the state's history." Despite the resemblance to the North Face of Longs Peak, the mountain that adorns the Colorado state quarter is officially an amalgam image depicting no set peak.

The other four design finalists for the Colorado state quarter included were:

- "Mesa Verde," featuring Mesa Verde National Park with cliff dwellings
- "10th Mountain Division," depicting a soldier/skier of the famed U.S. Army division that originated in Colorado and was at least partially responsible for the modern-day development of Colorado's ski industry

- "The Centennial State," which featured a stylized letter "C" entwined with a mountain columbine and the Rocky Mountains in the background
- "Pikes Peak," featuring the gold-rush slogan, "Pikes Peak or Bust," and a prospector's pick and shovel

## GREAT SAND DUNES TO ADORN COLORADO'S NATIONAL PARK QUARTER

As geographically ambiguous as Colorado's official state quarter is, there will be no numismatic argument regarding the setting for the state's entry into the "America the Beautiful" series, which kicked off in 2010.

Dovetailing off of the amazing success of the 50 State Quarters Program," the U.S. Mint decided to instigate a new series of quarters that would feature a national park or other noteworthy federally protected/designated site from each of the states. The quarters are being released in the order in which the parks or sites were designated as such by the federal government. Hot Springs National Park, Arkansas, was the first quarter issued. (Note: Common understanding is that Yellowstone was the country's—indeed the world's—first "national park." Au contraire. Sort of. The national park system had not even been conceived, much less executed, when what is now Hot Springs National Park achieved federal protected status as a "national reserve" in 1832, a full forty years before Congress voted to protect Yellowstone.)

Colorado's entry into the America the Beautiful quarter series will depict Great Sand Dunes National Park & Preserve—home to the continent's highest sand dunes—which was established as a national monument in 1932 before being designated the country's 58th national park in 2004. It will be the 24th America the Beautiful quarter issued, set for release in 2014. The Great Sand Dunes quarter will be released just after Utah's Arches National Park (established 1929) quarter and just before Florida's Everglades National Park (1934) quarter.

NOTES

1. It might seem counterintuitive that the U.S. government can make a profit from minting more coins. But, in one of those bizarre situations that makes it perfectly plausible that, as of May 18, 2009, the federal government's debt stands at $11,295,620,800,875, there's this perplexing economic concept called "seigniorage," which is defined as "the profit gained by a government when it issues its own currency." The U.S. government discovered at the launch of the 50 State Quarters Program that a large number of people were collecting each new quarter as it rolled out of the Mint. Since it costs the Mint less than five cents

to actually produce a quarter, the government essentially made a 20-cent profit each time it replaced in circulation a quarter that had been collected and, thus, taken out of circulation. Makes you want to run right out and put all your retirement funds into T-notes, right?

## SOURCES

U.S. Mint; "Numismatic Study of the Colorado Quarter" by Dave Heim, which appeared in the March–May issue of the *Front Range Coin Club Newsletter;* Wikipedia; dcist.com; dc-coin.com; www.usatoday.com; the Associated Press.

# SUPERFUND SITES

Not every aspect of life in the Colorado high country is worthy of inclusion in a John Denver song or a tourist brochure. Colorado, like literally every other state in the country, has a whole slew of what have become known as "Superfund" sites. Matter of fact, Colorado has been home over the years to a total of 209 Superfund sites, which, while not minimizing the undeniable environmental implications of that statistical reality, places the state at only number 19 nationally.

"Superfund" is a vernacular term for sites that fall under the purview of the Comprehensive Environmental Response, Compensation, and Liability Act (CERCLA), a federal law designed to clean up abandoned hazardous waste sites. It was signed into law by President Jimmy Carter in December 1980. Superfund provides broad federal authority to clean up hazardous releases or threatened releases that may endanger the public health or the environment. CERCLA authorizes the Environmental Protection Agency (EPA) to identify parties responsible for contamination of individual sites and to compel those parties to clean them up. When responsible parties can't be located, the EPA is authorized to clean those sites up itself, using a special $9 billion trust fund that was established by the Superfund Amendments and Reauthorization Act of 1986.

CERCLA was enacted by Congress in response to the infamous Love Canal tragedy in New York State and the environmental disaster at the Valley of the Drums in Kentucky.

CERCLA authorizes two kinds of response actions by the EPA.

- **Removal actions** are typically short-term responses, where action may be taken to address releases or threatened releases requiring prompt response. Removal actions are classified as (1) emergency, (2) time-critical, or (3) non-time-critical. Removal responses are generally used to address risks that are very local in nature, such as abandoned drums containing hazardous substances and/or contaminated surface soils posing acute risks to human health and the environment.

- **Remedial actions** are generally more long-term in nature than removal actions. These are the actions people refer to when they say, sometimes derisively, that the "EPA is coming to town." Remedial actions are intended to permanently and significantly lower the risks or threats of release of contaminants that are serious—sometimes stunningly so—but lack the immediacy of removal actions. These include preventing the migration of pollutants and neutralizing of toxic substances, often on a large scale. Remedial actions can be conducted only at sites listed on the EPA's National Priorities List (NPL). NPL sites can be considered Superfund sites on steroids.

Nationally, as of January 4, 2010, there were 1,270 NPL sites, with an additional 340 sites that have been de-listed and 63 new sites proposed for inclusion as NPLs.

The majority of Superfund sites that have ever been listed in Colorado are found on the Front Range[1]. The City and County of Denver leads the way with 31 sites, followed closely by Jefferson County with 25, Adams County (18), Boulder County (11), El Paso County (10), Arapahoe County (9), Weld County (7), Pueblo County (6), and Douglas County (5).

Superfund sites for Colorado mountain counties since 1980 are the following[2,3]:

- **Chaffee:** 6 total Superfund sites (Chalk Creek Mining District, Cozinco, Koppers, Smeltertown Site, Smeltertown Zinc, Smeltertown Wood Treatment)
- **Clear Creek:** 1 (Central City–Clear Creek)
- **Conejos:** 1 (Cedar Resources)
- **Costilla:** 1 (Battle Mountain Gold)
- **Delta:** 3 (Love's Spraying Service, Delta Tank Fire, Hotchkiss Chlorinateds)
- **Dolores:** 1 (Rico–Argentine)
- **Eagle:** 3 (Eagle Mine, Southern-Pacific-Tennessee Pass, World Alpine Championships Hazmat HQ)
- **Fremont:** 4 (Lincoln Park, College of the Cañon, Prospect Heights area, Rockvale Water Supply)
- **Garfield:** 3 (Carbondale PCBs, New Castle H2S, Union Carbide Corp.)
- **Gilpin:** 1 (Clear Creek Pinto Bean)
- **Grand:** 2 (Granby Landfill–BLM, Grand County EDB)
- **Gunnison:** 4 (Ruby District South, Ruby District West, Ruby District North, Great West Gold and Silver)

- **Hinsdale:** 2 (Crooke Brothers Smelting Works, Henson Creek Mines)
- **Lake:** 5 (Climax Mine, Leadville Drums, California Gulch, Leadville Trailer Courts, Upper Arkansas River lagoons)
- **La Plata:** 2 (Durango Lead Smelter, La Plata H2S)
- **Mesa:** 4 (Western Slope Refining, Hansen Containers, Grand Junction Projects Office, Lower Valley Air Park)
- **Mineral:** 3 (East Willow Creek and Willow Creek, West Willow Creek, Creede Mining District)
- **Moffat:** 1 (Craig Mercury)
- **Montezuma:** 5 (Cortez Ore, Ute Drum, Towaoc Daycare site, Ute Mountain–Ute Maintenance Drum, Montezuma County Pesticides)
- **Montrose:** 2 (Montrose Rocket Fuel, Uravan Uranium Project–Union Carbide)
- **Ouray:** 2 (Corkscrew and Gray Copper gulches, Canyon Creek watershed)
- **Park:** 1 (London Mine)
- **Pitkin:** 1. (Smuggler Mountain)
- **Rio Grande:** 2 (South Fork Landfill, Summitville)
- **Routt:** 1 (BLM–Oak Creek Landfill)
- **Saguache:** 3 (U.S. Forest Service Bonanza Mining District, Kerber Creek, Forest Service–Saguache Mill Site)
- **San Juan:** 4 (Navajo Reservoir, Kendrick & Gelter Smelting Company, Red Mountain Pass Zinc, Upper Animas Mining District)
- **San Miguel:** 3 (Silver Bell Mine and Mill, Carbonero Mine, Vanadium Mill Site–Newmire)
- **Summit:** 4 (Breckenridge Auto Body, French Gulch, Keystone Groundwater, Silverthorne Mercaptan)
- **Teller:** 5 (Florissant TCE & Heptachlor, Gillette Gold Extraction Company, Independence Mine, Teller County EDB, Manitou Graben Dump)

NPL sites in Colorado mountain counties, as of June 3, 2009, are the following:

- **Captain Jack Mill.** Proposed listing: April 30, 2003. Final listing: September 29, 2003. Fifteen abandoned drums located near an inactive mining site approximately 1.5 miles from the town of Ward, in Boulder County. The drums are in a deteriorating condition and draining into a nearby creek.
- **Central City–Clear Creek Site in Clear Creek County.** Proposed listing: December 30, 1982. Final listing: September 8, 1983. Dissolved copper, cadmium, and acid drainage is contaminating Clear Creek, affecting surface drinking water supplies downstream. It is interesting to note that Clear Creek is the

creek that eventually flows through Golden, home to Coors beer, which has long advertised the purity of the water it uses during its brewing process.[4]

- **Eagle Mine.** Proposed listing: October 15, 1984. Final listing: June 10, 1986. The 235-acre Eagle Mine site is an abandoned mining and milling facility located along the banks of the Eagle River approximately five miles south of the town of Minturn, in Eagle County. The site consists of the abandoned town of Gilman and numerous former mine-waste disposal areas. It is interesting to note that there is a proposal to build a high-end real-estate-based private ski area pretty much right on top of this site.

- **Standard Mine–Ruby Mining District** (listed as three separate sites in the county-by-county listings above). Proposed listing: April 27, 2005. Final listing: September 14, 2005. Located west of Crested Butte, in Gunnison County, this NPL consists of a gold and silver mining district that was active from the late 1800s to the 1960s, causing heavy-metal contamination of Elk Creek— above Crested Butte's drinking water supply—Slate Creek and the Ruby Anthracite drainage.

- **California Gulch.** Proposed listing: December 30, 1982. Final listing: September 8, 1983. The site covers slightly more than 16 square miles and includes significant portions of the town of Leadville, including a portion of its historic district and a portion of the Arkansas River from its confluence with California Gulch downstream to the Lake Fork Creek confluence. The site was listed as a NPL because of concerns about the impact of significant mine drainage on surface waters in California Gulch and the impact of heavy metals in the Arkansas. Mine tailings and contaminated underlying soil of 28,000 cubic yards were removed in 2005 alone.

- **Nelson Tunnel/Commodore Waste Rock Pile.** Proposed listing: March 19, 2008. Final listing: September 3, 2008. Lying north of Creede, in Mineral County, this site is about five acres in size and consists of a draining adit and a large waste-rock pile, both containing high levels of heavy metals such as arsenic, cadmium, lead, and zinc, all of which are flowing into Willow Creek and the Rio Grande.

- **Uravan Uranium Project (Union Carbide).** Proposed listing: October 15, 1984. Final listing: June 10, 1986. This site consists of uranium and radium tailings, vanadium, ammonium, aluminum sulfate, radon gas and associated decay products, sulfuric acid, and fugitive dust all occurring outside Uravan in Montrose County. In other words: Don't perform aerobic exercises anywhere near here. Much of the funkiness factor has been mitigated.

- **Summitville.** Proposed listing: May 10, 1993. Final listing: May 31, 1994. When the words "Superfund site" are used in the Colorado mountains, the name "Summitville" will spring forth from the lips of many people, Rorschach test–like, in a tone of voice usually reserved for hobbits talking about Mordor. The Summitville site, located about 25 miles south of Del Norte, in Rio Grande County, covers approximately 550 acres. It was the site of significant gold mining between 1870 and 1959, when more than 257,000 troy ounces were removed. Summitville is known for the significant environmental damage caused by the leaking of mine by-products into local waterways and the Alamosa River. In 1984, the site was acquired by Galactic Resources Ltd. (a subsidiary of Summitville Consolidated Mining Company, Inc.). They began a large-scale, open-pit operation using new techniques to extract gold from otherwise uneconomic ore. The technique involved the treatment of pyretic ore with a sodium cyanide solution to leach the gold out of the ore. The solution was then removed from the ore and valuable metals were extracted using activated carbon.[5] About 10 million tons of ore were thus treated, resulting in the removal of about 294,365 troy ounces of gold and 319,814 troy ounces of silver. The site was closed in 1991, with about 160 million gallons of stored water "in need of treatment" (the EPA's words). In 1992, an estimated 85,000 gallons of this water leaked through a damaged pad liner and entered nearby creeks. Shortly thereafter, Galactic Resources declared bankruptcy, and the site was taken over by the EPA. It was estimated at the time that about 3,000 gallons of polluted water were leaking from the site every minute. The sum of $155 million was spent to detoxify the water and reduce leakage, $30 million of which came from the tattered remains of Galactic—meaning that U.S. taxpayers paid $125 million to clean up the mess left by a company that had only recently pulled a combined 20,000 kilograms of gold and silver from the site. Despite cleanup efforts, cyanide, heavy metals, and acid from the mine killed all aquatic life in 17 miles of the Alamosa River. It was the single worst cyanide spill in American history. Cleanup efforts continue. In April 2009, Colorado Senators Mark Udall and Michael Bennett, along with Congressman John Salazar, announced that Summitville would receive between $10 and $25 million more in taxpayer money under the American Recovery and Investment Act. The funding will be used to complete a new water-treatment facility.

The one de-listed NPL site in the Colorado mountains is:

- **Smuggler Mountain.** Proposed listing: October 15, 1984. Final listing: June 10, 1986. It was taken off of the NPL list on September 23, 1999. This site, consisting of about 110 acres near Aspen, was contaminated with old mine tailings, blowing dust, and ground and surface water contamination.

A proposed NPL site in the Colorado mountains, as of June 3, 2009, is:

- **Smeltertown sites** (listed as three separate sites in the county-by-county list above). This is a 118-acre site located one mile northwest of Salida, in Chaffee County. It is generally zoned industrial, but Chaffee County's industrial zoning allows residential development. Industrial activity began in 1902 with the construction of a lead–zinc smelter by the Ohio and Colorado Smelting and Refining Company. The smelter operated until 1919 and was dismantled in 1920, when the area was cleared of most structures. A portion of the property was utilized by a series of railroad-tie-treating companies until 1953.

Following is a state-by-state comparison of the total number Superfund sites listed since CERCLA was passed in 1980. Note that an overwhelming majority of the sites listed consist of removal actions that have been completed.

1.  California (total number of Superfund sites): 781
2.  New Jersey: 611
3.  Pennsylvania: 540
4.  New York: 530
5.  Florida: 525
6.  Massachusetts: 505
7.  Connecticut: 442
8.  Missouri: 427
9.  Illinois: 365
10. Georgia: 306
11. Tennessee: 272
12. Texas: 252
13. North Carolina: 250
14. Michigan: 241
15. Ohio: 240
16. Kansas: 239
17. Virginia: 227
18. Iowa: 219
19. Colorado: 209
20. Washington: 200

## NOTES

1. Although Jefferson, Boulder, El Paso, and Pueblo are undeniably considered Front Range counties, they all contain significant mountain territory, de-

spite the fact that the bulk of their populations dwell down on the flats. Several of the Superfund sites located in these Front Range counties, in fact, are located in mountainous terrain.

2. The majority of these sites were Removal Action sites that are no longer listed as Superfund sites. So, before you have a heart attack because one of the sites listed is 20 feet from your child's sandbox, you should eyeball the status of the sites listed. Go to http://cgi.hsh.com/superfund/superfund.fxp?state_code=COColorado.

3. A few of these individual sites are aggregated into one listing in the EPA's National Priority List (NPL).

4. In 2000, Coors agreed to spend more than $500,000 to try to mitigate an accidental discharge of 2,500 barrels of beer and wastewater from its Golden brewery into Clear Creek that killed somewhere between 10,000 and 50,000 fish. An agreement between Coors and the Colorado Division of Parks and Wildlife (CDOW) called for Coors to:

- Construct and monitor a wetland of at least two acres to filter the brewery's wastewater before it flows into Clear Creek. The wetland should reduce nitrogen and phosphorus in wastewater effluent and provide wildlife habitat.
- Purchase thousands of fish for stocking in Denver Metro–area waters. The number of fish, and the species, were determined by Coors and CDOW.

The settlement amount was far below the $35-per-fish ceiling set by state law, an amount that would have translated to a $1.7 million fine.

5. In 1994, at least partially as a result of what had happened at Summitville, the Summit County Board of County Commissioners enacted a countywide ban on cyanide leaching in the county. The ban took note of the possible effects cyanide leaching could have on the tourism industry of the nation's largest ski county. At least four other counties in Colorado were considering a similar ban. In January 2009, though, the Colorado Supreme Court overturned Summit County's ban, arguing that local governments cannot impose reclamation standards or ban the use of mining chemicals that are regulated by state and federal laws. (So much for local control.) The court ruled that the state has a "dominant interest" in the regulation of mining activities.

## SOURCES

http://cgi.hsh.com/superfund/superfund.fxp?state_code=COColorado; Environmental Protection Agency; http://coyotegulch.wordpress.com; http://www.cdphe.state.co.us/hm/sf-sites.htm; Wikipedia; legalnewsline.com; salazarvcoorsblogspot.com.

# STRANGE COLORADO FESTIVALS

It might seem a bit odd to some that the students of the University of Colorado–Boulder organize and host an annual tribute to convicted cannibal Alferd Packer. (Please see "Colorado Movies" section of this book for more detail.) Truth of the matter is, it doesn't take much of an excuse to get Coloradans thinking in terms of putting together and systematizing a local celebration/

event, especially if there is the potential of (1) drinking and (2) enticing money-bearing tourists to town on an otherwise dead fiscal weekend. Verily, Colorado is the event capital of the country. From the annual Telluride Mushroom Festival to Frisco's Spontaneous Combustion town bonfire, Colorado mountain dwellers are always ready to institutionalize a raucous good time under the guise of community event. Some, however, are stranger—at least superficially—than others and thus are worth mentioning in these pages. It should be noted that a couple of these events have passed away and made the journey to the big strange festival in the sky.

## FROZEN DEAD GUY DAYS

Frozen Dead Guy Days is an annual celebration in the Colorado mountain town of Nederland, 20 miles west of Boulder, which is, for reasons no one has ever been able to figure out, not only home to the state's very first traffic roundabout, but home to the state's very first traffic roundabout by more than 10 years. (Speculation is that a traveling roundabout salesperson came through town one intoxicated winter night.)

Frozen Dead Guy Days is based upon an actual frozen dead guy named Bredo Morstoel. In 1989, a Norwegian citizen named Trygve Bauge brought the recently deceased body of Morstoel, his grandfather, to the United States The body was preserved on dry ice for the trip. Then it was stored in liquid nitrogen at the Trans Time cryogenics facility in San Leando, California, from 1990–1993. In 1993, Morstoel was returned to dry ice and transported to Nederland, known among friends as Ned (its residents are often called Nedheads), where Trygve and his mother Aud planned to create a cryogenics facility of their own. When Trygve was deported from the United States for overstaying his visa, Aud continued to keep her father's body cryogenically frozen in a shed behind her unfinished house.

Aud was eventually evicted from that house for living with no electricity or plumbing, in violation of local ordinances. At that time, she told a local reporter about her father's body, and the reporter went to the Nederland town hall to let authorities know about Aud's concerns that her eviction would cause her father's body to thaw. Not surprisingly, the story caused a sensation. The Ned town government consequently passed an ordinance prohibiting the keeping of bodies or body parts within town limits. Because of the publicity, Nederland town officials grandfathered-in Bredo's remains. Trygve eventually secured the services of a local environmental company to keep Bredo's cryogenic sarcophagus up and running. The local Tuff Shed supplier built a new shed to house

Morstoel's mortal remains. He now lies in an apparent perpetual frozen state under 800 pounds of dry ice.

Proving once again that it doesn't take much for Colorado mountain dwellers to rev up an annual party, Frozen Dead Guy Days is celebrated from Friday through Sunday on the first full weekend of March. Coffin races, a slow-motion parade, a "Frozen Dead Guy" look-alike contest, and the ever-popular Grandpa's Blue Ball are held. A film documenting all of this frozen-dead-guy craziness, called *Grandpa's in the Tuff Shed,* is shown every year. An updated version of the film, *Grandpa's Still in the Tuff Shed,* premiered in Nederland on March 7, 2003.

Although Trygve and Aud filed a complaint against Nederland regarding money and naming rights in 2005, Frozen Dead Guy Days is still very much alive and kicking.

*Grandpa's in the Tuff Shed* (1998) and *Grandpa's Still in the Tuff Shed* (2003) were both produced, directed, and written by Robin, Kathy, and Shelly Beeck, with help from famed documentarian Michael Moore. *Grandpa's in the Tuff Shed* won the 1998 Best of the Fest Award at the Breckenridge Festival of Film.

Not only does Frozen Dead Guy Days have a couple of documentary films to its credit—it also has a song, performed by Sister Merry Harmony, boasting a chorus that starts, "Grandpa whatcha doin' in the shed? C'mon and admit it: You are dead!"

## MIKE THE HEADLESS CHICKEN DAYS

On September 10, 1945, a five-and-a-half-month-old Wyandotte rooster living in Fruita, Colorado, could not have known that his last moments of life were well nigh upon him. Clara Olsen was planning to feature the plump chicken on that very night's dinner menu and, thus, sent her husband Lloyd out to dispatch the bird—something he had done many times before. Knowing that his mother-in-law, who savored the neck, would be dining with the family, Lloyd positioned his ax in such a way as to leave a generous neck bone. "It was as important to suck up to your mother-in-law back in the '40s as it is today," Lloyd was fond of saying of that eventful eve. The ax was dropped, and the chicken twitched and staggered like most recently dispatched poultry: Mike, who at that point existed sans appellation, ran around like a chicken with his head cut off.

Then, surprise of all surprises, the bird shook off what was supposed to be a terminal event and never looked back. He did not die and, as a matter of fact, lived on for 18 more months. Lloyd had missed both the jugular and the brainstem but had managed to lop off most of the chicken's cranium. Lloyd, impressed by the now-noggin-less bird's will to live, figured out a way to use an eyedropper to feed and water the fowl, now known as Mike. Despite his mostly decapitation, Mike could still perch and, although he lacked the apparatus to successfully do so, still tried to preen himself. The Olsens took Mike on the road and made a small fortune, charging people 25 cents to eyeball Mike the Headless Chicken, who, at the time of his eventual demise (caused by choking), was valued at $10,000. Mike's success actually resulted in a spate of copycat beheadings administered by people hoping to cash in on the headless-chicken market. A pickled chicken head always accompanied Mike's public appearances, but it was a fake—a cat having already dined upon the original severed pate.

In 1999, the Powers That Be in Fruita, who were trying to come up with some sort of event to raise funds, decided to celebrate the life and times of what until that point could arguably be called the small town's biggest celebrity ever. Events at Mike the Headless Chicken Days, held the third weekend in May, include a 5k Run Like a Headless Chicken Race, an egg toss, Pin the Head on the Chicken, a Chicken Cluck-off, and Chicken Bingo, in which chicken droppings on a numbered grid choose the numbers.

This event has also given birth to a Web site—which has received more than 2.5 million hits—organized by, of all things, Mike's Fan Club, which solicits and posts a line list of chicken jokes, including: "What goes hahahahahahaha plop?" Answer: "Mike laughing his head off." (That would be the best of the batch.)

## DANDELION DAY

Despite the fact that, at least according to historic lore, it was introduced to the high country by miners back in the 1880s to help provide an abundant source of fresh greens to this naturally vitamin-C-challenged part of the country, the humble dandelion has fallen into severe disfavor in these days by subdivision homeowner association–mandated, weed-free, and well-coiffed lawns and Safeway stores filled to the brim with kiwi fruit and 47 kinds of vitamins. These days, homeowners try to eradicate dandelions with such vigor that people who otherwise consider themselves carriers of the green torch display absolutely zero in the way of compunction when it comes to using all manner of nasty chemicals to try to thwart a seemingly unthwartable dandelion onslaught.

One town, Carbondale, rather than castigating the plant that once helped stem the tide of scurvy in mountain country, embraces *Taraxacum officinale* with an annual festival every May to herald the arrival of spring. It began in 1998, when the Carbondale Environmental Board asked the town council to adopt the dandelion as the official town flower. The goal was to prevent the spraying of herbicides on town parks.

Carbondale's Dandelion Day begins with a 5K Dandelion Dash and includes a "Parade of the Species," which is a celebration of the Earth's diverse creatures. There is always live music, workshops about dandelions and their medicinal uses, a slow bike race, local produce, and organic farmers selling starter baskets.

## NOTHING FESTIVAL

No town in Colorado is more events-dense than Telluride, which sees one sort of festival or another literally almost every weekend of the year. The Telluride Nothing Festival, which has passed away due to—appropriately enough—a lack of sponsorship, was accidentally created by a local resident who was fed up with the number of festivals in general and the prospect of another huge event organized by a large promoter specifically. A tongue-in-cheek letter, sent to the city manager requesting a non-festival event permit, was actually taken seriously. So, the first Nothing Festival was held in 1991 and the locals loved it. They could, according to Nothing Festival non-organizers, "finally enjoy all the things that make life in a small town so special: no crowds and no traffic. And visitors could come to Telluride and not worry about event passes or parking hassles."

Although its non-itinerary varied from year to year, the Nothing Fest, held in July, included non-events such as:

- Sunrises and sunsets as normal
- Gravity to continue to be in effect
- The Earth's rotation to be increased to add a few thrills
- The laws of physics to be on display
- Duct Tape Seminar: How to defeat weapons of mass destruction for under $110
- Sense of humor search
- Terrorist threat level to be increased to red when every other American is a lawyer, the other half are realtors, politicians cease lying to you, and fast-food restaurants super-size once again and add even more fat to their "food."

According to the Nothing Fest Web site:

- The Telluride Nothing Festival has no need for a large, expensive staff, or even a small, cheap one. Usually, festivals have security staffs, but instead of going with a predictable non-security staff, the Telluride Nothing Festival goes with an insecurity staff. That way, everyone is qualified and will automatically become a staff member!
- No wristbands or permits are needed at the Telluride Nothing Festival. If you want to look official, just tie a little piece of string

around your wrist—red for backstage (if any), blue for camping, orange for all events, etc. If you want to look really silly, dress only in black and white, have a small placard on a string around your neck, and don't forget the nametag.

- All parking regulations, including Telluride's dreaded solar-powered parking meters, are in effect during Nothing Fest. Fest organizers did ask the town to suspend metering just for the fun of it and to show folks visiting what it used to be like to live in a small, quiet town. Their response: "Naaaaaaaaaah! We need the money!" Telluride locals think that the meters are not really about parking. They are, rather, about revenue stream.
- The end: Thank you for not participating!

## THE HEENEY TICK FESTIVAL

Speaking of weirdly named Colorado festivals, who can forget the late, great Heeney Tick Festival? Media reports have erroneously reported for years that the festival, which ran from 1981 to 2001, was named after ticks (which, well, you can see how that misconception came about, given the festival's name and all). The festival was actually launched to celebrate the fact that long-time Heeney local Faith Tjardes had actually survived a case of dreaded Rocky Mountain spotted fever, which is transmitted by—you guessed it—ticks.

Tjardes, who contracted her case of spotted fever while ascending nearby Green Mountain in June 1981, wrote a story about her ordeal for the *Summit County Journal.* The town of Heeney, located on the shores of Green Mountain Reservoir, was in need of a fundraiser to help raise cash for the local Lower Blue Volunteer Fire Department, and Tjardes's survival tale provided a perfect excuse for celebrating all things *dermacentor.*

The Heeney Tick Festival, which took place below the Green Mountain Dam, always hosted much in the way of food, drink, music, merriment, and arts and crafts, as well as a parade and the crowning of the annual Queen of the Tick Festival. (Tjardes herself was, appropriately enough, the first Tick Queen.)

After 20 years, the Heeney Tick Fest finally died—of all things— from national security concerns that had nothing whatsoever to do with ticks or intoxicated revelers. After 9/11, the federal Bureau of Reclamation declared the Green Mountain Dam, which it administers, a piece of "national critical infrastructure" and closed all public access, except driving over the dam in a vehicle. Vehicles are not allowed to stop on the dam, nor are pedestrians allowed on it. The dam is still patrolled by Summit County Sheriff's Department personnel who are paid federal overtime dollars to protect a dam that few people visit and that lies upriver from a whole lot of beautiful nothing.

# CRITICAL INFRASTRUCTURE

The Colorado Office of Preparedness and Security, part of the Governor's Office of Homeland Security, is justifiably reluctant to release a list of all facilities deemed in the national interest as "critical infrastructure" (my request for that list was greeted with a stony silence followed by audible teeth-gnashing and a very unambiguous demand to know just exactly why such skinny was relevant for a book project such as this). However, at least two high-country dams—Green Mountain (administered by the federal Bureau of Reclamation) and Dillon (administered by Denver Water)—are indeed on that list.

Under a directive issued by the National Strategy for Homeland Security, adopted into law when the Department of Homeland Security was established after 9/11, there are 13 critical infrastructure sectors: agriculture, food, water, public health, emergency services, government, defense, industrial base, information and telecommunications, energy, transportation, banking and finance, chemical industry, and postal and shipping.

The owners of the individual critical infrastructure sites are the ones who determine what protective measures are necessary to decrease their vulnerabilities.

With regard to high-country dams (and this, as the following wording attests, comes straight from the mouths of several Homeland Security types):

> *Any of the long-term security measures are taken as a result of the possibly severe consequences of a failure, regardless of the threat. These security measures can change based on the dam owner's knowledge of a specific or a general threat to their dam. The state does not keep track of what measures each dam owner in Colorado has taken at various times to mitigate the vulnerabilities to their dam, however the state works closely with those dam owners if any specific threats are identified through what is known as the "intelligence fusion center." The state will also help the owners in determining threats and assessing the vulnerabilities of their dam and will make recommendations for mitigation. Most of those assessments and recommendations are classified under the Protected Critical Infrastructure Information (PCII) program and are not publicly available due to obvious reasons of security.*

The security situation with regard to the Dillon Dam, located in Summit County, has been borderline Keystone Cops-ish. In 2006, in the middle of the night, with no warning to a local citizenry used to using the Dillon Dam Road to get from one part of the county to the other, Denver Water closed the Dam Road to all vehicular traffic, which resulted in threats of legal action on the part of the Summit County government. Locals were incensed.

A compromise was reached after weeks of very public acrimony (just what Homeland Security likes). Now, the Dam Road is closed from 10 P.M. till 6 A.M. It is also closed to large trucks, RVs, and trailers—meaning that would-be terrorists now have to plan their assault during daylight hours using normal cars and trucks. Tire-puncturing security strips have been installed, and at least once already, they have actuated for no apparent good reason, causing considerable damage to an innocent Honda Civic.

Local police personnel are hired by Denver Water, using federal Homeland Security grants, to keep an eye on the Dillon Dam 24/7.

---

## "ROCKY MOUNTAIN SPOTTED FEVER" GIVES THE ROCKIES A BAD NAME—IT SHOULD BE NAMED "SOUTHEAST SPOTTED FEVER"

Rocky Mountain spotted fever is the most lethal and most frequently reported rickettsial (a form of especially funky bacteria carried by fleas, lice, and ticks) illness in the United States. Most transmission occurs via the bite of the American dog tick (*Dermacentor variabilis*) and the Rocky Mountain wood tick (*Dermacentor andersoni*).

Rocky Mountain spotted fever remains a serious and life-threatening disease. Despite the availability of effective treatment and advances in medical care, approximately 3 to 5 percent of those infected still die. About 800 cases are reported in the United States each year.

Initial symptoms may include fever, nausea, vomiting, severe headache, muscular pain, and lack of appetite. Later symptoms may include the spotted rash that gives the malady its name, abdominal pain, and joint pain.

Appropriate antibiotic treatment, usually doxycycline, is generally administered immediately after the disease is diagnosed, generally for a minimum total course of 5 to 10 days.

Rocky Mountain spotted fever is inappropriately named because more than half of the diagnosed cases are found in the southeastern part of the country—although cases have been reported in all states except Hawaii and Alaska. The disease was first identified in 1896 in the Snake River Valley of Idaho, and that is how its name originated.

Rocky Mountain spotted fever is not to be confused with Colorado tick fever—also called mountain tick fever, mountain fever, and American mountain fever—which is an acute viral infection transmitted from the bite of an infected wood tick, our old friend *Dermacentor andersoni*. Those infected usually experience a two-stage fever and illness that can continue for one to three days, diminish, and then return for another episode that lasts for one to three days. Initial symptoms include fever, chills, headaches, pain behind the eyes, light sensitivity, muscular pain, generalized malaise, abdominal pain, nausea, vomiting, and a flat or pimply rash. During the second phase, a high fever can return with an overall increase of the initial symptoms.

This virus has the ability to live in the blood for as long as 120 days. Its incubation period is usually three to six days, but can be up to 20 days. There is no specific treatment for Colorado tick fever. Usually, the symptoms themselves are treated via acetaminophen and analgesics.

---

## BRECKENRIDGE ST. PATRICK'S DAY PUB CRAWL

These days, numerous towns and resorts throughout mountain country offer St. Patty's Day pub crawls—usually, sad to say, extremely watered-down, family-friendly versions that are specifically designed to make certain that no women, children, or old people are repulsed or even made slightly uncomfortable. But the pub crawl that set the mountain-town standard was the infamous Breckenridge Pub Crawl, and, when it finally died a last, gasping death in 2004, the mold was broken.

Fundamentally, the event, which began in 1968, was organized as a fundraiser for various worthy local causes. Prizes included all-expenses-paid vacations, season ski passes, and various other schwag. There is no way to spin the fact that this was an event focused around some serious drinking—during its heyday, participants had to visit a total of 17 bars (in no set order), at which they had to chug one 12-ounce green beer—but it attracted some very serious high country athletes. Several Olympians even participated, making this the only pub crawl that mixed world class drinking with world-class athleticism. Most participants (there were more than 500 one year) simply mixed walking with running as they made their wobbly way between those 17 bars.

As the wild 1960s and 1970s fizzled their way toward the more marketable 1980s, concerns grew within Breckenridge's more buttoned-down business community about such once-unheard-of concepts as liability and image. Every year, the erstwhile-unanswered calls for restraint and dignity started echoing louder and louder. Those 12-ounce green beers started shrinking in size until they literally became shots of suds. The straw that broke the camel's back occurred in the early 1990s, when one inebriated participant vomited on the hood of a car occupied by an elderly couple from Kansas that was sitting at a stoplight. The couple complained to the police, and that was pretty much the nail in the event's coffin. It limped along for another couple of years, but, by 1994, shortly after the long-time host bar, Shamus O'Toole's Roadhouse Saloon, was converted into a community theater (a metaphor if ever there was one), the plug was pulled, and Breckenridge's St. Patrick's Day Pub Crawl crawled off into infamy.

## THE STRANGE FESTIVAL THAT THANK GOODNESS NEVER HAPPENED

On June 4, 2004, much to the shock and horror of Colorado mountain dwellers, a man named Marvin Heemeyer, a welder who lived in Grand Lake but whose shop was located in Granby, used a Komatsu D355A bulldozer that he had spent literally an entire year myopically modifying into a mayhem-maker straight out of *Terminator* to rampage through Granby. In the course of several hours, Heemeyer used his 'dozer, which was armored with layers of steel, concrete, and bonded Plexiglas, to destroy the town hall, the town library, a former judge's home, the home of the elderly widow of a deceased former mayor, the local newspaper office, and numerous other downtown buildings. He also destroyed several police cars.

The rampage ended only after Heemeyer's bulldozer got stuck in the basement of a hardware store into which he had just been pushed by another local, who, in one of those scenes where a person would be tempted to say, "Only in Colorado," owned and operated an even bigger bulldozer than the one Heemeyer was driving. Law enforcement tried in vain during Heemeyer's reign of destruction to shoot through and immobilize his bulldozer. But it was covered in thick grease, making it almost impossible for police to stand on the machine as it made its way through Granby. More than 200 rounds of ammunition were fired at Heemeyer's bulldozer, to no avail. Explosives, including C4 packs and flash-bang grenades, were detonated directly on the bulldozer, but Heemeyer had done such a good job of armoring his machine that they had absolutely no effect.

Colorado Governor Bill Owens had 200 National Guard troops on alert. There was talk of using Hellfire anti-tank missiles right there in downtown Granby, which, by the time Heemeyer was stopped, resembled a war zone. It took law enforcement 12 hours to cut through the hatch with an oxyacetylene torch. They extracted the driver's cage with a crane, at which time they learned that Heemeyer had taken his own life by shooting himself in the head. Inside the bulldozer, law enforcement found a .50-caliber semi-automatic Barrett M82 rifle pointing out the rear, a semi-automatic variant of the FN FNC in front, a .223 Ruger Mini-14 to the right, a 9mm Kel-Tec P-11 semi-automatic pistol, and a .357 magnum revolver, which Heemeyer used to kill himself after his 'dozer was pushed into the hardware store basement by the even bigger 'dozer.

The cause of Heemeyer's crazed escapade was that he was angry with the Granby town government for passing a zoning variance request that allowed for the construction of a cement plant on land adjacent to his welding shop. Heemeyer's access to his shop would have been affected by the construction of that cement plant.

Representatives from the U.S. Department of Defense were impressed enough that they flew to Granby to study the modifications to Heemeyer's bulldozer, which included the use of external video cameras protected by three-inch-thick sheets of bulletproof plastic and a sophisticated interior cooling system.

It was a flat-out miracle that no one was hurt during Heemeyer's rampage (besides Heemeyer, of course). In all, he destroyed 13 buildings and caused more than $7 million in damage. News teams from all over the country descended upon Granby, a town not exactly used to being in the national spotlight. Although the town was justifiably traumatized by the event, that fact did not stop several local people from seriously proposing that Heemeyer's bulldozer be put on permanent display and that a yearly festival, to be called something like "Bulldozer Days" or "Marv Days," be used as a way of drawing tourists to Granby.

This was one instance when cooler and more reasonable heads prevailed. The idea of "Marv Fest" was summarily nixed with prejudice before it even germinated, and the bulldozer was unceremoniously dismantled with its parts dispersed to many scrap yards to dissuade souvenir hunters. So, while Colorado still is home to Frozen Dead Guy Days and Alferd Packer Days, at least Marvin Heemeyer's destructive exploits have been allowed to fade into the darkness of history sans a festival named in his honor.

## SOURCES

imbd.com, nederlandchamber.org; miketheheadlesschicken.org; Wikipedia; postindependent.com; telluridenothingfestival.com; Personal interview with Summit County history buff and long-time Heeney resident Keats Ann Scott, augmented by a June 1981 copy of the *Summit County Journal;* the Colorado Office of Preparedness & Safety; personal e-mail exchange from Major General Mason C. Whitney (ret), Director, Governor's Office of Homeland Security; medicinenet.com; hazy memory combined with summitdaily.com.

Although one would be hard-pressed to outrank business names in the Colorado mountains that bear some variation on the "Fourteener" or "High Country" themes, when it comes to actual products, "Aspen" reigns supreme.

Part of that reality, of course, stems from the sophisticated perception associated with the town Aspen, and part of it stems from the fact that "aspen" is also actually the name of a very prevalent tree with serious Colorado mountain connotations.

Either way, products with "Aspen" as part of their name are many and varied. Here are a few.

- Aspen Cologne for Men by Coty. Despite its haughty nomenclature, it sells for as little as $9 a bottle at Target. It also includes a warning that the contents are flammable.
- Aspen Bidets. For only $200, you can wash your private parts in style. An optional Aspen Butt Dryer costs only $70 more.
- Aspen Toilet Paper Holders. Because there's a very palpable top end when it comes to actual toilet paper—meaning it's a hard item to use to impress one's blue-blood chums in and of itself—the only option available to well-heeled Aspenites looking to dazzle their guests, then, is to purchase an iron Aspen Toilet Paper Holder from Quiescence. Only $188.
- Chrysler Aspen. The all-wheel-drive Aspen, with a MSRP of $35,000 to $45,000, comes with such haute couture must-haves as floor mats and a clock. Rarely seen in Aspen, where Hummers and Priuses dominate the asphalt landscape.
- Aspen Pure Water. Available in more than 10 states, it comes straight from the Continental Divide. The fact that the company is based in Alamosa matters not one bit, as Alamosa is a fine and dandy town that just happens to not be, well, Aspen.
- Aspen Edge Beer. Introduced by Coors in 2003, Aspen Edge was one of the first "low-carb" beers. Despite its attractive, mountain-adorned label, this beer never really caught on, even in Aspen. It was discontinued in 2006. Additionally, Aspen Gold beer came out of Spokane, Washington, in the 1970s. Naked Aspen beer comes out of Minnesota.
- Aspen One Wristwatch. Perhaps the most over-the-top Aspen-named product. It goes for $38,900, with a diamond version available for $49,900. Only 3,267 were released (that's supposedly the altitude of Aspen in meters), and it rings a little alarm at 4 P.M. to remind you to change the watch's ski strap to the watch's après-ski strap. It also has a specially designed compass to pin-

point your location on Aspen Mountain. The buyer's name gets engraved on a plaque on the backside of Aspen Mountain. The manufacturer, Swiss-based Aspen Jewelry and Watches, leased the rights to use the name "Aspen" from the Aspen Ski Area. The fact that supermodel Elle Macpherson introduced the product in February 2007 adds to its high-class perception.

- Aspen is actually a name parents sometimes give to their offspring. In 2006, Aspen was the country's 543rd most popular name for boys and the 572nd most popular name for girls.

## SOURCES

Various Web sites, with input from Catherine Lutz, one-time managing editor of the *Aspen Daily News*.

# SMOKING BANS: IT ALL STARTED IN COLORADO'S MOUNTAIN COUNTRY

As of August 2009, 24 states had enacted statewide bans on smoking in all enclosed public places, including bars and restaurants. Another seven states had banned smoking in most public places, but authorized adult venues, such as bars and casinos, could allow smoking if they chose. Nineteen of the 60 most populated cities in the country have enacted bans that disallow smoking in all public places, including bars and restaurants. Many people consider it just a matter of time before public smoking goes the way of the dodo from sea to shining sea.

And it all began in 1985, in the heart of the Colorado Rockies, when Aspen passed the country's first smoking ban. That ban, which only prohibited smoking in restaurants, seems downright quaint by today's often draconian standards—mainly because it exempted bars from the ban—but it got the ball rolling.

In 1996, Boulder became the first Colorado city to enact a smoking ban that included restaurants *and* bars.

By 2004, a significant number of Colorado cities and counties—many located in the mountains—had enacted smoking bans, including unincorporated Boulder County, Breckenridge, Dillon, Fort Collins, Frisco, Alamosa, Arvada, Aspen, Boulder, Montrose, Silverthorne, Snowmass, unincorporated Summit County, Superior, and Telluride.

On July 1, 2006, Colorado became the thirteenth state to enact a statewide smoking ban. The Colorado Clean Indoor Air Act bans smoking in all enclosed workplaces, including bars and restaurants. The act only exempts private residences and automobiles unless they are used for the public transportation of children or as part of a health care/day care program, limousines for private hire, hotel/motel rooms designated as smoking rooms, retail tobacco stores, cigar bars, designated areas in airports, outdoor areas, and workplaces not open to the public that have three or fewer employees.

Curiously, casinos, all of which are located in the mountain towns of Central City, Black Hawk, and Cripple Creek, were exempted from the statewide smoking ban, an oversight that was rectified in January 2008, when casinos were added to the long list of places where smoking is not allowed in Colorado.

One of the most captivating components of the Colorado Clean Indoor Air Act is that local governments were given permission to regulate smoking more strictly than the state.

In March 2009, Boulder did just that, extending its smoking ban to include enclosed porches, balconies, and patios, while also prohibiting smoking within 15 feet of any building entrance.

No matter one's feelings toward smoking bans, it all started under the snowcapped peaks of the Rockies.

### SOURCES

City of Aspen Community Relations Department; *Time Magazine;* Wikipedia; Smoke Free Summit.

# COLORADO'S MOUNTAIN HISTORIC DISTRICTS

Colorado's mountain towns boast much in the way of historic architecture and archeological sites, and most mountain towns try mightily to preserve buildings, mine sites, and Native American ruins for both aesthetic and marketing reasons. Studies show that cultural tourism is the fastest-growing segment of the industry; therefore, establishing and preserving historic parcels, most of which are dominated by the mining heyday of the mid- to late-1800s, translates to measurable cash flow.

There are three types of historic districts in Colorado: State Register Listed, National Register Listed, and National Historic Landmark.

Almost every historic district in Colorado's mountain towns falls into the National Register Listed category, although structures within those districts might be listed individually or additionally on the State Register. As well, most mountain counties have sites that are listed on the national and/or state registries that might be out of the designated historic districts. National Historic Landmarks are the crème de la crème of historic sites, and their importance has to be national in scale. Of the more than 80,000 individual sites listed on the National Register, only about 2,430 are National Historic Landmarks.

Only two mountain towns have their entire historic districts listed as National Historic Landmarks: Telluride and Leadville.

All told, Colorado has more than 1,300 properties and historic districts that are listed on the National Register alone. Those sites are distributed over 63 of the state's 64 counties.

Following is a list of the historic districts in Colorado's mountain towns, the years the historic districts were legally established, and the size of those districts, both in terms of acreage and number of properties/sites. Again, it must be stressed that almost every mountain town has additional historic listings outside of its designated historic district. All of the following historic districts are National Register Listed unless otherwise stipulated.

- Telluride (National Historic Landmark): 1961; 576 properties; 90 acres
- Central City–Black Hawk–Nevadaville: 1966; 535 properties; 600 acres
- Manitou Springs; 1983: 444 properties; 329 acres
- Georgetown–Silver Plume: 1966; 393 properties; 3,288 acres; includes the corridor for the Georgetown Loop Railroad as well as numerous mine sites outside town
- Crested Butte: 1974; 374 properties; 55 acres
- Ouray: 1983; 353 properties; 114 acres
- Cripple Creek: 1966; 322 properties; 1,674 acres; includes significant acreage spread out on mine sites outside town
- Leadville (National Historic Landmark): 1961; 251 properties; 6,000 acres; includes significant acreage spread out on mine sites outside town
- Breckenridge: 1980; 249 properties; 102 acres
- Lake City: 1978; 219 properties; 119 acres
- Durango: 1980 and 1984; 210 properties; 72 acres
- Boulder: 1980 and 1984; 172 properties; 68 acres
- Salida: 1984; 124 properties; 50 acres
- Trinidad: 1973; 121 properties; 131 acres
- Cokedale: 1985; 117 properties; 450 acres
- Eldora: 1989; 72 properties; 140 acres
- Morrison: 1976; 71 properties; 51 acres
- Victor: 1985; 50 properties; 22 acres
- Gold Hill: 1989; 50 properties; 18 acres

- Aspen: 1984; 47 properties; 32 acres
- Idaho Springs: 1984; 46 properties; 9 acres
- St. Elmo: 1979; 45 properties; 70 acres
- Pine–Buffalo Creek: 1974; 37 properties; 741 acres
- Silverton: 1966; 29 properties; 735 acres; includes significant acreage spread out over mine sites outside town
- Grand Junction: 1984; 24 properties; 15 acres
- Redstone: 1989; 23 properties; 640 acres
- Monte Vista: 1991; 11 properties; 20 acres

Following is a random smattering of the literally hundreds of individual Colorado mountain-town historic sites, just to show how varied these listings are.

- **Alamosa:** Husung Hardware Building (listed on the National Register in 2000). Constructed in 1936 with a terra cotta façade and stylized ornamentation, this two-story brick building possesses the distinct characteristics of Art Deco, a style not well represented in the small towns of Colorado.
- **Boulder:** McKenzie Well (National Register, 2005). This was the site of the 1901 discovery of the Boulder Oil Field, the first discovery of oil in the multi-state Denver Basin. The field reached its peak in 1909 with an annual output of 85,000 barrels of oil.
- **Salida:** The Chaffee County Courthouse and Jail (National Register, 1979). Constructed in 1882, the buildings reflect the Italianate style. Both have walls of red brick, and the roofs are hipped.
- **Chaffee County:** The Winfield Mining Camp (National Register, 1980). Located about 12 miles up the Clear Creek Road, this well-preserved 120-acre town site was established in 1881. By 1890, it had a population of 1,500.
- **Clear Creek County:** Georgetown Loop Railroad (National Register, 1970; State Register, 1994). Built in 1877 to haul silver ore, the Colorado Central Railroad also enjoyed popularity as a tourist attraction, which it remains. The Devil's Gate High Bridge, considered an engineering feat and the most famous element of the railroad, allowed climbing trains to circle back over the lower track as the rail bed rose from Georgetown to Silver Plume.
- **Georgetown:** Hotel de Paris (National Register, 1970). Originally constructed as a bakery in the 1870s, this two-story brick building is stuccoed, and its symmetrical façade includes tall, narrow, segmented arched windows on both floors.
- **Basalt:** Archeological site outside town (National Register, 1982). This site is believed to have functioned as a prehistoric campsite.
- **Eagle County:** Camp Hale (National Register, 1992). Served as the training site for the U.S. Army's famed 10th Mountain Division during World War II. After the war, many of those who

trained at Camp Hale were active in the development of Colorado's ski industry.

- **Central City:** The Central City Opera House (National Register, 1973). Opened in March 1878, the two-story Renaissance Revival–style stone building is the oldest surviving and first permanent opera house in Colorado.
- **Rocky Mountain National Park:** East Inlet Trail (National Register, 2005). This was one of the more difficult trails in Rocky Mountain National Park during the early part of the twentieth century, but, due to its scenic beauty, it still attracted scores of tourists. The dangerous nature of the trail led to Depression–era funding for improvements.
- **Grand Lake:** Shadow Mountain Lookout (National Register, 1978). Located on the summit of 10,128-foot Shadow Mountain, the lookout is the last of four fire-detection towers constructed in Rocky Mountain National Park during the Great Depression.
- **Hot Sulphur Springs:** Denver & Rio Grande Railroad Snowplow AX-044 (State Register, 1998). In 1918, The Denver & Rio Grande Railroad constructed Snowplow AX-044 to meet its specific needs for dependable snow-removal equipment to maintain its mountainous routes. Sixty years of continuous service on such difficult terrain as Tennessee Pass demonstrates the success of the plow's design.
- **Winter Park:** Rollinsville and Middle Park Wagon Road (National Register, 1980). David H. Moffat, one of Colorado's most important financiers and industrialists in the late-nineteenth and early-twentieth centuries, was associated with the Denver, Northwestern & Pacific Railway, which brought the first rail service over the Continental Divide from Denver to Middle Park. Utilizing the nineteenth-century Rollinsville and Middle Park Wagon Road, construction began on the rail bed over 11,670-foot Rollins Pass in 1903. Trains continued to battle the steep grades and fierce winter storms until the 1928 completion of the Moffat Tunnel, which is still in use.
- **Crested Butte:** Crested Butte Denver & Rio Grande Railroad Depot (National Register, 2001). Constructed in 1883, this combination passenger and freight depot remained in use until the 1954 abandonment of the Crested Butte narrow-gauge branch of the D&RG.
- **Gunnison:** Gunnison Hardware (State Register, 1993). Local master stonemason Frederick Zugelder built the store in 1882 to serve as the freight office for the Denver & Rio Grande Railroad. It became Gunnison Hardware in 1898. Built in the Italianate style, the building now serves as the Gunnison Arts Center.

- **Marble:** Marble Mill Site/Colorado Yule Marble Company (National Register, 1979). Constructed between 1896 and 1905, the mill produced the marble that was used in the construction of the Lincoln Memorial and the Tomb of the Unknown Soldier.
- **Lake City:** Capitol City Charcoal Kilns (National Register, 1999). Constructed of brick in 1877, the kilns, outside Lake City, were used in the production of charcoal. They are the last remaining charcoal kilns in Hinsdale County.
- **Durango to Silverton:** Durango–Silverton Narrow Gauge Railroad (National Historic Landmark, 1961). This narrow-gauge railway, constructed in 1880–1882, connected the rich silver mines of the Silverton Mining District with the smelters in Durango. The line also formed an important transportation link for moving ores to processing plants and supplying the high-mountain community with the necessities and comforts of life. The railroad continues to operate as one of Colorado's best-known summer tourist attractions.
- **Red Mesa:** Ute Mountain/Mancos Canyon Archeological District (National Register, 1972). The archeological resources of Mesa Verde and this adjoining area constitute the largest archeological preserve in the United States. This 125,000-acre tribal park contains thousands of pueblo ruins and cliff dwellings. The ruins of Mancos Canyon are some of the best-preserved remains existing from the Anasazi culture of the Four Corners region.
- **Leadville:** Leadville National Fish Hatchery (National Resister, 1980). The hatchery was established in 1889 by Executive Order of President Benjamin Harrison as the first national fish hatchery in the Rockies. An 1890 one-story hatchery building of native red sandstone remains on the site.
- **Creede:** Rio Grande Depot (Creede Museum) (State Register, 1994). After reaching Creede in 1892, the Denver & Rio Grande Railroad provided the mining district with an outlet for its ore while providing a conduit for the goods and services that made life possible in this remote town. The depot, built in 1903 as a replacement for the original facility, functioned until 1949.
- **Ouray:** Beaumont Hotel (National Register, 1973). Opened in 1887, the three-story brick-and-wood resort building was designed by architect O. Bulow. The interior was modeled after Denver's Brown Palace Hotel and featured a rotunda encircled by balconies, cathedral-glass skylights, rosewood paneling, and an oak staircase.
- **Ridgway:** Sherbino Building/Theater (State Register, 1991). Significant for its role in the social and cultural heritage of Ridgway, this simple one-story building was designed by Gus Kullerstrand

and built in 1915 by Louis Sherbino. In 1968, a boardwalk shielded with a fiberglass-shingled roof was added to accommodate the filming of the John Wayne movie *True Grit.*

- **Alma:** Alma School (State Register, 1996). The 1925 Alma School, a rare local example of the Mission style, showed the dedication to education of the residents of the nation's highest-elevation incorporated municipality.
- **Fairplay:** South Park Lager Beer Brewery (National Registry, 1974). Constructed by Leonard Summer in the mid-1870s, the primarily stone, one-story building was associated with the Summer Saloon. Because such local saloon owners usually imported their stock from Denver, the brewery represents a somewhat unusual undertaking for such a small and remote mining community.
- **Aspen:** Hotel Jerome (National Register, 1986). This three-story, red brick building occupies a prominent corner location in the heart of Aspen. Completed in 1889, the building features numerous round-arch window openings and an unusual parapet. The construction was financed by Jerome B. Wheeler, one of Aspen's most-notable financiers. The hotel gained additional prominence in the early 1970s when famed gonzo journalist Hunter S. Thompson, who lived in nearby Woody Creek, used it as an ex-officio headquarters for his infamous campaign when he ran for sheriff of Pitkin County.
- **Aspen:** Ute Cemetery (National Register, 2002). Beginning with the first burial in 1880, the cemetery became a resting place for many of Aspen's earliest settlers. When the community established two other more formally designed cemeteries, Ute Cemetery remained the town's burial ground for residents of modest means and uncelebrated accomplishments.
- **Routt County:** Summit Creek Guard Station (National Register, 2004). Built in 1912, this modest cabin represents the transition between the 1890–1910 pre-design phase and the 1911–1932 pre-Civilian Conservation Corps phase of U.S. Forest Service construction.
- **Steamboat Springs:** Rabbit Ears Motel Sign (State Register, 2006). The 1953 Rabbit Ears Motel sign remains an enduring and established visual feature of the community and serves as a source of local identity. The large neon sign with its distinctive rabbit face has survived several periods of downtown modernization to become a much-beloved local landmark.
- **Silverton:** Frisco–Bagley Mill (State Register, 2005). Constructed in 1912, the massive Frisco Mill is important for its distinctive architecture. The 150-ton ore-concentration mill, with its massive post-and-beam construction, is an unusual example of a

prefabricated industrial building. Its pieces were pre-cut, pre-fit, and coded with numbers and letters before being shipped to the site for assembly.

- **San Miguel County:** Fort Peabody (National Register, 2005). Straddling the Ouray and San Miguel county lines near Telluride at an elevation of more than 13,000 feet, Fort Peabody is associated with Colorado's hard-rock labor strikes of 1903–1904. A local Colorado National Guard unit constructed this redoubt in early 1904. Consisting of a small guardhouse, a flag mount, and what some have characterized as a sniper's nest, troops occupied the defensive fortification until martial law was revoked in June of that year. Built for a single purpose—to prevent members of the Western Federation of Miners, union sympathizers, and previously deported men from entering San Miguel County by way of Imogene Pass—the site illustrates how quickly (and often illegally) mine owners and management gained control over local government and the Colorado National Guard to run roughshod over the legal, political, and economic rights of union members.

- **Breckenridge:** Boreas Pass Railroad Station Site (National Register, 1993). The site, located at an elevation of 11,481 feet, was a key element of the Denver South Park & Pacific Railroad's route that ran from Como to Breckenridge and then on to Leadville. The DSP&P completed this narrow-gauge line in 1883. The station functioned as a major hub both during construction of the route and during its period of operation from 1882 to 1937. The most prominent surviving structure is the one-and-a-half-story log section house, which has been restored by the Summit Huts Association for use as a backcountry winter ski hut.

- **Dillon:** Porcupine Peak Site (National Register, 1980). Located on a river terrace, this prehistoric site is significant for its numerous occupational components, extensive time range, and archeological evidence suggesting a variety of cultural activities.

- **Frisco:** Staley–Rouse House (State Register, 2007). The 1909 Staley–Rouse House is a rare example of vertical and horizontal structural log construction in a domestic design. The juxtaposition of the vertical logs on the first story with the horizontal logs on the second story is exceptionally uncommon. The use of difficult keyed half-notching may reflect Nordic influences in the house's design and construction.

## SOURCE

Colorado Office of Archeology and Historic Preservation, which is part of the Colorado Historical Society.

# LEGALIZED GAMBLING IN
# COLORADO

Gambling is as much a part of Colorado lore as beaver-pelt-attired mountain men, bank robbers, crazy prospectors named Mad Jack, and cowboys and Indians. Were a person to rely totally upon popular-media renditions of days of yore, one would be inclined to wonder how industry of any kind was conducted, given the fact that the entire population of what is now the Mountain Time Zone was seemingly perpetually engaged in playing cards and shooting craps.

However, during the McKinley administration, gambling of all kinds was made illegal in Colorado, as it was in most of the states. In 1990, though, Colorado voters, by a 574,620 to 428,096 margin, gave an electoral thumbs-up to return legalized gambling to the Centennial State in three towns and three towns only: Central City, Black Hawk, and Cripple Creek. (The first casinos were legally allowed to throw open their doors in those three mountain hamlets on October 1, 1991, literally seconds after the terms of the ballot initiative went into effect.) Additionally, legalized gambling came to the Southern Ute Reservation in 1992 under the provisions of the federal Indian Gaming Regulatory Act of 1998, which directed state governments to allow on reservations within the states any kind of gambling that was legal anywhere within those states.

The run-up to re-legalized gambling in Colorado began in the early to mid-1980s, when times were not so good economically in the Rockies. Charities were looking for any vehicle they could conceive of to increase their diminishing coffers. So, you started seeing a preponderance of casino-night-type events. It wasn't long, though, before the state government got involved. Loathe to step on the toes of charities, state regulators determined that casino nights could legally operate as long as there was not even the appearance of single-play winnings; i.e., that after, say, a hand of blackjack, you could directly cash out whatever you just then won. As long as there was some sort of aggregation of winnings, where, say, at the end of the night, if you "won" 1,000 "dollars," you got a trip to Vegas—then it was OK. Well, at that point, the cat was out of Pandora's Box.

In 1985, the first statewide attempt to legalize gambling in Colorado was put to the state's electorate. It was a constitutional initiative that called for gambling to be legal only in Pueblo County, and the tax revenues skimmed off by the state were to be dedicated solely to the medically indigent and public schools. (That is one constant theme of almost every subsequent attempt to legalize gambling in Colorado—that the proponents name some worthy cause as the recipient of the tax revenue. That way, if you're voting against the measure, you're voting against the medically indigent, you self-centered scoundrel!) That initiative was thumped at the polls, 819,533 to 406,989.

The next attempt to legalize gambling in Colorado was in 1990, when a statewide ballot initiative was passed that allowed limited-stakes gaming in the mountain towns of Central City and Black Hawk, both in Gilpin County, and Cripple Creek, in Teller County. The lion's share of the tax revenues generated by gaming in those towns was, according to the wording of the initiative, supposed to go to historic preservation. Thing is, the initiative itself was worded so ambiguously that, within a few years, the monster new casinos that now define Black Hawk somehow fell under an acceptable definition of "historic preservation." Within a few years, elected officials in Black Hawk were using gaming proceeds to renovate their own houses. And rumors of Vegas mob infiltration of Colorado's gaming industry started wafting throughout the state almost immediately.

It was not long before other gaming-related initiatives started appearing on statewide ballots. In 1992 alone, there were four statewide ballot initiatives focused on gambling. Three of those initiatives were focused on expanding the areas where legalized gambling could transpire. The other 1992 gambling-related amendment that went before Colorado voters stated that, even if the people of Colorado voted in favor of allowing legalized gambling in additional jurisdictions, it could not take place without a supportive vote from the residents of those jurisdictions. That initiative, which passed 1,075,521 to 339,521, despite aggressive opposition from the gaming industry itself, at least partially mitigated the ability of out-of-towners to force gambling onto local populations that did not want casinos in their midst. That marked the last time a gaming-related initiative passed in Colorado until 2008. The three other proposed initiatives in 1992—which, in the aggregate, would have expanded legalized gambling to an additional 32 towns and counties—were all thumped by 2-to-1 margins.

In 1994, there was an attempt to allow slot machines in airports and limited-stakes gambling in Manitou Springs. It was defeated—get this—1,007,557 to 90,936. That is a posterior kicking by anyone's standards.

In 1996, another proposed statewide initiative, this one to allow gambling in Trinidad, was jungle smacked—958,991 to 440,173.

In 2003, an attempt to allow video gaming terminals at racetrack locations—facilities that were already not exactly churches—was soundly thrashed, 766,893 to 180,959.

In 2008, the anti-gambling tide that had defined Colorado politics ever since the 1990 initiative that allowed limited-stakes casinos in Central City, Black Hawk, and Cripple Creek turned. Initiative 121, which appeared on the statewide ballot as Amendment 50, passed 1,261,562 to 890,920. Amendment 50 allowed a change to the most fundamental component of the 1990: limited stakes. The passage of Amendment 50 allowed for an increase in the maximum allowable bet from $5 to $100. It also allowed casinos to stay open 24 hours a day, seven days a week. Pro-gaming forces had argued that, since 1991, when the first legal casinos opened in Central City, Black Hawk, and Cripple Creek, gaming-based competition had expanded in other states so significantly that Colorado, with its limited stakes and its limited hours of casino operation, was operating at a competitive disadvantage.

However, because of the local-rule initiative that had passed in 1992, the provisions of Amendment 50 could not be made manifest until the citizens of Central City, Black Hawk, and Cripple Creek had their electoral say. In December 2008, the people of Cripple Creek voted 174 to 10 in favor of adopting the terms of Amendment 50. In January 2009, the people of Central City voted 212 to 16 in favor of Amendment 50. That same month, the people of Back Hawk voted 54 to 6 in favor of Amendment 50.

## SOURCES

Wikipedia.com; americangaming.org; ballotpedia.org; state.co.us/gov_dir/leg_dir/lcsstaff/research/CONSTbl.htm; personal interviews with the town clerk of Black Hawk and the county clerks of Gilpin and Teller counties.

# MOUNTAIN COUNTIES MOST OFTEN VOTE BLUE

In Colorado, the litmus-test locale when it comes to perceived liberal tendencies is, of course, Boulder. Often referred to as the "People's Republic of Boulder," the home to the University of Colorado is considered by many people to be the state's designated political and philosophical counterweight to Colorado Springs, which, given the fact that it is home to Focus on the Family and more military installations than you can shake a stick at, is perceived in Colorado as being extremely conservative.

Thing is, when it comes to casting ballots—on almost every level, from the President down to the local dogcatcher—Colorado's mountain counties, especially those that are home to ski areas, have become veritable bastions of blue-leaning electoral inclinations, to the point that places like San Miguel County, home to Telluride, and Pitkin County, home to Aspen, often surpass even Boulder when it comes to voting for Democratic candidates and overtly liberal causes.

For most of Colorado's recent history, Republicans have carried the day when it comes to presidential elections. In 1960, Nixon carried Colorado over Kennedy (with mountainous Lake, San Juan, San Miguel, Saguache, and Hinsdale counties bucking the trend and going in favor of Kennedy). In 1964, Colorado joined the national landslide of Lyndon Johnson over Barry Goldwater (with Hinsdale being one of only three Colorado counties to go for Goldwater).

In 1968, Nixon carried Colorado over Hubert Humphrey by nine percentage points, with Lake and Mineral being the only altitudinous counties to go for Humphrey. In 1972, Colorado joined Nixon's posterior kicking of George McGovern, with Pitkin being one of only two Colorado counties to cast its lot with hapless George. In 1976, Colorado went for Ford over Carter, with Gilpin being the only mountain county to go for the Southern Baptist peanut farmer from Georgia.

In 1980, Reagan whupped Carter from sea to shining sea, with all Colorado mountain counties joining that landslide. When Reagan trounced Mondale in 1984, the mountain counties once again overwhelmingly went with the Gipper.

But the tide began to turn in 1988. Even though George H.W. Bush took Colorado 728,000 to 621,000 over Michael Dukakis, Pitkin, Lake, Gilpin, Boulder, and San Miguel counties went with the diminutive governor of Massachusetts.

In 1992, Clinton became the first Democratic presidential candidate to take Colorado (629,000–562,000 over Bush I) since Johnson. The ski/mountain counties overwhelmingly went for Clinton, who lost Colorado to Dole in 1996 by a mere 25,000 votes. However, the 1996 election saw a Democratic-leaning solidification of ski/mountain counties, with Routt, Eagle, Summit, Clear Creek, Gilpin, Boulder, Lake, Pitkin, Gunnison, Saguache, San Miguel, and Mineral counties all casting their electoral lots with Slick Willy.

In 2000, even though George W. Bush took Colorado 883,000–738,000 over Al Gore, Pitkin, Lake, Summit, Boulder, and Gilpin counties lined up behind the Inconvenient Truth. It is also interesting to note that, in the 2000 presidential election, hyperliberal Ralph Nader took 6.9 percent of the vote in Eagle County, 13 percent in Pitkin County, 8 percent in Lake County, 10 percent in Summit County, and 11 percent in Boulder County—some of the highest county percentages for Nader in the entire nation.

In 2004, however, the liberal-leaning mountain/ski county block solidified. While W. again took Colorado, 51 percent to 47 percent, over John Kerry, in the mountain/ski counties, Kerry did well. He took Eagle County, which had, the previous election, gone for Bush. He also took Summit County (59 to 39 percent), Lake County (55 to 42 percent), Pitkin County (68 to 30 percent), Routt County (54 to 44 percent), Gunnison County (56 to 41 percent), Clear Creek County (53 to 44 percent), Gilpin County (56 to 41 percent), Boulder County (66 to 32 percent), La Plata County (52 to 45 percent), and San Miguel County (71 to 26 percent). The core of Colorado's highest counties had suddenly coalesced into one of the most blue-leaning areas in the entire Mountain Time Zone, if not the country.

That coalescence reached an electoral crescendo in 2008, when Obama took Colorado 54 percent to 45 percent. In Summit County, the nation's largest ski county (home to Copper Mountain, Breckenridge, Keystone, and Arapahoe Basin), Obama won the presidential vote 65.7 percent to 32.8 percent over McCain. That hyperblue trend was echoed throughout Colorado's major ski counties. Obama won Pitkin County, home to Aspen Highlands, Ajax, Buttermilk, and Snowmass ski areas, with 73.7 percent of the vote. The blueness of San Miguel County, home to Telluride, was even more striking, with Obama getting a staggering 77 percent of the vote, and in Eagle County, home to Vail and Beaver Creek, Obama received 61 percent of the vote. In Routt County, home to Steamboat Springs, Obama took 63 percent. And so it goes through La Plata County, home to Durango Mountain Resort; San Juan County, home to Silverton Mountain Ski Area; Gunnison County, home to Crested Butte; and Lake County, home to Ski Cooper.

The only Colorado counties with noteworthy ski-area presence that did not vote for Obama were Grand, home to Winter Park/Mary Jane and Sol Vista, which went for McCain by all of 127 votes, and Chaffee, home to Monarch Ski Area, which went for McCain by five votes.

And it has not just been presidential elections that have reflected this liberal high-country trending in the past few elections.

In 2010, while Democrat Michael Bennett was elected senator by the skin of his chinny-chin-chin (47.76 percent to 46.82 percent over Republican Ken Buck), he carried by substantial margins all of the major ski counties, with the exception of Grand. All told, the only mountain counties that went for Buck in 2010 were Custer, Garfield, Grand, Jackson, Mineral, Park, Rio Grande, and Teller.

In 2008, Democrat Mark Udall was elected to the U.S. Senate 51.9 percent to 43.4 percent over Republican Dan Schaeffer. In

Summit County, Udall won by a margin of 64.4 percent to 31.8 percent; in Eagle County, he overtook Schaeffer 59.2 percent to 36.9 percent; and in Pitkin County, he beat Schaeffer 72 percent to 24.7 percent, almost exactly the same winning percentage as in Boulder County, which went for Udall 72.9 percent to 23.8 percent. In San Miguel County, Udall got a staggering 73 percent of the vote. Udall took every Colorado county that is home to a ski area, including Chaffee and Grand counties, both of which went for McCain.

This was the culmination of senatorial trending that began several elections ago.

In the 2004 senatorial election, which saw Democrat Ken Salazar beat Republican beer magnate Pete Coors 51 percent to 46 percent, Eagle, Summit, Lake, Pitkin, Gunnison, and Boulder counties all went overwhelmingly for Salazar. Most other mountain counties also went for Salazar. In the 2002 senatorial election, which saw Republican Wayne Allard beat Democrat Tom Strickland, Routt, Boulder, Gilpin, Summit, Lake, Pitkin, Gunnison, and San Miguel counties all went for Strickland. Allard won Eagle County in that election, but by only 56 votes.

In 1998, Ben Nighthorse Campbell, then running as a Republican (after switching his party affiliation midway through his previous term), handily won his reelection over Democrat Dottie Lamm. The only mountain counties that went for Lamm in that schizophrenic election were Boulder, Pitkin, and San Miguel. In the 1996 senatorial election, Allard beat Strickland by a sizeable margin statewide, but Strickland took Summit, Eagle, Lake, Pitkin, Boulder, Gilpin, Gunnison, San Miguel, and Saguache counties. When Campbell was first elected senator in 1992 as a Democrat (over Republican Terry Considine), he took all of the mountain counties. And when Hank Brown trounced Democrat Josie Heath in the 1990 U.S. Senate election, Gilpin, Pitkin, Lake, Gunnison, and San Miguel counties leaned blue and went for Heath.

The mountain counties have also trended blue when voting for governor the past few elections, with only Bill Owens doing well over 8,000 feet in his jungle-slapping of Democratic rival Rollie Heath in 2002. Only Boulder and San Miguel counties went for the hapless Heath in that gubernatorial election. In 1998, although Owens won the statewide election for governor, he did badly up high, with Routt, Garfield, Eagle, Summit, Lake, Boulder, Gilpin, Clear Creek, Pitkin, Gunnison, San Miguel, San Juan, Hinsdale, and La Plata counties all going for Democrat Gail Schoettler.

In 2010, Denver Mayor John Hickenlooper took 51 percent of the state gubernatorial vote over Tom Tancredo, American Constitution Party (37 percent), and Republican Dan Maes (11 percent).

(Note: Maes' showing was so poor that, had he received 20,000 fewer votes, the Republican Party would have been de-certified as a major party in Colorado for the 2012 and 2014 elections—meaning that the GOP would have had to go through a tedious petition process to have been placed upon ballots throughout the state.) Hickenlooper pretty much dominated the altitudinous counties, receiving less than 50 percent of the vote in only Grand, Jackson, Custer, and Dolores counties. Hickenlooper, who surely scored extra points in mountain country because of his brewpub-owning past (Denver's Wyncoop Brewery), took 73 percent of the vote in San Miguel and Pitkin counties, 70 percent in Boulder County, 65 percent in Summit County, 63 percent in Routt County, 60 percent in Alamosa, Gunnison, and Eagle counties, and 57 percent in Lake and Huerfano counties. These lopsided margins were only exceeded by Denver's 75 percent vote in favor of Hickenlooper.

In the gubernatorial elections of 1992 and 1994, the mountain counties went overwhelmingly for Democrat Roy Romer, one of the most popular governors in Colorado history.

Three other recent elections underscore the left-leaning electoral tendencies of the high-country counties.

In 2010, Amendment 62, which called for the definition of personhood as beginning at conception, was placed on the ballot. It was trounced statewide about as badly as anything can be trounced, with 70 percent of Colorado's voters casting a thumbs-down. The main counties voting against Amendment 62 were located in the mountains, with San Miguel County voting 84 percent against it, Pitkin and Boulder counties voting 83 percent against it, Summit County voting 81 percent against it, and Gunnison County voting 80 percent against it. Denver was the only other Colorado county voting more than 80 percent against Amendment 62.

In 2006, there was a statewide referendum calling for the legalization of small amounts of marijuana. It lost, 913,000 to 636,000 votes. But that ballot initiative won hands-down in Routt, Eagle, Lake, Summit, Pitkin, Clear Creek, Gilpin, Boulder, San Miguel, San Juan, and La Plata counties, among others. (Draw your own conclusions on that one.)

Again in 2006, a statewide initiative called for the definition of traditional marriage as being between one man and one woman. It passed statewide, 855,000 to 699,000, but it got a thumbs-down in most of the ski counties.

The mountain counties have become such a reliable electoral base for those with blue-leaning inclinations that at least twice in the past decade there have been efforts, mostly successful, in the then-Republican-controlled state legislature to redistrict the area to water down those liberal voters. In the end, those efforts have had significant effects on state senate and house seats as well as U.S. congressional elections. When it comes to all other statewide elections, though, the mountain/ski counties have recently shown their true political colors.

Addendum: After spending many hours poring over Colorado election results clear back to 1880, the biggest head-scratcher I came across was that the candidates for something called the Colorado Prohibition Party drew more than 7,000 votes in both the 1990 and 1994 gubernatorial elections. Those candidates, not surprisingly, did not do so well in the mountain counties.

## BLUE-BASED ELECTORAL TRENDING FOR SKI COUNTIES IN OTHER MOUNTAIN STATES

Colorado is not the only Mountain Time Zone state with ski counties that vote overwhelming blue these days.

- Obama took the state of New Mexico 57 percent to 42 percent over McCain in 2008. Taos County, home to Taos Ski Valley, Ski Rio, Red River Ski Area, and Sipapu Ski Area, went for Obama by a whopping 81.5 percent to 17.2 percent. Obama took almost 77 percent of the vote in Santa Fe County, home to Ski Santa Fe. Both of those counties went big-time Democrat from the top of the ballot to the bottom.

- The blue-leaning nature of ski counties in the Mountain Time Zone even bled into red states. Two counties in Wyoming went for Obama in 2008: Albany, home to Laramie (a college town), and Teton, home to Jackson Hole Mountain Resort, where Obama took 61 percent of the vote.

- In Montana, which as a state went for McCain by 13,000 votes, Obama took Gallatin County, gateway to Big Sky Ski Area, and Bridger Bowl Ski Area.

- In Idaho, only three counties went for Obama: Latah, home to the University of Idaho; Teton, home to Driggs (the access town for Grand Targhee Ski Area and a major bedroom community for Jackson); and Blaine, home to Ketchum and Sun Valley.

- Two counties in Utah went for Obama: Grand, home to outdoor-recreation-crazed Moab, and Summit, home to Park City Mountain Resort, Deer Valley Resort, and the Canyons Resort.

SOURCES

uselectionatlas.org; usatoday.com; the *Taos News*.

# CHANGING YOUR NAME

Colorado has long been a state to which people move with the idea of some degree of self-reinvention. For some, this merely means establishing a new list of life goals: take up telemark skiing, start making craft soaps, become a Buddhist. For others, it means going all the way and changing one's name.

The two best-known contemporary examples of a person changing his name in Colorado's mountain country are Henry John Deutschendorf, Jr., who, in the early 1960s, legally became John Denver (rejecting a suggestion from friends—who had already convinced the then-20-something Deutschendorf that, if he was serious about making it as a professional musician, his clumsy patronymic needed to be jettisoned posthaste—that he go with "John Sommerville")[1], and Richard Gordon Bannister, who was known for more than 24 years in his adopted home of Crested Butte as Neil Murdoch. It is an understatement to say that Bannister's name change, unlike Denver's, was not on the legal up-and-up.

Bannister had been charged in 1973 with smuggling 26 pounds of cocaine after U.S. Customs agents seized from the trunk of his car four hand-carved wooden statues sent from Bolivia to Bannister in Taos, New Mexico. He was freed on $20,000 bond, and that was the last time members of the judicial system saw him again until 2001, when he was finally arrested in Taos using yet another alias, Grafton Mailer.

Bannister, who had already served time in the 1960s after a drug conviction in Pennsylvania, first arrived in Crested Butte in 1974. At that time, no one in this once-funky mountain hamlet so much as batted an eye when yet another dropout from the real world showed up sans plausible life-history story[2].

Unlike many people who would have hidden in the shadows for the rest of their natural lives, Bannister, who was 34 at the time, quickly became a big, boisterous part of Crested Butte's social geology. He played a pivotal role in giving birth to an entire new sport: mountain biking. In the mid 1970s, he started attaching cannibalized parts to battered Schwinn frames and test-driving them on trails around town. Before he knew it, he'd become a fat-tire forefather. His shop, Bicycles Etcetera, is now generally considered to have been the second mountain-bike-oriented bike shop in the entire country. In 1982, Murdoch helped launch Crested Butte's annual Fat Tire Bike Week, now one of the largest mountain-bike festivals in the country.

# THE LEGAL JOURNEY

The process of changing your name in Colorado is a fairly straightforward journey through a legal paperwork morass. The most common reasons for changing your name are marriage and divorce, which generally only cover last names. By possessing a marriage certificate or divorce decree, step one of the process of legally changing your name has begun. Additional paperwork and notification requirements for the newly married or divorced can easily be found at newlastname.org/co-colorado.

The process of changing your name for purposes other than marriage or divorce is more challenging. First of all, it is against Colorado state law to seek to change your name for the purpose of avoiding or evading prosecution. Thus, if you have anything, shall we say, in common with Bannister/Murdoch/Mailer, you probably ought to change your name on the sly.

Petitions for a legal name change are generally made to the local district or county court in the county of the petitioner's residence. The petitions, verified by affidavit, need to include the petitioner's current full (and hopefully real) name, the new name desired, and a concise statement of the reason for the desired name change. In legalese, "The court shall order such a change to be made and spread upon the records of the court in proper form if the court is satisfied that the desired change would be proper and not detrimental to the interests of any other person."

Verily, there are only a handful of reasons the court can use to deny a proposed name change. These include but are not limited to:

- Unworthy motive
- The possibility of fraud on the public
- The choice of a name that is bizarre, unduly long, ridiculous, or offensive to common decency and good taste
- The interests of a wife or child of the applicant would be adversely affected

If a court has decided to deny a name-change request, it is required by Colorado law to hold an evidentiary hearing to determine if "good and sufficient cause" exists to deny the application.

Once the court approves the proposed name change, the applicant, whether a newly ordained John Denver or New Harvest Moon Spirit of Life, is further required by law to publish notification of the change in a legal newspaper at least three times in the county where New Harvest Moon Spirit of Life lives within 20 days after the order of the court is made.

---

After 24 years, however, Bannister's charade began to unravel. Showing once again how it is almost impossible to completely drop out from society, Bannister had been unable to make it through his life on the lam without having a Social Security number, which he had stolen from a Pennsylvania man who, coincidentally or not, owned a bicycle shop. As a result of a routine credit check in spring 2008, the man came to suspect that someone else was using his Social Security number. The Pennsylvania man filed a complaint, and an agent with the Social Security Administration hunted the number down and drove to Crested Butte, where he interviewed Bannister at the local police department. Bannister was fingerprinted, photographed, and then released, at least partially because the local police chief vouched for him.

When the Social Security Administration agent returned to Denver, he ran Bannister's fingerprints, and—voila!—he got a hit on the outstanding warrant issued after Bannister jumped bail in 1973. Bannister knew that his cover was blown. He handed his keys to his roommate and bid her adios, saying she would never see him again. He had a friend drive him to the Four Corners Monument with only his trusty mountain bike and a small stash of clothing, then asked his friend to drive away so that he couldn't tell police which way Bannister had literally pedaled off into the sunset, destination known only to him.

When agents from the U.S. Marshal's Office arrived in Crested Butte the next day, they had missed Bannister by less than an hour. He had managed to disappear again. Bannister's next nomenclatural self-redefinition lasted only a couple of years. Acting on a tip from a suspicious local business owner, federal agents arrested Bannister–Murdoch–Mailer in 2001. He was sentenced to nine years in prison, to be followed by three years of probation.

The people in Crested Butte justifiably reacted weirdly to the Bannister saga. Most folks defended him. An ex-mayor was quoted as saying, "Neil Murdoch had a spotless record for a quarter century. Yeah, he made some big mistakes. But this is one of those rare cases where a criminal has rehabilitated himself."[3] Bannister was presented in absentia with a lifetime achievement award in acting by the Crested Butte town theater for playing the role of Murdoch for 24 years.

## NOTES

1. Read more about Denver in the "Rocky Mountain High" section of this book on page 88.

2. Unlike many parts of the country, it is still considered bad manners in most Colorado mountain towns to inquire too enthusiastically after a person's background. If you ask a person, for example, where he or she is from, and the response consists of nothing more than a grunted, snarled, "back East," best to leave it alone and change the subject to the Broncos.

3. An episode of the critically acclaimed TV show, *Northern Exposure,* dealt with this concept of place/time-based reinvention of self. In the episode titled "Crime and Punishment," which aired on December 14, 1992, Chris Stevens (played by actor John Corbett)—aka Chris in the Morning—is suddenly arrested on an outstanding warrant for breaking parole by leaving his native West Virginia many years before without the consent of his parole officer. Chris's defense rests almost entirely upon his lawyer's argument that the man standing before the court that day had changed so much for the better that he was, in fact, not the same person who decades prior had hot-wired a car in West Virginia at age 18, despite the fact that his fingerprints and DNA were the same as that person. The court, after hearing from townspeople about how important Chris was to the community, opted in the end to not enforce the arrest warrant, going so far as to praise Chris for turning his life around. This anecdote has relativity to Colorado's mountain country in a way that transcends its admittedly specious connection to the Bannister/Murdoch/Mailer situation. *Northern Exposure* was set in the mythical town of Cicely, Alaska. It was mostly filmed in Roslyn, Washington. But many people over the years have argued that the actual concept/notion/idea of Cicely, Alaska, was born from the familiarity the show's creators, Joshua Brand and John Falsey, supposedly had with the isolated Colorado mountain towns of Ouray and Paonia. The comparison between Cicely, Alaska, and Paonia is especially intriguing, because one of the prime components of Cicely was the fact that the town's radio station, KBHR, had a window fronting Main Street (Pennsylvania Avenue in Roslyn, where the KBHR studio is still maintained in situ as a shrine to *Northern Exposure*) so that locals could walk by and wave at Chris in the Morning. Chris, his nom de guerre notwithstanding, seems to have been the only DJ employed at KBHR and, therefore, was on the air many evenings, too. KVNF (90.9 FM in Paonia), a creative grassroots, volunteer-based, community-based public radio station, had been serving western Colorado since 1979. And, much like *Northern Exposure's* fictional KBHR, it fronts the town's main drag, Grand Avenue. (It does not have a big window through which passersby can see the DJs at work, however.) Brand and Falsey have been unable over the years to directly address questions about which town Cicely was actually based upon, because, two years into the show's seven-season run, a legal suit was filed contending that the idea for *Northern Exposure* was actually stolen. (The court records from that suit were sealed.) From that point on, Brand and Falsey were very tight-lipped about the show's origins, so they have never admitted to or denied the Paonia/Ouray connection to the show, which won two Golden Globes for Best Drama and which was nominated for a total of 21 national-level awards.

## SOURCES

"What does a mountain-biking pioneer do when his cocaine-smuggling past finally catches up with him? He rides like hell"—an excellent article by noted author Hampton Sides in the September 1998 issue of *Outside* magazine; "'Murdoch pleads guilty after 3 decades on the run," by Patrick O'Grady, in *VeloNews;* coloradonamechange.com; namechangelaw.com; marriage.about.com; newlastname.org; consumerreports.org; Denver.bizjournals.com; names.mongaby.com; *The Northern Exposure Book* by Louis Chunovic; personal correspondence with Joshua Brand.

# HOME AWAY FROM HOME
# (EXTRADITION)

When Royal "Scoop" Daniel III suddenly and inexplicably went missing from his Breckenridge law office in 2007, local law-enforcement personnel feared the worst. After initially exploring every variation on the foul-play theme imaginable, Breck's men in blue finally learned that Daniel might not have met a bad end after all; rather, they learned, he might have fled the country because of some alleged nefarious fiscal transactions. By early 2010, law enforcement believed that Daniel might be kicking back in Brazil, a country that he had visited often and that happens to have no extradition treaty with the United States—meaning that, if Daniel indeed is living in the land of Carnival, there is nothing the U.S. government can legally do to bring him back to face the legal music in Colorado.[1]

Although the overwhelming majority of us will never have cause to so much as ponder the concept of international extradition treaties in any manner more personal than trying to understand the latest episode of *Law & Order*, it never hurts to keep a mental tab on which countries are beyond the long arm of American law, because, well, you never know what may happen in the course of a lifetime.

Probably the most famous folks with a Colorado connection to head to another country with the express intent of avoiding prosecution were Robert Leroy Parker and Harry Alonzo Longbaugh, the infamous Butch Cassidy and the Sundance Kid. Although little of the tandem's extra-legal exploits transpired in Colorado, Cassidy's first verified bank robbery took place on June 24, 1889, when he and two other cohorts relieved Telluride's San Miguel Valley Bank of $21,000. (Parker, along with two other ne'er-do-wells, may have been responsible for the November 3, 1887, almost farcical robbery of a train near Grand Junction. Apparently, the train's safe-master convinced the robbers that no one aboard had the safe's combination, so the only spoils heisted were the personal possessions of the passengers, which amounted to about $150. But there seems to be no historical verification that Parker was indeed involved in this low-rent enterprise.)

It wasn't until 1896 that the Wild Bunch, which eventually included the Sundance Kid, committed its first robbery as a unified gang, and that was in Idaho. The first act of Wild Bunch larceny that actually involved the Sundance Kid, who hailed from, of all places, Pennsylvania, transpired in Wyoming.

As anyone who has watched the 1969 movie, *Butch Cassidy and the Sundance Kid* (much of which was shot in southwestern Colorado)—which won six Academy Awards and was nominated for Best Picture—knows, the dynamic duo eventually left the United States to seek additional vocational opportunities in South America. On February 20, 1901, they hopped a boat out of New York, and, along with Sundance's paramour, Etta Place, sailed to Buenos Aires. After a stint as respectable ranchers in Argentina, they reverted to their nefarious bank-robbing roots and were eventually shot to death by the Bolivian army on November 3, 1908. (Of course, there is significant dissension among historians about whether or not Butch and Sundance actually did perish in that place on that date.)

During the early years of the twentieth century, the concept of extradition treaties between countries was in its infancy, especially in the hinterlands of South America. So, all Butch and Sundance had to do to evade the law was assume a series of aliases, and they were pretty much in the clear—right up until they perished in a hail of bullets, that is.

These days, with Interpol, the Internet, and a global economy and all, Butch and Sundance would have had to scrutinize the lay of the legal land a bit more thoroughly if they wanted to find a safe haven, for both Bolivia and Argentina now have extradition treaties with Uncle Sam.

At this point, it would be prudent to include a disclaimer: I stress that people ought not to be thinking in terms of which countries do and do not have extradition treaties with the United States, unless it's for entertainment purposes only. But, if you do find your thoughts wandering down this slippery slope, there are a few things you ought to understand.

The list of countries that do not have extradition treaties with the United States is long (at least 64 countries) and constantly changing. As well, it is often crime-and-punishment specific. Certain countries—Canada, European Union nations, and Mexico among them—will not extradite suspects back to the United States if there is a chance those suspects will face the death penalty. So, unless you're fleeing, well, a first-degree murder rap, don't go to Canada, Mexico, or the European Union.

Also, it is worth noting that—if you are in a position where you find these words more than casually captivating—just because a country does not have an extradition treaty with the United States does not mean it will let American citizens fleeing the law into its country.

More importantly, though, from a Colorado mountain perspective, the overwhelming majority of the nations that do not have extradition treaties with the United States are seriously short of lift-serviced skiing. I mean, if you're going to find yourself on an "extended vacation" in a country that very coincidentally does not have an extradition treaty with America, then you might as well do your research and choose one where you can perform a few turns.

Most U.S. extradition-treaty-challenged countries are not only short on skiing but fall into a macro category that doctoral candidates in international relations would likely classify as Third World cesspools—places where a lack of skiing is the least of their concerns. This category of countries includes Burkina Faso, Equatorial Guinea, Myanmar, Somalia, and my personal favorite, Bangladesh.

Sure, some nations that lack extradition treaties with the United States may sound acceptable as a "retirement option" for those on the lam. These include Indonesia, the Maldives, Cape Verde, and Samoa. But, again, if your rapidly packed luggage includes skis and/or a snowboard, these ain't the countries for any law-evading winter recreationist to even consider. No, if you like to ski or ride, and you feel a need to outrun the law, you're pretty much stuck with these countries that lack extradition treaties with the United States:

- **Afghanistan.** Some folks might be turned off by the, well, war, and the constant threat of al-Qaida and the Taliban, as well as all of those unexploded land mines, but, boy oh boy, this place has it all when it comes to mountains. You've got to earn your turns, as there's no lift-serviced access, but at least it'll just be you, al-Qaida, and the Taliban out there enjoying untrammeled lines. You definitely *will* get first tracks.
- **Armenia.** This miniscule Caucasus country actually has a ski area named Tsaghkadzor, which is served by three lifts and which long served as the training ground for the Soviet alpine ski team. Tsaghkadzor's highest chair gives access to a wide-open hillside with some great views of post–Soviet industrial decay, including what looks like an abandoned nuclear power station! At least it's better than the inside of an American prison! Maybe.
- **The People's Republic of China.** Who knew, but the host of the 2008 Summer Olympics is home to dozens of ski areas, including one, Alshan, that's conveniently located on the very remote border of Inner and Outer Mongolia. The upside of considering the PRC as your extradition-free destination of choice is that job opportunities abound. Pay's not great—slightly more in terms of buying power than being a dishwasher in Vail or Aspen—but, in addition to a regular paycheck, you'll get to be politically repressed.
- **Iran.** Located less than two hours from Tehran, Shemshak Resort boasts two lifts and three T-bars. It's Web site proclaims that it's a mogul lovers' paradise, which, translated from Farsi, means

"no on-slope grooming on premises." Relocating to the extradition-treaty-free slopes of Iran also brings with it the opportunity to chase snow bunnies and shred betties adorned with the latest in Islamic ski fashion. And the après-ski parties are to die for.

- **Andorra.** This diminutive nation in the Pyrenees offers several dozen ski areas, all very close, we should note, to Spain and France, which most certainly *do* have extradition treaties with the United States. If you arrive frantically fleeing American jurisdiction sans automobile, you should be perfectly comfortable in Andorra, which, at 181 square miles, is the world's sixth smallest nation, making it easy to get around on foot.

Other extradition-treaty-free nations that offer skiing, in one form or another, include Serbia, the Russian Federation, Morocco, and Syria. If you think even for one second that this is the sort of information you one day may find applicable to your immediate reality, might I suggest that, first, you place a large amount of money in an offshore bank account and, second, that you take a preemptive tour of these unique "ski destinations" before you actually find yourself living in Syria, awaiting the arrival of the latest snowmaking technology.

### NOTES

1. In late 2011, Daniel was finally arrested trying to re-enter the U.S. from Tijuana, Mexico. He had apparently been living in Acapulco. Mexico definitely has an extradition treaty with the U.S.

### SOURCES

Wikipedia, www.answerbag.com, http://answers.google.com, www.timesonline.co.uk, www.piste-off.com, www.skiarmenia.com, http://gochina.about.com, www.heliskinepal.com, www.iranmania.com, www.j2ski.com, www.igluski.com, www.goafrica.about.com, http://lexicorient.com/morocco, www.syria.cimbing.ch, www.imbd.com

# LISTING COLORADO

For more than a decade, the process of publishing variations on the "Top 10 List" theme has become a staple for magazines, newspapers, and Web sites. These lists cover the gamut from best towns for ski bums to live in to best golf courses. The methodology for compiling these lists likewise covers the spectrum, from aggregating objective reader surveys to freelance writers subjectively trying to cover as much geographic ground as possible. Rare is the top-anything list that does not include a Colorado mountain reference.

- Boulder was named America's second-healthiest city in the January 2010 issue of *Men's Health* magazine.
- Western State College in Gunnison was rated the country's 76th "coolest school" (out of 100) in the August 16, 2010, issue of *Sierra Magazine*.
- In the August 5, 2010, issue of *Golf Magazine*, three Colorado mountain courses made the list of "Top 100 Courses You Can Play." The Red Sky Ranch Norman Course in Wolcott came in at number 24, followed by the Lakota Canyon Ranch course in New Castle (number 75) and the Redlands Mesa course in Grand Junction (number 94).
- Carbondale, Pagosa Springs, and Colorado Springs were all listed in the September 2008 issue of *National Geographic Adventure* as being among the best towns in which to live and play in the Rockies. Gunnison was named the number-2 mountain town in the same issue.
- Divide was named one of the country's "Best Small Towns" in *National Geographic Adventure*'s story, "Where to Live and Play 2006: 31 Towns Perfect for You."
- In its October 6, 2009, issue, *Ski* magazine included 11 Colorado areas on its "Top 30 Ski Resorts" list. Vail came in at number 3, followed by Beaver Creek (number 5), Snowmass (number 6), Steamboat (number 10), Telluride (number 11), Aspen (number 14), Breckenridge (number 15), Aspen Highlands (number 17), Copper Mountain (number 18), Keystone (number 21), and Winter Park (number 23).
- *National Geographic Adventure* named Carbondale "The Ultimate Rocky Mountain Hideout" in 2004.
- Boulder came in at number 4 in *Kiplinger*'s July 2010 article "10 Best Cities for the Next Decade."
- Colorado was rated the country's least-fat state in 2010 by Calorie Lab.
- In 2003, *Ski* magazine named Frisco one of the country's best towns for ski bums to live.
- Colorado Springs was named by *Outside* magazine in its August 2009 issue as the country's healthiest city. Denver received honorable mention in that same issue.
- Colorado Springs was named by *Forbes* magazine in May 2009 as the country's 5th-greenest city.
- In 2007, *Sunset* magazine listed Crested Butte as one of its "Top 10 Dream Towns."
- Crested Butte was number 8 on *"Outside*'s Best Towns 2008" list. Boulder was listed as the best all-around town in *Outside*'s 2006 "Live Here Now: 20 Dream Towns" issue. Durango was listed in

that issue as the best mountain-biking town. Fort Collins came in at number 3 on *"Outside's* Best Towns 2005" list. Salida was named one of *Outside* magazine's "Best Towns 2004."

- In May 2009, *Forbes* rated Boulder as the top city in the country "to live well."
- In 2008, *USA Today* named Aspen as the country's top partying and nightlife ski town. In 2004, *USA Today* listed Aspen as the number-2 partying and nightlife ski town in the country.
- Colorado's mountain towns really scored when *TravelLady Magazine* listed Aspen, Crested Butte, Telluride, and Beaver Creek among its "Top 10 Most Romantic Towns in the West."
- AskMen.com listed Aspen as number 2 on its best resort town list.
- MountainYahoos.com listed Telluride as its number-1 ski-resort town in 2007. Aspen was number 2 and Steamboat Springs number 5.
- In 2008, *AARP The Magazine* rated Boulder as the country's sixth "Healthiest Hometown." Fort Collins/Loveland received honorable mention. In that same issue, Boulder was named the country's "Skinniest" (lowest average body mass index) town, while Fort Collins/Loveland came in 10th in that category.
- Fort Collins was named one of the "15 Best Places to Reinvent Your Life" by *AARP The Magazine* in 2003.
- *Money* magazine rated Fort Collins as the number-2 best place to live in the country in 2008. *Money* named Fort Collins number 1 in 2007. Fort Collins also came in 14th on *Country Home's* "Best Green Cities" list; it was named the country's 25th best running city by *Runner's World* magazine and the 56th most walkable city in America by *Prevention* magazine.
- Seven Colorado towns made *Outdoor Life* magazine's 2008 list for the top hunting and fishing towns in the country. Fort Collins came in at number 14, followed by Rifle (number 17), Durango (number 28), Craig (number 41), Grand Junction (number 44), Evergreen (number 45), and Gunnison (number 84).
- Glenwood Springs was named one of the country's top fishing towns by *Field & Stream* magazine in 2008.
- Trinidad was named one of the "Top 10 True Western Towns of 2008" by *True West* magazine.
- Colorado was well represented on SkiNet.com's list of the "Top 10 Ski Towns." Aspen came in at number 1, followed by Crested Butte (number 3), Telluride (number 4), Steamboat Springs (number 6), and Breckenridge (number 7).
- Vail and Breckenridge both made SkiNet.com's "Top 10 Ski Town Oktoberfest" list.

- *Skiing* magazine in 2007 named three Colorado towns—Steamboat Springs (number 2), Breckenridge (number 8), and Aspen (number 9)—on its "Top 10 Ski Towns in America" list.
- Crested Butte came in at number 3 on *Sunset* magazine's "Top 10 Dream Towns" list.
- Crested Butte, Beaver Creek, Keystone, and Steamboat Springs all made bestskiresorts.com's 2008 "Best Ski Resorts" list.
- The Park Hyatt Beaver Creek Resort & Spa, Aspen's St. Regis Resort, and Vail's Cascade Resort & Spa made the "Editor's Top 10 North America" list for "Top Ski Resorts" on professionaltravelguide.com.
- In 2003, bestever.com named Breckenridge the "Best Ski Town in America."
- Epinions.com named Crested Butte number 10 on its "Top 10 Most Adventurous Ski Areas" list.
- Glenwood Springs came in at number 11 on *Paddler* magazine's "Why Aren't You Here?" list. "You might have it good where you live, but joining the lucky residents of these 13 towns could be the best decision of your life. Start packing."
- Colorado scored big on XCSkiResorts.com's "Top 10 Recommendation Lists." Beaver Creek's cross-country ski area was listed number 1 under the "Great Scenery Category." Crested Butte's Nordic area was number 3 under the "Great XC Ski Towns" category. Steamboat Springs's Vista Verde Nordic area came in number 10 under the "XC Ski Resorts That Cater to Families" category. Vista Verde also came in at number 10 under the "Great Cuisine" category, number 10 under the "XC at an Alpine Ski Resort" category, and number 4 under the "Luxury XC Resorts" category. Beaver Creek came in number 1 in the "XC at an Alpine Ski Resort" category. Home Ranch, in Clark, came in number 2 in the "Luxury XC Resorts" category. Under the "Full Spa Service" category, Devil's Thumb Ranch, outside Tabernash, came in number 2, followed by the Keystone Nordic Center (number 5) and the Vail XC Center (number 10).
- In 2005, skisnowboard.com named Crested Butte the number-6 area in the country for expert skiers and snowboarders. In the "Intermediate" category, Snowmass came in number 2, followed by Steamboat Springs (number 5) and Vail (number 7). In the "Beginners" category, Buttermilk came in at number 1, followed by Durango Mountain Resort (number 4). In the "First-Timers" category, Winter Park came in at number 2, followed by Durango Mountain Resort (number 3), Buttermilk (number 4), and Telluride (number 9).

- *Backpacker* magazine rated the First Flatiron, outside Boulder, as the "Wildest Spot to View July 4 Fireworks" in 2003.
- *Bike* magazine named the Edge Loop, outside Fruita, as one of America's 10 best mountain-bike trails.
- The Weather Channel (TWC) ranked Rocky Mountain National Park as the 6th best national park for wildlife viewing. In TWC's "Top 10 National Parks for Rock Climbing," Black Canyon of the Gunnison came in at number 4, followed by Rocky Mountain National Park (number 5). TWC listed Trapper's Notch, in the Flat Tops Wilderness, number 6 in its "Top 10 Secluded Campgrounds" category. Rocky Mountain National Park came in at number 4 in TWC's "Top 10 Winter Family Getaways" category. The Gunnison National Forest was listed at number 4 in the "Top 10 Fall Forests" category.
- Colorado was ranked the 19th-healthiest state by the United Health Foundation in 2008, a drop of three spots from 2007. The report listed Colorado's health "strengths" as: low prevalence of obesity, low levels of air pollution, low rate of preventable hospitalizations, and low rates of cancer deaths and cardiovascular deaths. The state's health "challenges" included: high geographic disparity within the state and a high rate of uninsured population. The report further listed health-based "significant changes": In the past year [2007–2008], the violent crime rate in Colorado decreased by 11 percent; in the past year, per capita public health funding increased by 34 percent; in the past five years, immunization coverage increased by 25 percent; and, since 1990, the percentage of children in poverty declined by 42 percent.

## SOURCES

Websites for all of the magazines, foundations, and books mentioned in this chapter.

# INDEX

# ABOUT THE AUTHOR

M. John Fayhee is the editor of the *Mountain Gazette*. A one-time contributing editor at *Backpacker* magazine, Fayhee's work also has appeared in *Forbes-Life Mountain-Time, High Country News, Aspen Sojourner Magazine, Outside, Sierra, Sports Illustrated, USA Today, Men's Fitness, New Mexico Magazine, America West Airlines Magazine, Horizon Air* and many other local, regional, and national magazines and newspapers. He is the author of many books, including *Along the Colorado Trail, A Colorado Winter,* and *Bottoms Up.* Fayhee also has hiked the Colorado Trail and the Colorado section of the Continental Divide Trail.

CPSIA information can be obtained at www.ICGtesting.com
Printed in the USA
LVOW082022230812

295727LV00003B/1/P